James Wallace
The Kelly Gang Sympathiser

Peter Newman

First published by Busybird Publishing 2024

Copyright © 2024 Peter Newman

ISBN:
Paperback: 978-1-923216-45-7
Hardback: 978-1-923216-47-1
Ebook: 978-1-923216-46-4

This work is copyright. Apart from any use permitted under the *Copyright Act 1968*, no part of this publication may be reproduced, stored in a retrieval system or transmitted in any form or by any means, electronic, mechanical, photocopying, recording or otherwise, without the prior written permission of Peter Newman.

The information in this book is based on the author's experiences and opinions. The author and publisher disclaim responsibility for any adverse consequences, which may result from use of the information contained herein. Permission to use any external content has been sought by the author. Any breaches will be rectified in further editions of the book.

Cover design: Busybird Publishing/Bill Denheld

Layout and typesetting: Busybird Publishing

Busybird Publishing
2/118 Para Road
Montmorency, Victoria
Australia 3094
www.busybird.com.au

This book is dedicated to Arthur Hall, whose publication The Headmaster of Hurdle Creek set me off on a quest to find out more about James Wallace and the role he played in the Kelly story.

Peter Newman

ACKNOWLEDGEMENTS

Writing this book about the life of James Wallace has taken me to some interesting places and I have met with many people who, like me, have a keen interest in the Kelly story. There are a number of people I must thank:

- Lorraine Hall and Elaine Wallace (grand-daughter of James Wallace), with whom I have enjoyed periodic lunches over the years at which we discussed Elaine's knowledge of her grandfather and where my further research into his life has taken me.

- Other members of the extended Wallace family, including Judy Wallace, Dianne Ellis, Roger Wallace and Mary Sayers, all of whom have also been generous with their time and information.

- Bill and Carla Denheld with whom I have been friends for nearly a decade after Bill took me to Stringybark Creek to show me the true site of the police murders, as opposed to the locations signposted by the authorities.

- David MacFarlane who runs the blog site *Ned Kelly: The True Story* (previously called *Ned Kelly – Death of the Legend*). David's blog has played an important role in correcting mistruths about the Kelly story.

- Wangaratta-based surveyor Rob Steel OAM, who shares my interest in the history of North-Eastern Victoria and who has provided much assistance over the years in deciphering the information contained on those early 'put-away' parish maps.

- The late Alan Gibb, fifth-generation farmer at Bobinawarrah (and an expert on Australian wattles!)

- who guided me to the 'hut behind the school' site in the Carboor Range, and who was very helpful in answering my questions about the history of the Hurdle Creek area.

- The late Ian MacFarlane (no relation to David MacFarlane), author of *The Kelly Gang: Unmasked*, who was always willing to provide information and guidance, and with whom I also enjoyed discussing other (non-Kelly) historical events.

- Stuart Dawson, whose scholarly research, including *Ned Kelly and the Myth of a Republic of North-Eastern Victoria*, has done much to correct the misinformation and nonsense about the Kelly story.

- Trent Cupid, for an exhausting day's exploration of the Woolshed Valley showing me the actual sites of significance (rather than those marked as part of the Ned Kelly touring route), including the site of Tom Straughair's foundry.

- Sharon Hollingsworth for initial proof-reading and fact-checking of my manuscript. Sharon knows more about the Kelly story than just about anyone else I know, despite being based in North Carolina and never having visited Australia!

Over the years, I have spoken with many others who have joined me in the search for some obscure site related to the Kelly story or who have been helpful in other ways.

Finally, most thanks must go to my wife Maryanne and my sons Tom and Matthew for encouraging me to complete this story. I apologise to them for my obsession.

Contents

Introduction		1
1	Woolshed	4
2	Different paths	14
3	Hurdle Creek	20
4	Tensions leading up to the Kelly outbreak	31
5	Helping a friend	39
The Outlaw by Sir Walter Scott		43
6	The robbery of theNational Bank at Euroa	44
7	Kelly Gang sympathisers	48
8	Sympathiser arrests	51
9	Another bank robbery(Jerilderie, NSW)	55
10	Publicity for the Kelly Gang	57
11	Wallace's activities after Jerilderie	75
12	Nicolson's secret agents	80
13	Wallace's letters to Nicolson	83
14	Preparing for Glenrowan	122
15	A Pardon for Joe?	129
16	A letter from Mr Connor	131
17	Wallace's removal from Kelly country	136
18	A new life in Yea	140
19	The Royal Commission (Wallace on Trial)	144
20	The fallout from the Royal Commission	207
21	The search for evidence of Wallace guilt	218

22	The Crown Law Office calls for the Wallace file	235
23	Wallace appeals his dismissal	237
24	Unwanted publicity	242
25	Flight to Queensland	253
26	The Band of Brothers	263
27	Animosity towards Mr Bolam	267
28	Return to Victoria	270
29	The Kerang years	282
30	Valedictory	290
31	A new life with Bonnie	293
32	Death of James and Bonnie	306
33	Wallace family cover-up	313
34	Conclusion	316

APPENDIX 1
Wallace's land selection dealings — 319

APPENDIX 2
Transcript of the Cameron Letter — 326

APPENDIX 3
Transcript of the Jerilderie Letter — 337

APPENDIX 4
The Traveller — 360

APPENDIX 5
Wallace letters to Nicolson — 367

APPENDIX 6
Letter to the *Herald*   390

APPENDIX 7
M Connor letter to Mr Graves MLA   396

APPENDIX 8
Detectives Reports on Wallace investigations   401

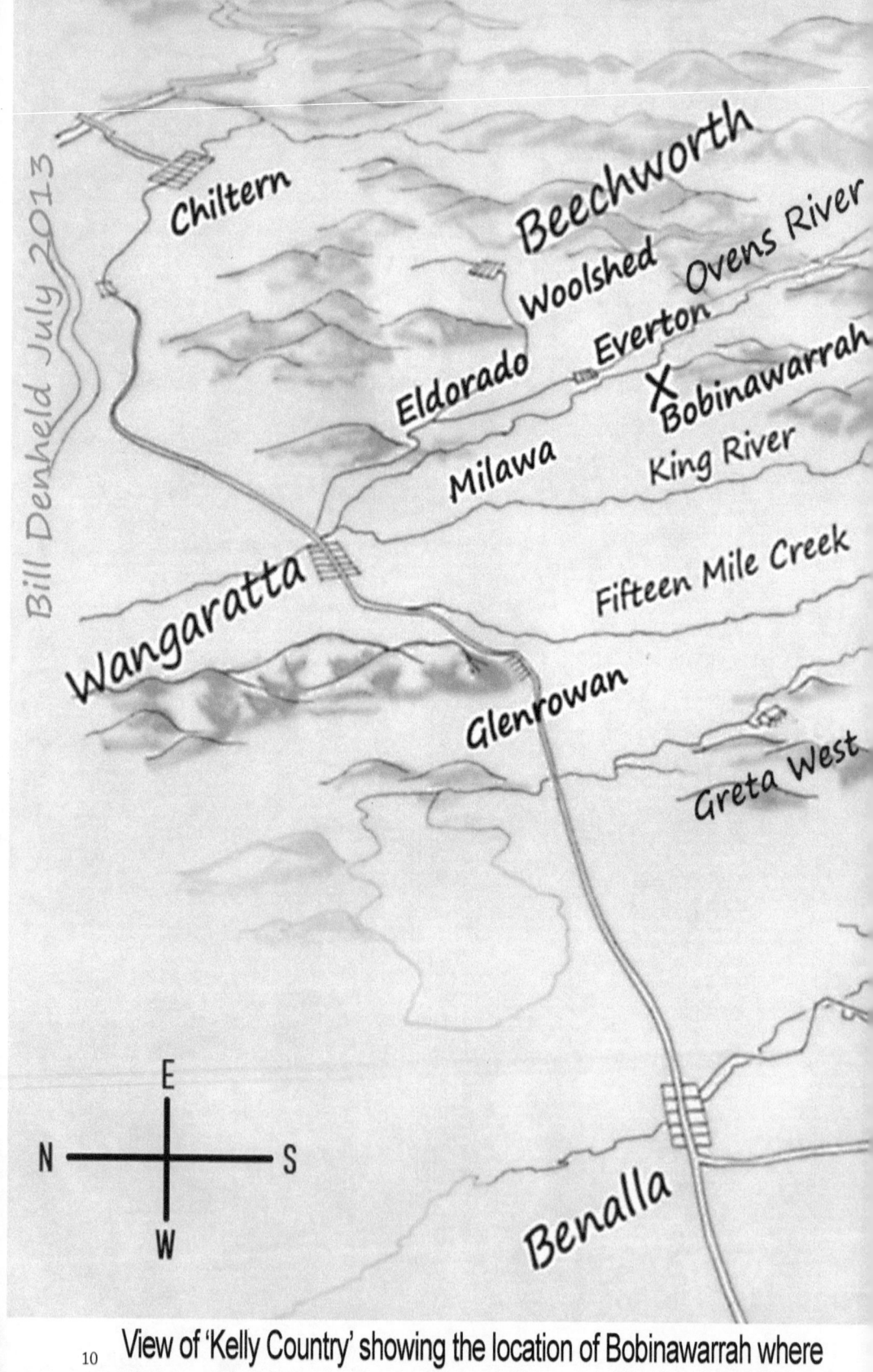

View of 'Kelly Country' showing the location of Bobinawarrah where

James Wallace was the head teacher at the Huedle Creek State School.

Introduction

I have been interested in the story of the Kelly Gang since childhood and I have avidly collected Kelly books and memorabilia for many years. In my secondary school years, I remember a school camp near Beechworth during which we walked from the Sheep Station Creek area down into the Woolshed Valley and along Reedy Creek to El Dorado. I was aware the area had an association with the Kelly story, including as the home of gang member Joe Byrne and as the place where Joe murdered his friend Aaron Sherritt in the lead up to the gang's final showdown at Glenrowan. Our walk would have taken us right past the Byrne property and the site of Sherritt's murder, but at the time I had no idea where any of these sites of significance were. I do, however, have a vivid recollection of finishing our walk at the old El Dorado State School where the James Wallace of this book began his teaching career.

Despite my interest in the Kelly story and despite some minor references to James Wallace in Ian Jones's books *Ned Kelly: A Short Life*[1] and *The Friendship that Destroyed Ned Kelly – Joe Byrne and Aaron Sherritt*,[2] I didn't know a great deal about the man. One day, though, I came across a publication titled *James Wallace (1854–1910) – The Headmaster of Hurdle Creek,* by Arthur Hall and Julie Stevens.[3] Hall had spent 20 years researching James Wallace – it started as a family history exercise,

---

1 - *Ned Kelly: A Short Life*, Lothian Books, First published 1995, Ian Jones.

2 - The Friendship that Destroyed Ned Kelly – Joe Byrne and Aaron Sherritt, Lothian Books, First published 1992, Ian Jones.

3 - *James Wallace (1854–1910) – The Headmaster of Hurdle Creek*, 2005, Arthur Hall and Julie Stevens. Julie Stevens is generously credited as a co-author, but readily acknowledges her contribution as being that of typist and research assistant. The main driver of the publication was Arthur Hall, whose interest in James Wallace was due to his mother being a great-niece of Barbara Allan (the wife of James Wallace), and to his daughter's marriage in 1978 to a great-grandson of James and Barbara Wallace.

but evolved into something more as he came to realise how important James Wallace was to the Kelly story. His publication contained a lot of information that was totally new to me. As the head teacher of the Hurdle Creek State School located in the middle of Kelly country, Wallace protected the Kelly Gang during the two years they were at large, primarily because of a friendship with gang member Joe Byrne, which dated back to their school days in the Woolshed Valley.

Wallace supported the gang in many ways. I believe he played a role in the planning of the gang's bank robberies at Euroa and Jerilderie. I also believe he made a major contribution to the writing of two lengthy letters (which would later become known as the Cameron and Jerilderie letters) and other publicity that sought to present the gang in a more positive light. Wallace also acted as a double agent, all the while assisting the gang whilst acting as a secret agent for the police. For some of the time that the gang remained at large, Wallace hid them away in a hut in the ranges behind his school. Wallace also helped the gang collect the plough mouldboards used in the making of the armour worn at Glenrowan. All these actions by Wallace are explored in this book.

Arthur's publication also included information about Wallace's attempts to secure a pardon for Joe; the adverse findings against him by the Royal Commission on the Police Force of Victoria (which was set up in the aftermath of the Kelly Gang's destruction); his flight from Victoria and eventual return; and the breakup of his family as he took up with a woman named Bertha ('Bonnie') Bonn. In the last decade of his life, James and Bonnie travelled throughout Australia and New Zealand as Bonnie gained fame as a clairvoyant and spiritualist who called herself Madame Spontini.

After reading Arthur Hall's publication, I wanted to meet with him to find out what more he knew about Wallace. Unfortunately, by this time Arthur had passed away; however, his wife Lorraine referred me to her friend Elaine Wallace (granddaughter of James Wallace), who she said was the keeper of Arthur's research papers. Elaine was about to move to a retirement unit and was very pleased to give me the two plastic tubs containing Arthur's research material, which has been of great assistance in writing this book.

It is amazing that James Wallace's role has been so overlooked by historians and that he has received so little attention in Kelly literature, despite being the only sympathiser to have had adverse recommendations made against him by the Royal Commission. He was not mentioned in Kenneally's *The Complete Inner History of the Kelly Gang and their Pursuers* (1929)[4] or in Max Brown's *Australian Son* (1949),[5] and barely mentioned in Ian Jones's books. To my knowledge, Arthur Hall's publication and another titled *Pioneer Teachers of the Kelly Country* (2016)[6] by Len Pryor and his son Geoff Pryor were the first publications whose authors fully appreciated the role James Wallace played.

James Wallace was a complex man – highly intelligent, charismatic, forceful and energetic. This book gives an insight into his importance in the Kelly story, as well as his extraordinary life after the demise of the Kelly Gang.

---

4 - *The Complete Inner History of the Kelly Gang*, first published in 1929, by JJ Kenneally. The book has been republished multiple times, with the most recent publication being in 1980 (edition 9). The title of the book has also changed with the various publications – including *The Inner History of the Kelly Gang – and how justice was administered in their time* (1934 edition), and *The Complete Inner History of the Kelly Gang and their pursuers* (1946 edition).

5 - *Australian Son*, first published 1949, Phoenix House in association with Georgian House, Max Brown.

6 - *Pioneer Teachers of the Kelly Country*, 2016, Australian Scholarly Publishing Ltd, LJ and GW Prior.

1
Woolshed

Sixteen years after explorers Hume and Hovell passed through, a squatter named William Cropper built a shearing shed on land at Reid's Creek. The year was 1840. The locality would become known as Woolshed.

In 1852, gold was discovered in Reid's Creek. Alluvial miners were soon working the creek and its tributaries, including Woolshed Creek, Spring Creek and El Dorado Creek. These streams and tributaries were part of the Ovens River catchment, and the area became known as the Ovens Diggings. The town of Beechworth emerged almost overnight to meet the needs of the miners and others attracted to the district.

The Woolshed Creek Diggings – photograph taken by Walter Woodbury in approximately 1857.

Woolshed boomed between 1852 and 1855 with the population growing close to 5000. The town was almost as well known as Ballarat, Forest Creek and Bendigo. There were over 20 hotels at which miners could slake their thirst and a large number of stores and victualing establishments supported the burgeoning population. The town also hosted 10 blacksmiths who made and repaired the mining equipment and shod the horses. The buildings were all ramshackle and hurriedly built, and disappeared quickly once the rush was over.

Many of the early Woolshed settlers were from Ireland and Scotland. They had come to this new land intent on leaving behind lives of hardship in the old countries. However old-world animosities could not be left behind so easily.

The Wallace, Byrne and Sherritt families all settled in Woolshed around 1860, with their children getting to know each other through their attendance at the Woolshed school. With James Wallace, Joe Byrne and Aaron Sherritt all going on to become central players in the Kelly saga, it is useful at this point to provide some background about each family and how they came to settle at Woolshed.

The Wallace family

Charles Moreland Wallace and his wife Marion came from a small Scottish town called Stranraer. They arrived in Melbourne in 1853. Charles had been to Melbourne before, courtesy of his work as first mate on one of the fast clippers owned by the East India Company. However, it was probably poverty and lack of opportunity back in Scotland that mainly influenced them to emigrate, with neither Charles nor Marion having come from well-off families. Indeed, Charles's father James was employed as a lowly shoemaker.

Despite the likelihood that the goldfields attracted Charles and Marion to this unfamiliar land, circumstances saw them living in a shanty-town in the Melbourne suburb of Collingwood for the first six years of their new life. Their first child James was born there on 14 February 1854, followed by Andrew in 1856.

It was only at the end of 1859 that the family made the move north to the Ovens diggings. The family arrived at Woolshed in 1860 just as the town's heyday was over.

Charles tried his luck seeking gold along Reid's Creek, but the easy-to-find alluvial gold had already been well and truly picked over. His mining life soon ended when he contracted a respiratory disease that came close to killing him. By 1864 his occupation had changed to storekeeper.[7]

In 1869, the family moved downstream to the town of El Dorado, located about midway between Wangaratta and Beechworth. There, Charles set himself up as a local produce merchant.[8] The family then consisted of six sons: James (aged 15), Andrew (13), Charles (10), William (8), John (6) and Hugh (4). Gilbert, the last of the Wallace's seven children was born in El Dorado in November of 1869.

Charles Wallace was known a firebrand with a dislike for the English. His former home-town of Stranraer was a ferry-port connecting Ireland with Scotland, and as such was a stepping stone for many Irish 'migrants' escaping persecution and famine in Ireland. Stranraer was thus a town where Scots and Irish alike could vent about the persecution and hardships they suffered under the English-yoke. The Wallace family would likely have brought their old-world animosities with them and been very sympathetic to the plight of Irish families like the Byrnes.

Given the relationship that would exist between the Byrne and Wallace families in Woolshed, it is interesting that the Byrne family of Woolshed and another family of Wallaces which also hailed from Stranraer, Scotland, feature in the history of Braidwood in NSW. Indeed, Braidwood's main street is named Wallace Street in honour

---

7 - The 1864 records for the Woolshed school lists James Wallace as a pupil. The records also include the occupations of the pupils' fathers, with James's father's occupation being listed as storekeeper.

8 - A granite-lined well that Charles constructed behind his premises was known locally for over 115 years as 'Wallace's well'. After the well was filled in, the location of the Wallace property was largely forgotten. The book *El Dorado gold ... an Australian story* (2001), edited by Sandra Buchan, includes a map at page 34 that shows the location of homes and businesses in El Dorado circa 1897, on which the location of the Wallace property is identified at the Wangaratta-end of the Main Road (item 38 on the map).

of that family. It would have been very interesting had the Braidwood and Woolshed Wallaces been related, given that a gang of bushrangers called the Clarke Brothers featured in Braidwood's history. The Clarke Brothers, like the Kelly Gang, gained notoriety after ambushing a police party that had been sent to search for them. The Clarke Brothers also enjoyed a modicum of support from sympathisers, including initially (prior to their ambushing of the police) from the very well-off Wallace family of Braidwood.[9]

The Byrne family

Patrick and Margret Byrne came to Woolshed after marrying in Goulburn in 1855. Patrick's elder brother John and his wife Mary also settled in Woolshed at about this time. Both the Byrne families would have eight children,[10] with the eldest in both families being named Joseph. Patrick and Margret's son Joseph (Joe) was born in 1856, and would one day find infamy as a member of the Kelly Gang. John and Mary's son Joseph had been born two years earlier in Goulburn. The two Joseph Byrnes would later cause the authorities some confusion when they were searching for the Kelly Gang.

By the late 1860s, Patrick and Margret had established a small dairy farm on the south side of Reedy Creek. The Byrne family suffered a major change in fortunes, however, with Patrick's premature death in 1870 while Margret was pregnant with their eighth child.[11] Patrick's early death left Margret to support their eight children on her own. For 14-year-old Joe, the loss of his father meant he had to cut short his education and become the man of the household.

---

9 - An amateur historian named Jack Thomas did research many years ago that led him to believe that the Wallace families in Braidwood and Woolshed were related. Jack Thomas called it 'the Braidwood connection' and put forward a theory that the Kelly Gang had spent some of the time whilst they were on the run in the Braidwood area. Jack Thomas's research papers are in the hands of the author. However, a search by the author of genealogical records for both the Braidwood and Woolshed Wallace families going back four or five generations has failed to identify any connection between the two families. It is possible, of course, that there may be connections further back than four or five generations; however, such distant links would be fairly meaningless insofar as this Wallace story is concerned.

10 - Patrick and Margret's children were: Joseph (b. 1856), John (b. 1858), Catherine (b. 1860), Patrick (b. 1862), Mary (b. 1864), Dennis (b. 1866), Margaret (b. 1869) and Ellen (b. 1871).

11 - Ellen Byrne, born 1871.

The Byrne family had no reason at all to be kindly disposed towards English authority. As already noted, Patrick and John Byrne had both named their first-born sons in honour of their father Joseph, who had been transported to Australia as a convict in 1834 after being sentenced to life imprisonment for the crime of unlawful oaths – another way of saying he had been convicted of being an Irish Nationalist or 'Whiteboy'.[12] The Whiteboys were a secret Irish agrarian organisation who used violent tactics to defend tenant-farmer land rights for subsistence farming, with the name Whiteboys bestowed due to the white smocks its members wore in their nightly raids. The Whiteboys sought to address rack-rents, tithe collection, excessive priests' dues, evictions and other oppressive acts. As a result, they targeted landlords and tithe collectors.

Joseph Byrne's transportation had torn his family apart and caused lingering resentment. During his incarceration, his wife and daughter both died back in Ireland, leaving his sons Patrick, John, James and Michael without either parent. After being granted his ticket of leave in 1843, Patrick settled in Braidwood, NSW, with his sons whom he had not seen for a decade joining him that same year after leaving Ireland as assisted immigrants. Had the Woolshed Wallaces and the Braidwood Wallaces been related (which we have already noted was not the case) it would have made for some interesting possibilities, given the Byrne family's connection to that town.

Margret (née White) had also had a tough upbringing, having been one of the 'Irish Famine Girls' forced to emigrate to Australia due to her parents being unable to care for her during the Great Irish Famine. Having arrived in Sydney, Margret had initially been employed in a workhouse at the Hyde Park Barracks, before being placed as an indentured servant with a grazier in Bungendore NSW, near modern-day Canberra. It is hardly surprising, given what his grandparents, parents and he himself had been through, that Joe Byrne would one day turn to crime and become a member of the Kelly Gang.

---

12 - Irish: na Buachaillí Bána.

The Sherritt family

John and Agnes Sherritt were also from Ireland. Like the Wallace family, it was the lure of gold that brought them to the Ovens goldfields. They and their one-year-old son Aaron moved from Melbourne to Woolshed around 1856.

The Sherritts were of a different religious and political disposition to the Wallace and Byrne families. Whereas Patrick Byrne was a Catholic who had been transported for being an Irish nationalist, John Sherritt was of the Protestant faith and had been an 'Orangeman' – a member of a secret society that operated in the north of Ireland to defend the British sovereign and support the Protestant religion. Not only that, but John Sherritt had also been a member of the Irish Constabulary. The Sherritt and Byrne families therefore had little in common, although this did not prove to be a barrier in their children forming friendships, and likewise with the Wallace children.

Friendships are formed

Before compulsory education, the children of many settlers in places like Victoria's North East would end up helping out on the family's selection, or be faced with the prospect of itinerant work.[13] Lack of opportunity was just as bad here as it was in the old countries, and education was the key to a better life. The Wallace family, and Marion especially, pushed their sons to make the most of the education opportunities available.[14] James and Andrew were therefore enrolled at the local Woolshed school, a rough, saplings-and-bark building in which a single teacher named Cornelius O'Donoghue taught about 40 children.[15]

---

13 - Compulsory education was not introduced in Victoria until 1873.

14 - Not only were the education opportunities in these times limited, but teachers were not formally trained and the quality of teaching was highly variable. A good source of information about schooling in the North East in these early days is the book *Pioneer Teachers of the Kelly Country* by LJ & GW Pryor (2016).

15 - Cornelius O'Donoghue was appointed to the Woolshed school in 1863 and would remain there until 1883. He taught James, Joe and Aaron, and was one of the first on the scene after Sherritt's murder. He has sometimes been referred to as a Kelly sympathiser, but the reality is that as a Woolshed resident he needed to co-exist with those who were friendly with the families involved.

It was at this school that James became friends with both Joe and Aaron.[16]

Reid's Creek School

For a short time after 1864, James and Andrew Wallace transferred to the Roman Catholic school in Beechworth, despite them being Protestant. In 1866 they transferred again, this time to the Reid's Creek Church of England Common School.

After the family's move to El Dorado in 1869, the five eldest Wallace boys attended the El Dorado Common School No. 246 – a new brick school had replaced the original slab hut school built in 1863. The new school had a staff of nine and an enrolment of over 400 pupils in its first year. El Dorado's population started declining, however, almost

---

16 - James Wallace, Joe Byrne (and his cousin, also named Joe Byrne) and Aaron Sherritt were enrolled at the Woolshed School in 1864. As was the practice of the day, school inspectors regularly assessed the standard of both pupils and teachers. When an inspector visited the school on 14 March 1864, James and both Joe Byrnes were recorded as being present, but not Aaron Sherritt. James Wallace always achieved consistently high marks when tested, while Joe Byrne usually performed creditably. There is no record of Aaron ever having sat a test, it being common for schools to discourage the attendance on testing days of students who were likely to perform poorly. *Pioneer Teachers of the Kelly Country*, pages 175–176.

from the time the new school began operating – a victim of the decline in alluvial mining.[17]

El Dorado School No. 246 in the valley of Reid's Creek. Photo taken in 1900.

The Woolshed Valley in the 1870s was an adventurous place. The Wallace, Byrne and Sherritt families were strung out along the length of the valley – the Wallace family in El Dorado; the Byrne family further upstream about midway between El Dorado and Beechworth; while the Sherritt family owned a large selection in the Sheep Station Creek area located on the high ground to the south of the Woolshed Valley.[18] From Sheep Station Creek it was easy access to the Beechworth-Wangaratta Road and from there, hamlets like Everton Upper, Everton, Tea Gardens (now Markwood), Moyhu and Hurdle Creek, and south-west to the Kelly home at Greta.

Steep gullies provided a quick means of access between the Woolshed Valley and Sheep Station Creek. Byrne's Gully, so named because it terminated behind the Byrne property, was one such gully and was used extensively by Joe. Local knowledge and Joe's (and the future

---

17 - The El Dorado school building still exists and is now used as a folk museum.

18 - Sheep Station Creek joins with Reid's Creek not far below the impressive Woolshed Falls.

Kelly Gang members') ability to traverse terrain like Byrne's Gully would later give them an advantage over the police. Many of the police brought in from Melbourne to join the hunt for the gang were poor horsemen with little experience of the bush, while those who were more skilled were disadvantaged by not having the local knowledge of the gang members. As a result, the police tended to keep to the main roads and tracks, while the gang was able to take to the rougher country when travelling from place to place. Indeed, a policeman who later gave evidence to the Royal Commission expressed disbelief that the gang members were known to navigate Byrne's Gully on horseback.[19]

Halfway along Byrne's Gully there is a prominent granite rock that is visible from the Woolshed Valley floor. The rock is a local landmark known as 'London'. At its base is a small cave that could be used as a cosy bivouac shelter for two people. A small waterfall adjacent to London rock requires careful skirting if further progress is to be made up the valley. This was home turf for Joe Byrne, James and the Sherritts. An area of flattish land located not far from the top of the waterfall, but far enough removed to not be visible to those using the gully for access, is said to have been used by Joe as a secret holding yard for stolen horses. A rocky wall on the high side of the slope and cliffs on the low side kept horses confined, while access into the yard was only available via a narrow path that could be closed off and hidden by placing branches across the entry point.[20]

Large granite boulders are scattered over the sides of the Woolshed Valley and, as with London, some of these boulders offer cave-like shelter. Caves that would later be used by the police to watch over the Woolshed settlement (not the Byrne house) became known as the

---

19 - *Royal Commission on the Police Force of Victoria – Minutes of Evidence*, 1881 (Minutes of Evidence). Q13661–Q13667. When Senior Constable Patrick Mullane (who had been stationed at Beechworth) gave evidence at the Royal Commission, he was asked by Nicolson if he knew of London rock and the steep gully behind Mrs Byrne's house, and if he was aware that Aaron Sherritt and the outlaws were able to ride down that gully. Assistant Commissioner Nicolson said he himself had seen Aaron do it. Mullane was somewhat incredulous that this was possible.

20 - The holding yard was discovered in 1962 by a party led by Ian Jones, who claims it was used by Joe Byrne as a holding yard for stolen horses. All the indications suggest that this area was indeed used as some kind of a holding yard, but whether it was used for this purpose by Joe is uncertain – it would seem rather unwise for Joe to have a holding yard for stolen horses so close to his home.

Police Caves. The Kellys are said to have used another cave to keep watch over the Byrne house. The Police and Kelly caves would become known to the wider public after the Kelly outbreak ended.

Woolshed supported a large Chinese community, including near the Byrne household. Some were gold fossickers, but most were market gardeners who supplied the Woolshed population with vegetables and other produce. James, Joe and Aaron were all familiar with Chinese members of the community, with Joe reportedly speaking some Cantonese and developing an opium addiction. Relations with the Chinese were not always harmonious, however, with Joe and Aaron being charged in 1877 for assaulting a Chinese man named Ah On. They had been skinny dipping in the dam where Ah On took his water, and a dispute arose that caused Ah On to chase them with a bamboo rod. Aaron retaliated by throwing a large rock that cracked open Ah On's skull.

The knowledge Joe and the other members of the Kelly Gang and their friend James Wallace had of the Woolshed Valley, together with the support they received from some of its residents, was advantageous to the Kellys during the two years they were at large.

2
Different paths

James completed his education at El Dorado State School No. 246 in 1869. He was 15 years old. He returned the following year as a trainee teacher – a 'pupil teacher' as they were called then.

The head teacher at the El Dorado School was a man named Thomas Trembath, a Cornishman who had trained in Glasgow. He commenced at the school in 1863 at the age of 22, at which time, with the assistance of a work mistress, he was responsible for 32 children. In the year that James completed his education at the school, the enrolment had grown to over 400 pupils. The new brick school that had been built only a few years earlier was hopelessly overcrowded. However from this time on, the enrolments started to fall as residents left the district as a result of the closure of a number of El Dorado mines.

Although often unpaid, pupil teaching was seen as a stepping stone to a paid and secure teacher position. Many pupil teachers started from as young as 13 or 14 years of age, and would often continue in that role for four or five years. In due course, James's brothers Andrew, Charles and William would all commence as pupil teachers at the El Dorado State School. Charles, however, died of typhus in 1875, while Andrew's teaching career was short-lived due to an epilepsy condition. William was still working, by then as a teacher, at the El Dorado school at the time of the Kelly outbreak (in 1878).

Around the time James commenced his teaching duties at El Dorado, a young constable named Anthony Strahan was transferred from Beechworth to El Dorado Police Station. The fact that the police station was next door to James's school meant the two men would have been known to each other. With James's father Charles being an El Dorado store owner, Strahan would also have known the family by reputation, whether he shopped there or not.

Ned Kelly would later accuse Strahan (in what would become known as the Jerilderie Letter) of letting it be known he would shoot Kelly like a dog without first giving him an opportunity to surrender. It was one of many justifications Kelly cited for his murder of three policemen at a place called Stringybark Creek. If James had a hand in the writing of the Jerilderie Letter (which is discussed later in this book as something that was more than likely), then it would seem very likely that Anthony Strahan failed to make a good impression on young James.

James eventually obtained his Licence to Teach in 1873. This meant he had successfully sat examinations in reading, composition, grammar, geography and arithmetic, and had shown familiarity with the readers used in the schools. The Licence to Teach qualification was an Education Department prerequisite for appointment as a head teacher – a somewhat grandiose title for a position that usually meant being the only teacher.[21]

Out of school hours, James found time to associate with his old friends, including those like Joe and Aaron who led what could be called colourful lives. James also had a serious side to him, which saw him writing newspaper articles and letters to people in authority about a wide range of matters. He developed what would become for him a lifelong interest in spiritualism, a practice that by the late 1800s was becoming increasingly common and accepted. An associated interest was mesmerism, and he would later recount to the Royal Commission how he had used Aaron as a mesmerism subject.[22] A granddaughter would later recall the family talking of how James could summon them through mind-power alone, although a more likely explanation is that he possessed a strong and dominating personality and family members were anxious to please him.[23]

Unlike James and his brothers, the opportunities open to Joe Byrne were limited. While he attended the ramshackle school at Reid's Creek, he showed some early academic promise, obtaining similar results to

---

21 - In the early days of compulsory education in Victoria, teachers were often appointed as head teachers and remained in that position for many years before actually obtaining their licence.

22 - Minutes of Evidence. Wallace's answer to Question 1477.

23 - Elaine Wallace (James Wallace's granddaughter).

James's. However, with the tragic premature death of his father, Joe's school days were brought to an early end – as the eldest son, he became obligated to support his mother and siblings. In these circumstances, it is easy to appreciate how he went off the rails.

Joe's first court appearance was in 1871 on the charge of illegally using a horse, for which he had to pay a fine of 20 shillings to avoid jail. Then in 1876, he and Aaron were convicted of stealing a bullock and were sent to Beechworth Prison. And in February 1877, Joe and Aaron again came before the courts, this time for the assault of Ah On.

Joe was a complicated man. He had several convictions and had already served time in gaol well before getting involved with the Kellys. He was an opium addict and a well-known ladies' man. He also had a vicious temper, as evidenced by his assault on Ah On and another incident in which he severely injured one of his sisters after belting her with a bridle. A neighbour of the Kellys would later describe him as 'a dangerous man ... a man who would fire on any one that would attempt to arrest him.'[24] In the Royal Commission report he was described as someone who was in trouble from the age of 16 years and who from the first appeared to have developed vicious and cruel propensities.[25]

Joe and Aaron's theft of the cow was known in those times as cattle duffing or poddy-dodging. It happened a lot, with the need to feed one's family making it justifiable in the eyes of some settlers. Yes, it was criminal and illegal, but laws were always being broken and it was notable how not all laws were enforced equally. As an example, the laws introduced by the government with the aim of breaking up large squatter landholdings to make land available to selectors were often ignored. This was a regular occurrence, with no repercussions for that particular class of lawbreaker.

James was also not averse to a bit of cattle duffing. Aaron Sherritt's older brother John would later tell the Royal Commission of how he came to mistrust Wallace after finding out that he had slaughtered

---

24 - Joe was described as a dangerous man by Brickey Williamson, one of the men who would be arrested after the attempted murder of Constable Fitzpatrick at the Kelly's home at Eleven Mile Creek – the act that triggered the Kelly outbreak.

25 - Second Progress Report of the Royal Commission of Inquiry into the Circumstances of the Kelly Outbreak, Chapter 1 – The Kelly Family.

one of the cows he had been agisting on Wallace's selection at Hurdle Creek.

As for Aaron Sherritt, he was never academically inclined and needed little encouragement to drop out of school early.

Through a lens

A photograph of James Wallace, taken in 1900, appears on the front cover of this book and is the only known photograph of him that still exists. It was taken when he was the Manager of the *Kerang Times*, and is extracted from a group photograph in which he and another newspaper man were posing with the councillors and staff of the Kerang Shire Council. James was only 46 years old, but he looks a decade older. More is said about his appearance later in this book when discussing Wallace's Kerang years.

The absence of a photograph of James in his younger years is disappointing. There was a wedding-day photograph of James and his wife that had survived until comparatively recent times. That photograph once sat proudly on the mantelpiece of James's parents-in-law, Ebenezer and Martha Allan, at their house at Tea Garden Creek (now known as Markwood), and remained in the family until it was discarded a few years ago by a younger member of the family who was unaware of the photograph's significance. The photograph had been taken only a few years before the Kelly outbreak and would have been an important record of James as a young man. According to one of James's granddaughters, the Wallace men of that generation were big, impressive-looking men with large personalities.[26] She said this of her own father and from being acquainted with several of his brothers, and believes that James would have been similar in terms of physique and personality.

The 1870s photographs of Joe and Aaron are '*carte de visite*' portrait shots, which were taken by Beechworth photographer James Bray, who also photographed future Kelly Gang member Steve Hart. Bray established his studio at a time when photography was in its infancy.

---

26 - The granddaughter concerned is Elaine Wallace. Elaine's father was Hugh Wallace who was the ninth child of James and Barbara Wallace.

His matchbox-sized portraits are often the only pictorial records of people from those times and were treasured by the families and loved ones of the subjects, and perhaps also by the subjects themselves. It is hard to believe a man like James Wallace would not also have posed, but if he did, the portrait of him has been lost to time.

Bray's photograph of a suited-up Joe Byrne shows a tall and dapper-looking man. It would have been the only photograph of Joe if it weren't for the ones taken two years later of his corpse strung up for public viewing outside the Benalla courthouse.

Bray's photograph of Aaron Sherritt shows a strong, confident-looking bushman with a touch of the larrikin about him. The hat strap under his nose shows him to be a member of the Greta Mob. Superintendent Francis Hare, the man who was in charge of the Kelly manhunt for much of the time they were at large, would later describe Aaron in the following terms: 'He was a remarkable looking man. If he walked down Collins Street, everybody would have stared at him – his walk, his appearance, and everything else were remarkable.'[27]

Gaol can be a great apprenticeship for budding criminals. It was there that Joe and Aaron befriended a young man named Dan Kelly who was doing time for similar crimes. The Kellys, of course, were involved in a wholesale stock-theft racket in which the ringleader was Dan's elder brother Ned. Once released, Joe spent a lot of time with the Kellys at their selection in Greta West. Aaron also initially spent time with them, but for the most part was content to work on the family selection at Sebastopol.

Despite all his faults, James Wallace was a devoted friend to Joe and did all that he could to protect him.

---

27 - Minutes of Evidence – Francis Hare responding to Question 1270 describing his first encounter with Aaron Sherritt at Benalla about five or six days before the Jerilderie robbery.

3
Hurdle Creek

In 1873, James, aged only 19 years, was promoted to run the newly established Hurdle Creek State School No. 1076 at Bobinawarrah, situated south-east of Oxley between Milawa and Moyhu and about 15.5 miles away from his family at El Dorado. Bobinawarrah is an Aboriginal name which means water cascading in the hills.

The Oxley Plains were opened to selectors in the 1850s. The land closer to Milawa was taken up first, with early selectors including the Allan family who owned a property called Ballan Boga at Tea Garden Creek (later renamed Markwood). The land further south along Hurdle Creek was opened up later for selection, and was taken up by families including the Swinburne, McGreggor, McAliece, Doig and Gibb families, whom would have been well-known to James Wallace. The descendants of some of these Hurdle Creek pioneers still farm or live in the area today.

With the passing of the 1872 Education Act, education became compulsory and caused the Victorian Government to embark on a massive school-building agenda to ensure children in all districts were served by an accessible school. The new school at Hurdle Creek was one such school, built to cater for the selector families whose children's education was sporadic, due to Hurdle Creek's distance from Milawa and Oxley. The school was constructed of brick and set a new standard for rural schools. It also came with a detached residence for the schoolmaster. It is likely that judicious lobbying by James and his family had managed to secure him this prized school, as there were many more-experienced teachers in the North East who would have jumped at the opportunity. James was never one to hold back when it came to improving his situation.

Hurdle Creek State School No. 1046, with the head teacher's residence in front. This photograph was taken in 1895, and is the only known photograph of the school.

James initially lived alone at Hurdle Creek, but soon met and married a young woman named Barbara Allan, daughter of the Allan family at Ballan Boga. They married on 26 March 1874 at St Paul's Church in Wangaratta. Barbara's parents obviously approved of the match, as evidenced in 1877 when they named their fourth child James Wallace Allan in honour of their son-in-law.

At the time of his marriage, James had only recently celebrated his twentieth birthday, while his new bride was only two months shy of her own twentieth birthday. James's best man was a fellow teacher named Crawford McAliece, whose family were selectors at Hurdle Creek.[28] Mary Ann Swinburne, whose family also owned a selection at Hurdle Creek, was bridesmaid.

Although they were living at the school house, James aspired to owning a selection like their new friends at Hurdle Creek. In 1875, he marked out a 152-acre parcel about a mile down the road from the school and at the southern edge of the agricultural district. The land

---

28 - Crawford McAliece was also a teacher. He married a Mary Ellen Haworth at Bobinawarrah in 1877, and lived most of his life in the district. He was a popular umpire for the Ovens and King Football League in the late 1890s and early 1900s, and was the chairman of the district's School Board of Advice in the early 1900s.

he selected was separated from the bush-covered Crown Land to the south by a rough track (known today as Box Forest Road). He marked out the corners of the land with a combination of posts and stone cairns, and applied to the Land Board for a License to Lease.[29] Further information about the Wallace selection is included at Appendix 1.

Selection was hard work. License conditions required a selector to build a residence and reside on their property. If these conditions were not met to the Land Board's satisfaction, there was a danger of the selection being relinquished by the Crown. Although James built a residence on the land in 1876 as his lease conditions required, he was given an exemption from having to reside on the land due to his residency at the school.

James's younger brother Hugh (born in 1866) came to live with James and Barbara at Hurdle Creek when he was about 12 or 13 years old, most likely in the schoolhouse. Hugh was not academically inclined like his brothers and would only ever hold down a job as a farm labourer. He came to live with James and Barbara to look after the stock and help out on the selection in other ways. John Sherritt owned the stock he looked after, which was paddocked on the property to keep the grass down.

The Carboor Range and other ranges surrounding the agricultural districts were unsuitable for agriculture and were for this reason retained as Crown Land. The ranges were the source of timber for the buildings and fences required by the new settlers, and there had been some splitters at work in the ranges not far from James's selection. They had built a hut in a minor gully, which became known for obvious reasons as Sawpit Gully. It was the location of one of the few perennial springs in the Carboor Range. The existence of the hut would have been known to James and the other selectors at Hurdle Creek. James would almost certainly have explored his local area and visited the hut, given access was via an indistinct track that commenced near the southern boundary of his selection.

---

29 - The land selected by James Wallace was described as Allotments 5A & 5B, Section 1, County of Delatite, Parish of Moyhu. The land had an area of 152 acres 3 roods and 26 perches. James applied to the Land Board on 9 November 1875 for a Licence to Lease under Part II of the Land Act 1869.

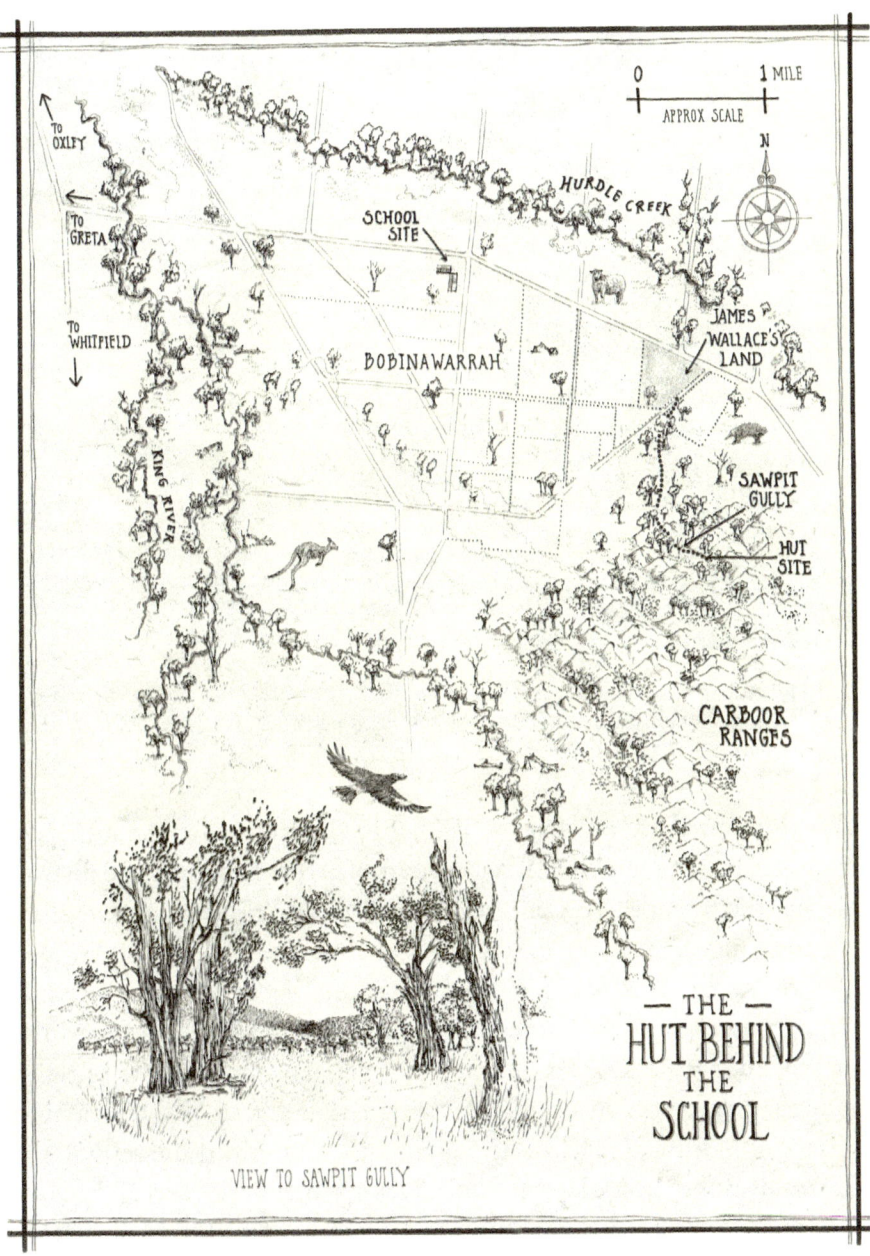

Map showing the Bobinawarrah/Hurdle Creek district, and the locations of the Hurdle Creek State School No. 1046, the Wallace selection, and the splitter's hut in Sawpit Gully within the nearby Carboor Range. [30]

---

30 - Map drawn by Alex Hotchin, Cartographer.

Photo taken from the school site looking south-east towards the gap in the ranges that leads to Sawpit Gully and the 'hut behind the school' site. (Denheld, 2013)

After the splitters harvested the timber in the vicinity of the hut, they moved on and the hut was all but forgotten. Most people in the district had too much work to do on their selections and no reason to venture into the ranges. As a result, during the time the Kelly Gang was at large, they were able to make occasional use of the hut unnoticed. It was only much later when detectives investigating Wallace found the hut that they were able to draw a link between him and the outlaws' occupancy. Locals then started referring to the hut as 'the hut behind the school'—although the hut site is actually miles from the school, the gap in the range through which the track to the hut passes can be seen from the former school site. This was compounded by the association of the hut with Wallace the schoolmaster.

Ned Kelly and Joe Byrne were later said to have visited Wallace at his school residence at various times to pick up provisions. The visits would have been outside of school hours and probably at night, given that most of the district's residents were not sympathetic towards the gang. As far as provisioning the gang, this is more likely to have taken place from Wallace's selection than from the school. It is said that Hugh Wallace used to drive stock over the outlaws' tracks after they had visited to pick up provisions, hiding the evidence of their passing.[31]

After their marriage, James and Barbara wasted no time in starting a family. Charles James Wallace, named in honour of James's father Charles Moreland Wallace, was born in 1875, exactly nine months after their marriage.[32]

After Charles, other children followed in quick succession – Martha in 1876 (who died in infancy), Ebenezer Arthur (Prince) Wallace in 1877 and George Gilbert Wallace in 1878.

Those early years at Hurdle Creek were a busy time for the Wallace family. While James attended to his teaching duties, Barbara was responsible for the household and also ran the Bobinawarrah Post Office during school hours from a small annexe at the front of the school.[33] The post office opened in December 1874 at James's instigation and with the support of local residents. The mail was carried by horseback from Wangaratta three times a week. By 1878, the Hurdle Creek school and its attached post office had become the main focal point for the local community.

The reports of school inspectors, not just in Victoria but also later when he worked in Queensland, invariably described Wallace as energetic and displaying a lot of initiative. A school inspector who visited Hurdle Creek in 1875 reported on him as follows:

> *A good teacher – a good deal above the average of country schoolmasters. He is active, energetic, and careful. Preserves good order, when a little older, and with a little more experience, will make an able, efficient servant to the Department.*

---

31 - An affidavit later signed by Hugh Wallace (but obviously written for him by James) states that if there had been tracks left by the outlaws, then he (Hugh) would have noticed them. The fact that James included this detail in Hugh's affidavit indicated to historian Arthur Hall that there probably were tracks, and that it was Hugh's job to obliterate them. It seemed to Arthur Hall that it was an otherwise unnecessary detail to have included in the affidavit.

32 - Charles Wallace died of heart failure in Adelaide in 1912, aged only 37 years.

33 - Post Office No. 863, which operated as a sub-branch of the Milawa Post Office.

As if running one school was not enough, in March 1878 James commenced teaching on a half-time basis at a new school (Hurdle Creek West School No. 2536) that the Education Department had just built to service the western part of the Hurdle Creek district. He had managed to secure this additional school by enlisting the support of the Hon. JH Graves MP.[34] The new school was needed due to difficulties that parents in the western part of the district faced in getting their younger children to the Hurdle Creek School, particularly during the busy harvesting time.

Under the arrangement James entered into with the Education Department, the Hurdle Creek School was run as a full-time school, while the Hurdle Creek West School, which had an enrolment below what was needed to employ a full-time teacher, was run as a part-time school. James could do this by teaching mornings at the Hurdle Creek School and then putting the work mistress (Barbara) in charge for the afternoon to allow him to teach at the other school.[35] James benefitted financially because teacher salaries were calculated according to the number of students taught and the new arrangement increased his student numbers from 30 to 45. He was now paid a special salary of £3.10 a week (£182 per annum) on top of which Barbara earned £30 a year for her work-mistress role. James was earning about £30 a year more for running these two low-enrolment schools than teachers were receiving for running a single school with a much higher enrolment. He also had the added advantage of a detached residence to reside in, when most school residences were rather ramshackle affairs attached to the school building itself. The family was also receiving an additional income for running the post office, and it is likely that James was also being paid for some of the newspaper articles he started writing for papers like the Wangaratta Despatch. The Wallace family was raking it in![36]

---

34 - The Hon. Graves MP wrote a memo to the Education department on 2 February 1878 saying that he wished for Mr Wallace to be appointed to the new school at Hurdle Creek when ready. A transcript of the letter is included in *The Headmaster of Hurdle Creek*, page 50.

35 - A school with greater than 30 pupils was entitled to have a work mistress.

36 - RC Minutes of Evidence – Q14759-Q14761.

Over the nine months the Kellys were at large and James acted as a police agent, he also claimed expenses that the future Royal Commission estimated at £180. Working for the police effectively doubled his salary over that period. Legitimate questions can be asked about his motivations. We know that the information he provided to the police was next to useless, and it is hard to accept that this was not deliberate. Was he out to enrich himself, while at the same time helping to protect his mate Joe? Or was what he did part of some broader agenda related to the selector movement? Or perhaps it was a combination of both? Arthur Hall, author of *The Headmaster of Hurdle Creek*, believed that the emergence of Free Selector Associations around 1875 hardened James's anti-British sentiments and caused him to think a lot about the republican sentiments being expressed by some of these associations. Arthur believed that James sought to take advantage of the upheaval caused by the Kelly outbreak to further advance the republican cause. Despite this belief, lack of evidence meant he didn't say so in his book.[37]

As stated, James was a man of great initiative. Only a month after taking on the running of the additional school, he arranged to accompany his students on an excursion to Ballarat to visit the Juvenile Industrial Exhibition. Upon his return, he sought permission from the Education Department for the Hurdle Creek School to be used as a public library and reading room outside of school hours. When the Department finally agreed some five months later, he then immediately organised a 'Promenade Concert' to raise money to purchase books.

From his early days as a young teacher, James cultivated an extensive list of contacts throughout the North East. His role as head teacher and post master at Hurdle Creek gave him exposure to hundreds of selector families and meant he was an important pillar of that society. An educated and articulate man, he also developed relationships with a range of important men in the wider community.

---

37 - The idea that the Kelly Gang had a republican agenda was put forward by Ian Jones in *Ned Kelly: A Short Life* (1995). Ian Jones was for many years acknowledged as the expert on all things related to the Kelly story, so the idea that Ned Kelly had republican tendencies became almost a given, and it is possible that Arthur Hall was unduly influenced by this line of thinking. Any thought that the Kelly Gang had republican ideas has been comprehensively debunked in *Ned Kelly and the myth of a republic of North-Eastern Victoria* (2018), by Stuart E Dawson.

One such person was Mr James Howlin Graves, MLA for Delatite. Graves was a strong advocate for the selector movement and made a number of representations for James over the years, including getting him appointed to run the new school at Hurdle Creek West on a part-time basis. Two years later, after the police and the Education Department initiated moves to relocate James out of the district, Graves would send another letter to the Education Department endorsing his brother William as his replacement. He sent that letter after being prompted to do so by James. Graves had no idea, however, that Wallace was protecting the Kellys. Ultimately Graves was appointed to the Royal Commission on the Police Force of Victoria, which resulted in him forming a very different view of James Wallace.

Another politician James turned to for help was James Goodall Francis MLA.[38] In April 1880, James would close his schools without permission to travel to Melbourne in the hope of persuading Francis to support a plan that would see Joe Byrne granted a pardon in exchange for betraying the rest of the gang. Wallace would later report to Aaron Sherritt that the proposal was rejected, with Francis telling James that when the gang was caught, Joe Byrne would hang.

For five years prior to the Kelly outbreak, James ran his school at Hurdle Creek without any issues. He was well liked by the selector families in the district, who would have been delighted that their children were being taught by a teacher of James's calibre. Barbara's family lived not far away at Tea Garden Creek. Friends would also visit, including Joe and Aaron.

James maintained his friendship with Joe, despite Joe having a criminal record. Because of his friendship with Joe, it is likely that James would have also been acquainted with Ned and Dan Kelly and many of their extended network of relatives and friends. The Kellys had a reputation in the North-East that James would have been well aware of. However, as the Kellys and their associates were from the same class as the Wallace, Byrne and Sherritt families, there may have been an element

---

38 - https://adb.anu.edu.au/biography/francis-james-goodall-3566

of class loyalty that would see James turn a blind eye.[39] Loyalty to friends is important, and perhaps James took the view that a friend of Joe's was also a friend of his. We shouldn't forget, though, that James was a young man at this time. Perhaps with the benefit of hindsight he may have chosen to be more discerning about his associations. His sympathiser activities caused him many difficulties in his later life.

James was far from alone, though, in his attitude towards the Kellys. *The History of Greta*, a small publication written in 1940 by a Greta resident named Samuel Ellis, indicates that the residents of Greta, including many respectable people like Samuel's own parents, shared a similar attitude. Samuel was born in Greta in 1873, and attended school there from 1878. His parents Thomas and Annie were both born in Ireland. His father Thomas had for a time been a police constable in Melbourne where he was a friend of Henry Pewtress, who would later be in charge of the Mansfield Police Station.[40] Thomas and Annie were prominent members of the Church of England, where Thomas would sometimes conduct the service at Greta's Christ Church. Samuel, in turn, would later become a foundation member of the Greta Primitive Methodist congregation. It could be said that Samuel had Greta in his blood and was therefore well placed to write the district's history.

Samuel's publication only runs to 35 pages. It gives a brief account of the white settlement of Greta and of happenings familiar to locals. It is very much aimed at Greta folk, being a sort of documentation of their shared experiences and attitudes. It was clearly not directed at a broader audience, as some of the content would be incomprehensible to people outside of the community. The 'chapter' on the Kellys is interesting as it seems to be a reflection of what Greta locals of Samuel's vintage thought of the Kelly years. It acknowledges that what happened was tragic, but also suggests that the Kellys, while no angels, were not entirely to blame as they were harshly treated as members of a poor Irish family.

---

39 - Assistant Chief Commissioner Charles Nicolson was very aware of the need to recruit agents (or spies) from the same class of people that the Kellys themselves belonged to.

40 - Henry Pewtress was in charge of the Mansfield Police Station in 1879 when the Kelly Gang murdered three policemen at Stringybark Creek.

Surprisingly for a man of his background, Samuel's account of the Kellys is rather partisan. There is a real 'us and them' idea running through his writing – with 'their' Kelly showing qualities of admirable forbearance, excellent planning and execution, and an obvious ability to out-general the police. The police, on the other hand, were peremptory, out of their depth, dependent upon the 'wily' Aboriginal trackers, and much preferring discretion to valour.

Significantly, Samuel wrote about how people in the neighbourhood showed no fear of being molested by the Kellys and simply went about their duties during daylight or darkness. He also wrote that the Greta tradesman who manufactured the armour, who he doesn't name but who the locals would have known was a man named Delaney, was 'not a belligerent … but (someone who) acted within his neutral rights.'

Samuel's publication, both in what he says and in how he expects his local readers to react, implies a general sympathy for Kelly in the Greta district. He gives a hint of some local active support given to the Kellys, referring here to a friend of the Kellys leading their horses. The general impression, though, is that people, himself included, were generally barracking for Kelly rather than actively involved. In essence, barracking for the Kellys was widespread, while active supporters were much fewer. And then there were some like Delaney who fell somewhere in between and would help out a little if asked. As an upright citizen himself, Samuel Ellis is almost apologetic when he says that things were different then: 'They are wild times of which I write … adventurers from distant lands had not yet realised that law was the foundation of freedom, though it be sometimes harsh and unequal.'

Samuel ends his publication with an epilogue that consists of a full quotation of Sir Walter Scott's poem 'Edmund's Song'. Samuel says he finds the poem almost prophetic, perhaps because it contains romantic sentiments that people like him found attractive about Edward Kelly. The fact that the poem-as-epilogue takes up nearly 10 per cent of 'The History of Greta', is perhaps indicative of the way Greta locals must have viewed the Kelly outbreak. 'Edmund's Song', as we will see in a later chapter, also had some significance to the residents of Hurdle Creek (Bobinawarrah) – the area in which James Wallace ran his schools.

4

Tensions leading up to the Kelly outbreak

There were many reasons for the local 'us and them' sentiments that shine through in Samuel Ellis's little publication.

The end of the 1850s gold rush created tensions as many diggers and their families looked to farming as another way of making a living.[41] The good farming land was mostly under the control of squatters and pastoralists who had been given long-term leases over the land they occupied for nominal rentals as low as £10 a year. Squatters occupied much of the land in the North East in the area that would one day become known as Kelly country. The towns and settlements of Kilfera, Tarrawingee, Taminick, Glenrowan, Bontharambo, Oxley, Laceby, Boorhaman, Myrrhee and El Dorado were all named after extensive squatter runs that preceded them.

Squatting had created enormous riches and the squatters naturally did all they could to maintain their wealth. After Victoria separated from New South Wales in 1851, the squatters dominated the Legislative Council (the Upper House) of the Victorian Parliament, and therefore had a monopoly on land and power. However, despite their best efforts, a series of Land Acts were passed when the balance of power in the Upper House occasionally shifted in favour of the reformists.[42] The Land Acts sought to break up the vast pastoral runs to deliver land into the hands of small farmers.

Land Acts passed throughout the 1860s resulted in the Crown Land occupied by squatters being broken down into smaller parcels, which

---

41 - The gold rush saw the Victorian colony grow rapidly from 77,000 people in 1851 to 540,000 in 1861 as eager miners from Europe, China and other Australian colonies surged to the new goldfields.

42 - Nicolson Land Act 1860, Duffey Land Act 1862, Grant Land Act 1869.

were then made available for selection. The blocks could be anywhere from 40 acres to 640 acres (a square mile) and were subject to set conditions regarding residence, cultivation, method of purchase, and cost. These were arrangements under which James Wallace's father-in-law Ebenezer Allan selected 'Ballan Boga' and under which James also acquired a selection.

The aim of releasing land to selectors was to create new and prosperous rural communities of yeoman farmers. However, the term 'selector' quickly became synonymous with rural poverty. The reality was that many selectors had little or no real farming experience and struggled on selections that were too small to sustain farming. The Kelly selection at Greta is an example of an inappropriate selection. Even if the Kelly family had worked hard, their selection would have only supported a subsistence lifestyle. It was far easier for Ellen Kelly to run the property as a sly grog shanty than to make a serious effort at farming.

Selectors and squatters were often on a collision course as selections were excised from existing squatting runs. The squatters used a number of techniques to thwart the breaking up of their land. Extensive use was made of 'dummies' – a slang term used to describe those with no intention of becoming farmers but who were used by the large squatter-landowners to apply for selections that would effectively remain in their hands. Perhaps the greatest of the squatters' weapons was to deny selectors access to water by maintaining control of land adjacent to waterways or containing a spring. Many disputes arose over access to water. These tensions contributed greatly to the 'us and them' attitude evident in Samuel Ellis's publication.

James Wallace's father-in-law Ebenezer Allan found himself in a land dispute with a more powerful landowner. In 1879, the local Land Board refused Ebenezer's application for a new allotment. The unstated reason for the refusal was that one of the members of the Board wanted the land for himself. Luckily, Ebenezer had in James Wallace a son-in-law with the literary skills required to write a letter of protest to Francis Longmore, the Minister for Lands.[43] His protest was upheld and he was allowed his selection. Ebenezer's case, however,

---

43 - The letter bearing Ebenezer Allan's signature was dated 10 July 1879.

was a typical example of the bias many selectors faced when dealing with the local Land Boards. This kind of conflict further contributed to the 'us and them' attitude.

James concluded his letter to Longmore with a paragraph in which he pandered to Longmore's vanity by noting that he had gained a name and fame as the 'Selector's Friend'. James would find out one day that Longmore was certainly not his friend – as the Chair of the Royal Commission on the Police Force of Victoria, Longmore and his fellow commissioners would come to make a finding of 'reprehensible conduct' against James that would see him dismissed from the Education Department and forced to flee the state.

Many selector families on the Oxley Plains at this time lived a hand-to-mouth existence. While the squatters benefitted from ridiculously low annual licence fees, the selectors were paying much higher licence fees for smaller parcels of generally inferior land that often lacked water. The conditions attached to their licences were also onerous. Up until 1878, licence conditions required a selector to reside on their land. However, the inadequate returns from farming forced many men to take seasonal work away from home to make enough money to support their families and meet the annual payments to the Lands Department. The need to seek work elsewhere often caused selectors to fall behind in meeting their obligations to fence, cultivate and generally improve their land. The Land Boards were aware of the difficulties and were usually prepared to look the other way, but the practice of using the police to check for compliance with licence conditions sometimes caused issues, particularly if the selectors were known to the police for other reasons. This also hardened the attitude of some selectors towards authority.

Disputes with squatters and difficulties with authority were not the only issues facing selectors in these times. The police presence in the North East was sparse and the quality of many police officers was poor, which led to an element of lawlessness in which families like the Kellys turned to cattle duffing and horse stealing. The victims of these crimes were not just large landowners. Other selectors were often the victims of stock theft. However, the absence of effective law enforcement caused law-abiding selectors to think twice about informing on criminal activity out of fear of retribution.

Larrikinism also added to the tensions in the North East. The 1870s saw the early mines in Woolshed, Sebastopol, El Dorado and Stanley become worked-out, as the children of the first miners were reaching adulthood. The children of the early selectors were also coming of age at this time, with many of them dissatisfied at the idea of working the family selection for what was essentially a subsistence lifestyle. A drought was making selector life even more difficult. The combination of these factors led to unemployment and disillusionment, and created an underclass of discontented young men who gathered in larrikin groups like the Greta Mob, of which Joe, Aaron and the two Kelly brothers were members. Joe and Aaron were typical of many who fell through the cracks.

> *They were young men, vigorous and active, with minimal education and few marketable skills. They were usually good horsemen and keen bushmen who could 'rough it' and survive. But they had poor prospects and became restless and frustrated. A little cattle duffing and horse 'borrowing' eased the tension for some and provided irregular incomes.*[44]

The divide between the haves and the have-nots, the hardships of selection, and the dislocation of young men (and women) coming of age during this period all contributed to that 'them and us' attitude that probably contributed to why so many people would become Kelly sympathisers. Another factor was that the failure of the police to quickly catch the Kellys resulted in the gang becoming media sensations, which in turn saw many otherwise law-abiding people in the district start to admire them for their exploits and derring-do.

The discontent among selector communities found expression in the formation of Free Selectors Associations around Victoria from 1875 onwards. In 1877, the Upper Murray Free Selector's Association was formed to fight Council and Land Board abuses, apparently with

---

44 - Pioneer Teachers of the Kelly Country, (2016) LJ & GW Pryor, page 82

some success. Although some have suggested that James played an important role in the Free Selector's Association, there is no hard evidence of this. However, unpublished material left by Arthur Hall, author of *The Headmaster of Hurdle Creek*, leaves no doubt that he believed James Wallace was a champion of the selector movement in North-Eastern Victoria from a very young age. Hall believed that James had ample time prior to his marriage to reflect on the vital issues affecting the selector class and his hopes for the future, and that he was highly influenced by the views of men like John Dunmore Lang who filled the editorials and political columns of *The Age* and *Argus*, and by political giants like David Symes and Gavin Duffy. Symes and Duffy, in particular, were strong advocates for independence from England, with Hall in his unpublished material expressing the view that James had been highly influenced by their views, noting that James adopted anti-British sentiments, which were on show later in his journalistic career. After becoming aware that his friend Joe Byrne had been involved in the Stringybark Creek outrage, Hall believed that James saw this as an opportunity to advance a republican cause and that this resulted in him contributing to numerous newspapers including the *Wangaratta Despatch*, *Yea Advocate*, *Ovens and Murray Advertiser*, *Kerang Times* and probably others.

Despite his own personal success, James maintained his friendships with Joe and Aaron and continued to mix with them outside of his teaching hours. They would probably have visited James at his school house at Hurdle Creek. Perhaps in the light of the events that were soon to come, James should have reconsidered his position, but with the bonds of friendship being as strong as they were it is understandable that he didn't. In the end, James never gave up on his friendship with Joe – although both he and Joe would ultimately turn on their friend Aaron as they became aware that he had sided with the police.

Whatever James thought of the Kellys, things took a turn for the worse on 15 April 1878. That was the day Ned Kelly shot a policeman named Constable Fitzpatrick who was in the course of arresting Dan Kelly on a charge of horse stealing. The botched arrest set in place a series of events that would see the formation of the Kelly Gang and a two-year effort by the authorities to apprehend them.

Joe was at the Kelly property at the time of the shooting, but had not been identified. For reasons unknown, Joe joined the two Kelly brothers as they fled into the Wombat Ranges in the aftermath. Another young man named Steve Hart joined them later. A warrant against Ned Kelly for attempted murder was duly issued by the police.

15 April 1878 was also a personally significant day for James and Barbara, with the death on that day of Barbara's 14-year-old brother George Allan. The death certificate records George's death as being due to remittent fever. James is recorded on the certificate as the witness.

News of the shooting at the Kelly property spread fast through the selector community. With the school at Hurdle Creek being a focus of the community, James would have soon learned of Joe's involvement in the fracas. It would have been difficult for James to hear about this while the family was also coming to terms with George's death.

The Kelly brothers, together with Joe and Steve, hid themselves away in the Wombat Ranges at a place known as Bullock Creek. For six months they spent their days there sluicing for gold and distilling whisky from a maize crop they had planted. They also spent considerable time honing their shooting skills as if preparing for a violent encounter. Their whereabouts were known to their kin and friends who were frequent visitors and upon whom they relied for supplies and news.

James and Aaron would certainly have known of Joe's whereabouts. And because at this stage the police had not yet identified Joe, he may even have visited James at Hurdle Creek over this period, given that the hideout at Bullock Creek was only a hard day's ride away, and Hurdle Creek was on the way to Woolshed, Beechworth and other places Joe was likely to visit.

By this time, James and Barbara were the busy parents of three young children. In their dual roles as schoolmaster and postmistress they were working hard to support their growing family and were active in their local community. Despite this, James often left Barbara and the children at home on weekends and during school holidays as he travelled around the district visiting friends and acquaintances. The Golden Ball Hotel, halfway between Hurdle Creek and Beechworth, was one of his favourite drinking venues, and he was also known to frequent various hotels in Beechworth. Like Joe and Aaron, he was comfortable in the bush and it is not inconceivable that he might even have visited Joe and the Kellys at Bullock Creek.

The Kelly family had already had many brushes with the law, and with a charge of attempted murder hanging over him, Ned must have known that freedom would be short lived. The authorities, in particular a detective named Michael Ward, had been making extensive enquiries and had a good idea of where they were hiding out. Six months on from the Fitzpatrick incident, two search parties were sent out to apprehend them – Senior Constable Shoebridge led one from the north, and Sergeant Michael Kennedy led the other from the south. Shoebridge's party included a constable named Anthony Strahan who would have been well known to the Wallace family (and also to Joe Byrne), having been stationed at El Dorado during the years James was a pupil teacher there (the El Dorado Police Station was located next door to the school).

The Wombat Ranges is rugged country through which easy passage was only possible using the network of trails that followed the watercourses running through the area. The main trail ran along Stringybark Creek. The Kelly camp at Bullock Creek was on the other side of a ridge that separated the two creeks. After friends tipped the gang off about the two search parties, the gang either discovered for themselves or received word that the Mansfield police party was camped adjacent to the Stringybark Creek trail near the remains of two old huts. They chose to take the initiative and confront the party.

The gang made its move on the police camp on 26 October 1878, unaware that the police party had split up and that only two of the police were in the camp. Ned Kelly quickly shot dead one of the two policemen – Constable Thomas Lonigan – without giving him the chance to surrender. Later in the day when the other two police officers returned to the camp, one of them (Constable Michael Scanlon) was shot dead immediately as he reached for his weapon and the other (Sergeant Michael Kennedy) was chased down and murdered almost a mile away. It was only sheer luck for the fourth member of the party (Constable Thomas McIntyre) that he was able to escape during the confusion and bear witness to what had happened.

Had the Kellys simply disarmed the police party, any freedom they gained would have been short lived. Perhaps they thought killing the police party was their only way of evading justice, although the finger of suspicion would have been pointed at them anyway and nothing would have changed the fact that Ned was still wanted for the attempted murder of Constable Fitzpatrick. Whatever their thinking, what happened at Stringybark Creek was chaotic and undisciplined. And James Wallace's friend Joe was caught up in it.

The day after the murders, news of the outrage spread like wildfire throughout the colonies. James Wallace would have been shocked. It was one thing to know that Joe was associating with the Greta Mob and the Kellys, but murder was something else entirely. However, James would stand by his friend and do all in his power to support the gang during their period at large.

Officialdom acted quickly with the Victorian Parliament passing the Felons Apprehension Act on 15 November 1878. The Act placed Ned and Dan Kelly and their two as yet unnamed accomplices officially beyond the normal protection of the law. In other words, they were outlaws.[45] It was about this time that the outlaws also came to be known as the Kelly Gang, with the government offering a reward of £800 (£200 each) for their arrest and conviction. Joe Byrne and Steve Hart had at this stage not yet been identified as members of the gang.

---

45 - An article by Stuart Dawson published in the journal of the Australian and New Zealand Law and History Society examines the origins of the Felons Apprehension Act under which the Kelly Gang was outlawed after their murder of three police at Stringybark Creek on 26 October 1878. http://nedkellyunmasked.com/wp-content/uploads/2021/11/Ned-Kelly-Outlawed-Dawson-corrected-FINAL.pdf

5
Helping a friend

After the Stringybark Creek murders, the Kelly Gang took flight for NSW. Unable to cross the flooded Murray River near Bungowannah on 31 October 1878, the gang narrowly avoided capture by wading into the floodwaters and hiding amongst reeds.[46] They decided their best option was to turn back and head for home where their extensive family and other connections could offer them refuge. Their route took them past Sheep Station Creek near Woolshed, where a bark stripper sighted them on 3 November.[47] The following day, the gang passed by the northern edge of Wangaratta and headed for the Warby Ranges.[48] The men were exhausted and in a very precarious state and could easily have been captured if not for the incompetence of Inspector Brook Smith who was in charge of the Wangaratta district.

The Kelly Gang most likely made it back to the safety of Greta around 7 November. Despite the improbability of them being anywhere near Woolshed, on that same day a police party set out for Woolshed in response to a false report that the gang was hiding out in a hut opposite Aaron Sherritt Snr's hut (Aaron's father). The police party grew larger and larger as word spread among the wider district. There were said to be up to 50 police officers involved in what the newspapers would derisorily call the Sebastopol Charge as the party descended on the hut concerned. Finding the hut empty, the party then descended upon another nearby hut, before eventually moving on to Mrs Byrne's house. Although Joe Byrne had not at this stage been positively identified as

---

46 - A table of reported appearances of the Kelly Outlaws is included at page 690 of the Police Royal Commission Second Progress Report. The gang was sighted at 'Margery and Peterson's near Bungowannah' on 31 October 1878, with this report being received by the police on 2 November 1878.

47 - The gang was sighted by a bark stripper at Sheep Station Creek on 3 November 1878, but the report was only received by the police on 6 November 1878.

48 - The gang was sighted at a Wangaratta Bridge and railway crossings on 4 November 1878, with the police receiving reports on this on 4 and 5 November.

one of the gang members, the police obviously had reason to think he was involved.

Chief Commissioner Standish met with Aaron Sherritt in the aftermath of the Sebastopol Charge and sounded him out about his preparedness to act as a police agent. The gang, of course, was at this time back in Greta being sheltered by family and friends.

On the day of the Sebastopol Charge, James was busy at his school preparing for a fundraising concert to be held the following evening (Friday 8 November 1878) to raise money for his proposed Bobinawarrah Public Library. Arthur Hall, author of *The Headmaster of Hurdle Creek* believed that Joe visited him around this time to ask for assistance.

The Stringybark Creek shootings and the subsequent flight of the Kelly brothers and their two unidentified associates had of course been dominating the news. The murders had caused an outrage, but stories had been circulating even before the murders that presented the Kellys in a more sympathetic light. There was talk of police persecution and harassment. And a story spread that Fitzpatrick had had ulterior motives for visiting the Kelly property six months earlier, and that he had attempted to seduce Ned's 14-year-old sister Kate.

In due course, Ned Kelly would put his grievances into print, but at this stage the stories spread by word of mouth and in the occasional newspaper report. When seeking to secure the assistance of his friend, it was in Joe's interests to run with the Kelly's version of events.

On the night of the school concert, the Stringybark Creek shootings, the Sebastopol Charge and the declaration of the four fugitives as outlaws would have been the subject of much discussion. Their notoriety was such that the Kelly name was known to most in the district even before the murders at Stringybark Creek. Many may even have known the Kellys personally, given the number of friends and relatives they had in the North East. Although Joe Byrne and Steve Hart had still not been identified at this stage, some of the local selectors would have known they had been with the Kellys at Stringybark Creek, and that Joe was a friend of their children's teacher.

The concert was a great success according to the *Ovens and Murray Advertiser*.[49] Interestingly, the night's entertainment included a recitation by one of the local selectors of Sir Walter Scott's poem 'The Outlaw'[50] – the same poem that Samuel Ellis would include in *The History of Greta* some 60 years later, albeit under a different title – 'Edmund's Song'. Obviously that poem was significant not just to the residents of Greta, but also to the residents of Bobinawarrah/Hurdle Creek. The similarities between the outlaw in Scott's poem and Edward Kelly would have been hard to miss, as would the fact that the poem is heavily sympathetic to the outlaw and is set in a land where he roams quite apart from the Queen of England. James Wallace was obviously confident his audience would be amused by the selection, despite the recent horrors of Stringybark Creek. It is interesting that this particular poem was recited publicly at a local fundraiser as the hunt for the Kellys intensified. It indicates that the romanticising of the Kellys that has continued to the present day commenced at the start of the Kelly outbreak.

The success of the concert enabled James to apply to the School Board for a library and reading room.[51] From this point on, James started providing active support to the Kelly Gang, with the school at Hurdle Creek becoming an important point of contact for the district's sympathisers.

James was prepared to take extraordinary risks to help Joe. By providing the Kelly Gang with supplies and information, he helped them remain at large for twenty months. At the same time, and at his own instigation, he also 'helped' the police by acting as a secret police informer. A respectable school teacher and family man like James was the kind of person the authorities would have least expected to provide assistance to the gang. James was playing a double game in which the stakes were very high.

It may seem strange that the Kelly Gang members chose to remain in the area rather than escape and seek a new life elsewhere. However,

---

49 - The *Ovens and Murray Advertiser*, Saturday 16 November 1878.

50 - The poem was recited by Mr S Downey, the owner of an 85-acre selection on the Whorouly-Bobinawarrah Road. (Land file no. 5528, section 33 of Land Act 1869 relates.)

51 - James's letter to the School Board is dated 12 November 1878.

they had lived outside of the law for so long with the support of their extended family and friends that they apparently believed this could continue. Despite a reward for their capture, which was ultimately increased to £8,000, the gang was able to remain at large for the next two years.

The Outlaw by Sir Walter Scott

O, Brignall banks are wild and fair,
    And Greta woods are green,
And you may gather garlands there,
    Would grace a summer queen:
And as I rode by Dalton Hall,
    Beneath the turrets high,
A Maiden on the castle wall
    Was singing merrily:—

'O, Brignall banks are fresh and fair,
    And Greta woods are green!
I'd rather rove with Edmund there
    Than reign our English Queen.'

'If, Maiden, thou wouldst wend with me
    To leave both tower and town,
Thou first must guess what life lead we,
    That dwell by dale and down:
And if thou canst that riddle read,
    As read full well you may,
Then to the green-wood shalt thou speed
    As blithe as Queen of May.'

Yet sung she, 'Brignall banks are fair,
    And Greta woods are green!
I'd rather rove with Edmund there
    Than reign our English Queen.
'I read you by your bugle horn
    And by your palfrey good,
I read you for a Ranger sworn
    To keep the King's green-wood.'
'A Ranger, Lady, winds his horn,
    And 'tis at peep of light;
His blast is heard at merry morn,
    And mine at dead of night.'

Yet sung she, 'Brignall banks are fair,
    And Greta woods are gay!
I would I were with Edmund there,
    To reign his Queen of May!

'With burnish'd brand and musketoon
    So gallantly you come,
I read you for a bold Dragoon,
    That lists the tuck of drum.'
'I list no more the tuck of drum,
    No more the trumpet hear;
But when the beetle sounds his hum,
    My comrades take the spear.

'And O! though Brignall banks be fair,
    And Greta woods be gay,
Yet mickle must the maiden dare,
    Would reign my Queen of May!

'Maiden! a nameless life I lead,
    A nameless death I'll die;
The fiend whose lantern lights the mead
    Were better mate than I!
And when I'm with my comrades met
    Beneath the green-wood bough,
What once we were we all forget,
    Nor think what we are now.'

Chorus

Yet Brignall banks are fresh and fair,
    And Greta woods are green,
And you may gather flowers there

Would grace a summer queen.

6

The robbery of the National Bank at Euroa

Based on information that would be provided to the police by a man named William 'Brickey' Williamson, the Kellys may have previously entertained thoughts about committing a bank robbery. If so, they now needed to put those thoughts into action as funds were urgently needed in order for them to stay at large. The National Bank at Euroa was selected as the target. The robbery needed to be done quickly given the increasing number of police officers being brought to the North East to join the search for the gang.

'Brickey' Williamson was a neighbour of the Kellys and had been at the Kelly homestead at the time of the Fitzpatrick shooting. He was serving a six year sentence in Pentridge Prison in Melbourne for his part in the incident and was now cooperating with the police in the hope of an early release. Brickey told the police that he thought the gang would attack one of the banks at Seymour.[52] When this information was passed on to the newly appointed Assistant Chief Commissioner Charles Nicolson, he immediately increased the police presence at Seymour. Brickey was wrong though – the actual target was the National Bank at Euroa.

On 8 December 1878, two days before the Euroa raid, the gang was reported as being seen at 'Chappells'. This was the Reidford Hotel,

---

52 - In the Royal Commission minutes of evidence, there are a number of questions and answers relating to information given by the prisoner Williamson on 15 November 1878 about the likelihood of a bank at Seymour being targeted by the Kellys. Assistant Chief Commissioner Nicolson, who was in charge of the police operations at the time, was criticised by Chief Commissioner Standish for his failure to act on the information in a timely manner; however, it became clear (Q16889 and Q16890) that he did not receive the information until 28 November, by which time it was too late for him to take precautions against such an attack.

which was run by two brothers named Jim and Jack Chappell.[53] Chappells was conveniently located opposite a ford or crossing point on Reid's Creek.[54] It had done a roaring trade when Captain Standish's men had gone there for liquid refreshment after the debacle of the Great Sebastopol Raid, unaware that most of the locals who drank there were well acquainted with the Kelly Gang members. They certainly knew Joe Byrne well, as he was a local like them.

The reported sighting at Chappells was a red herring though, as the following day the gang would hold up Faithful Creek Station (also known as Younghusband's Station) a few miles north of Euroa before conducting their bank raid the day after.

The Euroa Bank robbery took place on Tuesday 10 December. To prevent word getting out about the planned raid, the previous day the gang had bailed up the workforce at Faithful Creek Station as the men returned to the homestead for lunch. They locked the men in the station's storeroom overnight, guarded by Joe Byrne. Several strangers not known to the station workers were locked in with them. With no way of knowing if the strangers were actually sympathisers, the prisoners made no move to overpower their guard.

The Melbourne-Wangaratta railway and telegraph line ran along the east side of Faithful Creek Station. The gang cut the telegraph wires before the robbery to prevent communications between Benalla and Euroa. Workmen sent out to repair the line were duly captured and added to the party of prisoners, as were several others who happened to be passing by.

In a nice touch, one of the strangers visiting Faithfuls Creek Station happened to be a hawker named Gloster, who would later be identified as a sympathiser. Gloster just happened to have some new outfits in his cart that would allow Ned and Dan to dress up as well-off young gentlemen. Leaving Joe behind to guard the prisoners, the young

---

53 - The hotel was the last hotel to operate in the Woolshed Valley, but was lost in bushfires over Christmas 1899.

54 - The crossing (made from solid granite) became known as Wick's Crossing after Anton Wick moved to a new house at this locality after the murder of Aaron Sherritt. However, at the time of Aaron's murder by Joe Byrne, Anton Wick lived at a house located further upstream on the opposite side of the creek to the 'murder house'.

gentlemen, driving separate carts, headed off to Euroa. Steve Hart was already in town to watch the bank and ensure things ran smoothly.

Ned, Dan and Steve bailed up the National Bank staff and succeeded in getting away with £2000 in cash and a large quantity of gold sovereigns. They returned to Faithfull Creek Station, taking with them the bank manager Mr Scott, his wife and seven children, Mrs Scott's mother, the children's nurse and two servants. After threatening the prisoners with death if they dared leave the station before a specified time, the gang then left on horseback, flaunting their horsemanship by jumping the station fences as they headed towards the Strathbogie Ranges. Sympathisers ensured that their tracks could not be followed.

The Euroa robbery took place a little more than a month after the gang members had straggled back to Greta after the Stringybark Creek murders. Even if the Kellys had previously entertained the idea of a bank robbery, the limited time that had elapsed since Stringybark Creek and the fact that they were in a state of exhaustion and stress, makes it unlikely that they planned the Euroa robbery on their own. These reasons, and because of the fact that they needed to move from place to place to avoid detection over the weeks since they returned home, pointed to someone else being the mastermind. Arthur Hall, the author of *The Headmaster of Hurdle Creek*, and Len Pryor, co-author of *Pioneer Teachers of the Kelly Country*, believed that James Wallace was the primary architect of the raid (and also the Jerilderie bank raid that followed). As noted later in this book, the likelihood that James was that author of what became known as the Cameron Letter is a good reason to think he was also the mastermind behind the planning of the Euroa bank robbery (or at least had significant input into the planning). The level of detail that went into the planning of the Euroa robbery (and later again for the Jerilderie bank robbery) was consistent with what might be expected of Wallace – a man who, as we will see later when looking at the letters he would write to Assistant Commissioner Nicholson, thrived on detail! Examples of the planning that went into the Euroa robbery included: recruiting men to watch the police movements at Euroa prior to the robbery; the taking of prisoners at Faithful Creek; the seemingly happenstance appearance at Faithful Creek of a hawker who just happened to have in his wagon the clothes the Kellys needed to dress like gentlemen; and the recruitment of men to ride over the outlaw's tracks as they made their escape over the Strathbogie Ranges.

Another example of the high-level planning that went into the robbery was the provision of (mis)information to make the police believe the gang would seek to cross the Murray near Albury on the day of the robbery. Sometime before the raid, the postmaster at Hedi Post Office just happened to intercept a letter outlining such a plan. That letter was handed to the policeman in charge of that district (a Senior Constable Kelly, who had no connection whatsoever to Ned Kelly), who duly passed it on to Assistant Commissioner Nicholson. Hedi, also sometimes called Edi, was a small settlement on the King River about 10 miles to the south of Bobinawarrah. James may well have written the letter (or arranged for another to write it) and as a postmaster himself and therefore familiar with the way letters were handled, would have known how to ensure the letter was intercepted.

The Hedi letter caused Assistant Commissioner Nicolson and Benalla-based Superintendent John Sadleir to immediately depart Benalla for Albury on the day of the robbery. As their train passed through Glenrowan, they noticed they were being watched by people they knew were sympathetic to the outlaws, but so confident were they with the information in the letter that they dismissed this. They also dismissed a report that the telegraph line opposite Faithfull Creek Station happened to be down.

The Euroa robbery went off without a hitch, except that the hitherto unidentified fourth member of the gang was positively identified as Steve Hart by one of the Scott's servants, a young girl named Fannie Shaw who had gone to school with Steve.

The public perception of the Kelly Gang changed after the Euroa raid, with reports circulating that Ned Kelly was anything but the monster the press had painted him as after Stringybark Creek. The wife of the bank manager contributed a great deal to that change of perception, describing Kelly as a good people manager and as someone who would have made a magnificent general had he not been a bushranger.

7
Kelly Gang sympathisers

The Kelly Gang, as noted earlier, enjoyed considerable support among the local population. The author with Kelly historian Bill Denheld has compiled the map below that shows the location of those people identified in the police blacklist of Kelly sympathisers.[55]

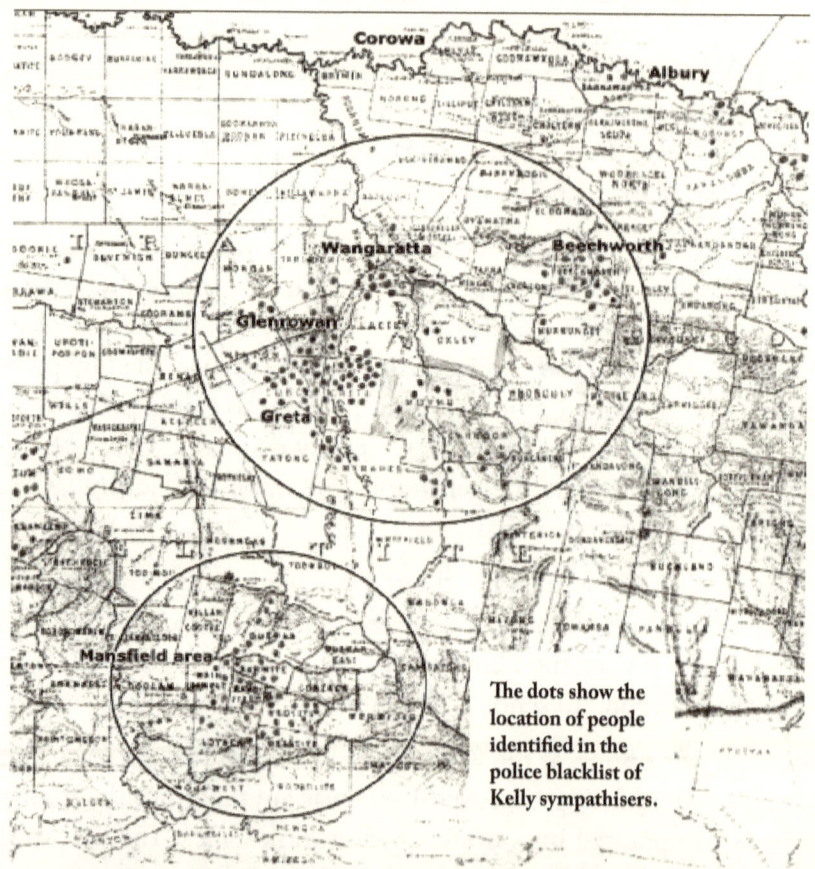

The dots show the location of people identified in the police blacklist of Kelly sympathisers.

Map showing locations of known Kelly sympathisers.

---

55 - The first step in compiling this map was to identify the Kelly sympathiser's selections and/or places of residence on the relevant Parish Plans. The respective Parish Plans were then joined together and ultimately scaled down to produce a single map covering the whole of the Kelly country.

As the map depicts, there were certain locations in which Kelly sympathisers were quite prevalent. There was a large concentration of sympathisers in a belt extending south from Wangaratta, through Glenrowan and Greta and along the Fifteen Mile Creek towards Myrrhee. There was another concentration in a belt which extended east from Myrrhee towards Moyhu and Carboor, and a further concentration around Beechworth. There was also a particularly large concentration of sympathisers around the Mansfield area. Sympathisers were also scattered along the Murray between Albury and Wodonga and the Baranduda Range. There would, of course, have been many others who were not on any police blacklist, but were sympathisers nonetheless due to family connections or friendships with other sympathisers.

It would have been impossible to live in Kelly country and not be exposed to the many sympathisers. The prevalence of sympathisers meant that a sensible option for those who were not sympathisers was to remain neutral.

Len Pryor in *Pioneer Teachers of the Kelly Country* speculates on the relationships some school teachers in Kelly country might have had with the Kelly Gang members and their sympathisers and allies.[56] By way of example, he cites a teacher named Thomas Wall who had been Ned Kelly's teacher at Beveridge when Ned was there as a student in the mid-1860s.[57] In 1879, Wall was placed in charge of a new school at Bungeet near Lake Rowan.[58] The Kellys had some very reliable friends in this area, including fathers who had petitioned for the school. Thomas Wall must have had some knowledge of the gang's movements, and might even have met his former student from Beveridge days. One of his sons (Daniel Wall) was a close friend of a young man named Joe Ryan, a nearby selector and a sympathiser who was well known to the police – if there is such a thing as guilt by association then Daniel was guilty as a Kelly supporter.

---

56 - *Pioneer Teachers of the Kelly County* (2016), LJ & GW Pryor, pages 173–205.

57 - The school at Beveridge was Common School No. 711 and was housed in the Catholic Church at Beveridge.

58 - Bungeet State School No. 2148.

Another school teacher with links to the Kelly story was Cornelius O'Donoghue, the head teacher at the State School at Woolshed.[59] In 1864, his class lists showed three of his pupils to have been 'Joe Byrne (son of a miner)', 'James Wallace (son of a storekeeper)' and 'Aaron Sherritt (son of a dairyman on Sheep Station Creek)'. He had also been uncomfortably close to some of the significant events in the Kelly saga, including the Sebastopol Charge and later the murder of Aaron Sherritt. Cornelius had lived with and taught the children of the families along Reedy Creek for 18 years, and, as such, would have known many people who were sympathisers and many who were not. He would most certainly have been well aware of what was going on in the district and would have heard of things that would have been of interest to the police. Because he remained silent he was said to have been a Kelly sympathiser; however, it may have been more a case that he chose not to take sides in order not to fall out with those he had to live with.

James Wallace would have faced the same predicament as teachers like Thomas Wall and Cornelius O'Donoghue, except that in his case things were more complicated because he also happened to have a close friendship with Joe Byrne.

---

59 - Woolshed State School No. 1900.

8
Sympathiser arrests

In the aftermath of the Euroa bank robbery, the hunt for the Kelly Gang intensified. Police Commissioner Standish travelled to the North East to personally oversee the search, assisted by Superintendent Francis Hare. Assistant Commissioner Nicolson, who had previously been in charge, was relieved from duty, exhausted from having already spent months hunting the gang.

Concerned about the growth in sympathy towards the Kellys, and perhaps also in response to growing condemnation in the press about the failure of the police to capture the gang, Commissioner Standish made the decision to arrest prominent sympathisers under the provisions of the Felons Apprehension Act 1878. Section 5 of the Act provided that those who harboured or provided aid to the outlaws could be punished by up to 15 years imprisonment.

Standish asked his officers to prepare lists of those in the district who they considered to be sympathisers. On 2 January 1879, warrants were sworn for the arrest of over 30 men. Most were arrested simultaneously over the next two days. Some of the men were only detained for a short period before being released, but 23 men were charged and remanded in custody at Beechworth Gaol. The remanded men are listed in the table below:[60]

The remanded men included some of the leading Kelly sympathisers, such as Tom Lloyd Jr, Jimmy Quinn, Issiah 'Wild' Wright and Joe Ryan. It wouldn't have escaped the notice of many who moved in the same circles as these men that Aaron Sherritt, a known associate of the outlaws, had not been arrested. They wouldn't have known at this stage that he was working as a police agent, but the fact of his non-arrest must have had some wondering where his loyalties lay.

---

60 - The table showing the remanded men is taken from *The Kelly Outbreak 1878–1880*, John McQuilton, page 114.

Name	Date Arrested	Reason	Remands	Date Released
J. McElroy	3 Jan. 1879	Associate	7	25 Feb. 1879
J. Quinn	3 Jan. 1879	Relative	15	22 Apr. 1879
F. Hearty	3 Jan. 1879	Associate	15	22 Apr. 1879
R. Strickland	6 Jan. 1879	Associate	15	22 Apr. 1879
D. Delaney	4 Jan. 1879	Suspected associate	2	22 Jan. 1879
W. Woods	4 Jan. 1879	Suspected associate	2	22 Jan. 1879
J. Lloyd	3 Jan. 1879	Relative	15	22 Apr. 1879
P. Quinn	6 Jan. 1879	Relative	15	22 Apr. 1879
J. Hart	3 Jan. 1879	Relative	9	11 Mar. 1879
I. Wright	3 Jan. 1879	Associate	15	22 Apr. 1879
H. Perkins	4 Jan. 1879	Supplied gang	2	22 Jan. 1879
J. McMonigal	3 Jan. 1879	Associate	7	25 Feb. 1879
D. Clancy	3 Jan. 1879	Associate	15	22 Apr. 1879
J. Clancy	4 Jan. 1879	Associate	15	22 Apr. 1879
M. Harvey	4 Jan. 1879	Associate	15	22 Apr. 1879
R. Miller	3 Jan. 1879	Relative	1	18 Jan. 1879
J. Ryan	4 Jan. 1879	Relative	7	25 Feb. 1879
B. Gould	14 Dec. 1878	Associate	5	To Euroa
W. Stewart	10 Jan. 1879	Anonymous tip	1	11 Jan. 1879
J. Stewart	10 Jan. 1879	Anonymous tip	1	11 Jan. 1879
T. Lloyd	3 Jan. 1879	Relative	5	25 Feb. 1879
J. Cain	10 Mar. 1879	Associate	5	22 Apr. 1879
T. Lloyd jun.	10 Mar. 1879	Relative	5	22 Apr. 1879

Sources: Beechworth Record of the Court of Petty Sessions, Case List Book, Burke Museum, Beechworth; Sadleir's Diary, Sadleir Papers, L.C.S.L.V.

Interestingly, Wallace had approached Captain Standish around the time of the Sebastopol Charge (November 1878) offering his services as a police agent. He was well aware of how work as an agent could be used to his advantage. He may have known or suspected Aaron had already been recruited in the aftermath of the Sebastopol fiasco. His offer was rejected, though, with Standish letting him know he would be pleased nevertheless to receive any information about the outlaws that he might become privy to.

Standish would later tell the Royal Commission on the Police Force of Victoria that his real reason for rejecting Wallace's offer was that he had had first-hand experience as to why he could not be trusted. That mistrust was due to a lie Wallace told him during the course of a visit he had made to Wallace's residence at Bobinawarrah. When he (Standish) had asked Wallace if he had seen Aaron recently, Wallace replied that he had not seen him for weeks. On returning to Benalla later that day, Standish found Aaron waiting at his office to meet him. When he told Aaron that he had just come from visiting Wallace, Aaron told him that he too had just come from visiting Wallace. That made him realise that Wallace could not be trusted.

Undaunted, Wallace wrote to Assistant Commissioner Nicolson on 5 January 1879, offering his services to him instead.[61] His letter may have been motivated by the mass arrest of sympathisers over the preceding two days. The fact that he wrote to Nicolson indicates that he was unaware that he had been replaced by Superintendent Hare. Nicolson was not in a position at this time to act on James's offer, but he would do so later in the year when Hare was himself forced to step down.

While the arrest of the sympathisers was at first popular with the public, it eventually caused problems for the police as the arrested men were each week brought before a magistrate and continuously remanded. Public opinion soon turned as rumours spread that keeping these men on remand was the cause of ruined crops and unnecessary hardship to their families, despite these men being mostly farm labourers rather than selectors. Eventually the presiding magistrate at Beechworth had no choice but to order their release. All were released on 22 April 1879, their prison experience having further embittered them against the police and made them more determined to help the Kellys.

The Police Royal Commission Second Progress Report would later have this to say about the sympathiser arrests:

> *... without any effort to obtain information for the purposes of the prosecution, the necessary legal machinery was put in motion to make the arrests. In making these arrests no proper discretion was exercised. Several persons were taken into custody against whom no evidence could be obtained, while a number of persons known or suspected of being in close and intimate relations with the gang were allowed to remain at large. As a consequence, when the cases were called on, remand after remand was applied for and granted, until finally the magisterial bench at*

---

61 - Minutes of Evidence, Q14493.

Beechworth discharged the prisoners. Those apparently arbitrary proceedings were not salutary in their effects. They did violence to people's ideas of the liberty of the subject; they irritated and estranged probably many who might have been of service to the police; they failed to allay apprehensions of further outrages on the part of the gang, or to prevent them from obtaining the requisite supplies; they crippled the usefulness of the officers, who had to be called away from active duty in connection with the pursuit to attend the petty sessions at Beechworth, when remands were applied for; and, what was of more significance, the failure of the prosecutions led the public to believe that the conduct of affairs was mismanaged.[62]

---

62 - Police Royal Commission Second Progress report, commentary extracted from Chapter X – 'Captain Standish and Supt Hare in charge of the pursuit'.

9
Another bank robbery (Jerilderie, NSW)

On 8 February 1879, the Kelly Gang conducted a second bank raid – this time a branch of the Bank of NSW at the small town of Jerilderie in NSW. As with the raid at Euroa, the robbery was conducted with panache. Senior Constable George Devine and Probationary Constable Henry Richards of the NSW Police were captured and kept confined in their own lock-up, while the gang made use of their police uniforms to trick the bank manager into opening his door at midnight. As in Euroa, the gang also rounded up some of the townspeople and held them hostage at the Royal Hotel, where Ned subjected them to a lecture in which he told them the raid was to demonstrate the futility of arresting the sympathisers and to embarrass the New South Wales force.

The raid netted the Kelly Gang some £2,000. In an act intended to demonstrate sympathy with the plight of small selectors, the gang also burnt mortgage papers they took from the bank's safe.

While in Jerilderie, Ned Kelly tried unsuccessfully to locate the editor of the local newspaper to force him to publish a letter that would later become known as the Jerilderie Letter.

After the robbery, the Kelly Gang left Jerilderie, leaving no clue about their direction of travel, and no tracks that the police forces of either New South Wales or Victoria could follow. Trusted selectors provided food and shelter, allowing the outlaws to travel light and to cover fifty miles or more in a night. They simply disappeared into the bush once again.

The Jerilderie raid exceeded Euroa in many respects, especially with the gang appearing in police uniforms. Planning had required great attention to detail, and must have occupied many hours during the summer of 1878 to 1879. The logistics were incredible. The gang is believed to have travelled to Jerilderie via the west side of the Warby Ranges, before crossing the Murray River into NSW about four and a half miles west of Yarrawonga at a place called Burramine. The trip to Jerilderie and back would have taken about 10 days, requiring changes of horses and the picking up of supplies from trusted selectors along the way. Everything was planned to coincide with the phase of the full moon, which enabled travel through the night.

As with the Euroa bank robbery, it is likely that James Wallace played a major part in the planning of the Jerilderie robbery. As noted in the next chapter, it is probable that James had input into the writing of the letter that Ned Kelly wanted to give to the editor of the local newspaper for publishing. A great deal of organisation and planning went into the raid and, again, James was one of the few amongst the sympathisers with the required organising capabilities.

After Jerilderie, the police faced growing public and official pressure to capture the Kelly Gang. The New South Wales Government and the Bank of NSW contributed to the Victorian reward for the gang's capture, bringing the total amount offered to a very substantial £8000.

The Victoria Police grudgingly accepted an offer from Queensland to provide a contingent of Aboriginal trackers. They arrived in Benalla in March 1879 under the command of Sub-Inspector Stanhope O'Connor, who developed an uneasy relationship with the Victorian Police commanders. As a result, the Victorian police never properly utilised the skills of the Aboriginal trackers. The Kellys, however, were very aware of the capabilities of the trackers, whose presence forced them to exercise extreme caution in travelling about. The presence of the trackers and increased police efforts would cause the gang to mostly disappear from public view for almost a year. Despite the large number of their relatives and friends, the gang no longer enjoyed the same liberty they once did.

10
Publicity for the Kelly Gang

A number of attempts were made between December 1878 and July 1879 to present the Kelly Gang in a more positive light:

1. A letter (which would become known as the Cameron letter) dated 14 December 1878 (only four days after the Euroa bank robbery) was sent to Donald Cameron MLA.

2. Ned Kelly took a letter (which would become known some 50 years later as the Jerilderie letter) to their second bank raid in Jerilderie NSW in the hope that he could persuade the local publisher to have it printed.

3. Twelve days after the Jerilderie robbery, the proprietor of the Mansfield Guardian published a treatise titled *The Kelly Gang or The Outlaws of the Wombat Ranges*. This publication was significant because it gave an impartial account of the Kelly outbreak, and included information about 'the other side of the story' that could only have come from someone who knew or had access to the Kellys.

4. A further letter presenting the Kelly Gang in a more positive light was published in the *Ovens and Murray Advertiser* on 12 July 1879.

For the reasons discussed below, it is likely James Wallace had a role in all of the above.

The Cameron Letter

A few days after the Euroa robbery, a letter purportedly from Ned Kelly and dated 14 December 1878, was sent to Donald Cameron MLA.[63] A copy of the same letter was also sent to Superintendent John Sadleir, the officer in charge of police in the North-Eastern District.

The letter seems to have been prompted by criticisms Cameron made in parliament on the 14 November 1878 about the lack of progress by the police in their hunt for the gang. Cameron had said things in his speech that could be construed as indicating support for Ned Kelly, although this was more likely part of a political game than any genuine concern for the Kelly Gang.

Ned Kelly could barely write, so it can be said with certainty that he did not write the letter. Although some of the hostages at Faithfull Creek Station reported seeing Joe at work on a long letter, Joe's literary skills were also not good enough for him to have composed a letter like the one written to Cameron. The content of the letter was also indicative of it having been written by someone who was better placed to have kept his ear to the ground as far as news was concerned. James Wallace had the literary skills and was also a keen follower and commenter on the news. He was a childhood friend of Joe Byrne and a man of whom it would later be said knew more about the Kellys than anyone else. Wallace was also an inveterate letter writer and was found later by the Royal Commission on the Police Force of Victoria to have been the likely writer of another letter (the Connor letter) which was sent to another MLA. So, whilst there were undoubtedly others in the North-East with the ability to have written the Cameron letter (and the other letters and writings discussed in this chapter), it is more likely than not that James Wallace at least played a major part in the writing of this lengthy letter giving Kelly's side of the story. And if we accept that Wallace was the writer of the Cameron letter (and the other letters) then it is probably fair to assume that he must have believed there to have been some truth in what Ned Kelly was telling him.

---

63 - Donald Cameron was the Member of the Legislative Assembly (MLA) for the electoral district of West Bourke (which was one of the three electoral districts that made up greater Melbourne). The electoral district of West Bourke extended north to the Great Dividing Range. Its northern extension included the town of Lancefield and the feature known as Big Hill (half way between Beveridge and Kilmore).

The Cameron letter is significant because it represents the first effort to correct the public opinion about Ned Kelly. It is a long, turgid letter, which would be outdone by the longer Jerilderie letter, neither of which were made available at the time for public consumption.

A complete transcript of the Cameron letter is included at Appendix 2, but is summarised below.

The Cameron letter starts with Ned complaining that the information that had been sworn against him in regards to shooting Fitzpatrick was false, and that his mother, brother-in-law and another neighbour (Brickey Williamson) were all innocent of the charge of aiding and abetting him. It then goes into a long and convoluted description of the incidents that had led to the Fitzpatrick incident, with most of his grievances being about wrongs that had been done to him by large landowners like Whitty, Farrell and Burns (Byrnes).

James Whitty was a prosperous squatter in the Greta area. John Farrell was a son-in-law of Whitty and owned land contiguous with Whitty's own holdings. Andrew Byrnes (no relation to Joe Byrne) was a squatter with landholdings at Moyhu, which covered some 3000 acres contiguous to Whitty's land. Andrew Byrnes was also a justice of the peace, a councillor with the Shire of Oxley (representing the Western Riding of the Shire of Oxley from 1874 until 1893), and involved with the Moyhu Racing Club, the Moyhu Cooperative Dairy Company and the Wangaratta Show Society.

Ned's complaints about these men were typical of the kind of complaints many selectors had with some of the larger landowners and squatters:

> *Whitty and Burns, not being satisfied with all the picked land on King River and Boggy Creek, and the run of their stock on the certificate ground free[64], and no one interfering with them, paid heavy rent for all the open ground, so as a poor man could not keep his stock, and impounded every beast they could catch, even off Government roads. If a poor man happened to leave his horse or a bit of poddy calf outside his paddock, it would be*

---

64 - 'Certificate land' was land over which a grantee named in a document issued by the government would become entitled to a grant of the land upon fulfilling certain conditions.

> *impounded. I have known over sixty head of horses to be in one day impounded by Whitty and Burns, all belonging to poor men of the district. They would have to leave their harvest or ploughing and go to Oxley, and then perhaps not have money enough to release them, and have to give a bill of sale or borrow the money, which is no easy matter.*

The outlaw's perceived injustices were further detailed when he described how a policeman named Farrell had stolen a horse from his family and had kept it in Whitty and Jeffrey's paddock.[65] This was the reason that he (Ned) stole Whitty's horses and sold them to a man named Baumgarten and to others. He was effectively saying that he had been provoked into entering the horse stealing racket.

The information Ned gave in this letter about his horse stealing provided him with an alibi for why it was not possible for him to have been in Victoria on the day Fitzpatrick was shot. Despite that, he related at length what actually did transpire that day. His mother and others, according to Ned, had been convicted on the evidence of the 'meanest man that ever the sun shone on'. He then further denigrated Fitzpatrick by saying that he had been told by the police that he was a man who was hardly ever sober, and among other things that he had sold (prostituted) his sister to a 'Chinese man'.

Ned told how, having returned to Victoria, he then joined his brother and another man at Bullock Creek after hearing there was a £100 reward on him and that he faced hundreds of charges of horse stealing, as well as the charge of shooting a trooper. He said he had heard that the police had been talking about how they would shoot him first and then cry surrender, and told of how the police used to come to the house when there was no one there but women and threaten to blow him to pieces, and that they used to repeatedly rush into the house with their revolvers and destroy the family's provisions, mishandle the girls and abuse and insult them.

---

65 - The reference to a policeman named Farrell would seem to be an error on the part of the writer, as there is no record of a policeman by that name in the North East. Robert Jeffrey was a prominent grazier at Moyhu and neighbour of James Whitty. Corfield, page 233.

Ned gave his version of how the events at Stringybark Creek had unfolded. What had happened there could not be called wilful murder, for he was compelled to shoot the police in his own defence or else lie down like a cur and die: '… those men came into the bush with the intention of shooting me down like a dog, yet they know and acknowledge I have been wronged.'

Ned gave other instances of having been wronged. He had been arrested by a constable at Greta and wrongly found guilty of receiving a horse knowing it to be stolen. He had been wrongly convicted of assaulting a hawker whose horse he was accused of borrowing. His brother Dan was also wrongly convicted of wilfully destroying property, for which he was sentenced to three months imprisonment. The Kelly family, it would seem, were never in the wrong!

Ned warned that if his people did not get justice, he would be forced to seek revenge while God gave him strength to pull a trigger. He said that witnesses who could prove Fitzpatrick's falsehood could be found by advertising, and that if this was not done immediately horrible disasters would follow:

> *Fitzpatrick shall be the cause of greater slaughter to the rising generation than St. Patrick was to the snakes and frogs in Ireland. For had I robbed, plundered, ravished & murdered everything I met my character could not be painted blacker than it is at present but thank God my conscience is as clear as the snow in Peru…*

The Cameron letter concludes with Ned expressing astonishment that Members of the Legislative Assembly could be led astray by the police:

> *for while an outlaw reigns their pockets swelled with double pay and (the availability of) country girls. With no more paper at his disposal unless he robbed for it, he would cry a fair go if he got justice.*

He signed off with the words, 'With no offence (remember your railroads) and a sweet good bye from Edward Kelly, a forced outlaw.'

The reference to railroads is interesting. This letter was dated 14 December 1878, only two months after the police murders at Stringybark Creek and four days after the Euroa bank robbery, and yet here was a threat against the railways. It was as if Ned Kelly was contemplating some kind of action against the railways a full year and a half before the attempted derailment and mass murder of police at Glenrowan.

The Jerilderie Letter

Following the Euroa robbery, planning was soon underway for the second bank robbery at Jerilderie, planned for early February 1879. During the planning stage, a longer and more detailed version of the Cameron letter was written. Ned planned to take that letter with him to Jerilderie with the intention of forcing a local publisher to print the letter. The letter would later become known as the Jerilderie Letter.[66] A full transcript of the letter is included at Appendix 3.

As with the Cameron letter, the Jerilderie letter gave justification to Kelly's actions, including the murder of the three policemen at Stringybark Creek. It also described cases of alleged police corruption and called for justice for poor families. As mentioned earlier, Constable Anthony Strahan's threat to shoot him down like a dog was cited by Kelly as a justification for what transpired at Stringybark Creek. Strahan had made the comment in the heat of the moment while trying to interrogate one of Ned's uncles – a violent and dangerous man named Patrick Quinn. It was the type of language commonly used by Quinn and Kelly themselves.[67]

If James Wallace had had a hand in the writing of the Jerilderie Letter (which this author submits he did) then this indicates he had no qualms about letting it be known that Constable Strahan, whom James would have known reasonably well when they both lived in El Dorado, had made that statement. It would appear that James must have had some dislike for Strahan.

---

66 - The letter was first called the 'Jerilderie Letter' by author Max Brown in his 1948 biography of Kelly, *Australian Son*.

67 - *Justice in Kelly Country*, Lachlan Strahan (a great-great-grandson of Anthony Strahan), Chapter 14.

Unfortunately for Ned, the publisher (who he needed to print his letter) fled when he saw the Kellys approach. The letter was handed to someone else who promised to pass it on to the publisher; however, the authorities suppressed its publication and it was not until 1930 that it was published in full. The failure to get the letter published must have been extremely frustrating for Ned. However, several newspapers did print summaries written by people who had had the opportunity to read the letter.

As noted already in respect to the Cameron letter, Ned Kelly could barely write, so it can also be said with certainty that he did not write the Jerilderie letter. It has generally been said that Ned had dictated the letter to Joe Byrne. The bellicosity, madness and passion of the letter is consistent with the long-winded speeches Ned was prone to give whenever he had the opportunity (as he did at Euroa and Jerilderie). But did Joe write it for him? In his book *Nabbing Ned Kelly*, the author David Dufty has put forward plausible reasons as to why Joe Byrne could not have been the writer. These reasons include stylistic differences between the Jerilderie Letter and another letter Byrne wrote to Aaron Sherritt, as well as spelling and grammatical differences between the two letters. Dufty identifies James Wallace as the likely writer of the Jerilderie Letter, suggesting that he had the motive, the means and the opportunity:

> *He had a proven record of producing long handwritten documents as substantial as the Jerilderie Letter... he is the only person connected to the gang who we can be certain had the ability to do it. Furthermore, the circumstantial evidence overwhelmingly points to James Wallace as the writer.* [68]

If the Kelly Gang decided that they wanted to compose some lengthy documents, it makes sense, according to Dufty, that they would seek help from the most educated person they knew and trusted, and that person was James Wallace:

---

[68] - David Dufty in *Nabbing Ned Kelly* (2022) was the first to seriously suggest James Wallace as being the author of the Jerilderie Letter. It is one of two mysteries (the other being who made the armour) that he has addressed at the end of his book ('Mystery 2 – Who wrote the Jerilderie Letter?').

> *Sure, the content was Ned's, but as the confidante and resident scholar, Wallace probably influenced it. The letter would have taken many hours and multiple drafts (particularly given the neatness of the writing, and the almost complete absence of mistakes and corrections), in a hideaway somewhere. There would have been multiple sessions, re-readings and conversations about it.*

Dufty notes that a 2014 graphological analysis of the handwriting in a letter Byrne wrote to Aaron Sherritt and the writing in the Jerilderie Letter was inconclusive, including because the letter to Sherritt at only two pages long was too short for the stylistic differences to manifest themselves. He found through his own analysis, however, that there are many stylistic similarities between the letters Wallace wrote to Nicolson (known as the Fisher letters, discussed later in this book) and the Jerilderie Letter. In any event, Dufty suggests that Joe's letter to Sherritt may also have been written by Wallace, noting that Detective Michael Ward seemed to have doubts it had been written by Byrne. Ward was familiar with Joe's writing, as he had been the recipient of numerous threatening letters from him during the course of the Kelly hunt.[69]

Dufty concluded his section on the mystery of who wrote the Jerilderie Letter by suggesting that although the literary and rhetorical powers of Ned Kelly and Joe Byrne have been eulogised for almost a century and a half, it is entirely possible that, apart from classroom exercises, neither of them ever wrote anything at all. We know that isn't true in the case of Joe – the threatening letters he had written to Detective Ward show he had some writing ability. But as far as the Jerilderie letter is concerned, it is highly likely that James Wallace either wrote or played a significant part in its composition. As Dufty says, he had the motive, the means and the opportunity.

As far as motive is concerned, it is likely that Wallace, like many in the district, believed Fitzpatrick had been the cause of the outbreak. Perhaps having seen the hardship faced by many selectors in the

---

69 - These letters were at one time held by the Public Record Office Victoria (PROV), but have been lost or deliberately removed from the records.

district and having first-hand experience of this through growing up in the Woolshed Valley, he also saw an opportunity for the Kelly outbreak to be politicised. As for means and opportunity, Wallace had a school, library and meeting room at his disposal, and was well-known for being a prolific letter-writer. He also had easy access to the gang when they were hidden away at the 'hut behind the school' at Sawpit Gully.

The Kelly Gang or The Outlaws of the Wombat Ranges

Twelve days after the Jerilderie robbery, a book was published titled *The Kelly Gang or The Outlaws of the Wombat Ranges* (referred to hereafter as *The Outlaws of the Wombat Ranges*). The book was edited and published by GW Hall, the proprietor of the Mansfield Guardian. The preface indicated it was written by 'an author or authors unknown'.

Dr Stuart Dawson has noted in a historical note attached to his freely available transcript of *The Outlaws of the Wombat Ranges* that it is a massively important historical document in its claim to give an impartial account of the Kelly outbreak up to the time of its writing, particularly given Ned Kelly's failure to have copies of his 'Jerilderie letter' printed.[70] It is also significant that GW Hall, publisher of the pamphlet, would one day be appointed as a member of the Royal Commission on the Police Force of Victoria, which was set up to investigate the failings of the police force to capture the gang.

The book did not hold back from criticism of the gang's actions and of the Kellys' criminality, but also strived to give an impartial account of the Kelly outbreak. Chapter VI, for instance, presents the story of Constable Fitzpatrick's visit to the Kelly property 'as narrated by the other side', with that alternate story raising the possibility that the constable did not go there with any intention of arresting Daniel Kelly, but rather to take liberties with a member of the family (Kate Kelly). The book said the story required confirmation, but was consistent with a statement made by Edward Kelly at Jerilderie. The general opinion, according to the book, was that the constable 'did not altogether act the clean potato'.

---

70 - Dr Stuart Dawson prepared a transcript from an original copy of *The Kelly Gang or The Outlaws of the Wombat Ranges* held in the State Library of Victoria special collection. The transcript is downloadable for free at https://gutenberg.net.au/ebooks19/1900581p.pdf

Chapter VIII described the life of the Kelly brothers and their friends after the Fitzpatrick incident. It described how they confined themselves to the impenetrable natural fastness of the Wombat Ranges, supported by reliable and trustworthy friends.

> *To this part of the country, then, the Kellys retired, with a view of avoiding the consequences of a charge which they professed to be unjust, and which is now generally believed to be, if not groundless, at least gravely exaggerated and misstated.*

Their friends included Joseph Byrne and Stephen Hart, who were not 'wanted' by the police at the time they went into partnership with the Kellys, and so, 'It could be inferred had not joined with the design or anticipation of participating in any act whereby their liberties or lives might be jeopardised or forfeited.'

> *Indeed, it was thought by some that their presence in the deplorable tragedy of the 26th October was accidental, or, at any rate, they had no prevision of the terrible ending of the bloody encounter. Be that as it may, they are now as guilty in the eyes of the inexorable law as though they had planned and executed the slaughter unaided and alone.*

In Chapter IX, it was described how two parties of police had been despatched in pursuit of the Kellys. One of those parties was led by Sergeant Kennedy. It was noted that an opinion had been expressed more than once that Kennedy and Scanlan, with no idea of the Kellys having received a reinforcement, and with information that they were in the vicinity, had set out to capture them without the interference or assistance of their fellow troopers. The suggestion here was that Kennedy and Scanlan intended to split the reward money between themselves, cutting Lonigan and McIntyre out.

Two chapters (XXIV and XXV) towards the end of the book interrupt the flow of the narrative about the Jerilderie raid, and therefore seem out of place. These chapters introduce an 'unnamed traveller', who is referred to later as 'the wanderer' and 'Mr Blank'. This traveller is presumably the source of the information that presents the 'other side of the story'. The chapters relate the journey the traveller made to meet with the Kellys in a remote location within the Wombat Ranges. The journey started with the traveller wearily climbing the tedious spurs of Wombat Hill, from where a complicated set of directions saw him meet with the gang members at a location that would seem to be somewhere in the upper reaches of the west branch of the King River, upstream from Powers Lookout and Glenmore.

The author or authors of the pamphlet are unknown. However, the information about the Kellys' movements after the Fitzpatrick incident and up to and after the Jerilderie raid, including the support they received from sympathisers, could only have come from someone who knew or had access to them. Perhaps the author or one of the authors is the unnamed 'traveller', who is described as being:

> ...of medium height and build, somewhat past middle age, with dark brown hair and beard, hazel eyes, and a fair skin, save for the effects of the weather, he offered no point either of attraction or repulsion likely to induce a passer-by to take a second look at him under everyday circumstances.

The traveller's clothing and equipment was also described in some detail:

> His dress, to commence at the top, consisted of a broad-leafed, tall, soft felt sombrero, of an obfusc greyish-brown; an ordinary flannel singlet, covered by an olive-green Crimean shirt; trousers of a kind known in the slop-shops as 'coloured moles', kept in position by leathern waist-belt, and of a neutral shade, which might be described as dirty chocolate; grey military socks, and a pair of strong lace-up boots'...' and 'He carried on his shoulder a single coarse brown blanket, rolled up swag fashion, within the folds of which snugly reposed some tobacco, a maiden bottle of 'Three star' brandy, and a bottle, which, although three parts filled with 'Long John' whiskey, showed evident signs of having been tampered with and tapped since its purchase. The bottles were carefully The bottles were carefully wrapped in a few of the most recent copies of the Argus and Age newspapers.

> *From the two ends of this, fastened together with a saddle strap, depended what is known as a 'Sydney pot', containing water, and consisting of a quart billy, the closefitting lid of which formed a pannican. On the opposite side, slung to a strap passing over the other shoulder, hung a well-worn tourist's bag, made of leather, in one compartment of which were a few well-baked, solid scones, and a lump of hard corned beef; while the other contained two small calico bags, with tea and sugar, also a diminutive binocular field-glass, a good-sized note-book, the four of diamonds from a new pack, an ordinary large empty cardboard pill box, a few long hairs from the tail of a horse, and a bright white-metal table spoon. A coloured cotton pocket-handkerchief in his hat, and a strong clasp knife, some twine, a box of matches, a short black clay pipe, and a small compass in his trousers pockets, bring the inventory to a conclusion.*

As the traveller's identity is not divulged, the description of his looks and equipment was probably intended to mislead. The level of fine detail given is interesting. It is as if the writer could not help himself. Wallace was someone who went into this kind of detail. Indeed, Wallace later went to this same level of detail in a letter he sent to Nicolson in which he described a meeting he had had with a 'Chinaman' named Ah Shin who had had a chance encounter with a man who Wallace wanted Nicolson to think may have been Ned Kelly. This letter is discussed later, but for point of comparison with the above description of the traveller, here is Wallace's description of the man who might have been the 'senior outlaw' as described to him by Ah Shin:

> *… about six foot high – pretty well made, reddish beard & whiskers, black eyes, tweed trousers, top boots, dark coat, brownish felt hat worn down over his eyes with black band on chin, armed with no less than four revolvers hung around his belt – one of the revolvers of very unusual length – rode a red (bay or chestnut) horse.*

Wallace also went to a similar level of detail when he described how one of his brothers sighted Ned Kelly, which he then went on to describe to the Sherritt family.[71] It was a description of Kelly that Detective Ward found surprisingly, and suspiciously, detailed for a second-hand (and now third-hand) account:

> *He wore a brown overcoat, grey hood, trousers, leggings and soft felt hat, and rode Joe Byrne's grey horse.*

The section of *The Outlaws of the Wombat Ranges* (chapters XXIV and XXV) that relates the story of the unnamed traveller sits awkwardly with the rest of the publication. It is almost as if it were a last-minute addition. It was written by someone with high-level skills of composition, but also with a detailed knowledge of the Kellys and their movements, and of local sentiment towards them. James Wallace was such a person. It is also interesting that he would later tell the Royal Commissioners that he had sought out the gang with a view to writing a book, with the period of time he was referring to being about the time *The Outlaws of the Wombat Ranges* was being compiled.

If Wallace was the primary author of the Jerilderie Letter, as speculated by Dufty, then he would have been disappointed that it was not published as intended. There was insufficient time (12 days) between the Jerilderie robbery and the publication of *The Outlaws of the Wombat Ranges* for Wallace to have prepared the 'other side of the story' material that appeared in the latter document, assuming of course that he had a hand in either document. On the contrary, it would seem that the Jerilderie letter and the 'other side of the story' material were written at the same time. The letter was written to give voice to the illiterate Ned Kelly, while the more sober voice of the 'unnamed traveller' was written for inclusion in a book. Was it intended that both documents would be published at about the same time as part of a publicity blitz?

GW Hall was obviously seeking to put out a book quickly to capitalise on the Kelly story as it was to that point, but he could not have done so without input by someone like Wallace who had a detailed knowledge

---

71 - Dufty, page 259. This description was relayed verbally to Detective Ward by the Sherritts. Detective Ward gave details to the Royal Commissioners when giving evidence.

of the gang and their movements. If it was Wallace who wrote this material, then he must have provided it to Hall through an intermediary, as Hall made no mention during the course of the future Royal Commission (of which he was a member) of having known Wallace. One wonders if it might have dawned upon Hall during the course of the Commission's hearings that there were marked stylistic similarities between the 'unnamed traveller' material and the descriptions given by Wallace in his letters to Assistant Commissioner Nicolson (which are discussed later in this book).

After publishing *The Outlaws of the Wombat Ranges*, Hall moved to Benalla from where he would soon start publishing the satirical serial *The Book of Keli* in the Benalla Standard. *The Book of Keli* was a satirical account of the police pursuit told in mock-Biblical language, in which 'Captain Dishstand' with his chief officers, Nickelsilver and Harus, led the bumbling 'hosts of King Georgius' from disaster to disaster against 'the men of Keli'.[72]

Letter published in the *Ovens and Murray Advertiser*

The Kelly Gang's standing among some people in the North East was enhanced as a result of the successful Euroa and Jerilderie robberies and the failure of the authorities to bring them to justice. However, efforts to present the gang in a better light through the Cameron and Jerilderie letters and via GW Hall's book failed to impress the authorities. One of the gang's demands was an inquiry into the sentencing of Ellen Kelly (mother of Ned and Dan) for her role in the Fitzpatrick shooting, but neither the letters (which had been largely suppressed) or the book made any difference as far as that was concerned.

In an attempt to create interest in their case, a further letter addressed to the editor of the *Herald* newspaper in Melbourne was somehow directed to the *Ovens and Murray Advertiser* (Beechworth) instead.[73] An abridged version of the letter was published in the *Ovens and*

---

72 - Ian Jones, *Ned Kelly: A Short Life*, 1996 special edition, pages 201–202.

73 - The *Melbourne Herald* never published or acknowledged the receipt of this letter. Perhaps the same letter had been sent to both the *Melbourne Herald* and the *Ovens and Murray Advertiser*, but with both copies addressed only to the *Melbourne Herald*.

Murray Advertiser on Saturday 12 July 1879.[74] A copy is reproduced in full in Appendix 6.

The letter was written under the guise of a sympathiser, and would appear to have been written by the same author as the Cameron and Jerilderie letters given its use of identical phrasing to those two letters. The letter also displays a knowledge of the gang's history that would be unknown to anyone but the gang's closest sympathisers.

The *Advertiser* described the letter as evidently written by an illiterate person, due to the orthography being defective, the calligraphy in some portions almost undecipherable, and the composition rambling and sometimes unintelligible. It is known that Wallace could change his handwriting in the style of others, but if the handwriting in this instance was so bad as to be almost indecipherable, it is likely the letter was written by someone else. However, the fact that the content is consistent with what is contained in the Cameron and Jerilderie letters indicates the letter may have been written by Wallace and then copied by someone else, or perhaps had been dictated by Wallace. Whatever the case, the *Advertiser* said the letter showed that a very bitter feeling of animosity existed among the sympathisers against the police, with reasons being given as to why this should be. The *Advertiser* considered that the writer's demand for an inquiry was a justifiable request.

The letter noted that no case of horse stealing had ever been proved against any of the Kellys. It also pointed out that Ned's prior convictions for striking a man named Jeremiah McCormack and for receiving a stolen horse were on the evidence of two constables, one of whom (Constable Edward Hall) had twice been tried for perjury and the other (Constable Ernest Flood) who had since been sentenced to three years for horse stealing.[75] In respect to Dan, it noted that he had (only) been

---

74 - A photograph of the newspaper clipping is included at page 160 of McMenomy's *Ned Kelly, The Authentic History*.

75 - Constable Edward Hall had arrested Ned Kelly in 1870 on a charge of violent assault and the sending of an indecent letter to a female, and again in 1871 on a charge of stealing a horse (later changed to receiving a stolen horse). Hall had previously been posted to El Dorado where in 1858 he had been involved in an assault on a prisoner for which he was later charged for assault and perjury.

sentenced to three months for smashing a door with his fist.[76] These were the only convictions on the roll against the Kellys. Furthermore, the Kelly's shooting of the police was not cold blooded, as the police had gone out there to murder for the reward money, which at that time stood at £200. The public and the government, the writer said, had done their best against the Kellys, and the laws had been made to suit the police. The letter writer then came to his great grievance – the conduct of the police in the North-Eastern District. He described how good the business had been for the police in the 14 months that the Kellys had been outlawed:

> *Any scapegrace can get a pound a-day now. I know a great many of the special constables, not one of whom could earn their tucker before, but now can sport silk coats, and calls themselves mounted constables. Two, in particular, I could mention. One is well-known in the Beechworth and Greta districts, and his character needs no comment.*

The special constable referred to here was not named, but was obviously Aaron Sherritt. What followed was an overblown story, in part based on fact, of the things this special constable would get up to. The so-called sympathiser who wrote this letter therefore knew a great deal about Sherritt and the way he was being handled by the police. Wallace was in possession of this kind of information, and had also been doing everything in his power to make the police distrust Sherritt.

The remainder of the letter, as described in the *Ovens and Murray Advertiser* article, contained much of the rhetoric that was in the Jerilderie letter. The author professed the following:

- An inquiry was needed to show the public the true character of the special constables and others supposed to be hunting for the Kellys.

- If things were not altered, there would be plenty more bushrangers besides the Kellys.

---

76 - This was for his part in the break and entry of Goodman's Store at Winton, during which an attempted sexual assault was carried out against Mrs Goodman, for which Tom Lloyd Jnr was convicted and sentenced to a period of imprisonment.

- The police force was what ought to be outlawed, instead of the Kellys.

- The police were guilty of serious misconduct towards respectable men, women and even children.

- The police should wear uniforms to avoid them being fired upon by members of the public who might mistake them for being bushrangers.

- A fortnight prior to Fitzpatrick alleging he was shot at, a certain inspector of police had told an editor that he knew the Kellys were armed and that there would be shooting between the police and the Kellys within the fortnight.

- And if that was the case, that it was very strange that he should have sent a drunken trooper to arrest them without a warrant.

The letter concluded with the writer saying that he believed he had expressed the opinion of thousands, and that unless an inquiry was held, the Kellys would certainly revenge the insult offered to themselves and their mother. They were, he wrote, painted as black as print can paint them, but they harmed no man, woman, or child – their actions being more like those of four sisters of charity, than four outlaws.

> *If they had robbed, and plundered, and ravished and murdered the public and every man and woman they met, it would have been a very different thing, but in the way they have acted, after being treated as they have been, they deserve to be called men instead of outlaws. Their robberies are confined to banks, the police, and the Government.*

The article ended with the journalist writing that the extracts given from the letter had not been given *'verbatim et literatim'*, but had been altered sufficiently to render them intelligible. The newspaper had nothing to do with the letter writer's opinions as to the angelic nature of the Kellys, but noted that the public was concerned to know whether his allegations against the police were true or false.

Other publicity

As previously stated, Wallace was an inveterate writer of letters to newspapers. His writings included a satirical serial called 'Christmas in Kelly Land', which was published in the Wangaratta Despatch. Unfortunately, copies of 'Christmas in Kelly Land' no longer exist – a building used by the Wangaratta Despatch to store back copies of its papers was destroyed by fire many years later, and the copy of 'Christmas in Kelly Land' that had been forwarded to the Prosecutor's Office when it was considering a case against Wallace, subsequently went missing.

In the finest traditions of Irish balladry, the 'Ballad of Kelly's Gang' became a well-known song sung in hotels throughout the North East and beyond. The ballad was said to have been written by Joe Byrne before Jerilderie.[77] Another popular ballad called 'The Kellys Have Made Another Escape' was apparently written after Jerilderie by a girl known as Mary the Larrikin who was said to have been one of Joe's girlfriends.

---

77 - Ian Jones in *Ned Kelly: A Short Life*, 1996 special edition, page 201.

11
Wallace's activities after Jerilderie

Easter came and went, and the months passed into winter. After the excitement of the two bank robberies, things mostly quietened down in Kelly country. A minor stir occurred in June, however, when a constable fired at Aaron Sherritt while he was visiting Kate Kelly at the Kelly homestead, causing Aaron to flee by foot the 18 miles to James's residence at Bobinawarrah.[78] Sherritt at this time was on very friendly terms with the Kelly family and was courting Kate. The constable who shot at him presumably mistook him for one of the Kellys.

In July 1879, Assistant Commissioner Nicolson resumed command of the Kelly hunt. One of the first things he did was to visit James at Hurdle Creek (on 23 July 1879) to recruit his services. This was the second time James had been visited at Hurdle Creek by a police commander.

Nicolson's visit coincided with the police receiving a report that the gang's haunts included Hurdle Creek and the Hurdle Creek Ranges.[79] The report was not definitive, however, as it had also been reported that the gang had been seen in the Hedi Ranges, Gum Flat (at the southern end of the Carboor Ranges), Woolshed, Barambogie, the Pilot Ranges, Rat's Castle and Wooragee.

With James being the head teacher at the Hurdle Creek school, Nicolson may have assumed he would be well placed to obtain some useful information. James would later tell the Royal Commissioners

---

78 - *The Last of the Bushrangers* by Francis Augustus Hare, Chapter VIII. The book is available for download via Project Gutenberg. The fact that Aaron fled to Wallace's on foot (a distance of about 18 miles) is a testament to the remarkable endurance of bushmen like him in those times.

79 - Royal Commission Minutes of Evidence, Appendix 5 'Reported appearances of the Kelly Outlaws' – report received on 23 July 1879 describing the locations of some of the haunts of the gang.

that Nicolson asked him for his impression as to the gang's whereabouts, to which he answered:

> *I gave it as my opinion that they had gone into winter quarters; that is, that they were not travelling about, but were settled for the winter. I told the impressions and facts I had as regards their previous movements, life pursued, tactics observed, and mode of living, as far as I could learn from hints let drop by their friends.*[80]

James was probably telling the truth, as it was believed that the gang was at this time occupying a cabin in the Buckland Valley where they obtained provisions from a Chinese storekeeper. However, as with most of the information James would provide to the police, the information was non-specific and therefore unhelpful.

Visits from senior members of the police to the Wallace residence would not have gone unnoticed in Hurdle Creek where everyone had their eyes and ears open to matters of local interest. Upright members of the community would have been pleased to think that their local teacher was helping out. Fellow sympathisers, however, were likely aware that James was playing a double role.

James would soon start spending much of his spare time writing Nicolson long-winded letters reporting on what he had heard about the gang's whereabouts. The information was always encouraging, but invariably too late to be of any real use. The reality was that he was providing practical assistance to the gang over this entire period.[81] The letters continued for about six months, stopping shortly before the first plough mouldboard was stolen from a property at Glenrowan. Nicolson had by this time dispensed with James's services, following a dispute about expenses and a realisation that the information being passed to him was of little value.

---

80 - Minutes of Evidence Q14434.

81 - We are reliant on anecdote and hearsay for our knowledge of this, as Wallace was careful to leave no written evidence of this period, such as letters or diaries. When questioned about this at the Royal Commission, he said, (Q14432) 'I did not think it desirable to preserve any (letters).'

From evidence Nicolson would later give to the Royal Commission and from reported communications he had with James many years later, it seems that Nicolson never believed that James was acting as a double agent. That is curious given the reports Nicolson was receiving over this same period from Detective Michael Ward.

Wallace's letters to Nicolson are held by the Public Record Office of Victoria (PROV). The relevant file (the Wallace file) contains an index that lists 20 letters – the first being dated 18 August 1879, and the final being dated 5 March 1880. Only the first 11 of the 20 letters remain in the file, with the last of those being dated 12 November 1879. Those eleven letters run to 50 pages. One can only imagine what information the missing nine letters might have contained.

To protect their identity, Nicolson's agents were all given code names. Wallace's code name was Bruce. Although writing across the top of the letters in the Wallace file identify them as having been received from 'Fisher alias Bruce', it is not clear where the Fisher part of this pseudonym comes from. Bruce, though, is an entirely appropriate code name for a man of Scottish descent, being a jokey reference to the legendary Scottish historical figure Robert the Bruce. The alias was supposed to protect the writer's identity, although it would not have been difficult for someone to have put two and two together and identify James as the author.

Over the same period that James was in communication with Nicolson, Detective Ward was passing on his suspicions about James in his own reports to Nicolson. Ward had focussed his attention on the Woolshed families. He was suspicious of the Wallace and Sherritt families and watched their activities closely. In a letter dated 26 August 1879, he reported to Nicolson that James had come into Beechworth with his horse and buggy on the previous Saturday (23 August 1879) and had purchased a bag of bread and a case of brandy, half a dozen pocket handkerchiefs, a bottle of scent, and a package of arsenical soap. The purchases were over and above the needs of James's family.

Historians Arthur Hall and Len Pryor believed that on the occasions that the gang made use of the hut behind the school, they made pre-dawn trips into Bobinawarrah to collect provisions. They most likely collected the provisions from Wallace's selection, which was located at the edge of the Carboor Range and therefore closer to the hut than the school. It was Hugh Wallace's job, they believed, to drive cattle over the outlaw's tracks so as to conceal evidence of the visits.

Another anecdote about James's activities at this time would later come from a young man named Alex McGreggor, whose family held a selection adjacent to James Wallace's.[82] Alex left the district in 1879 to attend Ballarat Grammar School. While there, he received a letter from James that contained a sealed, stamped letter in Joe Byrne's handwriting addressed to Kate Byrne, c/o Beechworth Post Office, with an instruction to Alex to post this letter in Ballarat.

As all mail to the Byrnes was being monitored, James obviously intended the letter would be intercepted and that the authorities would be led to believe that Byrne was in the Ballarat area.[83] Alex would later tell detectives that he did as he was instructed, but was deeply troubled by what he had done. He told them that he had met James a short time later while both were fighting a bushfire, and told him that he thought it had been very foolish on his part to have sent the letter to him because he might have taken it to the police. Alex said Wallace laughingly replied that he knew that he wouldn't have done that and that he had only sent the letter as a joke.

A Mrs Fanny Cox would later make a statement that gave further reason to believe that James had been a sympathiser.[84] She made the statement in 1881 by which time she was married to one of the constables who had kept watch over the Byrne house at Sebastopol from a cave in the range above (the cave would later be known as the Police Cave). In her statement, she recounted a visit she had made to Wallace's house at Bobinawarrah in September 1879. During the visit, one of the Wallace children remarked while playing with her watch

---

82 - Alex Macgregor related this information to Detectives Considine and Ward as they searched for evidence against Wallace in 1881. The McGreggor family selection was located adjacent to James Wallace's own selection (refer to the Plan of Subdivision included at Appendix 1).

83 - There is no record of this letter interception having occurred.

84 - Mrs Cox was married to one of the constables who had been a member of the cave party watching over Mrs Byrne's house at Sebastopol. At the time she gave this statement to Detective Considine, her husband was a police constable at Katamatite.

chain that Ned Kelly did not have a watch and chain like hers. When she asked the boy if he knew Ned Kelly, he answered that he had been there previously and had given him a shilling. Mrs Cox said that Wallace must have overheard the conversation and asked her what the child had been saying to her. When she told him his son had been telling her that the Kellys have been paying him a visit, he told her not to take any notice of what the child had been saying. She said he appeared very annoyed and told his wife to put the child to bed, and that she later heard the child being slapped.

Further information about James's activities during 1879 and 1880 came to light due to the efforts of Detectives Ward and Considine, and is discussed later. Both were prominent in the search for the Kelly Gang, but unusual in that they acted independently of the general police force and reported directly to the Head of the Detective Branch in Melbourne rather than to Standish or Nicolson in the field. Detective Ward took his power as a free agent to extremes and was motivated by a strong desire to personally bring the Kelly Gang down.

Over the months of August and September 1879, James was known to have spent time collecting ploughs and mouldboards around his local neighbourhood. Anne Sherritt would later tell of how James had visited her family home at Sheep Station Creek not long after August 1879. He had asked her whether she had any mouldboards for sale, giving as an excuse that his father was a dealer in old metals and he was purchasing them for him. Anne said he showed her a mouldboard that he already had in a bag with him.

The fact that James was collecting mouldboards as early as 1879 indicates that planning for what would occur at Glenrowan was underway some nine months prior to that event. It begs the question as to how much Wallace knew about this plan. Anne incidentally was said to have been a very active sympathiser and was at one time engaged to Joe Byrne's brother Paddy. She related the story of James's visit to Detective Ward in 1881 – the murder of her brother Aaron had obviously changed her view of the gang.

# 12

Nicolson's secret agents

When James first wrote to the Chief Commissioner of Police Captain Standish, offering to use his summer holidays to assist in capturing the outlaws, he failed to mention that Joe Byrne was an old school friend. Standish would be very glad to hear anything that James might have to offer, but did not at that time require anything further from him by way of services.

Wallace later wrote to Assistant Commissioner Nicolson (on 5 January 1879), two days after the arrest of the sympathisers. Superintendent Hare was in charge of the Kelly hunt at the time, so Nicolson was not in a position to recruit Wallace. However, once he was back in charge, he called on Wallace at his home on 23 July 1879. Wallace later recalled to the Royal Commission that Nicolson told him:

> *... that the country looked to me, as a teacher and as a respectable member of society, that I should render all the assistance I could to suppress murder and robbery, and I understood him to wish me to take service with him. He then asked me if I would give them any other aid I could by collecting information, and beating up the houses in the neighbourhood which the outlaws were most likely to frequent. I decided to assist him in the interests of society.*[85]

Nicolson expected Wallace and his other agents to keep Kelly sympathisers in their local neighbourhood under surveillance. They were instructed to mingle, observe and report back. Wallace's daily routine was quite well suited to this, given his daily travels between the Hurdle Creek and Hurdle Creek West schools (a two and a half mile trip) and the fact he and Barbara managed the local post office. The

---

85 - Minutes of the Royal Commission, Wallace response to Question 14425.

public library and reading room also operated from the Hurdle Creek School after hours, giving Wallace plenty of opportunity to gather and pass on information. Wallace also made regular trips to Beechworth and frequented the local public houses, all of which was good for collecting information.

The Kelly Gang moved between refuges in the Sebastopol ranges, Greta ranges and the Warby ranges, usually remaining within a radius of some 15 miles. The school at Hurdle Creek was at the centre of this circle.

The Sherritt brothers (Aaron and John) were also engaged as agents. Aaron may in fact have been working as an agent from soon after the Sebastopol Raid. Having met with Captain Standish in the aftermath of the Sebastopol Raid, he had gone to visit him at Benalla several days prior to the Euroa bank robbery. Captain Standish was not there, however, and so Aaron ended up meeting with Superintendent Hare instead. Hare won him over and he agreed to deal with him instead of Standish. The extent to which Aaron was loyal to the police is somewhat murky, but it was always Hare's opinion that he was genuine.

In the weeks and months following Stringybark Creek and the two bank robberies, Aaron was a frequent caller at the Wallace household. Neither man was meant to know that the other was an agent, although it didn't take long for James to figure out that Aaron was. He would later describe Aaron to the Royal Commissioners as 'guarded and cunning' but prided himself on having an influence over him: 'If I wanted to get any information out of him I could do so.' He explained his power over Aaron as dating back to when he used him as a subject in mesmerism experiments when they were children.

Whilst James was supposedly assisting the police – something that Detective Ward 'accidently let slip' one day while meeting with locals at a hotel in Milawa – his true loyalties lay with Joe Byrne. The selectors who were sympathisers of the gang did not seem to doubt this. There was a lot of doubt, however, about Aaron. It seemed to be common knowledge, at least in the neighbourhood of Woolshed, that he was assisting the police, and he would later admit as much to Wallace.

Aaron told James far more than he should have. He admitted to playing a double game, but said that he was doing what he could to protect Joe. James was probably initially unsure where Aaron's loyalties lay. He would later tell the Royal Commissioners that he believed Aaron to have been a sympathiser, but it seems clear that James and the gang eventually formed the view that he was acting for the police. Even if Aaron had for a time played both sides, things eventually became so hot for him that helping the police bring in the Kellys was in his own best interest.

1

13
Wallace's letters to Nicolson

The letters written by James Wallace, in his capacity as a police agent, to Assistant Commissioner Nicolson are long-winded and full of flowery bombast. One can only imagine what Nicolson thought as he read them.

Wallace always had a lot to say, but what he said was of little value. He certainly liked to spin a yarn … similar, as mentioned, to the author(s) of the Cameron and Jerilderie letters and the writer of the chapters about the unknown traveller in *The Outlaws of the Wombat Ranges*.

Wallace's letters (complete transcripts of which are included in Appendix 5) are summarised and commented upon below, under headings that seek to encapsulate in a few words the thrust of each letter. In order to place the letters in context, reference is also made to events that occurred between the dates of the respective letters, as well as to some of the reports submitted to Nicolson by Detective Ward. Ward's reports show that he was alert to Wallace's double dealings over the entire period Wallace was communicating with Nicolson.

Wallace's initial letter, 5 January 1879

Wallace sent his first letter to Nicolson two days after the arrests of the sympathisers. Presumably the letter was an offer of services. We only know about this letter because Wallace referenced it in answer to a question he was asked at the Royal Commission.[86] The letter is not included amongst the other Wallace letters held by PROV (the first letter in that PROV file being dated 18 August 1879).

* * *

---

86 - Minutes of Evidence, Q14493.

Nicolson visited Wallace at his home at Hurdle Creek on 23 July 1879, after having taken back control of the Kelly hunt from Superintendent Hare.

***

On Saturday 16 August 1879, Detective Ward met Wallace on the Beechworth Road, near the Golden Ball (hotel). Wallace was going to Beechworth and told Ward that he would see him there that night, but failed to show. Ward reported on this encounter in a report to Nicolson dated 26 August 1879.

***

Comments made by Wallace in his letter of 18 August 1879 (see below), indicate that he must have met with Nicolson on either 16 or 17 August.

Wallace letter, 18 August 1879 – 'A screw loose in the Police Department'

This was Wallace's first letter to Nicolson where he was writing as an agent. The letter was written about three and a half weeks after Nicolson visited him at Hurdle Creek (on 23 July) and recruited him as an informer.

Wallace started the letter by agreeing with Nicolson that a bank robbery that had taken place three days earlier (on 15 August) in the central Victorian town of Lancefield could not have been carried out by the Kellys.[87]

The Lancefield robbery had been carried out by two men named Samuel Lowe and Christopher Bray, who were captured soon after. However, before their capture, there was considerable speculation that

---

87 - Lancefield, which the *Argus* newspaper report of the robbery described as a much more populous place than Euroa or Jerilderie, is located about 45 miles from Melbourne by rail and road.

the robbery had been carried out by the Kelly Gang, as the robbers identified themselves as the Kelly Gang when they bailed up the cashier.

The Argus newspaper of Saturday 16 August 1879 carried an extensive report of the robbery. It noted that Lancefield had long been regarded as a place that could be easily attacked by the Kelly Gang, with the police having several times cautioned the local bank manager to be in readiness for a visit from the outlaws.

Wallace gave Nicolson three reasons why he agreed with him that the robbery could not have been carried out by the Kellys. Firstly, he had ascertained that a horseman who had passed through (presumably Bobinawarrah) on the morning of the 11th (the Monday before) was the 'senior brother beyond a doubt', and that being the case, he would not have had time to reconnoitre, plan, and carry out the robbery. Secondly, the descriptions of the men did not correspond with the description of the Kellys. And thirdly, the 'modus operandi was altogether different to that of our boys' because the Lancefield robbery was a straightforward stick-up that lacked the subterfuge used by the Kellys at Euroa and Jerilderie.

In this first letter, as in many that would follow, Wallace reported a positive sighting – in this case of the senior Kelly brother. But the sighting was a week earlier and the report was therefore of no use. To keep up Nicolson's hopes, Wallace reassured him that 'The boys are or were for the past few weeks in the vicinity,' and that 'during that time they have visited a house within three miles of Beechworth on several occasions.' He added that 'the poet (Byrne) seems to have been ill – the exposure and occasional prolonged frosts not agreeing with his naturally delicate constitution.' And that 'the others are in good fettle and they are all in good spirits. I had hoped to have come across them last night but my horse is 'played out' and I have not yet come across another one to persist.'

Wallace then reported that there was a Kelly mole – 'a screw loose' – in Nicolson's police department. He thought this because a list of places (presumably of Kelly sightings) that he had given to Nicolson at their last interview was now in the hands of their friends. These people,

Wallace said, would like to know who the bloody hell had given out that information.

Wallace added that 'there is a delightful game of cross purposes being played on both sides that is worth the trouble of watching if there were no other motive.' There was no mention of names in this letter, but this was Wallace's first step to plant the seeds of suspicion in Nicolson's mind about the trustworthiness of Detective Ward, who Wallace was well aware suspected him of being a Kelly sympathiser. Wallace wanted to make Nicolson think that Ward had been the source of the information leak. As noted by Ian MacFarlane in *The Kelly Gang: Unmasked*, Wallace's mischief, as shown in his reports to Nicolson 'was cunning, far-reaching and poisonous'. [88]

In a final piece of mischief, Wallace concluded by telling Nicolson that he thought he could persuade someone to return Sgt Kennedy's chronometer to his widow, but that the person concerned was avaricious and would rather melt it down. He didn't mention a name at this stage, but in later letters Wallace would make it clear that he was talking about Aaron as being the person who had Kennedy's chronometer.

Wallace knew Nicolson had been speaking with the Sherritt brothers (Aaron and John), and had already made up his mind at this point that Aaron was a danger to the gang, and more alarmingly to Wallace himself. He needed to make Nicolson question the information Aaron provided. Who would Nicolson be most likely to believe – a respectable school teacher like James, or a man like Aaron who was a known associate of the Kelly Gang members and, for all Nicolson knew, still a sympathiser.

The information Wallace gave about the Kellys' recent whereabouts and the condition of the respective gang members would have been of great interest to Nicolson. One wonders, though, if Nicolson gave any thought to how someone like Wallace might have been privy to such information, or how it could be that he might have expected to have come across the gang the night before. At any rate, this first letter was a good start, and Nicolson must have thought Wallace's value as a police agent was promising.

---

88 - *The Kelly Gang: Unmasked*, (2018) Ian MacFarlane, page 181

***

On the night of 21 August 1879, Joe Byrne apparently visited Wallace at his home to ascertain from him where Aaron's loyalties lay. Aaron, who would come to hear of this meeting from Wallace, reported this to Detective Ward two nights later, who in turn passed the information on to Nicolson in a detailed report dated the 26 August.

***

On the night of Saturday 23 August 1879, a meeting took place at Beechworth's Wertheims Hotel between Wallace, Aaron Sherritt (who was also known by his nickname 'Tommy') and Detective Ward.[89] Ward sent a detailed report to Nicolson about this meeting on 26 August.[90] He reported that Wallace had come into Beechworth with a horse and buggy and had purchased a bag of bread, a case of brandy, half a dozen pocket-handkerchiefs, a bottle of scent, and a package of arsenical soap. He didn't need to say that the purchases seemed excessive for the immediate needs of Wallace's family of three.

Ward then detailed matters that Wallace had discussed privately with Aaron, which Aaron had then passed on to him:

- That Wallace wanted Aaron to go with him to him to Melbourne to try and get Graham Berry (the Premier of Victoria) and the Marquis of Normanby (Governor of Victoria) to sign a reprieve for Joe Byrne in return for Joe giving information to the police about where the other three could be caught. Wallace would arrange everything if Aaron agreed to go with the police (to capture the gang), but cautioned him (Aaron) that he should take care not to make himself a target (of the gang) by being at the front

---

89 - Tommy was Aaron Sherritt's nickname. In his dealings with Assistant Commissioner Nicholson, Aaron went by the codename Moses. Aaron's brother John went by the codename of Jones.

90 - Report by ME Ward (Detective No. 2358), North-Eastern District, Beechworth Police Station, dated 26 August 1879. The report was read out in full at the Royal Commission as part of Qu. 14773 to Wallace (with the Minutes of Evidence being the source).

(when the police moved in). Wallace suggested that Aaron should get £2,000 out of the reward for doing so.

- That Wallace told Aaron about two policemen who had passed on information that had got back to the Kellys. Constable Slater was described as 'the best friend the Kellys had' because after telling his friends about police movements the Kellys would hear about it soon after. Similarly, information another policeman named Sergeant Harkins let slip about a shanty four miles from Wodonga that was apparently used by the Kellys soon reached the Kellys and resulted in them changing their quarters.[91]

- That the gang's money was apparently running short, with Wallace wanting Aaron to go to Chiltern or Wodonga to sell their remaining gold. When Aaron replied that he was too well known to one of the policemen there, Wallace suggested as a way around this that Aaron get someone to go digging with him for a week or so in Stony Creek near Beechworth, so that they could then sell the gold as if they had found it themselves. Wallace had asked Aaron to go to his place at Hurdle Creek on the Friday evening (29 August), so arrangements could be made for selling the gold and for the trip to Melbourne (to seek a pardon for Joe).

- That Wallace had been visited that week (on the night of Thursday 21 August) by Joe Byrne, who wanted him to find out if Aaron was after them, and to tell him that he would know the consequences if he was.

- That Wallace had told Aaron that unless Joe could be got free (by being pardoned for giving up the other three), the gang would shortly stick up another bank, most likely at Oxley.

- That Wallace wanted to have a conversation with him (Ward), to try to find out what the police thought as to the

---

91 - *The Ned Kelly Encyclopaedia*, 2003, Justin Corfield, page 218. Harkins was one of the police party that nearly caught the Kelly Gang in October 1878 at the flooded Murray River, after the gang had fled from Stringybark Creek.

Kellys' whereabouts. Also, rather alarmingly, that Wallace had asked Aaron to shoot him (Ward), saying that the blame would be left on the Byrnes (which seems a curious request from someone who was keen for Joe to obtain a pardon).

The final part of Detective Ward's report described the meeting he had with Wallace and Aaron the previous Saturday (23 August) at Beechworth's Wertheim Hotel. (Wallace would the next day report to Nicolson with his own account of the meeting between him, Aaron and Ward — see below 'Wallace letter, 27th August 1879 — Casting further doubts on Sherritt and Ward'.)

Ward reported that Aaron had told him that Wallace had about nineteen or twenty National Bank notes on him. Sure enough, when Wallace paid for a round of drinks, he did so with a National Bank note. He first passed the notes to Ward with the comment that it was a pity he didn't have the numbers of the bank notes. Wallace then continued to spend money very freely during the night, before he and Aaron spent the night at the Imperial Hotel. They left at 7 am the following morning and went to Mrs Sherritt's. Wallace remained there until about midday, after which he left for home with Aaron accompanying him as far as the Golden Ball (the hotel midway between Everton and Beechworth).

Ward reported that Wallace asked him at their meeting whether he thought the Kellys were still in the country — a question Aaron had forewarned him was coming. When he answered that he thought they were, Wallace then broached the possibility of a pardon of one (Joe) in order to catch the other three.

Ward concluded his report to Nicolson by stating there was no doubt that Wallace was a warm supporter of the gang, and that strict watch would be kept on him when he next came in to Beechworth. Ward had been suspicious of Wallace from early on in the hunt for the Kelly Gang. The meeting he had with Wallace at the Wertheim Hotel reinforced those suspicions.

By the time of this meeting in Beechworth, it seems Aaron Sherritt was very much working on the side of 'law and order'. It seems likely, in fact, that Aaron was a reliable police informer from even before the Euroa bank robbery when he came to Benalla to speak with Chief Commissioner Standish, whom he had met in the aftermath of the Sebastopol charge. As Standish was not there on that occasion, he reported to Superintendent Hare instead, with whom he developed a good rapport from that point on. Hare reported to the Royal Commission that he trusted Aaron. Detective Ward also appears to have found him trustworthy. However, Nicolson's faith in both Aaron and Ward was compromised by Wallace's lies.

Wallace letter, 27 August 1879 – Casting further doubts on Sherritt and Ward

Wallace wrote this letter to Nicolson giving his account of the Wertheim's Hotel meeting (among other things) the day after Detective Ward had forwarded his own report. The information he gave would certainly have piqued Nicolson's interest and given him some doubts about the reliability of Aaron Sherritt (and perhaps also Detective Ward).

Wallace's account of the meeting at Wertheim's Hotel and the bank notes

Wallace told Nicolson that he had interviewed Mr Hare's protégé (Aaron) that night, and had spent the night with him at Beechworth. In contrast to Ward's report about the National Bank notes, he wrote that it was Aaron who had the notes – two National Bank notes in fact. Aaron, Wallace wrote, had told him the notes were 'square' and that he had obtained them in payment for services rendered to the police. Wallace then explained that he purposely cashed one of the notes in Ward's presence, whilst jokingly drawing his attention to it being a National and asking him what he would give to be told where it had come from.

It was reckless behaviour by Wallace to have flashed that bank note in front of Ward. He knew Ward suspected him of being a sympathiser, but did it anyway. However, a weakness in Wallace's account (which would tend to favour Ward's account if one had to decide who was most likely to be telling the truth) is why it would be that he was the one cashing the note – if it was Aaron's note, why would he have given it to Wallace to cash? Ward's report seems much more plausible. However, by giving Nicolson an alternative account, Wallace effectively neutralised any incriminating insinuations that Ward might direct towards him. Who would Nicolson believe? It was another example of Wallace's cunning.

Kennedy's watch

Having alluded in his previous letter to possibly being able to persuade someone to return Sergeant Kennedy's watch to his widow, Wallace now made it clear that that someone was Aaron. He wrote that in the early part of the evening Aaron had proposed that he (Wallace) should go home with him that night, so that he could show him Kennedy's watch and get his opinion as to the feasibility of getting it altered so it could not be identified. He wrote that Aaron had said it was at his mother's place for safe-keeping, and added that he told him there was a dark stain on the case and a sovereign pendant on the chain.

Wallace added, however, that Aaron would likely have been put on his guard following his interview with Ward. He was in effect telling Nicolson not to bother searching Mrs Sherritt's house, because with Aaron on his guard, it was unlikely the watch would still be there.

A letter in Joe Byrne's handwriting

As if the information about the bank notes and the watch was not enough, Wallace then related a story about Aaron asking him if he could imitate Byrne's handwriting, to which he had replied in the affirmative. He wrote that Aaron wanted a threatening letter written to a Mr A Crawford of Beechworth, which Crawford was to think came from Byrne.⁹² The letter was to warn Crawford to prepare for his end as they had been told that he had informed on Gustav Baumgarten for providing them with supplies.⁹³

Wallace explained that, at Aaron's request, he wrote a draft of the proposed letter and showed it to him. It was just as well Wallace told Nicolson this, as a threatening letter was in fact sent to Mr Crawford that was later shown to have been in Wallace's handwriting. As with the tale about the bank notes, Wallace telling this story to Nicolson neutralised any incriminating insinuations that Detective Ward might have directed his way.

As an interesting aside, if Wallace was indeed capable of imitating Byrne's handwriting, then this strengthens the possibility that Wallace and not Byrne wrote the Jerilderie Letter.

Visit to the Sherritts

After spending the night with Aaron at Beechworth, Wallace wrote that he went down to the 'old peoples' (Aaron's parents, John and Agnes) the next morning (Sunday) and stayed to dinner. The old lady, he said, was not at all communicative but appeared nervous and frightened. Wallace said that their son Jack was also rather reticent and distrustful at first.

It is hardly surprising the Sherritt's felt the way they did. The Sherritt family would have been aware by then of Wallace's duplicity, and it was

---

92 - The Mr A Crawford referred to was a respectable Beechworth businessman named Hiram A Crawford. Crawford is referenced in Corfield's *Ned Kelly Encyclopaedia* (at page 116), and further information about him can be found in his obituary, which appeared in the *Ovens and Murray Advertiser* on Wednesday 19 January 1916: https://trove.nla.gov.au/newspaper/article/90771212 Hiram Crawford appeared as a character witness for William Baumgarten when he had been charged with horse stealing, which is interesting given Baumgarten was part of the horse stealing ring that the Kellys were involved in, and which led to the arrest warrant for Dan Kelly being issued, the serving of which by Constable Fitzpatrick was the event that started the Kelly outbreak. Also of interest is that Hiram's daughter Emma was a friend of Kate Kelly and Aaron Sherritt, which shows that high social standing in those days was not necessarily a barrier to forming friendships with people lower in the social hierarchy.

93 - Gustav Baumgarten, was one of the two Baumgarten brothers who the police alleged were involved in Ned Kelly's horse-stealing racket. Whether Crawford informed on Gustav or not, it is interesting that he appeared as a character witness for Gustav's brother William Baumgarten after he was charged with horse stealing.

him they were nervous about. Perhaps by writing to Nicolson about their nervousness, Wallace might have been implying that they had something to hide.

Wallace also wrote that the outlaws had paid the Sherritts a visit. They had wanted food. Telling Nicolson this was another way of generating mistrust about Aaron's loyalties.

Wallace also reported that Jack Sherritt had told him that the police were on a new 'lay' – hoping to get Mrs Byrne to persuade Joe to turn informer. Jack added that the police might save themselves the trouble as the old woman (Mrs Sherritt) had declared 'she would rather see him shot or hanged any day than turn traitor'. Furthermore, Jack said that the outlaws were well aware of the 'move', and were not at all afraid of Byrne selling them.

Wallace concluded by telling Nicolson he had been out in the ranges all of the previous night. He added that he would reconnoitre at the Black Range Creek the following night and interview 'Mr B' on the Saturday morning. The Black Range is near Whitfield, to the south of Hurdle Creek. The Mr B who Wallace was referring was likely to be Mr Bourke who owned a property there.

* * *

Subsequent investigations into evidence of Wallace collusion with the Kelly Gang would find that at about this time (August 1879) he was buying excessive amounts of supplies, and that he was also collecting mouldboards with the excuse that his father was a scrap metal merchant. For him to have been collecting mouldboards at this time is interesting, given that the Glenrowan action was 10 months into the future.

Wallace letter, 1 September 1879 – Tells of his fantastical efforts to locate the gang

Wallace was on a roll with his letters. He waited only five days before penning his next letter to Nicolson.

Stating the obvious

He started by stating the obvious – that there was no doubt as to the Kellys being about. Indeed, from unguarded expressions let drop by the elder Sherritts (Agnes and John), he thought they had been bivouacking in some of the ranges between Sebastopol and El Dorado and that they were without horses. It was his view that they very seldom remained long in one place; that they moved about at night and slept in scrub or caves during the day. None of this information was helpful – everything Wallace was telling Nicolson was essentially common knowledge.

Efforts to locate the gang

The rest of this letter was a fantastical description of the efforts Wallace said he had taken to locate the gang over four nights in the previous week – Tuesday 26 August, Thursday 28 August, Friday 29 August, and then again on Saturday 30 August.[94]

On the Tuesday night between 11 pm and 3 am, he wrote that he had run through the likely places in the Hurdle Creek Range and had then reconnoitred Black Range Creek. As the Kellys were making use of the hut at Sawpit Gully around this time, it is quite possible that he had indeed been out in the Hurdle Creek Ranges on this particular night, perhaps meeting with the gang and taking them some provisions. Four hours would be about the time required for the round trip. Once again, this would be an example of Wallace's cunning, for if Nicolson accepted him at his word, then the police would search somewhere other than the Hurdle Creek Ranges.

The efforts Wallace went to on the Tuesday night were believable, but the account he gave of his searches on the Thursday, Friday and Saturday nights pushed the bounds of credibility. On the Thursday night, he claimed he visited Mackay's Springs and up the ranges as

---

94 - This period coincided with school holidays. It was getting close to a full moon on the nights that Wallace wrote that he was searching for the gang (full moon was on 1 September 1879).

far as Bullock Camp.⁹⁵ Then on the Friday night and early hours of Saturday, he claimed he rode along the gang's stolen horses track under the railway arch above Everton and along the ridges at the back of the Golden Ball Hotel, before checking out Sherritt's (Sheep Station Creek) and riding down to Byrne's lookout where he watched over the Chappells and Byrnes properties until sunrise. He then crossed the creek and took a series of gullies down into the Pilot Flat and along Deep Creek, getting to the upper Black Dog Creek about noon, his horse thoroughly knocked up.

At Black Dog Creek, Wallace claimed he camped until dark at the hut of an unnamed 'Chinaman', whom he recognised as being from Sebastopol and a great friend of the Byrnes, and who was loud in his expression of sympathy for the outlaws and ridicule for the search-party style of hunting them. Interestingly, his reference to the unnamed 'Chinaman's' criticism about the conduct of the search is similar to criticism that would later appear in a letter to James Graves MLA, which was purportedly written by someone named Mr Connor, but which the Royal Commissioners would suspect was written by Wallace.

Speaking of 'Chinamen'

Speaking of 'Chinamen', Wallace then related a story he claimed Aaron had told him. Aaron, he wrote, had heard from a 'Chinaman' that Ned had lately purchased some stores at a Chinese shop at Bright. Wallace wondered how many Celestials there would be who would supply the outlaws with food and hold their tongues about it. 'How would it be,' he mused, 'to let Fook Sing (sic, Shing) do a week's duty on the business?'

Fook Shing was a Chinese police detective who would later take part in the Kelly Hunt.⁹⁶ As noted by Ian MacFarlane in *The Kelly Gang: Unmasked*, at some stage it must have occurred to Commissioner

---

95 - Mackay's Springs were on land owned by AE Mackay to the east of the road now known as Farmers Road, which runs north out of the Beechworth-Wangaratta Road. From the northern end of Farmers Road various tracks then led to El Dorado and elsewhere into the Woolshed Valley. The author does not know the location of the Bullock Camp referred to by Wallace, but from Wallace's description it would appear that it was 'up (in) the ranges'.

96 - https://www.latrobe.edu.au/news/articles/2018/release/the-story-of-fook-shing

Nicolson that schoolmaster Wallace knew far more about police matters than he should.[97]

It is hard to believe Nicolson could have accepted all that Wallace said in this letter, particularly given the reports he was receiving about Wallace from Detective Ward. Wallace's reported expedition, starting from the Thursday night and ending on the Sunday morning, covered large parts of the Sebastopol and Chiltern Ranges. Who knows what he was really up to over these days, or even if he was covering the ground at all – he could have written about travelling through these ranges from memory, as this was country he knew well from his youth.

* * *

On 4 September 1879, Detective Ward wrote a confidential memo to Nicolson from the Beechworth Police Station.[98] He had seen Tommy (Aaron Sherritt) that morning, who had told him that he had stopped at Wallace's (this would have been his visit to Wallace's house on 21 August) in the expectation that Joe was going to call there, but Joe failed to show. Tommy, Ward reported, was certain that Wallace knew the gang's whereabouts and could find them when he liked, but that he would not sell Joe Byrne.

Ward also reported that Wallace and Tommy had made an appointment to go to Chiltern on the Friday evening (Friday 5 September). They would there meet a person who knew where Joe was (and would presumably take them to Joe). When he asked Aaron if he would have any objection to him being in Chiltern to see if Wallace would be there, Aaron replied, 'No you can come, and you might then get the gold when we are in the act of selling it.' Aaron also said the gang had told Wallace they would not try the Oxley bank now, as there were too many police there (two troopers every morning when the bank opened) and, as another drawback, that the ground was too soft. They

---

97 - The Kelly Gang: Unmasked, page 181

98 - Detective Ward's report was read to Wallace when he appeared before the Royal Commissioners (Q14791). Wallace replied that the report was totally untrue so far as he was connected with it.

were not going to do anything until the ground got harder, as they were frightened of the 'black boys'.

With respect to the threatening letter (that had been sent to Mr Crawford), Aaron told Ward that he believed from the description of the person who gave it to him, that it must be a man named Jack Fox, a friend of the Byrnes. Ward was not satisfied with this story, and believed that Aaron had likely had something to do with the letter's delivery.

With respect to Sergeant Kennedy's watch, Ward reported that Wallace had been told by Joe that this was in the possession of Grace Quinn (one of Ned Kelly's aunts). Joe apparently wanted to get the watch so it could be returned to Mrs Kennedy, as they were very sorry for the shooting of Kennedy.

Despite having some reservations about what Aaron had told him, Ward reported that Aaron had assured him that they would get the gang before too long. He was therefore giving money to Aaron to go to Chiltern to keep his appointment with Wallace, and said he would also like to go along to secretly watch their movements.[99]

Wallace letter, 9 September 1879 – 'You will have to do something with Aaron soon'

Only eight days after his last letter, Wallace wrote again to Nicolson. He had previously tried to make Nicolson doubt the reliability and loyalty of Aaron Sherritt, and continued to do so in this letter.

The gang is reprovisioned

Wallace wrote that 'Poet Sneak & Co' (Poet was Joe Byrne and Sneak was Dan Kelly) were up in the Sebastopol ranges again on the Saturday evening and that they had had a jolly carouse with two of the 'young S's' – presumably the young S's were Aaron and John Sherritt. He wrote that they had been reprovisioned and added, just to rub it in, that the pack horse carrying the provisions had been met when coming out of

---

99 - The proposed visit to Chiltern never eventuated.

Beechworth by (Inspector) Brooke Smith and a constable, but that no suspicions had been aroused.[100]

The threatening letter to Mr Crawford

As regards the threatening letter sent to Mr Crawford, Wallace wrote that this had been written by Byrne. He added for good measure that Byrne will never turn traitor, and that he swears 'to fight like a demon and die like a man with the assistance of God almighty'.

Wallace seems to have forgotten that he had previously told Nicolson (in his letter of 27 August) that he had, at Aaron's request, written a letter addressed to Mr Crawford that Crawford was to think had come from Joe Byrne. Aaron had asked him if he could imitate Joe's handwriting, to which Wallace had answered in the affirmative. And yet here he was now telling a different tale to Nicolson – that the letter had in fact been written by Byrne. Apparently, Nicholson did not pick up on this inconsistency.

It is surprising Nicolson didn't question Wallace about how he could know so much. It was one thing for him to have known Byrne in school days, but how could he know about the gang being reprovisioned, Byrne's supposed authorship of a letter, and other information that one would think could only be known from direct contact with the gang. It seems, however, that Nicolson didn't doubt Wallace – he virtually admitted this at the Royal Commission and at a meeting he would have with Wallace years later when Wallace was trying to clear his name.

His search for the outlaws

Wallace reported that he searched for the outlaws on the Saturday night down on the Black Dog; on the Sunday and Sunday night he

---

[100] - Inspector Brooke Smith was in charge at Wangaratta when the Kelly Gang passed through on 4 November 1878, about a week after the Stringybark Creek shootings. His incompetence in acting quickly to follow up on a reported sighting led to the gang evading capture on that occasion, and there were several other occasions when Brook Smith was in charge that also resulted in the gang remaining at large. In the Jerilderie Letter, Brook Smith was lampooned as a 'poodle dog half-clipped in the lion fashion'. A biography of Brook Smith appears in Corfield's *The Ned Kelly Encyclopaedia* at pages 438–440.

was round the Barambogie; and on the Monday he had searched the Pilot, Barnes' Gully, and Scarred Rock, etc.[101]

The area Wallace described is to the north side of the Woolshed ranges. The Black Dog is the area along Black Dog Creek that runs into the township of Chiltern. Barambogie is Mount Barambogie, and The Pilot is Mount Pilot. The area is extensive, and a long way from Hurdle Creek. One has to wonder how he could have managed to cover so much ground over the course of a weekend, although it is surprising the stamina that some people had in those times, and the distances they could cover whether on foot or horseback. It is quite possible, though, that Wallace was just making it all up – once again, it was an area he knew well from growing up in Woolshed and El Dorado.

And what did Wallace have to report of his search other than that he had missed the outlaws? Only that he had found traces on the Pilot of a recent campfire!

Wallace went on to give a confusing account of further efforts he had made to locate the gang. He told of his horse breaking its hobbles, leaving him to make it back home on foot. He wrote that he had visited some of the gang's old horse stealing dens and camps around Woolshed, before crossing the range to Sheep Station Creek. He saw nothing though. He finally got home at about 9.30 am on the Monday (the day he wrote this letter), thoroughly knocked up.

If all he wrote was true, then Wallace had been continuously on the move from Thursday night until Monday morning, with much of his travels on foot. And as if that were not enough, he planned to return that night, visit Whorouly the next night (Tuesday), and then put in a couple of days in Rat's Castle on the Saturday and Sunday where Byrne had offered (presumably in the past) to show him through the caves if he would swear 'to keep it dark'.

'You will have to do something with Aaron – he is playing you double!'

Wallace expressed concern about Aaron, telling Nicolson that he (Nicolson) would have to do something with him soon. Aaron, he said,

---
101 - Scarred Rock is probably Ingram's Rock, near Beechworth.

'was sweating horses right and left'. If he didn't get into some steady billet (work) where he could make an honest living, then he would develop into another outlaw before long. He added for good measure that, 'There is not the least doubt about his playing you double.'

Final miscellaneous matters

This was not one of Wallace's finest letters. Apart from losing the narrative when describing his searches for the gang, the letter became jumbled towards its end, with Wallace reporting, among other things, that 'young Jack S' (Jack Sherritt) was very desirous of meeting with Nicolson on a matter of great importance; that Mrs Byrne had been paid in National Bank notes for her good offices at the late trial;[102] that 'the boys' had been at Mrs Byrne's place, though not recently; and that he thought the boys were presently in the neighbourhood of Surface Gully, below Sebastopol, where there is ground cover.

Wallace wrote that Mrs Byrne had been much pestered about Joe's pardon (presumably the possibility of a pardon), and that it would be better to wait for a week or fortnight before he interviewed her in regards to that.

Wallace also wrote that he had strong hopes of being able to put 'Jumbo and Barney' (John Sherritt) on the trail soon.[103] He thought it would be better to take him down to Benalla to see him (Nicolson) – they could go down from the Wangaratta Show by the 4.46 pm train from Wangaratta, and return by the 8 pm train from Benalla. He added, 'There is not the slightest danger of his selling the boys. I cannot guess what business he can have with you.'

---

102 - The trial Wallace was referencing here would be the court case against Aaron for stealing a horse from one of the Byrne daughters.

103 - Wallace has referenced 'Jumbo and Barney' in the singular, and it appears given what follows that he was talking about John Sherritt. In the 19th century there was a famous circus in the United States that was known as PT Barnum's Circus, at which Jumbo the African elephant was a popular attraction (Jumbo and Barney!). This is purely speculation on the part of the writer, but it seems that 'Jumbo and Barney' may have been a nickname Wallace decided to use when describing John Sherritt.

Warning about Detective Ward

Wallace requested Nicolson to not let Ward know that he had received news (from Wallace) that the outlaws had been at Mrs Byrne's. He had strong reasons for this that he would explain to Nicolson when he next saw him.

Wallace's was trying hard to make Nicolson mistrust Ward. For his part, Nicolson was highly protective of his agents – even other police within his office were unaware of who his agents were. He did not need to be asked by Wallace to keep his confidences quiet, as it was something he did as a matter of course. The fact that Detective Ward never knew that Nicolson was using Wallace as an agent is testament to Nicolson's secrecy.

Wallace ended his letter by telling Nicolson what he surely wanted to hear:

> *I will very likely find them tomorrow night. If I do you will get a telegram at once from El Dorado or Beechworth. I will want a few more rounds of ammunition and perhaps a few pounds in cash. We are bound to have them soon now. I fancy I have got their routes and tactics correct.*

* * *

The Wangaratta Show was held on Saturday 13 September 1879. Wallace had said (in his letter dated 9 September) that he wanted to introduce Jack Sherritt to Nicolson at this show if he was going to be there.

* * *

The Milawa Ploughing Match was held on Tuesday 16 September 1879. After this ploughing match, Detective Ward reportedly spoke to a number of people at Gardiner's Hotel, Milawa, in the course of which he let slip (deliberately) that Wallace was working as a police agent.

Wallace letter, 19 September 1879 – Complains about Detective Ward's mischief

Wallace wrote this letter in response to a note posted by Nicolson on the 15th that must have referred to a rumour that Detective Ward had heard. The rumour, as it would later transpire, was that the outlaws had been seen at Hurdle Creek.

Wallace stated that he had heard nothing of the rumour, despite meeting a large number of people who had attended the ploughing match. He wrote that if there had been any truth to the rumour, he would be sure to have heard it as rumours of that kind soon travel. He added that Ward was probably responsible for the rumour.

Wallace then complained that after the ploughing match, Ward had spoken with various people at Gardiner's Hotel,[104] and that things had turned out as he had feared:

> *I knew well that if he found out what relations existed between you and me, he would do his best to spoil any chance of being useful to you.*
>
> *I have it on the very best authority from two different sources that he stated at the Ploughing match that I 'was a detective', that he 'was certain of it', that he 'had seen my name on the list'. He also told a Mr James Doig a farmer of this place that 'I was trying to get on as a detective' that he 'had seen my name on a departmental list'.*
>
> *How is it possible that my name could be seen on a list by him? He must just have conjectured it or else Captain Standish may have let him know. In any case he was not justified in any way in publishing the fact abroad in this manner.*
>
> *As far as anything I have said is concerned no one – not even my wife – could suspect that there is any communication between*

---

104 - Gardiner's Hotel, Milawa. The hotel still operates.

> *myself and the Department on the subject. If he has told the Sherritts or other Kelly Sympathisers the same story, he will have greatly lessened my chances of being of service to you, just when I thought I was about certain of success.*
>
> *If you have anyone else who bears the same relation to you that I do take care that Ward does not find out. If he does, he would do all in his power to spoil success. If he has told Aron, the outlaws will be possessed of the rumour by this time and I may expect a reminder from Byrne per post.*

Wallace wanted Nicolson to think that Ward was undermining him. He asked Nicolson to 'try to make Ward hold his libellous tongue'. He added that he had since met a man named Doig,[105] who confirmed that Ward had publicly stated in the Gardiners Hotel at Milawa that he (Wallace) was a detective, and that he had said this in the presence of four people: Colin Gardner JP, a teacher named James Kelly, and two farmers named John Barrie and A McCormick.[106]

Changing the subject away from rumours and the trustworthiness of Detective Ward, Wallace ended his letter by saying that he had a lot of information, on the authority of Jack Barry,[107] as to the outlaws being on visiting terms with Ned Burke of Black Range Creek.[108]

---

105 - Doig – a landowner at Hurdle Creek. Doig's selection abutted the Carboor Range where the 'hut behind the school' was located.

106 - Colin Gardiner JP was probably the Gardiner who lived at Oxley and who was the police agent code-named 'Tiller'. The teacher named James Kelly taught at a state school on Melbourne Road near Beechworth and was not related to Ned and Dan Kelly. John Barrie and A McCormick were local farmers.

107 - Jack Barry lived in the Black Range area and knew Ned Burke of Black Range Creek. According to Wallace, Jack Barry was also a great friend of Joe Byrne, and had worked at Byrne's uncle's farm at Whorouly, and had just now returned from Byrne's cousin's place at Wagga (Wagga Wagga).

108 - The Black Range is the range to the south of the Carboor Range. Ned Burke's property was to the north of Whitfield (near to Hedi). There is a strong possibility that Ned Burke was a sympathiser – a Mrs Bourke of Hedi (Ned Burke's wife) was included on a secret list of persons that had been compiled by the Lands Department (pages 194–195 *The Kelly Gang: Unmasked*) with the help of police. Those listed were considered as belonging to the criminal classes and were to be denied future land applications.

Wallace was on good terms with Ned Burke – he would go away with him later in the year (during the Christmas holidays) on a trip into the Wonnangatta Valley – so it seems strange that he would throw Burke to the wolves like this. It is likely, though, that Wallace knew Burke was already suspected of being a sympathiser, and therefore saw no harm in telling the police something they already knew as a way of enhancing his bona fides. For good measure, he concluded by telling Nicolson, 'I think I will do well to devote a little more attention to the Black Ranges than I have done hitherto. There is ground cover there and it has not been half searched.' Any excuse it seems to go for a wander!

Wallace letter, 21 September 1879 – Searching Hurdle Creek and Meadow Creek ranges

Only two days later, Wallace wrote to Nicolson yet again. He started by telling of how on the Friday night and Saturday morning he had gone through the Hurdle Creek and Meadow (Creek) ranges. He reported finding nothing but the tracks (a few days old) of a heavy-shod horse on the ranges near the One Tree Hill crossing over from the Hurdle Creek above McCallums in the direction of the Lower Meadow Creek.[109] He also reported finding traces of a camp fire (a week or fortnight old, if not older) at the head of Sawpit Gully. The area he was describing was the very area where the 'hut behind the school' was located. Perhaps the gang was there at the time Wallace wrote the letter, with Wallace calculating that Nicolson would accept his word that there was nothing to be found at this location.

On the Saturday night, he reported that he left for the Sebastopol ranges after a meeting at his home that ended at 10pm. It was a beautifully clear starlit night, much preferable for his purpose to a moonlit one. He rode and walked quietly through the hills above Sebastopol, but neither saw nor heard anything of note. He visited some huts of the Sherritt Brothers, but found all was quiet, despite a fire blazing brightly at one of the huts at the time of his 3 am visit. He

---

109 - Duncan McCallum owned a selection that abutted the Carboor Range where the 'hut behind the school' was located.

then went down Sebastopol Gully along the bed of the streamlet – a rough spot to ride through in the dark – and got to Mrs Byrne's just at daybreak.

At the mouth of the gully at the back of the Byrne property, Wallace wrote that he came upon the very fresh tracks of either two horsemen leading their horses or else two mounted men accompanied by two pedestrians. The tracks passed close to Mrs Byrne's house, before heading in a westerly direction. The tracks, Wallace wrote, were evidently made by the police who were watching Mrs Byrne's property. He then expressed his view that they had shown great indiscretion and been very careless to have left such noticeable tracks. In following the tracks the next day, Wallace wrote of how he came upon the fresh trail of a solitary individual on foot, which he then followed for about two and a half miles down the creek along the foot of the range. The trail appeared to go into a Chinaman's hut at the foot of a gully. Unlike the other tracks he had followed, this man had walked with more discretion, as after leaving the Byrnes's, he had kept on the grass for some distance before taking to the path. Always one for detail, Wallace wrote that the man whose tracks he was following had walked lightly and worn neat strong boots (about number seven in size). From the tracks, Wallace deduced that he could only have preceded him by a few minutes. Wallace wrote that he should have entered the hut, but that as all these confounded Chinamen knew him, and since Ward had libelled him, he thought it might do Nicolson's cause more harm than good if he did.

From the Chinaman's hut, Wallace said he put in about one and a half hours through the hills and then made for the El Dorado Road below the Kangaroo Bridge, where he again came upon similar horse tracks to those he observed near Byrnes, which he followed into the El Dorado Police Camp.

If any of what Wallace wrote in this letter were true, he must have possessed the tracking skills of an Aboriginal and the endurance of an athlete. It was a lot of ground to have covered over the course of a weekend.[110] If it were true, Wallace certainly had a real appetite for

---

110 - This period coincided with school holidays.

getting out into the bush and searching for the gang on Nicolson's behalf. It seems he much preferred this kind of adventure to spending time at home with Barbara and his growing family.

Wallace also related a bit of gossip about Jack and Bill Sherritt who he said had ridden into El Dorado in the previous week. He wrote that as they were returning, Jack's horse fell and threw him and that in the shock of the fall he dropped a concealed revolver on the road, which was seen by a bystander. He wrote that it was just possible that Bill was also armed, which, if so, was significant.

There was method to Wallace's story about Jack and Bill Sherritt. If the Sherritts had, in fact, been given a revolver by the police, then Wallace was letting Nicolson know that people knew this and would be asking questions about why they were so armed. And if the revolver had not been given to them by the police, then it would be the police who would be left wondering. Either way, it was more mischief making by Wallace.

Nearing the end of his letter, Wallace again raised the matter of the rumour he had written about in his previous letter. Referring to Ward, he wrote, 'I believe he told you a falsehood.' He concluded his letter by telling Nicolson that the school inspector would be examining his pupils on the coming Thursday and that it would take all of his time to prepare for that. Teachers were paid according to results, he wrote, adding that he thought he stood to lose from £5 to £10 through being so much engrossed in his work for Nicolson. It seems he was letting Nicolson know in advance that he might seek reimbursement for the expected loss of pay.[111]

***

On 25 September 1879, a Constable Alexander called at Hurdle Creek to make enquiries regarding a rumour that had been communicated to

---

111 - What Wallace was telling Nicolson about his loss of pay was a lie, as he was on a fixed salary.

Constable Arthur at Milawa, to the effect that the outlaws had been seen at Hurdle Creek.[112]

Wallace letter, 29 September 1879 – Wallace seeks a new teaching position

Wallace wrote this letter after receiving a letter from Nicolson responding to his letter of 21 September.[113] In his letter, Nicolson must have told Wallace that he had warned Ward not to spread rumours. Wallace wrote back that he was glad to hear that, adding that Ward might find it advisable to hold his tongue in the future.

Nicolson must have also told Wallace that the tracks he had followed had not been made by the police. Wallace said that put an entirely different complexion on the matter – he had not paid as much attention to the tracks as he otherwise would have done (ignoring the fact that his description in his previous letter had been extraordinarily detailed).

Wallace postulated that if they were not police tracks, then, 'The chances are that they were your missing friends. Who else would it have been manoeuvring round there at that suspicious hour?' He then expounded upon why there could be no doubt that the tracks had been made between midnight and daylight:

> *Up till 12 o'clock on the Saturday evening the sky was cloudy. On a cloudy night no dew falls. There was a heavy dew on the grass on Sunday morning which had fallen since midnight. These tracks were very plainly to be seen on the dewy grass, therefore they must have left the trail after the dew had fallen. Nothing could be plainer.*

---

112 - A month later (on 1 November 1879), Constable Anthony Alexander would be posted to the new police station that had just been established at Glenrowan. *Ned Kelly Encyclopaedia*, page 10.
Constable James Murdoch Arthur was posted to Benalla. He was involved in the search for the bodies of Constables Lonigan and Scanlan and Sergeant Kennedy, participated in the subsequent hunt for the Kelly Gang, and was present at the capture of Ned Kelly at Glenrowan on 28 June 1880. *Ned Kelly Encyclopaedia*, page 21.

113 - A copy of Nicolson's letter to Wallace no longer exists. Wallace would tell the Royal Commission he did not think it prudent to keep any correspondence.

With his love for a good story, Wallace added that another reason why he had judged the tracks to be police tracks was that they were accompanied by the tracks of a large dog (a hound). He hadn't mentioned the dog tracks before because he thought at the time that it was most unlikely the outlaws would have had a dog with them. He had thought the fact that the trail he had picked up ran all the way to the El Dorado Post Office (which was next door to the police camp) was sufficient circumstantial evidence to prove they were police.

With regards to the tracks he had followed to the Chinese man's hut, Wallace agreed with Nicolson that it was 'just possible as you suggest that it might have been a Chinaman' – he would visit the hut and ascertain. But now, having mentioned the Chinese man's hut at (Sebastopol), Wallace seized the opportunity to spin a new yarn to Nicolson about a story he had heard from a Chinese man that he had met down at Hedi:

> *Ah Shin, a chinese tobacco grower residing at Hedi, today informed me that on the Saturday after the Wangaratta Show (13th Sept) as he was walking through the Boggy Creek ranges (Moyhu) he was met about 2 miles from Tyrells and accosted by a man whose description very nearly tallies with that of the senior outlaw – about six foot high – pretty well made, reddish beard & whiskers, black eyes, tweed trousers, top boots, dark coat, brownish felt hat worn down over his eyes with black band on chin, armed with no less than four revolvers hung around his belt – one of the revolvers of very unusual length – rode a red (bay or chestnut) horse.*
>
> *This man came down from a hill to the road leading his horse and cross-questioned the Chinaman pretty severely – made him tell his name, occupation, etc, where he came from, where he was going etc. The Chinaman replied that he was looking for a job and the stranger said that he too was looking for work. The Chinaman mustered up courage to ask the stranger where he lived. The man answered 'anywhere'. Being too frightened to ask*

> *any further questions Ah Shin cut the interview as short as he could with civility and went on his way – he mentioned nothing to anyone about his interview with the stranger, thinking it possible that he might be one of the bushrangers. He feared that if such was the case that if he spoke of it he might be murdered by the Kellys or some of their numerous friends.*
>
> *Of course there may be nothing in it. The man may have been a policeman in disguise. Ah Shin estimated his age at about 40.*
>
> *I cannot understand how the man came to have a revolver of such a length – 2 ft or 2 ½ ft as described by Ah Shin. Perhaps fear exaggerated it.*

If that didn't get the police department interested, it would be hard to imagine what would!

Interestingly, this description of the stranger supposedly met by Ah Shin contains a similar level of detail to the description of the traveller in *The Outlaws of the Wombat Ranges*.

In this latest letter, Wallace again alerted Nicolson that there was a leak from somewhere in his department, telling him that someone had spread news of the police having got the scent of the boys about Greta a couple of months earlier. Once again, the news was old, so yet another example of useless information provided by Wallace.

Actually, Wallace didn't really have anything to report. 'I have discovered nothing new since last writing.' He wrote that he had to be very careful since Ward floated the report (about him being a police spy), and had to work almost wholly at night. However, once again, to keep up Nicolson's hopes, he added that he was confident of finding them (the gang) soon.

The concluding paragraph of the letter is interesting, with Wallace referencing a previous discussion he must have had with Nicolson about the possibility of the political head of his department bringing pressure to bear on the Minister for Education to secure his brother William a new teaching position.[114] He wrote that he himself had applied for the head teachership of the Three Mile School near Beechworth, which he was pretty confident of getting.[115] The new position, he wrote, would leave him in 'in a better position to work this business for you' because he would have more leisure and be more centrally situated. He wanted political intervention to be brought to bear in having his brother William Wallace of the El Dorado school appointed as his successor at Hurdle Creek.

> *Perhaps you could assist me to work the thing so. If it can be done I will guarantee, with his assistance, to pin down the outlaws within a month, or die in the attempt. Apart from this particular business I could assist you in many ways in stamping out the horse stealing game for instance which has been so long carried on, and will consider myself bound to do so if you assist me in the above matter.*

For Wallace to seek to be reassigned to Three Mile Creek is understandable, as it would place him closer to home (Woolshed Valley and El Dorado) and to the amenities of Beechworth. As for seeking to have his brother William take over the school at Hurdle Creek, was he seeking to just secure him a more responsible teaching position at a more modern school? Or was he seeking to relocate his brother to a district where he could better assist Joe and the Kellys?

Wallace letter, 1 October 1879 – Delays in delivering letters

In this letter, Wallace responded to a complaint Nicolson must have made to him about delays in letters being delivered from the Bobinawarrah

---

114 - The Minister for Education at this time was Major Smith, who just happened to be Nicolson's father-in-law and the man who bestowed upon Nicolson the honorary title of Assistant Police Commissioner (which was a source of consternation to Police Commissioner Standish).

115 - Three Mile Creek is located south of Beechworth, about midway between Beechworth and Murmungee.

Post Office.[116] Of course, being in charge of the Bobinawarrah Post Office placed Wallace in a unique position to intercept mail going in either direction, and to delay the mail if it might be in the interests of the gang to do so. Wallace was always ready with an answer, in this case blaming his wife for the delay:

Post Office Bobinawarrah

October 1st 1879

Sir,

I am duly in receipt of your favor of yesterday with enclosed envelope of a letter which passed through this office, and which you complain of as having been unduly delayed.

Posted in Benalla on the 9th under the present postal arrangements it should have reached Hedi on the 13th but was delayed a week here through an oversight of my wife's. Registered letters are kept apart from ordinary letters in a secure place. From the 12th to the 20th inst. I was away from Post Office due to the serious illness of my brother (I had to take him to Melbourne) and left the post office in charge of Mrs W. She being new to the work did not think of looking in the Registered Letter Repository and only dealt with the ordinary letters. Consequently, your letter was overlooked till my return.

You refer to similar delays having occurred before of your correspondence. I am quite positive that if such is the case they were wholly owing to the defective postal arrangements which now obtain on this line. You can ascertain what they are by referring to a 'Postal Guide'. It is impossible to imagine anything more stupid than present arrangements.

---

116 - This particular letter is not in PROV's Wallace file, but can be found at VPRS 4965/P0000, 435

I would respectfully suggest that you communicate with the Postmaster General on the subject of more frequent and more rational mail communication with Hedi. For instance, a letter posted at Hedi for you on Wednesday reaches here on the following Saturday night and lies here till Monday night when it leaves for Milawa where it passes another night's rest and is sent on to Benalla on Tuesday, occupying exactly a week in that short transit.

Regretting the unfortunate delay referred to.
I have the honor to be Sir,
Yours most respectfully
James Wallace
Postmaster

Wallace note, 6 October 1879 – Responding to a rumour

On this date, Wallace sent both a brief note to Nicolson and a letter. His note advised Nicolson of the visit Constable Alexander had paid to Hurdle Creek on 25 September. He wrote that Alexander told him he had been sent to make enquiries regarding a rumour that had been communicated to Constable Arthur at Milawa, to the effect that the outlaws had been seen there (Hurdle Creek). 'Some more of Ward's pleasantries I reckon,' Wallace wrote.

Nicolson had raised the rumour with Wallace a few weeks earlier. From evidence later given to the Royal Commission, it seems the outlaws – or at least Ned Kelly – had indeed visited Wallace around this time. An affidavit had been given by the daughter of a Beechworth hotelier, who, during the course of a visit to Wallace's residence, was told by one of his children that Ned Kelly did not have a watch and chain like the one she herself had. She also stated that Wallace used to stay at her father's hotel and that he had purchased tinned fish from her on several occasions.

Wallace letter, 6 October 1879 – Still searching hard

Wallace also wrote a letter to Nicolson on 6 October describing how he had been out almost incessantly since he had last written, having worked 'this side of Hedi, Meadow Ck, Hurdle Ck Ranges, Sebastopol Ranges & between Sebastopol and El Dorado'.

Despite his efforts, he had made only one discovery of interest. He described how he had left his home on horseback one night and ridden to Everton in time to catch the train to Beechworth. From Beechworth, he had then gone by foot and carefully reconnoitred the vicinity of Sherritts on Sheep Station Creek and the adjoining suspected camps. He wrote that he had visited Aaron's hut on his selection, which was 'the place where the boys used to camp before the Jerilderie raid'. He had visited the same hut three weeks earlier, at which time the floor was dirty and litter was scattered around. The fact that the floor was now clean indicated that the hut had recently been occupied. There was also evidence of a recent fire. Among the cinders he said he found a few green strips of the wild broom which had been used to sweep out the house – 'these were quite fresh and green not more than a couple of days pulled, proving by their scorched ends that the fire had been recent'.

Wallace also reported that he visited the Chinese hut that he had reported in his previous letter. However, 'there was no one in, and I did not feel justified in ransacking the place in the absence of the owner.'

Wallace letter, 27 October 1879 – Meetings with the Sherritts and with Pat Byrne

In this letter, Wallace wrote that he had stayed a night with someone named Walsh of Hedi who was reported to have seen the Kelly brothers. However, this was before the Jerilderie exploit.

Wallace wrote that he doubted Walsh's claim that he had not seen the Kellys since then, for he had 'lately acquired a very neat silver mounted Breech-loading pistol, rifled, or American manufacture (which) has a range of 150 yards,' which he said had been given to him by a friend. 'Perhaps you may have some record of such a toy from Euroa or Jerilderie.'

Things were otherwise quiet on Black Range Creek, with Wallace writing that he didn't think the Kellys had been there within a fortnight. Turning then to the Sebastopol ranges, he wrote that he thought the Sherritts suspected something, because the last time he called there he only saw the old man who told him the boys were not at home, which was not true as he had seen 'Master William' make tracks for the bedroom and hide there as he rode up to the house. He wrote that the old man was very constrained in his manner towards him, despite the fact that he had called at the old man's request to give him the pedigree of a particular horse he wanted. Wallace said that the same Sunday in Woolshed he also saw Jack and Aaron at a distance, killing a bullock.

Wallace wrote that he had met young Pat Byrne – Joe's younger brother – and had a yarn and a drink with him. They discussed the Kelly's whereabouts and had a laugh at Wallace's suggestion that they were likely to be somewhere between Sebastopol and Greta (which, of course, represented just about the entirety of what had come to be known as Kelly country). He wrote that he told Pat that he should caution the Kellys to be more careful than they had been in recent days, lest they soon be reined in. Pat said he would caution them, but added that they would have to make another 'rise' soon as their funds were low. Wallace added that he noticed Pat had a black greyhound bitch with him, which would account for the dog tracks he had previously reported to Nicolson. 'Doubtless young Pat was with them, or perhaps the dog might have followed Joe.'

Wallace reported that he had beat round that quarter (Sebastopol) the previous night, but that all was quiet. He did, however, see Pat and his dog at about midnight in Woolshed, accompanied by another whom he took to be Jack Sherritt. They were coming from the Chinese camp and going in the direction of Mrs Byrne's cottage. Almost as an afterthought, he added that in speaking to Pat in reference to the police search parties, Pat had remarked that on the previous evening (Saturday 18th) three or four strangers had come in to Beechworth by the late train. They looked like 'traps' (police) in disguise and were enquiring about the way to the Hibernian Hotel.

Wallace concluded by saying he fancied the Kellys were still on Nicolson's side of the King River.

Wallace letter, 31 October 1879 – Comings and goings of various persons of interest

In a brief note to Nicolson this day, Wallace wrote that at about 2.30 am on the Thursday morning (October 30), five horsemen riding pretty fast had crossed the Hurdle Creek Bridge opposite the Bobinawarrah State School. They came from the direction of Hedi and were making towards Milawa, but were going too fast to be identified.

He also wrote that on the Tuesday (28 October), Jack Johnson of Black Range Creek, Hedi, was seen at about 4 pm near the Pioneer Bridge heading in the Beechworth direction. And on the previous Sunday (26 October), that Francis Harty of Greta (or a man like him) passed through El Dorado and went up the Sebastopol Road.

The reference to Francis Harty would have been of interest to Nicolson given he was a known associate of the Kellys who had provided an alibi for one of the men present at the Kelly property when Constable Fitzpatrick was assaulted. He was also one of the sympathisers who had been rounded up and placed on remand earlier in the year, at which time he had publicly declared his support for Ned Kelly, saying, 'I would fight up to my knees in blood for him – I have known him for years. I would take his word sooner than another man's oath.'

Both of these sightings mentioned by Wallace were too old to be of any use whatsoever. Furthermore, Wallace qualified the sighting of Harty by saying it could have been a man who looked like him.

Wallace letter, 12 November 1879 – Request to help Tom Burke

This was a lengthy letter. Wallace started by telling Nicolson how hard and incessantly he had been working in his interests since he had last written. He also expressed his fear that the precautions Nicolson had taken at Beechworth (against a possible bank robbery) had been too conspicuous as the gang appeared to have relinquished that idea for the present at least.[117]

---

117 - The police had been warned that the gang had been contemplating the robbery of a Beechworth bank, and had therefore put in place certain precautions.

Wallace described how he had 'beaten up' the gang's haunts in the Sebastopol Ranges on three different nights since he had last seen Nicolson. He found no recent traces – their friends there appeared to be 'paying attention to their sleeping' (i.e. they had gone quiet). On each occasion he had passed through the arch (railway arch) above Everton where the gang used to cross, but despite looking carefully he could observe no tracks. He had also visited a place known as as the 'Disputed Camp' on the Hurdle Creek run between Bobinawarrah and Whorouly and 'paid attention' to various people who were suspected sympathisers.

On the last Sunday week, Wallace reported that he had met with Aaron Sherritt in Woolshed and had a long conversation with him. Among other things, Aaron had told him that the police were going to have more than one mustering match and run in all the sympathisers again; that Nicolson had been persecuting him about Kennedy's watch; that he and Ward were now on bad terms and that he now negotiated with Nicolson personally. Wallace concluded the summary of his discussion with Aaron by telling Nicolson that Aaron had boasted that he knew all about the unlaws.

Wallace also wrote that he had twice seen Jack Sherritt, who carefully avoided him on both occasions. He inferred from this that Jack suspected him of having played him false, and gave various reasons why this might be the case, including that Nicolson's precautions at Beechworth were too evident (the inference being that Jack thought that Wallace had passed on information that Jack had given to him regarding the gang's plans to rob a Beechworth bank). 'If the outlaws suspect me of working for you either directly or indirectly they will take care to be careful of Sebastopol,' Wallace wrote.

As usual, Wallace was doing all he could to discredit the Sherritts. In Aaron's case, by referring once again to Kennedy's watch and to Aaron boasting about knowing all about the outlaws. In Jack's case, by making Nicolson believe that he had some prior knowledge of the gang's plans to rob a bank at Beechworth.

It is likely that it was around this time that the gang (and Wallace) realised that discrediting Aaron was not enough, and that he would need to be silenced.[118]

Wallace then turned to the Burkes. He wrote that there had been a ball at Bobinawarrah on the Monday night, and that Mr William Burke of Black Range Creek, Hedi, had honoured them with his company, but had '… paid for his ticket with a Bank of New South Wales £1 note dated Sydney October 1878.' The insinuation, of course, was that the note had come from the Jerilderie bank robbery.

Wallace wrote that Burke had come purposely to see him, because he wanted a favour, which Wallace said he would be most happy to do if it lay in his power. The favour he sought was for his brother Tom, who some time back had pegged out a selection of 50 acres, but whose application had been refused by the Land Board at Tarrawingee. No reason was given at the time, but the Burkes later heard through a friend in Melbourne that Tom was suspected by the police of being a Kelly sympathiser, whose name, along with the names of about 100 other residents of the district, was registered in a blacklist at the Land Office. Wallace wrote:

> *William says that he is positive that his brother Tom was not connected in any way with the outlaws. He could take his oath that Tom had not spoken to them since the murders and that if*

---

118 - In evidence that would later be given to the Royal Commission (refer Minutes of Evidence Q13490–Q13508), an Education Department truant officer named Enoch Downes recounted a conversation he had with Mrs Byrnes during the course of a visit he made to the Byrne house on 12 November 1879 to investigate the absence from school by one of the younger Byrnes. During the conversation, Downes said he put it to Mrs Byrnes that her son had had no reason to have joined the outlaws, to which she answered that Joe had made his bed, and must lie in it. She referred to the horse-stealing case against Sherritt, and said that it was a dodge (shifty trick) of Ward's to bring Joe back again to have revenge on Sherritt. She said it was a dodge by Ward to catch the outlaws, but that they (the gang) would wait their own time – which Enoch took to mean that they intended to come back for Sherritt. Downes said he passed the information on to Ward, who told him that they would not come back for Sherritt for a while, but that it was just a matter of time. (This was November, and Sherritt was not murdered until June the following year, just before Glenrowan.) Towards the end of the Commission's questions to Downes, they asked him (Q13507) if he had the opinion that they (the gang) had the intention to murder Aaron Sherritt, to which he answered that he was certain of it. From the evidence given by Downes, it would seem that the gang had decided (and one would presume with Wallace's full knowledge) as far back as eight months before Glenrowan that Aaron Sherritt would be killed. It was clear to the gang at this early stage that Aaron was acting for the police.

he had seen them, it was purely by accident and not through any wish or fault of his own. He admitted that a number of those in the vicinity whose names were marked richly deserved it as they were guilty of aiding and abetting the outlaws. He therefore wished his brother Tom's case dealt with apart from the others – apart even from his own or his other brother Ned's, as Tom was totally innocent, and being so it was not right that the innocent should suffer for the guilty. I thoroughly believe him. Tom is a decent, honest, hardworking lad always employed about home doing the farm work and looking after the horses, and very seldom going out anywhere.

Knowing I was acquainted with some of the Members of Parliament he wished me to write to them on his brother's account. He wished me to write to Graves, Gaunson, Cooper M L and to Reid, Wallace and Wilson MoLC and also to draw out a petition to Parliament respectfully worded for the respectful presidents of the district to sign saying that Thomas Burke's case be enquired into.

I agreed to do what he desired, but suggested that he should first write a letter to the Chief Commissioner of Police stating the facts of the case and requesting him to enquire into it, for as he was positively certain that his brother was innocent the Court on enquiry would soon find out where the mistake had been made and as both Captain Standish and Commissioner Nicolson were reputed to be honourable and humane gentlemen, I was sure they would withdraw their objection. He coincided with me and said he would take my advice as it would be a much easier and simpler course than petitioning Parliament and enlisting the advocacy of MPs and thus bringing their name into public. I therefore wrote a letter for him to the Comm which young Tom was to forward on by first post. That letter will probably have reached you before this.

We arranged it will give me a sort of claim on their friendship and gratitude, which I can then abuse in your interest. I could almost take my oath that young Tom is innocent while I could almost as surely swear that Ned knows all and William a great deal about them.

Please contrive that your reply, if reply you do, leaves Benalla by the first mail on Friday. He will then be sure to get it and I will be able to work him on the strength of it.

Ian MacFarlane in *The Kelly Gang: Unmasked* noted that this was a most remarkable request, with Wallace demonstrating that Kelly sympathisers like the Burkes had access to the confidential inner workings of the Land Office in Melbourne and, in relation to this matter, the connection between police command and the blacklist. Then there was the implied threat of parliamentary interference through Wallace's contacts.[119]

Wallace's next item of business in this long letter was to tell Nicolson that he had gleaned some more very interesting information in reference to a proposed bank raid in the Lancefield style. He thought it was best, though, to withhold this information for a day or two (perhaps until they next met), intimating once again that there was a leak within Nicolson's office.

Other than William Burke's request for a favour for his son, Wallace said he had a long conversation with him about the outlaws. William was very wary and reticent at first, but eventually began to talk freely and gave him to understand that the boys were still about, and that they now had a much stronger party and were in a better position to deal with their pursuers, and that they would have to make another break soon as their cash was running low. From what William said, or rather hinted, Wallace fancied that the gang was now reinforced by two others – Tommy Lloyd Jnr, and an elderly man (possibly Evans 'the Avoca desperado' who has been in the district before). If true, then the gang would form a strong party as Evans was reported to be

---

119 - *The Kelly Gang: Unmasked*, (2012) Ian MacFarlane, page 180.

a determined ruffian and young Lloyd, in addition to being the best rider in Victoria, without exception knew the ranges better than any of the others.

Wallace said he had expressed to William Burke his great admiration for the outlaws and had boasted of his acquaintance with Byrne. Burke replied that his mother ('Old Mrs Burke') was very intimately acquainted with Joe's father and mother in the old country. Burke warmly pressed Wallace to visit, with Wallace saying that he promised to go up on Saturday and that he would go out on the Black Range on Sunday with Ned (Burke) to run wild horses. There was also to be a dance up the river (King River) on the Friday night, which he intended on going to as it would be a chance to learn something and there would be a number of 'Kelites' there.

And then to the subject of remuneration. Wallace reminded Nicolson that when he had asked him to act in his interests, he 'had promised to make good any extra expense he might be put to in consequence'. He calculated his expenses since he had last been paid as amounting to between £7 and £10 and requested that Nicolson remit that amount by return post if he could. He, in fact, asked if Nicolson could send him £10, promising that he would then not ask for more until the business was finished, which he assured Nicolson would be very soon. If Nicolson could send him that amount, then the extra could later be deducted from his share of the plunder (reward money). A £10 note would be most convenient but otherwise a cheque would suffice.

Wallace's final letters – 26 November 1879 to 5 March 1880

Wallace's letter of 12 November 1879 is the last of his letters still held in the Wallace file at the PROV. An index at the start of the collection indicates, however, that he wrote nine further letters to Nicolson on the following dates:

- 26 November 1879
- 18 December 1879

- 22 December 1879
- 5 January 1880
- 17 January 1880
- 26 January 1880
- 11 February 1880
- 17 February 1880
- 5 March 1880

During the Royal Commission, Wallace's letter of 26 January 1880 was discussed.[120] It seems there had been a dispute between Wallace and Nicolson about reimbursement of Wallace's expenses, and that Nicolson had also been dissatisfied with the information Wallace was providing.

Wallace responded to a question put to him at the Royal Commission by Nicolson by saying he had given him information at Benalla on 12 January, but that he (Nicolson) had told him that he was not in a position to pay him his full expenses, which Wallace said he had positively understated at £25.[121] All Wallace got that day was £6, with Nicolson telling him he (Nicolson) would need to consult with the Chief (Standish) about the balance and get back to him once he had an answer. He never did get back to him though.

The Royal Commission records Wallace saying that Nicolson had hinted at the time that his intelligence had been 'manufactured to raise money upon.'[122] Nicolson had also been dissatisfied with the way his information was coming, and that he had told him that his slowness in returning from the bush after his Christmas holidays (from a trip that Wallace and Ned Burke had made to the Wonnangatta River) had raised unpleasant suspicions.

---

120 - Minutes of Evidence, Q14764.
121 - Minutes of Evidence, Q14767.
122 - Minutes of Evidence, Q14769.

14
Preparing for Glenrowan

With no offence (remember your railroads), and a sweet good bye from Edward Kelly

enforced outlaw

So ended the letter sent by Ned Kelly to Donald Cameron MLA only four days after the Euroa bank robbery.

... I will be compelled to show some colonial stratagem which will open the eyes of not only the Victorian police and inhabitants but also the whole British army, and no doubt they will acknowledge their hounds were barking at the wrong stump, and that Fitzpatrick will be the cause of greater slaughter to the Union Jack than Saint Patrick was to the snakes and toads in Ireland.

These words were written in the letter Ned Kelly took with him to Jerilderie with the intention of having his grievances published in the newspapers.

The references to railways and colonial stratagems in the two letters that this author believes Wallace to have had a hand in writing, point to the possibility of the Kelly story being much more than simply a story about a group of young and disaffected men.

There was considerable support at the time for the Free Selectors Associations, and it has been suggested by some[123] that involvement in the Upper Murray Free Selectors Association took up a lot of Wallace's

---

123 - Arthur Hall (author of The Headmaster of Hurdle Creek) and Len Pryor (author of Pioneer Teachers of the Kelly Country).

time. There were many people involved with the Free Selectors Associations and whilst there is no evidence for Wallace having been involved, there is no reason to think he wasn't. However, it is a big jump to suggest Wallace was involved in the planning of some kind of selector-armed insurrection. Admittedly, however, those references to railways and colonial stratagems do leave the door open for the Wallace story to be revised, but without some definitive proof, we can only speculate.[124]

After Jerilderie, the gang disappeared from sight for more than a year. There were numerous reported sightings, but the tightening net due to the increased police presence and the use of informers, together with the gang's concerns about the Aboriginal trackers specially brought in from Queensland, made them unwilling to attempt another robbery.

James Wallace was active throughout the gang's hiatus. He was busy writing his letters to Nicolson, in which he hardly ever missed an opportunity to spread doubt about Aaron's reliability and frequently belittled Detective Ward. A rumour spread (September 1879) that the outlaws had been seen at Wallace's school. He was buying food in excess of his family's needs. And he was collecting mouldboards on the premise that his father was a dealer in scrap metals.[125] Wallace also closed his schools without permission and travelled to Melbourne in March 1880 in a desperate attempt to secure a pardon for Joe Byrne.

On 20 May 1880, nine weeks before Glenrowan, Wallace made an application for a mortgage over his lease (selection) for the sum of £125. This was the same day that Nicolson received a letter from his agent Daniel Kennedy, aka Denny, telling him that 'Feed was scarce

---

124 - Arthur Hall and Len Pryor certainly believed there was a political aspect to the Kelly story and that James Wallace was a key figure in that movement. Arthur Hall only included material in his book *The Headmaster of Hurdle Creek* if it was backed up by evidence. However, Mr Hall had also written some draft chapters pointing to a more significant role played by Wallace and to the school at Hurdle Creek being the centre of selector operations, which he did not include in his book due to the lack of supporting evidence. Likewise, a draft paper on James Wallace that was written by Len Pryor (but not published) also makes a case for James Wallace being at the head of a selector rebellion.

125 - It was in March 1880 that the police first received a report of mouldboards having been stolen from a farm (the Glenrowan farm of a Mr Sinclair), although the theft could have occurred much earlier. Wallace was collecting mouldboards more than six months before that reported first theft.

and a breakout is imminent' and that the mouldboards were being used to make armour.[126]

Nicolson knew something was afoot, but would never have thought the plan could have involved the derailment of a police special train and the massacre of those onboard as a prelude to a raid on the banks in Benalla. A section of railway line just past the hamlet of Glenrowan had been selected as the place for the derailment. The line at that point curved adjacent to a steep embankment. Removal of a section of the tracks at this point would cause the train to topple over the embankment and onto its side. The gang, wearing homemade armour and standing upon the railway embankment, would fire upon those emerging from the train wreckage. With the police despatched, the gang and its supporters would then be free to ride in to Benalla and raid the banks. The proceeds would pay for their ongoing liberty.

For the massacre to succeed, the gang needed to do something that would cause the authorities to send a trainload of police from Melbourne. Aaron Sherritt had been a marked man for a long time and it was decided that shooting him at his home at Sebastopol would be the bait.[127] Joe and Dan would do the deed. They would shoot him the night before the Glenrowan action, in the expectation that a train carrying police reinforcements would pass through Glenrowan the following day. On the same night, Ned and Steve would break the rails at the designated spot.

Many hands were involved in the collection of the mouldboards used to make the armour, and in the armour's actual manufacture. The use of armour is indicative of a high level of planning, with the armour's design proving that the idea for derailing a train was formed very early

---

126 - Daniel Kennedy was a police spy code named 'Denny'. He was a Greta selector and also worked at Bridget O'Brien's Hotel in Greta where he was in a good position to gather local intelligence. Kennedy had also at one time been a school teacher and in fact applied to take over as head teacher at Glenrowan State School 1742 after Thomas Curnow (the teacher at that school) had to leave the area because of the possibility of reprisals by associates of the Kelly Gang.

127 - As noted in an earlier footnote, Truant officer Enoch Downs gave evidence to the Royal Commission about discussions he had had with Mrs Byrne some eight months prior to Glenrowan in which she had made it clear that the gang was aware that Aaron was acting for the police, and that he would be dealt with when the time was right. (RC Minutes of Evidence, Questions 13490 to 13508, pages 488–489).

in the planning (the armour did not include leg coverings, because the legs would be hidden from view of those firing back from below).

There have been many theories put forward over the years about the inspiration for the armour and about who made it. Until recently, it was generally agreed that the armour was Ned Kelly's idea, with book after book quoting Joe Byrne as saying, 'Well, it's your fault; I always said this bloody armour would bring us to grief.' Nearly every book written about the Kelly Gang has attributed this statement, overheard by a constable named Phillips who had crept to the back of Jones Hotel during a lull in the gunfire, as having been made by Joe to Ned. And yet, the report of the Royal Commission and a transcript of the constable's statement, which was reproduced in the newspapers of the time, state that it was Ned Kelly who made the statement to Joe Byrne.[128] On first reading, Ned complaining about the armour and telling Joe it was all his fault points to Joe as being the instigator for using the armour. And if so, then perhaps the confrontation at Glenrowan was also Joe's idea. Or could it all have been someone else's idea? Could the idea of the armour (and even the Glenrowan confrontation) have come from Wallace? It seems unlikely that Wallace would have been collecting mouldboards as far back as eight months before Glenrowan without knowing what they were to be used for. Historians Arthur Hall and Len Pryor certainly believed that a case could be made for James Wallace as having been at the head of a selector rebellion. However, no proof of that has ever come to light. There are so many unanswered questions!

Much has been written over the years about the making of the Kelly armour. After Glenrowan, a number of blacksmiths – including Patrick Delaney at Greta, Charles Culph at Milawa, and Tom Straughair at Woolshed – were investigated. A detective sought to establish who made the armour but was met with silence, as the blacksmiths concerned would have been subjected to serious charges. However, Detectives Ward and Considine would eventually report that they knew with very little doubt that Tom Straughair was responsible.

---

128 - This is discussed by David Dufty in his book *Nabbing Ned Kelly*, (2022), pages 314-315. Constable Phillip's statement is included in the Royal Commission Minutes of Evidence, page 674.

The descendants of some of the suspected blacksmiths are very keen for their ancestors to be credited – being descended from a maker of the Kelly armour is seen by some as a badge of honour, or at the very least as something that gives their family a place in Victorian history. A theory that gained some traction, perhaps as a means of appeasing the supporters of one blacksmith over another, is that the four suits and/or their components were made by a number of different blacksmiths. However, the author David Dufty has dismissed the notion of an underground blacksmith fraternity on the basis that it only makes sense in the context of the discredited theory that Ned Kelly was the leader of a republican movement.[129]

Dufty has included two mysteries at the end of his book *Nabbing Ned Kelly*, with the first of those (Mystery 1) addressing the making of the armour. He dismisses speculation that the armour was made by Patrick Delaney or Charles Culph, and speculates that it was Tom Straughair who was responsible. Detective Ward, Dufty notes, reported that he knew 'with very little doubt' that Straughair was the blacksmith responsible. He was a friend to both Joe and Aaron, despite being much older, and was also friendly with Wallace.[130]

Straughair's forge was located almost directly opposite Aaron Sherritt's property and it is rather ironic to think that Aaron's fate had already been decided whilst the armour to be worn at Glenrowan was being made directly under his nose.[131]

---

129 - There was no republican movement. This has been comprehensively debunked in the paper 'Ned Kelly and the Myth of a republic of North-Eastern Victoria', 2018, Stuart Edward Dawson. Mr Dawson's paper is freely available at: https://gutenberg.net.au/ebooks19/1900551p.pdf

130 - Dufty notes that Straughair accompanied Aaron, as either a peacemaker or for backup, when he visited Maggie Skillion in 1879 to try to retrieve a horse.

131 - Signage identifying the location of Aaron's hut is installed as part of the Ned Kelly Tourist Trail. However, the actual site is in fact some distance further to the west, at a point where there is a slight bend in the road where the parking of cars could be a safety hazard. The authorities probably thought placing the signs near enough to the actual site was close enough. The site of Tom Straughair's forge is almost directly opposite the correct site of Aaron's hut. The site is heavily overgrown, but on close examination, scraps of iron can be found scattered throughout the site. It was at this site that Darren Sutton, a Beechworth-based amateur historian, found a scrap of iron that he believes is an offcut of the suit of armour that was made for Joe Byrne. Joe's suit of armour is kept at the Beechworth Museum and the offcut found by Mr Sutton exactly fits that suit, although the veracity of the offcut has been questioned (including by the CSIRO).

After Detectives Ward and Considine embarked on their investigations into Wallace's activities towards the end of 1881 and into 1882, they managed to establish a link between Straughair and Wallace. Their investigations are discussed in more detail later in this book, but in brief they established not only that Wallace had travelled about collecting scrap iron on the false pretext that his father was a metal collector, but that he was also a frequent visitor to Straughair. In one of their reports from January 1882, they stated:

> *Friday we had an interview with a confidential person at the Woolshed re the connection between Wallace and Straughair black smith, Woolshed relative to the making of Byrne's armour. We ascertained that Wallace was on very intimate terms with Straughair and used to leave his horse there when visiting Mrs Sherritts or Byrnes and also that Straughair used to work late at night. We have very little doubt that Straughair made Joe Byrne's armour but from the length of time that has elapsed there is no feasible chance of obtaining any proof about him.*

Dufty put forward the proposition that Straughair made all four suits of armour, and speculated about the inspiration for the armour. He submits that Straughair may have been inspired by the display of the armour of a German cuirassier (an armoured cavalry soldier) at

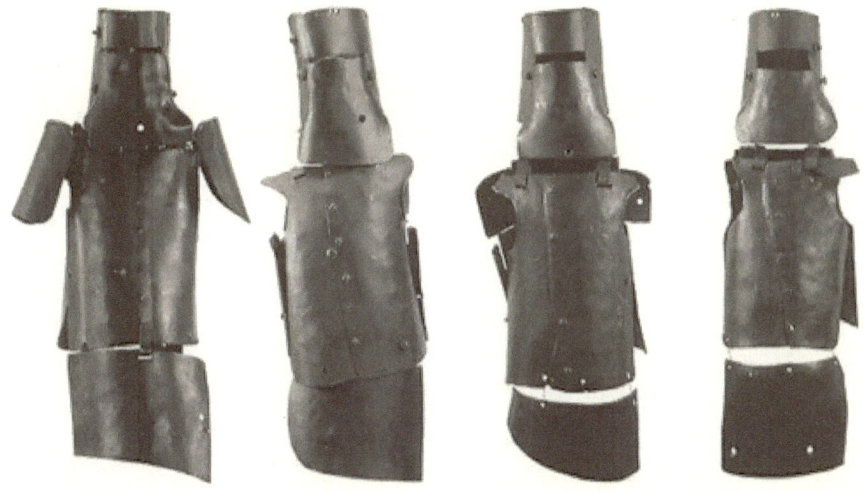

the 1873 Beechworth carnival, or by the samurai armour that was exhibited at the carnival the following year. He speculated that perhaps Straughair had embarked on the armour-making project some years earlier (well before the Kelly outbreak) as a hobby, having been inspired by those German and Samurai suits of armour. That would explain the differences in quality between the four suits of Kelly armour, with each suit of armour improving with practice.

If Straughair had indeed been an armour-making hobbyist, then it is likely Joe, James and Aaron would have been aware of it. Dufty speculates that, perhaps over drinks, the notion was born of using suits of armour in real combat. If that was the case, then far from the armour being an inspired idea thought of by Ned or Joe, it was simply an opportunistic happenstance.

Dufty's conclusion about the Kelly Gang's armour, which is as good an assessment as anything else that has been put forward, is as follows:

> *The origin of the Kelly Gang's armour need not be shrouded in mystery. Thanks largely to the work of detectives Ward and Considine, we know that in all likelihood, at least some of the armour, and (in my view) probably all of it, was made by the blacksmith Tom Straughair.*

15
A Pardon for Joe?

Wallace, despite collecting mouldboards and more than likely being aware of the gang's plans, appears to have had some misgivings. From those early days after the murders at Stringybark Creek, he did all he could to protect his friend Joe.

In August 1879, Wallace had broached the possibility of a pardon for Joe when he met with Detective Ward at Beechworth.[132] Ward had been forewarned by Aaron that Wallace intended to broach the subject. He had reported to Nicolson that Wallace wanted Aaron to go with him to him to Melbourne to try and get Graham Berry (Premier of Victoria) and the Marquis of Normanby (Governor of Victoria) to sign a reprieve for Joe in return for Joe giving information to the police about where the other three could be caught.

Detective Ward, perhaps having had the idea put into his head by Wallace, later unsuccessfully tried to encourage Joe's mother to persuade her son to turn informer. Despite this, Wallace decided to make a last-ditch attempt to seek a pardon for his friend.

At the end of the school day on Friday 16 April 1880, Wallace closed both his schools without official permission and informed his students there would be no school for two weeks. The next day he boarded the train to Melbourne where he arranged an appointment with James Goodall Francis MLA (Member for Warrnambool), who he hoped might be instrumental in obtaining a pardon for Joe.[133]

---

132 - Pardon is probably not the right word for what Wallace was seeking for Joe. Leniency would probably be more accurate, i.e. a reduced sentence in return for assisting in the capture of the other gang members; a guarantee that the prosecution would not seek the death penalty, etc.

133 - James Francis was known to be sympathetic to the selector cause, but this would have been irrelevant in respect of any decision to grant Joe Byrne a pardon.

Wallace took an enormous personal and professional risk in taking these actions and it is hard to believe he could have been so naïve as to think there was any hope of a successful outcome. It was a last-ditch attempt on his part to save the life of a friend who he realised was about to embark on a course of action that would surely result in his death.

The personal risk for Wallace was that his role in supporting the gang for the past two years might become known. The professional risk for him was that his unexplained closure of the schools would be a black mark against him by the Department of Education (it was) and that his visit to James Francis would raise eyebrows (it did become known to the police).

Wallace's efforts were, of course, in vain. The government was not interested in making deals where the Kelly Gang was concerned. On his return from Melbourne, Wallace told Aaron Sherritt that it was no use – that Mr Francis had told him there is to be no reprieve for Joe Byrne.[134] When Joe was caught, he would be hanged.

Wallace did not immediately return to the North East after visiting Francis. He remained in Melbourne for two weeks and perhaps during this time made visits to other people who he thought may have been in a position to help Joe or perhaps the selectors' cause. He also busied himself writing a letter that is discussed in the following chapter.

It was during this period in which Wallace was busy sourcing material for the making of the armour, seeking a pardon for Joe, and agitating to be assigned to a new school, that Wallace also applied to mortgage his lease for £125. He lodged his application for a mortgage on 20 May 1880, the same day that one of Nicolson's agents (Daniel Kennedy, code named Denny) wrote to him to tell him that armour had been made and tested and that 'feed was getting scarce.'

With nine weeks to go before Glenrowan, one would have to wonder why Wallace thought it necessary to mortgage his property. Was he seeking to cash up in case he needed to flee?

---

134 - There are no records of such meeting with Mr Francis. It is only the fact that Wallace reported to Aaron Sherritt that Francis had told him there would be no reprieve for Joe Byrne, as passed on by Aaron to Detective Ward, that we have reason to believe this meeting took place.

16
A letter from Mr Connor

Coinciding with Wallace's time in Melbourne, a mysterious letter signed M Connor was posted from Melbourne to Mr James (Abraham) Graves MLA (Member for Delatite).[135] A transcript of the Connor letter is included at Appendix 7.[136]

As the local member in the North East, Graves kept his office at Benalla. He was one of the many important men whom Wallace developed a relationship with – as noted early in this book, Graves made a number of representations for James over the years, including getting him appointed to run the new school at Hurdle Creek West on a part-time basis.

Graves was known to have often led deputations to the Chief Secretary's office on behalf of Kelly sympathisers, but had no sympathy himself for the Kellys as evidenced by him being a member of the committee for the Murdered Police Memorial Fund, and by a suggestion he made in parliament that the water in Kelly country should be poisoned and the grass burnt as part of the efforts to capture the gang. In 1881, Graves would also come to serve on the Royal Commission on the

---

135 - From May 1877 to October 1900, Graves was the member of the Legislative Assembly for Delatite, an area that included much of the Kelly country. He often led deputations to the Chief Secretary's office on behalf of Kelly sympathisers. In 1881 he served on the Royal Commission into the Victoria Police Force and gave evidence to the Commission on 10 August. His first direct involvement with the Kellys was when he was appointed to the committee of the Murdered Police Memorial Fund, which had been established to raise money for a memorial to the three policemen murdered at Stringybark Creek, and also to provide money for the families of Sergeant Kennedy and Constable Lonigan. On 11 March 1880, the police received a report from Graves, who was obviously relaying sightings of the Kelly Gang from constituents. At Glenrowan, Ned Kelly is said to have told Constable Bracken, 'There was one bugger in Parliament he would like to kill: Mr Graves ... because he suggested in parliament that the water in the Kelly country should be poisoned, and that the grass should be burnt.' Graves maintained a close interest in the Kelly outbreak for the rest of his life. Source: *The Ned Kelly Encyclopaedia* (Justin Corfield), page 200.

136 - VPRS 4965/P0000, 37. This is a copy of the letter in which the name of the sender (Connor) has been deleted.

Police Force of Victoria, at which he also gave evidence on the Connor letter and his dealings with Wallace.

The Connor letter was extremely critical of the methods used by the police force in their search for the Kelly Gang and singled out Superintendent Nicolson for particular condemnation. The letter called on Graves '... to bring under the notice of the Chief Secretary the present helplessness of the police force to capture the Kellys.' It went on to call for the dismissal of 'those men that are hired at a high salary.' It caused a great stir at Spring Street and police headquarters.

The Connor letter was almost certainly written by Wallace.

If Wallace's true motive in all his actions was to assist Joe Byrne, then it would be fair to ask why he would pen a letter pointing out the shortcomings of the police search and suggesting an alternative approach. Unless, of course, the police looked like they were making progress and the object was to cast doubts and bring about a change that might increase the gang's chances of avoiding capture. From the letters he wrote to Nicolson, we know that Wallace often engaged in such subterfuge.

Although Wallace was suspected of being the author of the letter, he denied this when Nicolson had the opportunity to question him about it at the Royal Commission. He admitted, though, that he had read the letter, with it transpiring through further questioning that Graves had sent him a copy and had asked his opinion on the contents! Graves said he did this because he believed Wallace may have known the identity of the writer '... because Wallace knew more about the Kellys than anyone else (and) ... My impression was that he could have told me who wrote it.'[137]

On the back of the copy of the Connor letter that Mr Graves provided to Captain Standish there are two strictly confidential memorandums written respectively by the Chief Commissioner of Police (Standish) and the Assistant Commissioner of Police (Nicolson) in which they give their views of the letter and some of the statements in it.[138]

---

137 - Minutes of Evidence, Q15499.

138 - Public Record Office of Victoria – Kelly Historical Collection – Part 1 Police Branch (VPRS4965), Record 37 – Letter to Mr Graves re the Kelly Search (VPRS 4965/P0000, 37).

The memos are interesting because they highlight the differences of opinion about Nicolson's use of Aaron Sherritt as an agent, and the deteriorating relationship between the two men who were at the top of police command. The two memos are reproduced below:

Memo of Commissioner Standish, dated 24 April 1880:

Strictly Confidential

The letter of which this is a copy was handed to me yesterday by Mr Graves. It was signed by the hand of O'Connor or Connor but Mr Graves told me he was positive it was written at the dictation of another man who resides at or near Violet Town & whose handwriting he recognised in the address of the envelope. Mr Graves, however, declined to give up his name.

I confess that I have long now arrived at the opinion that Aaron Sherritt is not to be trusted – nor indeed any of the family. They have been too mixed up with the outlaws & and there can be little doubt that if they had made up their minds to sell the outlaws they would have had the opportunity of doing so long ago. I must therefore request Mr Nicolson to discontinue any advances of money to A Sherritt or to make any further use of him.

At the same time, many of the statements in this letter must be viewed with caution & I may add that I do not attach the least credence to what the writer says of Det. Ward.

24-4-80 F.C. Standish

P.S. This communication to be returned after Mr Nicolson has noted its contents. FCS

Memo of Assistant Commissioner Nicolson, dated 26 April 1880:

Strictly confidential – *I think the Chief Commissioner will see that I must be the best judge of the amount of confidence to be placed in my agents in this business – and as long as I am in charge of the duty of searching for the Kelly Gang it is essential that I should be left to act upon my own judgement in such matter, within the limits already laid down by the Hon. Chief Secretary as to expenses.*

I am quite ready to use the services of any of the Sherritt family, with alacrity, if I think it is in their power to assist in furthering the business in hand. As regards the copy letter on the other side, what the writer calls 'the facts' are simply gross misrepresentations which I do not feel called upon to notice, beyond pointing out as an example the untruthfulness of what is referred to as 'the great charge of Sebastopol', at which the Chief Commissioner himself was present, and in command.

26-4-80 C. H. Nicolson, Assistant Commissioner of Police

The Connor letter was a last-ditch effort by Wallace to interfere with the police search for the Kelly Gang, and it was written during the time he travelled to Melbourne to visit James Francis MLA to seek a pardon for Joe Byrne. By this time, Nicolson had dispensed with Wallace's services as an agent, but was still making use of Aaron Sherritt and other members of the Sherritt family.

Whilst Chief Commissioner Standish accepted the writer's criticisms of Aaron Sherritt and recommended that no further use be made of him, Assistant Commissioner Nicolson was ready to continue using the services of any member of the Sherritt family.

By this stage in the Kelly saga, it was clear that Aaron, his brother John and other members of the Sherritt family were fearful of the Kellys and were doing all that they could to assist the police. In the early days of the Kelly drama, when their loyalties were divided between protecting their friend Joe and doing the right thing, they had played the same double game that Wallace himself was continuing to play. By this stage, though, and in fact a lot before this, the Sherritts were clearly on the side of law and order. The gang's threats on Aaron's life had taken a toll.

17
Wallace's removal from Kelly country

Through Wallace's abrupt closure of his schools and trip to Melbourne, he managed to draw unwelcome attention from key figures in the Education Department and the police force.

A terse letter from the School Board of Advice greeted Wallace on his return home.[139] It informed him that he had displayed very bad taste in the matter and that he should have made his application to close the schools earlier than he did. It also informed him that the Education Department Inspector was aware the school had been closed without permission, and had been surprised that he had taken a fortnight's leave of absence.

By this time, the Inspector-General of the Education Department – a man named Thomas Bolam – was becoming suspicious of Wallace, particularly after he discovered that Wallace had attended the Woolshed Common School with Joe Byrne (a fact already known to the police).

Bolam realised that Wallace's travels between the Hurdle Creek and Hurdle Creek West Schools would have given him many opportunities to meet with the outlaws, and that his running of the post office also provided him with a unique opportunity to access information. He passed his concerns on to the Chief Commissioner of Police (Standish) who he was surprised to find held similar suspicions and fears. Wheels began to turn that would remove Wallace from the North East.

Wallace had, of course, tried unsuccessfully the previous September to be reposted to a school closer to Beechworth, with his brother William

---

139 - The letter was dated 26 April 1880 and was signed by Fred Kettle from the School Board of Advice. A transcript of the letter can be found at page 71 of *The Headmaster of Hurdle Creek*, by Arthur Hall & Julie Stevens. Arthur Hall has indicated he was indebted to Lindsay Simpson of Docker for providing him with access to the letter (and several other letters from the School Board of Advice).

to replace him at Hurdle Creek. After becoming aware that plans were afoot to remove him from Hurdle Creek, he now naively sought to be promoted to a new state school at Benalla East, again suggesting that William take his place at Hurdle Creek.[140]

James wrote to the Education Department from Bobinawarrah on 19 June 1880 in support of his brother being appointed to Hurdle Creek. He gave many reasons why this was a good idea – William had the required qualifications and would work both schools; Barbara Wallace (James's wife) was pregnant once again and should remain in place for the next two months, but could continue her work-mistress role (and perhaps the post office role) to assist William if he was appointed; and finally, that the Department would save nearly £100 per annum in salaries by appointing William. The savings to the Education Department would be due to William being appointed at a lesser salary, as he had only recently completed his pupil teaching course.

Wallace also asked George Kerferd MLA to write to the Chief Secretary Mr Ramsay reiterating the savings to the Department if they appointed William.[141] That suggestion, though, had the opposite effect, with school inspector Gilbert Brown of the Education Department replying to Kerferd on 6 July 1880 that there were many more deserving teachers who may be interested in the position and that it would be unfair to deprive them of the opportunity that the vacancy offered.[142]

Why did Wallace go to such efforts to have his brother appointed at Hurdle Creek? Perhaps it was simply a desire to secure his brother a better school than El Dorado. More likely, though, he was seeking to put another sympathetic family member in charge, particularly given that Bobinawarrah (the locality in which the Hurdle Creek School was located) was the approach to the 'hut behind the school' that the Kelly Gang used on and off over the 20 months they were at large. If James had succeeded in having himself posted to the new school at

---

140 - A transcript of the letter can be found at page 70 of *The Headmaster of Hurdle Creek*, by Arthur Hall & Julie Stevens.

141 - adb.anu.edu.au/biography/kerferd-george-briscoe-3947

142 - A transcript can be found at page 73 of *The Headmaster of Hurdle Creek*, by Arthur Hall & Julie Stevens. Arthur Hall obtained the letter from the Education Department file held by the Public Records Office, Melbourne.

Benalla East and in having William placed in charge at Hurdle Creek, between them they would have had an enhanced ability to monitor police movements and keep the gang safe.

Thomas Bolam was probably the first to fully appreciate the situation.[143] He told Captain Standish that Wallace 'strained every nerve' to place his brother at Hurdle Creek. However, his efforts were to no avail. The Education Department directed that he was to transfer to Yea where he would be the head teacher at Yea State School No. 699. His brother William was also to be transferred out of Kelly country – he was going to be teaching at two half-time schools at Boundary Creek and Break O'Day, both located outside of Yea.

Captain Standish, Chief Commissioner of Police, shared the news of Wallace's pending transfer with Superintendent Francis Hare:

> *I close this letter to tell you that James Wallace has been transferred from Bobinawarrah to Yea. He tried to stipulate that he should be replaced in his present post by his brother, and the ever-plotting Mr Graves MP is endeavouring to get this done, but Mr Bolam, the Inspector General of Schools, has told me that the request will not be acceded to, and that a school master will be sent up by this afternoon's train to relieve Wallace tomorrow. I think it is just as well that this treacherous pedagogue should be removed from the district, as I am firmly convinced he would never sell his old pal, Joe Byrne.* [144]

On 24 June 1880, James penned a short letter to Gilbert Brown in Melbourne to say that he had that day been relieved of his duties by the new teacher John Reed, and that he would set out the next day for Yea.[145] Barbara and the children would stay behind at Bobinawarrah until he found accommodation in Yea and was in a position to send for them.

---

143 - *The Headmaster of Hurdle Creek* (2005), Arthur Hall, page 63.

144 - Captain Standish letter dated 23 June 1880 to Superintendent Francis Hare.

145 - A transcript can be found at page 74 of *The Headmaster of Hurdle Creek*, (2005) by Arthur Hall & Julie Stevens.

Wallace would have travelled to Yea via a combination of train and then a carriage from either Seymour or Broadford. He most likely would have taken the train at Everton Station, which was the closest station to Hurdle Creek. If so, his train journey would have taken him past the section of track on the approach to Glenrowan where the gang planned to derail the train in the coming days. Imagine his thoughts as he passed by that area. Alternatively, if Wallace had caught the train at either Glenrowan or Benalla, then he would have passed through Greta, with the possibility that he might have had contact with Ned Kelly or Steve Hart and other sympathisers prior to their leaving for Glenrowan (Joe and Dan Kelly were by this stage in Woolshed where they would shoot Aaron).

Meanwhile John Reed, Wallace's replacement at Hurdle Creek, was encountering some unforeseen problems. Wallace had only been able to run both schools as full-time schools because his wife Barbara would take over the running of the Hurdle Creek School in the afternoons while he went off to teach at Hurdle Creek West. But Barbara had now resigned! Without Barbara helping out, both schools could now only be run as half-time schools.

John Reed also faced another problem – he could not find any accommodation in the Hurdle Creek neighbourhood and therefore had to live at Milawa. As Milawa was six miles away, he had to hire a horse at a cost of £1 per week so he could do the rounds.

Reed had also intended to take over the running of the post office. Wallace, however, had not resigned that position, but had arranged for another local to run the post office instead. It was probably just as well, as John would not have been able to conduct the post office business anyway, given he was forced by necessity to live so many miles away and had to run two schools.

18
A new life in Yea

Wallace arrived in Yea late on Saturday 26 June 1880, the same evening Joe and Dan murdered Aaron Sherritt at Woolshed, before galloping across the Oxley Plains to join Ned and Steve and an unknown number of sympathisers at Glenrowan. He began his new position as head teacher at Yea State School No. 699 on 28 June, shortly after the conflict at Glenrowan had come to a bloody climax. He probably heard the news via the Seymour Telegraph Office and would have read the newspaper reports soon after.

One wonders what Wallace's thoughts would have been as the news about the gang's demise at Glenrowan sank in. He would certainly have been grieved to hear of Joe's death. Did he feel any remorse about Aaron? One suspects that he would have also felt a sense of anti-climax now that his central role in the Kelly saga had come to an end.

Wallace settled in at Yea quickly. By August 1880 he had commenced teaching night school at the request of the local community and was on the way to establishing himself within the community. He continued to have the same energy for teaching that various school inspectors had remarked on during his career.

After Wallace found suitable accommodation, Barbara and the children soon joined him.[146] Their first five months at Yea went smoothly and Barbara was pregnant yet again. It must have been a crowded household, with James's brother William also boarding with the family while teaching at both the Boundary Creek and Break O'Day State Schools (both half-time schools located about 17 miles apart).

With the execution of Ned Kelly on 11 November 1880, Wallace must have breathed a sigh of relief. Imagine the information Ned could have

---

146 - Wallace rented a cottage known as Hastings Cottage. Despite enquiries, the author has been unable to find out any further information about this cottage or its location.

given the authorities if, instead of rushing him to trial and execution, they had kept him alive and interrogated him. Wallace soon put pen to paper to write the following words that were published in *The Age* newspaper on 20 November 1880 as part of an editorial critical of the police efforts to capture Ned Kelly and his gang:

> *None can feel surprised at the result, for in the whole world's history of criminals, nothing so monstrously absurd as the hunt after the Kellys was ever before chronicled. Responsible leaders were continuously quarrelling like so many children in the absence of their mamas; petty officers occasionally assumed supreme command, and a force of men sufficient to storm Afghanistan either marched and exterminated on their own trail, like Colonel Bob Shorty's immortal brigade or else greatly enjoyed the grand scenery of the Wombats or Strathbogie, while Europe held its breath in awful suspense, and in trembling accents whispered about the dangers of the Australian bush. But the farce was not complete until Mrs Jones' whiskey captured the outlaws, and heralded a scene which will long remain a blot on the records of our colony. Horrible inhumanity is the only term that can apply to the cowardly action of burning the hotel, and roasting the lifeless occupants long after a lull in the firing had shown that the spirits of the outlaws had fled to receive judgement at a higher tribunal. But ghastly and sickening as such a picture is, a sense of humour is imparted to the scene if we consider the final set, when a body of artillery and a cannon were sent to assist a regiment of police in dislodging a wooden shanty of two beardless boys.*
>
> *The subject is a melancholy one, and would not be referred to in these columns only for the inconsistent conduct of the Melbourne press. When the Glenrowan outrage wound up the Kelly drama with cowardice which characterised it all through, the 'Seymour Express' was the only paper that denounced the actions of the Victorian police. The Melbourne papers on the contrary raised a*

> *yell of triumph such as marks a sacrifice in a Sioux Indian camp, and shouted in chorus that the honour of the colony was again upheld. Since then public opinion would appear to have altered their principles, and a few days since, we are informed 'it would be difficult to say which reflected most humiliation on the colony – the folly of sending for a canon to bombard a weatherboard house, or the horror of burning the house down, with living and, possibly wounded human beings, in it.' Variable indeed are the principles of Melbourne writers. We cannot close this article without expressing surprise that some heroes in the horrible wind up was dealt with in a different manner from the others.* [147]

In December 1880, Yea experienced a measles outbreak. Three of the Wallace children were infected, as were William Wallace and two of the female teacher assistants at James's school. Yea had no doctor and measles was a potentially deadly disease, so Wallace took it upon himself to close the school for the duration of the outbreak. Doing this was a brave decision, given what had happened the last time he closed his schools without permission.

In the midst of the measles outbreak, baby Marion Katherine Cleopatra Wallace was born safely on 4 December 1880. Named after her paternal grandmother, she was known throughout her life as Minnie.

In April 1881, Wallace arranged special permission for a three-day holiday at his school (12, 13 and 14 April) and took his students to Melbourne to see the International Exhibition in the new and spectacular Exhibition Building. William and the students at his schools also participated.

To the surprise of the Yea community, at the end of July 1881, their new head teacher was directed to appear before the Royal Commission that had been commissioned to investigate the failings of the Victorian Police to capture the Kelly Gang. He appeared before the Commission on 2 and 3 August. The Yea School Board of Advice closed the school

---

147 - This article, published in *The Age* newspaper on 20 November 1880, is one of four contributions to the Victorian press that Wallace later submitted in support of his application to the Queensland Education Department for a teaching position at Ipswich.

to allow him to attend, with the local community being puzzled as to why he was required. It was known, of course, that Wallace had come to Yea from Kelly country and some local residents commented that he had spoken a lot about Ned Kelly. Indeed, his knowledge was so great that it had even been said that he seemed to know Ned's thoughts and opinions on certain senior police officers.

Later in August, with the Royal Commission behind him, Wallace organised a concert in the Yea Shire Hall to raise funds for school prizes. Like the concert at his school in Bobinawarrah several years earlier, the concert was a great success. The *Alexandra and Yea Standard* reported that the performance of his students reflected great credit on Mr Wallace and that the evening raised the sum of £10.

Yea township in 1880. Sold lots and reserves are coloured. The uncoloured land within the border comprises the Yea Town Common. Lot owners and tenants (including James Wallace) could also acquire depasturing rights on this land. The location of Hastings Cottage, which the Wallace family rented, is not known.

19
The Royal Commission (Wallace on Trial)

James Wallace had likely thought that he was home free after Ned Kelly's execution. He would soon be disappointed. The political fallout from the whole sorry episode was far from finished and a Royal Commission on the Police Force of Victoria was established in March 1881 to enquire into the conduct and efficiency of the force during the Kelly outbreak. It was not an inquiry into the politics associated with the Kelly outbreak.[148]

Two school teachers would be called to give evidence to the Commission. One was Thomas Curnow, the schoolmaster in Glenrowan, and the other was James Wallace.

Thomas Curnow was one of many people who the Kelly Gang held prisoner at Glenrowan as they awaited the arrival of the police special train that they had planned to derail. The prisoners were held at Ann Jones's Glenrowan Inn. Curnow managed to gain the trust of Ned Kelly, who agreed to let him leave the inn to return to his home on the pretext that his wife was unwell. Once released, Curnow took a red llama scarf and a lantern down to the railway line and managed to wave down the train some distance out from Glenrowan. He warned Superintendent Hare and the other police on board the train that the Kellys had taken hostages at Anne Jones's Inn and that the train should not proceed beyond Glenrowan Station. Curnow was highly commended for his actions and the Kelly Award Board awarded him £550 the following year.

---

148 - Despite assertions to the contrary by some modern-day Kelly supporters, the Royal Commissioners did not blame the Kelly outbreak on the police force. They very much placed the blame on the Kellys and the criminal element that infested the area that became known as Kelly country.

James Wallace was called before the Commission for entirely different reasons – he was suspected of having played a key role in protecting the gang. As discussed earlier in this book, there many other schoolteachers and locals in the North East who had knowledge that the Commission could also have benefitted from hearing, but for whatever reason they were not called.[149]

Francis Longmore MLA, Minister for Lands, chaired the Royal Commission . The other members were James (Abraham) Howlin Graves MLA, George Randall Fincham MLA, George Wilson Hall MLA, William Anderson MLA, James Gibb MLA, and Edward John Dixon JP.

The Royal Commissioners were an interesting lot. Some of them could be regarded as progressives. Several of them (Longmore and Graves) were known to Wallace. If the Kelly outbreak had been about land reform, as some have suggested, then at least some of the commissioners would have to have been regarded as friendly. None of them, though, felt kindly towards the outlaws, or as it would turn out towards James Wallace.

The Commissioners

Francis Longmore MLA

Francis Longmore MLA, the Chairman of the Royal Commission, had been a long-time critic of the police force since the days of Harry Power's escapades, and had been particularly critical of Chief Commissioner Captain Standish.[150] Longmore was a radical who had supported breaking up the control of the squatters and opening up the land for small farmers. In fact, he was the instigator of a royal commission into land settlement, whose recommendations led to

---

149 - *Pioneer Teachers of the Kelly Country*, Len Pryor, page 168. Len discussed the selection of witnesses by the 1881 Royal Commission on the Police Force, and wondered about who made the decisions about who would be called to give evidence or not.

150 - *The Ned Kelly Encyclopaedia*, 2003, Justin Corfield, pages 315–316. Also refer to the *Australian Dictionary of Biography*: https://adb.anu.edu.au/biography/longmore-francis-4036

the Land Act 1878. He was also a supporter of the Irish struggle for independence and enjoyed the support of the colony's Irish Catholic community.

Longmore, in fact, had been the person who Wallace's father-in-law Ebenezer Allan had written to in 1879 complaining about the decision of the Local Land Board to deny him access to land containing waterholes and a watercourse. The letter, written to Longmore when he was the Minister of Lands, was obviously written by Wallace. Longmore was well aware of the hardships faced by local selectors, and the letter achieved the desired results.

James Howlin Graves MLA

James Howlin Graves MLA was the member for Delatite in the Legislative Assembly, and was also known as being anti-squatter.[151] His inclusion as a member of the Commission would have been encouraging to Wallace as they were personally acquainted. Graves had endorsed Wallace's appointment to run the new school at Hurdle Creek West.[152] When Wallace travelled to Melbourne to seek a pardon for Joe, he happened to meet Nicolson and Graves on the platform at Benalla Station, with Wallace then travelling with Graves between Benalla and Seymour.[153] And just prior to Glenrowan, Wallace also managed to get Graves to send a letter to the Education Department endorsing the appointment of his brother William Wallace as his replacement at Hurdle Creek.[154]

In addition, Connor (a pseudonym) sent his letter to Graves.

---

151 - *The Ned Kelly Encyclopaedia*, 2003, Justin Corfield, pages 200–201. Also refer to the *Australian Dictionary of Biography*: https://adb.anu.edu.au/biography/graves-james-abraham-howlin-3653

152 - Graves had sent a memo dated 2 February 1878 to the Education Department asking that James Wallace be appointed to the new school at Hurdle Creek (Hurdle Creek West). James was only 21 years old at this time, and it is interesting that he had the political leverage at such a young age to get an MP like Graves to intervene on his behalf.

153 - Minutes of Evidence, Q14826–Q14827. James Wallace answering questions put to him by Nicolson.

154 - Graves sent this letter to the Education Department on 22 June 1880.

During the course of the Commission's hearings, there was a change of government that resulted in Graves being appointment as the Commissioner of Trade and Customs.[155] At the Commission's hearing on 2 August 1881, the same day Wallace was called to give evidence, Graves intimated to his fellow Commissioners that his new duties meant he would be unable to attend the meetings and that he therefore thought he should resign from the Commission. At the request of the Chairman and other members of the Commission, he consented to continue to act.[156] His agreement to continue was only temporary, however, with the Minutes of Evidence showing that he advised his fellow Commissioners the following week (at the hearing on 9 August 1881) that he had forwarded his resignation to His Excellency the Governor.[157] On that same day, Graves was himself sworn and examined as a witness, on account of the Connor letter.

Because he had had past dealings with Wallace, Graves was no doubt dumbfounded to hear that Wallace was suspected of having assisted the gang to remain at large. Given Grave's history of having supported Wallace, and the fact that the Connor letter had been addressed to him, one wonders if there was more to his resignation than his new duties as Commissioner of Trade and Customs. Despite him having been an agitator for the Commission and having sat through most of its hearing days, Graves was not a signatory to the Second Progress Report.

George Wilson Hall MLA

George Wilson Hall MLA was an unusual member of the Commission.[158] He had been the editor-proprietor of the *Mansfield Guardian* at the time the Kelly Gang shot the three Mansfield police

---

155 - A new government led by the conservative Bryan O'Loghlen replaced the former Berry government on 9 July 1881. O'Loghlen became Premier, Attorney General and Treasurer in the new government. James H Graves was appointed Commissioner of Trade and Customs.

156 - Appendix 20 to the Minutes of Evidence – refer to the summary for Tuesday 2 August 1881 (page 715).

157 - Appendix 20 to the Minutes of Evidence – refer to the summary for Tuesday 9 August 1881 (page 716).

158 - *The Ned Kelly Encyclopaedia*, 2003, Justin Corfield, pages 213–214.

at Stringybark Creek, and had published the book titled *The Outlaws of the Wombat Ranges* shortly after the Jerilderie bank robbery.[159] That book, whilst acknowledging the criminality of the gang members and their families, also put forward the Kelly's point of view as told by an unnamed traveller (this author believes that Wallace was the likely source for that material). Hall, however, was not an apologist for the gang. In 1879, Hall moved to Benalla and became the owner of the *Benalla Standard*, and covered the capture of the Kellys at Glenrowan for the Melbourne *Argus* and his own newspaper.

Hall was elected MLA for the seat of Moira in July 1880. The Commission – of which Hall became a member – was set up in part as a result of his agitation for an inquiry into the police force's handling of the Kellys.

George Randall Fincham MLA

George Randall Fincham MLA was the MLA for Ballarat and was known as an 'exceedingly moderate liberal'.[160]

William Anderson MLA

William Anderson MLA was the MLA for Villiers and Heytesbury. He was appointed to the Commission partly as a counterbalance to Francis Longmire and George Hall.[161]

James Gibb MLA

James Gibb MLA was the MLA for Mornington.[162]

---

159 - *The Kelly Gang or The Outlaws of the Wombat Ranges* contains a preface signed 'The Authors' (plural), which is dated 22 February 1879. The book, published on 22 February 1879, references the Jerilderie robbery that occurred only 12 days earlier.

160 - *The Ned Kelly Encyclopaedia*, 2003, Justin Corfield, page 162.

161 - *The Ned Kelly Encyclopaedia*, 2003, Justin Corfield, pages 12–13.

162 - *The Ned Kelly Encyclopaedia*, 2003, Justin Corfield, page 180.

Edward John Dixon JP

Edward John Dixon JP was a former MLA for St Kilda (having lost the seat in April 1880). After the report of the Royal Commission was tabled in 1881, Dixon tabled his own minority report that attempted to vindicate Francis Hare and leave the way open for him to become Chief Commissioner of Police.[163]

Evidence given before Wallace was called to give evidence

The Commission hearings commenced on 23 March 1881. In all, 66 witnesses were called to give evidence. Questions about Wallace were put to all who had had dealings with him, starting with the very first witness who happened to be Captain Standish, Chief Commissioner of Police.

Captain Standish gave evidence on the first day of the hearing (23 March 1881). He spoke about how the Kellys were known to have had an enormous number of sympathisers in the district, and described the different policing methods used by Nicolson and Hare. In talking about Nicolson's employment of spies and agents, he complained that some of those turned out to be Kelly sympathisers, to which Nicolson responded that he needed to employ people who were close to the Kellys or of the same class. When Nicolson was given the opportunity to question Standish, he asked him about his recollections of a private interview they had at Benalla with one of Nicolson's agents soon after he (Nicolson) had been put in charge of the Kelly hunt. No name was mentioned, but the man concerned was Wallace. He had been given a considerable sum of money (from £25 to £30) said to be for the purchase of a horse, and an order to any telegraph masters to permit the bearer to send a message to him (Standish) in Melbourne.

Nicolson, in his evidence (on 24, 25 and 29 March), also spoke of how the prevalence of sympathisers necessitated doing everything in secret. He referred to another discussion he had had with Standish, this time after Euroa, when he had spoken about his proposed mode

---

163 - *The Ned Kelly Encyclopaedia*, 2003, Justin Corfield, page 126.

of operations and had suggested that they employ a 'class of man' like Aaron Sherritt, whom they had met on the morning of the Sebastopol raid. Sherritt was employed soon after.

Nicolson told the Commissioners how he gradually came to employ secret agents. He described how, in the lead up to Glenrowan, his agents, including the one who wrote about the armour (Daniel Kennedy, aka 'Diseased Stock') were giving him almost daily information, such that he expected the Kelly matter to come to a speedy termination. That was why he had asked for a month's extension after Standish had sought to have him replaced again by Hare, shortly before Glenrowan.

It doesn't come out in Nicolson's evidence, but it was around the time he sought to be kept in charge of the Kelly hunt (20 April 1880 or thereabouts) that Wallace's communications with him ceased. It was about this time that Wallace travelled to Melbourne to seek a pardon for Joe and that the mysterious Connor letter to Mr Graves was sent – that letter of course being highly critical of Nicolson's handling of the Kelly hunt. The reality was that the police at this time, under Nicolson's command, were closing in on the gang and Connor (Wallace) wanted Nicolson replaced with someone less effective!

When Hare was called to give evidence (on 31 March, and 1, 5 and 6 April 1881), he was asked if he had ever had a paid agent in his service who was a state school teacher, to which he answered that he had had nothing to do with him and that it was Captain Standish and Mr Nicolson who had. Hare was reluctant to name Wallace, saying a desire had been expressed by Mr Graves and Mr Nicolson that the names of informers should not be mentioned. When asked if he knew afterwards that it was found that the state school teacher in question was a sympathiser with the Kellys, he replied that he hoped the matter would not be pressed, and asked that the press should not write about the teacher because that would create future difficulties for the police in recruiting agents. In response to a question about the duration of the transaction with the teacher, he answered that it extended over about six or seven months, commencing around the time of the Jerilderie robbery. When asked if the person was still in the employ of the Public Service, he answered that he was, but in another district.

Henry Moors, Chief Clerk with the police department's Benalla office, served under both Nicolson and Standish. When he was called to give evidence (6 April 1881), he was asked whether he had seen any correspondence with the head of the department in reference to a state school teacher in the employ of the police in the North-Eastern District. It was put to him that the teacher concerned had written many letters, to which Moors answered that it was the kind of correspondence that would not come through the office. He was also unaware of any money being paid to any school teacher for information.

After hearing from Standish, Nicolson, Hare and Moors, the Commission instructed the Secretary for the Royal Commission to write to his counterpart at the Education Department requesting information about the school teacher they had heard was acting as a secret agent for the police:

Royal Commission on Police Force
Melbourne, April 8, 1881
Secretary
Education Department

Sir,

I have been instructed by the Police Commissioner to apply to you for any papers or correspondence with the Secretaries Department having reference to the actions of a certain state school teacher in the Benalla district who was employed as a secret agent of the police in the search for the Kelly outlaws, and who owing to representations from the locality was subsequently removed to another district.

The Commissioner has not been placed in possession of the name of the teacher in question.

Yours truly,

Jas. Williams

Secretary

Evidence continued to be heard throughout April, May and June 1881 from many other police involved in the Kelly hunt, as well as from others who played a part in the saga.

Superintendent John Sadleir, stationed at Benalla, also worked under the command of both Nicolson and Hare. His evidence (13 and 14 April, and 3 May) included details about the relationship between Aaron Sherritt and Joe Byrne. Just as Wallace did all in his power to protect Joe, that was apparently also true in the early days for Aaron. Aaron, Sadleir said, wanted a guarantee that Joe Byrne would be saved. The best that Captain Standish could offer was that he would recommend to the government that Joe Byrne's life should be saved, not his liberty, and that he should be tempted through Aaron Sherritt to lead the police on to the other three. According to Sadleir, the saving of Joe's life was the only terms Aaron asked for.

Sadleir was asked if he or Captain Standish sought to make arrangements with any other individual apart from Aaron Sherritt. He answered that they had tried to make an arrangement with Mrs Byrne. He said they pointed out to her that her son had got his neck into a halter, and that she could save him if she liked. Her answer, though, was that, 'He had made his own bed, let him lie on it.'

Sadleir was asked many questions about the sympathisers who supported the gang, and about how the gang was provisioned. He answered that there were a hundred families, or heads of families, ready to supply them. He also mentioned a report from a reliable agent about Mrs Skillion, the sister of the Kellys, preparing provisions in excess of the requirements of her own household. Wallace was obviously not the only one buying provisions in excess of his own household's needs!

The Commissioner's final questions to Sadleir related to the dismissal of Nicolson's agents when Hare took over operations prior to Glenrowan. When asked about 'Bruce' (Wallace), Sadleir replied that he thought he had been 'got rid of at that time'.[164] When asked if he could think of any reason why he was got rid of, he answered, 'I think he was trying to swindle the police out of money – that is, he was trying to get money for false information.'[165]

---

164 - Minutes of Evidence, John Sadleir's response to question 2553.

165 - Minutes of Evidence, John Sadleir's response to question 2554.

Sadleir said he had never seen the man 'Bruce' or had any communication with him, so what he had to say about the man was hearsay. He said he thought it was Captain Standish or Mr Nicolson who communicated with the man. This shows the lengths Nicolson went to keep his agents safe. In fact, when Nicolson was replaced by Hare shortly before Glenrowan, he took the 'Bruce' papers (and papers from his other agents) with him for safe keeping, knowing that it was Hare's intention to dispense with all agents.[166]

Detective Ward also gave evidence on 3 May, and later again on 21 July, but was not asked questions about Wallace. The Commissioners saved those questions until a later date, at which time they would also give Ward the opportunity to cross-examine Wallace.

Mrs Sherritt Snr (Agnes), mother of Aaron, gave evidence on 20 July 1881. She said the gang turned against Aaron after Mrs Byrne discovered he was assisting Detective Ward, a man to whom she had taken a strong dislike.[167] She told the Commissioners that Mrs Byrne had found out because Aaron's schoolmate Wallace had told her. The Commission room was then cleared of reporters so she could give further evidence in private about this. She explained that Wallace had visited her house one afternoon when Detective Ward and a Beechworth draper, to whom she owed money, happened to also be there. She gave them all a cup of tea. The following day or two, her daughter went down to Mrs Byrne's and was asked by her how it was that they (the Sherritts) were so friendly with Ward as to give him tea.

---

166 - This became evident when Nicolson questioned Sadleir (Q2594) about the information he had left in his office for Mr Hare when the latter resumed command of the Kelly hunt. Nicolson asked Sadleir if he remembered seeing a large package of papers and of him saying to Mr Hare that he would like to keep them as they would be of no use to him. Sadleir replied that he did remember that with respect to the Bruce papers. Nicolson was keen to keep those papers because he knew Hare intended to dispense with all of his agents, of whom he had five at that time (including 'Diseased Stock'). Nicolson was seeking to keep his agents safe.

167 - There had also been a previous quarrel between Aaron and Mrs Byrne some eight or nine months earlier, after which time the gang had threatened to shoot him. It appears things settled down after that quarrel –Aaron made a present of a horse to one of her daughters. However, the daughter then exchanged that horse for another, which caused Aaron to take and sell the new horse that she had got in exchange. That then caused Mrs Byrne to take out a warrant for him. The police arrested Aaron and he stood trial in Beechworth, but was acquitted. It seems that the relationships between the Sherritt and Byrne families were difficult! The issue with the horse, though, was not the reason for the fallout between Aaron and the gang – the issue there was that he was working for the police.

She had got that information from Wallace (Jimmy Wallace, as she called him).

Mrs Sherritt told the Commissioners that Wallace used to tell her son he was writing a book. He would ask her son to tell him all that he knew – the particulars of what the police were doing. He promised Aaron that he should have half the profits from the book.

Further evidence given by Mrs Sherritt revealed that a complicated relationship existed between Aaron, Joe and James.[168] She believed it was Wallace who led Mrs Byrne to understand that Aaron was helping the police. She told of how Joe met her children as they were going to school one day and asked them to tell her not to let Aaron sleep inside for a fortnight because Kelly was going to come in to shoot him. This indicates that Joe was at this stage seeking to protect Aaron (just as Aaron had sought initially to protect Joe).

The Commissioners asked Mrs Sherritt if Byrne and Sherritt were very friendly.[169] She answered that they were, and that Wallace had also been an intimate friend. She added, though, 'My son was an innocent fellow, and easily led astray. If you asked him a question, he would tell it to an intimate acquaintance like Wallace.' When asked if, from all she had heard, she considered that Wallace acted as an enemy, she answered that she did.[170] When asked if she knew anything of what occurred about the time her son was shot by Byrne, she answered that she had only heard what she had told Superintendent Hare – that she had heard from Byrne's sister that they were going to do something that would astonish not only Australia, but the whole world.[171]

From further questions put to Mrs Sherritt and her answers to those questions, it is apparent that the gang, including Joe, had decided to kill Aaron.[172] This time there was no warning that Aaron should not sleep in his hut. Mrs Sherritt then recounted a meeting she had with Joe. Her plough horses had one morning got into a neighbour's paddock

---

168 - Minutes of Evidence, Q13177–13180.

169 - Minutes of Evidence, Q13180.

170 - Minutes of Evidence, Q13181.

171 - Minutes of Evidence, Q13182.

172 - Minutes of Evidence, Q13183–Q13214.

and when she went to get them, she found Byrne waiting there. He came over to speak with her and told her that he had come to take her son's life and also the life of Detective Ward. Although she pleaded for her son's life, telling Joe that he would do him no harm, Joe's mind was made up. She and her son John went into Beechworth and told Detective Ward what had transpired. A few days after that, she had the chance to tell Nicolson what had passed. Nicolson told her that her son would lose his life if he was not removed from where he was.[173]

Mrs Sherritt Jnr (née Ellen Barry) gave evidence after Mrs Sherritt Snr. When asked if she knew Wallace the schoolmaster, she answered that she did.[174] When asked if Wallace had come to her place (the hut she shared with her husband Aaron) during the time the police were there, she answered that he didn't, but that he had gone to her mother's place.[175] When asked about his attitudes towards the outlaws, she answered that he seemed to have a hatred against them, and that she did not think he knew where they were or anything about them. Some people, she said, seemed to think he was assisting the outlaws, but she believed that to be false. She said she had heard something about him being a sympathiser, but did not know how true that was.[176]

Mrs Ellen Barry (Ellen Sherritt's mother) was called to give evidence after her daughter. She had been with Aaron and her daughter on the night Aaron was killed, and most of the questioning related to the events of that night. She was also asked if she had heard anything about why the gang wanted to shoot Aaron, but had no knowledge of that. In amongst the other questions, she was asked if she had ever seen Wallace the teacher about. She answered that he had come to her

---

173 - The warning was ignored. Aaron's widow (Mrs Sherritt Junior) was asked by the Commissioners (Minutes of Evidence, Q13242) if she knew that Aaron had been asked to keep away from his hut for a fortnight for fear he would be shot. She answered that she wasn't aware. She had previously told the Commissioners, though, (Q13228) that Aaron had 'seemed to be afraid if he went out in the bush, but he had never once thought of their coming to shoot him at the house the way they did'.

174 - Minutes of Evidence, Q13298.

175 - Minutes of Evidence, Q13299. She was asked (Q13303) if she was on friendly terms with Aaron's mother, she answered that they had not spoken since her marriage to Aaron. It wasn't stated to the Commissioners, but the reason they had not spoken was due to the Sherritts disapproval of their son having married a Catholic.

176 - Minutes of Evidence, Q13300–Q13302.

place a couple of times to see Aaron when he was living with her (for a few months after he was married and before he went to live in his own house). He always spoke with Aaron outside of the house and Aaron never told her what passed between them.[177]

Evidence given by Wallace

Wallace appeared before the Royal Commission on the 2 and 3 of August 1881.

If James had thought the Royal Commissioners might have gone easy on him due to his prior dealings with some of them, or due to some of them having political views that were aligned with his own, he was sorely mistaken. The failure of the police to bring the four young outlaws to justice was an embarrassment for the government, and the Commissioners went about their task aggressively.

After all they had heard about him over the preceding four months, it appears the Commissioners had already well and truly decided that Wallace had been a sympathiser. Wallace was to be subjected to an aggressive line of questioning.

The questions put to Wallace, together with his answers, are reproduced in full below, with the only addition being the insertion of headings to improve the readability and to identify the line of questioning being pursued. The Commissioners had obviously spent considerable time preparing their questions, with the progression of the questions being designed to steadily put Wallace under more and more pressure. This is only apparent if all the questions are shown in full. Showing Wallace's answers in full is also important, in particular, because it shows that he could handle himself well under pressure and was able to answer the questions without incriminating himself.

---

177 - Minutes of Evidence, Q13430.

Day 1 of Wallace examination (2 August 1881)

Preliminaries

14415. By the Commission. – What are you? – *State school teacher at Yea, formerly at the Hurdle Creek, Oxley, near the King River.*

14416. You are aware that the pursuit of the Kellys was carried on very actively some time ago in the North-Eastern district? – *Yes.*

His dealings with the police

14417. The Commission understand that you were in communication with the police upon some occasions? – *I was in communication with the police, but was never in their pay. I never asked for any pay nor received any. I declined the offer. I did receive some money, but only for actual expenses.*

14418. How much did you get? – *I could not say.*

14419. Would you be surprised if you heard? – *From £70 to £80, I daresay, altogether.*

14420. You say you were not specially employed by the police? – *I was not employed; not receiving any remuneration whatever, and I was paid my actual expenses.*

14421. What agreement did you make when you agreed to give them information? – *I will read an extract from my diary at the time I made the arrangement with Mr. Nicolson.*

14422. Had you any arrangement with any one before Mr. Nicolson? – *No, none whatever.*

14423. No other officer? – *No, none that I remember.*

14424. What led to any communication that took place between you and the police? – *In December 1878, after the commission of the Mansfield murders by the Kelly Gang, and seeing the difficulty the police had in capturing them; hearing also that they would commit further outrages, and knowing I might be able to assist in the suppression of crime, I wrote a letter to Captain Standish offering my assistance to him. Of course I understood the offer to him that it was free, gratis, not with any intention of participating in the reward or receiving any remuneration for my services.*

14425. What motive had you? – *Simply in the interests of society, to suppress crime.*

14426. What special qualification had you? – *I knew Byrne; he was an old schoolmate of mine, and I knew the country. I had my suspicions that Byrne was one of the gang, and I knew the places they would be likely to go to, and the ranges they would be likely to frequent, and the friends who would be most likely to assist them.*

14427. Have you a copy of that letter to Captain Standish? – *No.*

14428. The first letter you wrote to Captain Standish was of what nature? – *Offering my services.*

14429. To do what? – *To assist them in capturing the outlaws.*

14430. Were you acquainted with either of the Kellys? – *No; not at all.*

14431. Having made the offer to Captain Standish in writing, what answer did you receive? – *I received a very courteous reply from Captain Standish declining my offered services. He would be very glad to hear anything, but he at present did not require anything further.*

14432. Have you preserved that letter? – *No, I did not think it desirable to preserve any.*

14433. Having declined that, what led you subsequently to offer any assistance to the police? – *On the 23rd July 1879, I was honoured by a visit from the Assistant Commissioner of Police, Mr. Nicolson. He said he called to have a few minutes' conversation with me in reference to the outlaws. He remembered seeing a letter from me in December last.*

14434. That is the letter you have already alluded to? – *Yes. He referred to the fact of my having been a schoolmate of Byrne's, to my knowledge of the district generally, and asked me when I had seen Byrne last, and several other particulars. He wanted to know my impression as to the present whereabouts of the gang. I gave it as my opinion that they had gone into winter quarters; that is, that they were not travelling about, but were settled for the winter. I told the impressions and facts I had as regards their previous movements, life pursued, tactics observed, and mode of living, as far as I could learn from hints let drop by their friends.*

14435. You say you told him the facts? – *No, I did not mean the facts exactly, but the impressions I formed – that would be a better word.*

His contacts with and knowledge of the outlaws

14436. Was there anything, beyond hearsay, that led you to give this information to the police? – *Nothing beyond hearsay; no personal knowledge.*

14437. You had never seen Byrne? – *Not since the commission of the murders.*

14438. Had you ever heard from him directly or indirectly? – *Indirectly through others I had heard of him.*

14439. Indirectly, from Byrne did you ever receive any direct message? – *Yes, latterly; not then.*

14440. Up to that time you have been speaking of, had you ever, through a second party, received a message direct from Byrne? – *I did.*

14441. What was its character? – *It was with reference to a saddle that Ned Kelly had stolen from me some time previously, for one thing, offering to replace it, stating they were sorry that I had been victimized, having been a schoolmate of Byrne's.*

14442. Anything else? – *On another occasion I forwarded a message from Captain Standish to Byrne through the same medium.*

14443. On this occasion, when you received the direct intimation from Byrne and the others, regretting you had been a victim about the saddle, was there any allusion whatever made to any other subject in which they were interested? – *No more whatever at that time. As I was just about to observe, I forwarded a message from Captain Standish to Byrne some time afterwards.*

14444. You received a direct intimation from them through a third party? – *Yes.*

14445. What action did you take? – *I took no action whatever.*

14446. Did you get the saddle? – *I did not.*

14447. Did you make any response in any shape or form? – *None whatever.*

14448. Who was the bearer of this news? – *Aaron Sherritt.*

14449. He brought this information direct from Byrne? – *So he said.*

14450. About what time was it; can you fix the date? – *No.*

14451. Approximately? – *I think it was after the Euroa robbery.*

14452. Did you know at that time that Sherritt was helping the police? – *I knew, as most other people did in the district, that he was helping the police.*

14453. You received this information from them; how did you do so? – *By a call from him. He frequently called at my place during the time he was employed by the police.*

14454. What was the nature of the conversation that took place then? – *We had so many conversations.*

14455. You say this information given you by Sherritt was after the Euroa robbery? – *Yes, between that and the Jerilderie robbery.*

14456. How many weeks after? – *I cannot say exactly. I should say it would be sometime in January.*

14457. Did Sherritt on that occasion give you any information at all which led you to form an opinion as to where these men were located? – *He did.*

14458. Can you tell us where that was? – *That they did not remain long in one place, but were frequently about Sebastopol ranges, Greta ranges, and up the King River, and sometimes down to Yarrawonga and the Warby ranges.*

14459. Did Sherritt describe to you the positions these men were then occupying specially? – *I believe he did.*

14460. Will you be kind enough to give them to us in the order he gave them to you? – *The ranges in the immediate vicinity of Sherritt's, down towards the Yellow Creek, and frequently were in the ranges between Sebastopol and Chiltern.*

14461. That was all within one neighbourhood, a radius of how many miles? – *Fifteen miles.*

14462. Did Sherritt give you any other information as to what the outlaws were doing or likely to do at this particular time? – *Perhaps not at that particular time; I did not make a note of it, but I know he frequently spoke of them.*

14463. At this time? – *Yes, he did. He said they did not remain long in one place; they beat backwards and forwards, sometimes in Sebastopol and sometimes in Greta, but still within this radius of fifteen miles round there.*

Kennedy's watch

14464. Did he give you any other information of an interesting character at this time? – *Yes, he spoke of the murders at Mansfield, and stated that he (Sherritt) had Kennedy's watch in his possession.*

14465. Did he show it you? – *No, he did not; he promised frequently to do so, but did not.*

14466. Did you ever see that watch? – *No, I did not. I should have secured it if I had.*

14467. Did you ever hear of the history of the watch? – *What do you mean by the history?*

14468. Do you know whether the watch was a presentation watch? – *Aaron said there was an inscription on the watch—stains on the watch—and wished to know from me what would remove those stains.*

14469. Did he tell you what the inscription was? – *No.*

14470. Did you ever hear of what it was? – *No.*

14471. Did you hear what the inscription was that would lead you to remember if it was a presentation watch? – *Subsequently I did. I think, in speaking to Mr. Nicolson, he said it was a presentation watch with an inscription on it.*

14472. Sherritt asked you if you knew anything that would take off the inscription? – *He used the word 'stains.' I understood him to mean inscription by that. Sherritt was guarded and cunning.*

14473. Did you give him any information about that? – *None. I advised him to hand over the watch to the police for the sake of the widow.*

14474. Did he give any other information then? – *Since he frequently stayed for hours and talked for hours, he must have done so.*

14475. I want you to confine yourself to that one interview? – *I cannot do that.*

14476. That must have been the most interesting you ever had? – *Not by any means.*

I used to dabble in mesmerism

14477. I cannot help thinking during the public excitement you would attach greater interest to that one than any other. Does your memory lead you to narrate to the Commission any other subject-matter of interest which Sherritt talked of at that time? – *He told me he was then in the employ of the police. I might simplify matters considerably by saying that when I was young I used to dabble in mesmerism. Aaron Sherritt, being, of course, a schoolfellow, was often with me in those experiments, and he was a 'subject' of mine. Naturally he had a great deal of confidence in me, and I had an influence over him, and he would frequently come there, and if I wanted to get any information out of him I could do so.*

14478. Did you mesmerize him then? – *No; I did on former occasions. His confidence in me was the result of that in former years.*

14479. He did not narrate anything of importance about the outlaws on that occasion beyond what you have said? – *Only just that they proposed sticking up other banks; but really I had so many interviews I could not fix upon that particular interview.*

14480. You are not mistaken when you say on that occasion he said the outlaws intended sticking up other banks? – *Yes, that information was conveyed in my confidential letters to Mr. Nicolson.*

14481. Having got that information, what action did you take? – *At that time I believe I was in communication with Mr. Nicolson.*

14482. You cannot fix the date of this interview? – *I cannot possibly; it is two years ago.*

Dealings with the police

14483. How many days after this interview did you interview the police and give the information that was of so interesting a character? – *That would appear from my letters, which you have in your possession.*

14484. The information you conveyed was in writing? – *Most probably.*

14485. Was it, or was it not? – *I cannot say. I frequently had interviews with Mr. Nicolson, and frequently wrote letters to him.*

14486. Did you, after this interview, have any personal communication with any officer of the police or any agent of police before you committed yourself to writing and gave the information which is contained in your letters? – *The only officer I had any direct or indirect communication with was Mr. Nicolson.*

14487. Was it before you committed yourself to paper about this interview of Sherritt's? – *I believe I had an interview with him then. I had so many, I could not possibly specify without referring to the letters.*

14488. You used to write under an alias? – *Half-a-dozen; that was the arrangement with Mr. Nicolson, and he wrote to me under the alias.*

14489. When you got information you generally wrote to Mr. Nicolson? – *Yes.*

14490. These letters before us will explain everything? – *Yes; and as to asking me about certain interviews with Aaron Sherritt, it is impossible for me to fix anything with distinctness.*

14491. I want to know what action you immediately took on obtaining this valuable information? – *It was communicated, no doubt, by letter, but I cannot say possibly because there was so much of a similar kind sent. I cannot fix the date; it is a tax on my memory it cannot stand.*

14492. From the knowledge you had of Sherritt and your influence over him, you received the information and believed it to be thoroughly reliable? – *Yes, but you are narrowing this all down to one day. It would be better to let me start from the beginning. Aaron was a schoolmate of mine, and he passed my place so frequently, and almost every time he called and had a conversation with me.*

14493. How many interviews had you either with Captain Standish, Mr. Sadleir, or Mr. Nicolson before you wrote your letter dated 5th January 1879—[handing the letter to the witness].—Is that your handwriting? – *Yes.*

14494. Is that the first letter you wrote to anyone connected with the police about the Kelly Gang? – *I do not think so; I did not keep a record.*

14495. To whom did you write any letter prior to that? – *Captain Standish; that I have already referred to.*

14496. Did you write any to Mr. Nicolson before that? – *I do not think so. I think I had several communications before that; but, inasmuch as I did not keep a record of dates, I cannot be precise without referring to my notes.*

14497. Did you, in the first instance, before writing to Captain Standish, have a personal interview with him at Benalla? – *Certainly not.*

14498. Did you, after writing the first letter to Captain Standish, have a personal interview with him at Benalla? – *I did.*

14499. Will you tell us the nature of the conversation? – *It was a general conversation with regard to the outlaws.*

14500. What was your proposal to him? – *I cannot recollect what proposals I made.*

14501. You must have gone with a definite idea of doing something? – *I had some information for him, I believe, with reference to a proposed crossing of the Murray by the outlaws which I thought would be interesting to him, but which he had already obtained from some other sources.*

Relationship with the Byrne Family

14502. Did you tell Captain Standish that Byrne was a schoolmate of yours? – *Most probably did.*

14503. Did you tell him of your own friendly terms with the Byrne family? – *I cannot say I told him; he might have inferred that.*

14504. At that time, you were on personal friendship and the best of terms with the Byrne family? – *I had been some time away from the particular vicinity of the Byrne family, and Joe Byrne was the only one I had seen at the time.*

14505. You had the means then of being on visiting terms with the Byrne family at that time? – *Yes, I had.*

14506. Is it probable that you did not inform Captain Standish? – *It is probable that I did inform him I was on friendly terms with the Byrnes.*

14507. Did you tell him what means you had of obtaining information as to the whereabouts of the outlaws at that interview? – *Probably I did.*

14508. Did Captain Standish make any arrangement with you from that time to supply him with any information you might obtain? – *I think not. Another matter at that interview with Captain Standish was with reference to a friend of mine—a pupil of mine at the time—named Slater, whom I recommended him to employ —to put him on the police force—stating I thought he would be able to give help from his knowledge of the country, and being an intimate friend of Byrne's.*

14509. Did you make that one of the conditions for your supplying information? – *No; I did not by any means. I did not make any conditions.*

14510. After Captain Standish declined to have anything to do with that, how did you have to do with Mr. Nicolson? – *He came to me once, one Friday.*

14511. Before the 5th January? – *Yes, it must have been, because I had had no communication with him.*

14512. Had you previously sent to him verbally? – *No.*

14513. Do you remember what Mr. Nicolson asked you when he called? – *Yes; he told me that the country looked to me, as a teacher and as a respectable member of society, that I should render all the assistance I could to suppress murder and robbery, and I understood him to wish me to take service with him; that it could be arranged that I could have leave of absence, but I declined to do so. He then asked me if I would give them any other aid I could by collecting information, and beating up the house in the neighbourhood which the outlaws were most likely to frequent, and I agreed to consider his proposal.*

14514. After considering, what did you do? – *I decided to assist him in the interests of society.*

14515. Did you state at that interview with Mr. Nicolson what special means you had of affording him information? – *I think so.*

Day Two of Wallace examination (3 August 1881)

The second day of Wallace's examination was conducted in private.

Overtures to help the police

14516. By the Commission. – There is a letter dated 5th January 1879? – *That ought to be 1880; and, in speaking of the interview I had with Sherritt, with reference to the stolen saddle, it should have been subsequent to the Jerilderie robbery, towards the beginning of March I should say now; I cannot be precise as to dates.*

14517. In that letter I have marked the place off, about receiving the bank note that you cashed – [handing a letter to the witness dated 27/8/79]? – *Yes; I remember the circumstances.*

14518. There is one party you, have mentioned there; I suppose it was someone who had been employed by Mr. Hare—'Interviewed Mr. Hare's protégé.' I suppose that was Sherritt? – *Yes; I said 'Mr. Hare's protégé' because he showed such an affection for Mr. Hare, and spoke of him in such high terms.*

14519. What were the overtures made by you in your first communication to Captain Standish; what was the nature of your offer? – *My offer was to offer my assistance to him to assist him in the capture of the Mansfield murderers; stating I knew them by sight, and knew Byrne intimately, and knew the country.*

Mr. Sadleir. – I understood it in a less definite way, that he meant it that he had a few weeks' holiday.

The Witness. – *Yes; that is true.*

Mr. Sadleir. – And he would be glad to put his leisure at the service of Captain Standish.

The Witness. – *Yes, just prior to the Christmas holidays, in 1878.*

14520. The Commission (to Mr. Sadleir). – In that letter did Mr. Wallace state that he would expect to be compensated in any way?

Mr. Sadleir. – I am pretty sure there was no reference to that.

Mr. Hare. – No, I know there was no reference to that.

There is a screw loose in your department

14521. By the Commission (to the witness). – Was there any correspondence from the time you wrote to Captain Standish, between Captain Standish and yourself, or Mr. Nicolson, before you wrote this letter of the 18th August 1879? – *I cannot recollect the date. I had a visit from Captain Standish at my place on one occasion, but I could not exactly give the date.*

14522. You can say there was no regular correspondence kept up? – *No; there was only one letter to Captain Standish.*

14523. Was it dated 18/8/79. Here is one statement:—'I think it more advisable to communicate details to you personally, as there is a screw loose in your department somewhere.' Will you tell the Commission what you meant to infer by that? – *I wanted to convey to Mr. Nicolson that the police information got abroad, that the outlaws' friends and Sympathisers were aware of the police movements, and that I was myself in communication with the police, was openly asserted in a public-house at Oxley.*

14524. Were you under the impression at the time that the information you supplied to Mr. Nicolson was made use of by some members of the police force not in the interests of the public? – *Yes, not in the interests of the public.*

14525. Were you aware at the time who the officer of police was who did that? – *I could not state precisely, only I knew the information I had supplied was floating about—I know the list of places I gave to Mr. Nicolson of the probable retreats of the outlaws was shown me by Aaron Sherritt afterwards.*

14526. But was he not at that time in the confidence of the police as well as yourself? – *He was. It was generally understood so.*

14527. Then would it not be probable that the information you supplied would be given him to assist him? – *Yes; but the form might have been altered so that he could not have detected whence it came.*

14528. You say further on – 'There is a beautiful game of cross purposes being played on both sides that is worth the trouble of watching, if there were no other motive'—what do you allude to there? – *I meant with reference to the game that was played on both sides, the resources they had to deceive each other, both the police and the outlaws. I had in my mind's eye then the trial of Aaron Sherritt at Beechworth for stealing a horse of Mrs. Byrne's, which he admitted to me was a 'got-up' case on the part of some members of the police on one side, and worked by the outlaws as well on the other.*

Who were the sympathisers?

14529. What reason had you to know that the outlaws were acquainted with all these movements at that time? – *From Sympathisers—from hints dropped by them.*

14530. By whom? – *I cannot say.*

14531. It is for you to say—we are supposed to be in private now—who were the Sympathisers and from whom did they obtain the hints? – *From the outlaws.*

14532. Give us one? – *Aaron Sherritt and Edward Burke.*

14533. Aaron Sherritt was in the confidence of the police? – *Just so.*

14534. Then you could not treat him at that time as a Sympathiser? – *I did.*

14535. Did you know him to be a Sympathiser? – *I knew him to be a Sympathiser, that was my belief, that he was playing double.*

14536. Did you communicate that to Mr. Nicolson – 'That he was in communication with the outlaws'? – *I did frequently—vivâ voce.*

14537. By letter? – *I think so, also.*

14538. The next paragraph in the letter is – 'I think I can persuade someone to return the chronometer to the widow'? – *That was Sergeant Kennedy's watch.*

14539. Who is this 'someone'? – *Aaron Sherritt.*

14540. What influence had he with the outlaws? – *He had the watch in his possession, according to his statement, and according to other information I got.*

14541. Did you ever see it? – *No.*

14542. What led you to that belief? – *His assertions to that effect, and his description of it.*

14543. He was a man you would believe when he said that? – *Yes.*

14544. Why did not you convey to Mr. Nicolson that you believed Aaron Sherritt had the watch? – *I did do so.*

14545. You say here – 'I can persuade someone'— these are riddles? – *Those letters were written for Mr. Nicolson, and as long as he understood them, that satisfied me.*

14546. Did you tell Mr. Nicolson about this time that Aaron Sherritt had the watch? – *I did.*

14547. He would understand that? – *He did. He would have asked me if he did not understand it. No doubt you will find reference to it in other parts of the correspondence.*

14548. Then the only one you had information from was Sherritt? – *Oh! No.*

14549. Who? – *There were many others. Some I would decline to mention under any circumstances.*

14550. What were the names? – *Edward Burke, of Black Range.*

14551. Was he in communication with the outlaws? – *He was, according to his own statement.*

14552. What is he? – *A selector.*

14553. Is he still in that district? – *He is, I believe. I have not been there for twelve months.*

14554. What is the name of any other Sympathiser you had an opportunity of seeing? – *John Sherritt.*

14555. He was in communication with the outlaws? – *I believed him to be so.*

14556. All through? – *Well, yes, all through. At least, according to his statement, he could communicate at any time, perhaps not directly, but indirectly through their relatives; but I do not think that he was willingly a Sympathiser. It was more through his friendship for Byrne, not through countenancing crime.*

14557. Did you, after the murders at the Wombat, visit Mrs. Byrne's place? – *Yes.*

14558. Do you remember the last time you visited the Byrnes? – *I was not inside; I passed the house very early one morning.*

14559. Do you remember the last time you visited there? – *Yes, I think so I would not be certain.*

14560. When was that? – *I could not give the date; you may find it in my letters.*

14561. You frequently visited there? – *No; I was not on intimate terms.*

14562. Never took tea? – *No.*

14563. Did you ever dine at the place? – *No.*

14564. Were you on friendly terms outside? – *Yes, outside. I had not seen Mrs. Byrne for a long time. I met the other members of the family.*

14565. Did you consider you were on terms of confidence with them? – *Yes, to a certain extent. Of course, they were guarded in their communications.*

A meeting with Byrne

14566. Did you ever see either of the outlaws after the time of the Wombat murders? – *I met one one evening. I met Byrne one moonlight night on the Oxley road, going in the direction of Sebastopol from Greta. My school was right in a line from the two places, and of course they would follow the track. He was by himself.*

14567. Did you have an interview with him? – *I had no interview with him. I was in company with others, and of course I did not state it was Byrne—simply said 'Good night,' and he passed on. I recognized his form and voice.*

14568. Did you inform the police? – *I did.*

14569. Immediately after? – *Not exactly immediately after, but within a few days, I think.*

14570. If you were working in the interests of the police, why did not you take immediate steps to inform them about that? – *Doubtless because I would think that no good could come from informing them. I had no confidence in the detective in charge at Beechworth. I would think that he might burke that evidence, so to speak, in order to frustrate the capture of the outlaws through any other means than his own.*

14571. Would it be to the detective you would give the information? – *Certainly not.*

14572. Then why had you fear in giving the information to the officer of the police you were previously in communication with? – *I cannot say, except it was I thought no good would come of it. I was expecting to see the others, and no good would accrue from taking Byrne alone. It would have been the worst thing that could have happened.*

14573. How far from the telegraph office were you then? – *Sixteen miles.*

14574. What office? – *Wangaratta.*

14575. That was at night? – *Yes.*

14576. You saw the direction Byrne was riding in? – *Yes, to Sebastopol.*

14577. And you waited some days? – *I cannot say the exact time. I know I mentioned the circumstance to Mr. Nicolson.*

14578. Did you see either of the gang any other time except that? – *I believe, I am not positive, I met Ned Kelly one morning sometime after I had dropped communication with Mr. Nicolson.*

14579. That would be the latter end of 1879? – *About that time, I think.*

14580. Did you see Byrne on any other occasion than the one you have already described? – *No.*

14581. Do you remember Captain Standish being at your place? – *I do, on two different occasions.*

14582. Do you remember he was there not long before the bank robbery at Jerilderie? – *I do, he was in my house.*

14583. Are you sure you did not see Byrne about that time? – *I am positive, as far as I can recollect.*

14584. Will you swear that Byrne was not in your house that day? – *Certainly.*

14585. You swear now positively you never saw Byrne but on one occasion? – *Yes, positively.*

Communications with the outlaws

14586. Did you have no direct communication with any of the outlaws? – *What do you mean—by letter, or word of mouth?*

14587. By letter or word of mouth—was there no confidence between you and the outlaws by which you could have communication? – *No direct communication.*

14588. Are you prepared to swear positively that after the murders you had no direct communication? – *No direct; I had indirect through others.*

14589. Is there any one you can think of, except those you have named, that you had communication through? – *Yes, I believe there is one.*

14590. Who is it? – *John Sherritt; I do not recollect any more.*

14591. You are quite sure you had no personal conversation with either of the outlaws any time after the day of the murders at the Wombat? – *None beyond what I have said about Byrne and Kelly, and I was not certain about Kelly. I met a man with a muffler on the road, and I heard afterwards Kelly had seen me.*

14592. You were familiar with him? – *Yes.*

14593. Could you make a mistake about him? – *Oh, certainly.*

14594. How far off was he? – *About fifty yards.*

14595. Do you think you could make a mistake at that distance as to any gentleman in this room? – *Yes, if they were in disguises. If I dressed you up in the garb of a woman, I would not know you.*

14596. He was not dressed as a woman? – *No, a grey coat, and a muffler round his face and nearly round his eyes; very little of his face was visible.*

14597. That would attract your attention and cause you to be more observant of who he was? – *Yes, I noted him as he passed.*

14598. If he was so disguised, did not that attract your attention? – *It did. I thought it looked like Kelly, but I could not swear that.*

14599. Have you any doubt in your mind but that it was? – *My impression that it was he was strengthened afterwards by hearing he had met me on that road.*

14600. Did you keep a horse? – *Three or four of them.*

14601. From whom did you hear that information that Kelly saw you at this time? – *From Ned Burke, at Hedi.*

14602. How long after your impression of having seen him? – *Two or three months after, I dare say.*

14603. Did you communicate that to the police? – *No, I did not; I did not see the necessity of it.*

14604. Although you were fully persuaded he was the man the police were looking for? – *No.*

14605. Did you feel fully impressed it was the leader of the outlaws? – *I felt slightly impressed.*

14606. Did you send the police word of that? – *I did not.*

14607. Even if you had a slight impression, as an officer in the public service and occupying a respectable position as a teacher of young people, did not you conceive it your duty to give the fullest and most expeditious information you could? – *Not in that case.*

14608. In every case? – *I have done so.*

14609. About Byrne—you did not communicate intelligence till two or three days after? – *Yes. Knowing the place so well, and also the means being used to capture them, I did not judge it necessary at the time to tell that about Kelly.*

14610. About the other man you were certain? – *I would not swear about that. I thought I recognized his voice and figure, still I would not swear it was he.*

14611. You keep a horse? – *I do.*

14612. And were within sixteen miles of the telegraph? – *Yes.*

14613. And you did not think it necessary to mount a horse and go and tell about it? – *The horse I was riding had just come a long distance. If I had wished to do so I should have had to borrow a horse, and if I had given information it would have been no use.*

14614. You did not feel in bodily fear of those men? – *No, never.*

14615. Then you were in a different position from many of the inhabitants in that respect? – *I recognized the possibility of my being shot if I gave information. I would have chanced that; but it was not through fear, but just through not seeing the desirability.*

14616. Are you quite sure you did not see any of those men on any other occasion? – *Quite sure.*

14617. Were you aware, from any confidential communications from a number of Sympathisers, of the locality where the outlaws were residing? – *Yes, several times, and I always communicated that to the police.*

14618. At all times, immediately? – *I think so, as far as I can recollect.*

14619. We have here all the reported appearances of the Kellys—[handing a printed paper to the 3rd witness].—Can you identify your information about Joe Byrne with any of those?—[The witness examined the printed paper]. – *It was not sent in by letter.*

14620. By the Commission (to Mr. Nicolson). – Can you help us as to the time about the information about Wallace seeing Joe Byrne? – *It was some time, I should say, about the month of October 1879, and I had heard that Mr. Wallace had seen Byrne, or had reason to believe he had seen him; and I asked him if it was the case, and he told me he had not. I asked him first if he had been at his house, and he said not, and he had not seen him, except one night when he was driving; and as he passed during the night by his own house he saw a man pass he believed to be Joe Byrne, and he bade him 'Good night.'*

14621. Did he mention how long it had occurred? – *This was a matter that had occurred some considerable time before.*

14622. All this time he had been writing to you and giving you information? – *He was writing from time to time.*

14623. Can you give an idea how long a time had elapsed between the time and the information? – *My impression now is that it was a considerable period, three or four weeks.*

14624. Altogether beyond the possibility of its being of any service? – *It was of no service then.*

14625. By the Commission (to the witness).—You are quite certain you never went to Byrne's house to take any meals. There is a paragraph here in this letter (27th August 1879) – 'I went down to the old people's next morning (Sunday) and stayed to dinner'? – *That is Sherritt's, not Byrne's.*

14626. Then you appear to have relied entirely on Sherritt? – *No, not entirely.*

14627. Principally? – *Yes, principally.*

14628. You state— 'The old lady was not at all communicative, but appeared nervous and frightened. Had a walk out with Jack for his father's horse (K. K.'s lost chestnut). He was rather reticent and distrustful at first.' That was John Sherritt.

'I asked him how the outlaws were so foolish as to go into the house while the children were there'? – *I think that refers to the night after the trial of Aaron Sherritt for the theft of Mrs. Byrne's horse.*

The National Bank banknote

14629. There is another passage with reference to Aaron Sherritt changing a National Bank note. Was it the National Bank stuck up at Euroa or Jerilderie? – *It was the National Bank at Jerilderie.*

14630. 'He said they were 'square,' and that he had obtained them in payment of service rendered to the police. I changed one of them for him, and cashed it purposely in Ward's presence at Wertheim's, Beechworth. I jocularly drew that gentleman's attention to it as being a 'National,' and asked him what he would give to be told where that came from.' Was that done with the view of putting Mr. Ward on his 'mettle' to find out where the note came from? – *I think so, and as a sort of collateral evidence that Sherritt had those notes in his possession. No doubt if Ward did his duty he would report that at once to Mr. Nicolson, being the officer in charge, and that would corroborate my statement that I had seen the notes in Aaron Sherritt's possession.*

14631. It was with that view? – *Yes.*

14632. What was your own impression about that note at the time? – *That he had received it from the outlaws. He made no secret of it.*

14633. It formed a portion of the notes taken from the Euroa bank? – *Yes.*

14634. Again, you go on to speak about the watch: – 'As to the watch, in the early part of the evening, he, of his own accord, proposed that I should go home with him that night and he would show it to me, to get my opinion as to the feasibility of getting it altered so as to defy identification.' You say you never saw the watch? – *Never saw it.*

14635. You do not know anything more about it? – *Nothing more than that Aaron had it in his possession; and Jack Sherritt also said he had seen it. They both said at different times they wanted to get it altered.*

14636. Did Jack say so? – *Yes, he did.*

14637. There was no doubt he had seen it then, and there was an inscription on it? – *No doubt whatever.*

14638. 'He said that there was a dark stain on the case and a sovereign pendent to the chain.' There is a very important clause here: – 'He had an interview with Ward after this, and I fancy he was put on his guard by that gentleman.' What is the meaning of that? – *That refers to Aaron Sherritt.*

14639. What was your meaning? – *Aaron Sherritt told me that Ward had told him (I know he told others —several) that I was assisting the police and endeavouring to capture the outlaws, that I was giving them information; and I had an idea that from his character if he knew I was making enquiries about the outlaws he would put them on their guard, so as to prevent them giving me any information.*

14640. Did others inform you as well as Aaron Sherritt that Ward had said so? – *Yes. I was informed that he had stated so publicly in Gardner's hotel, at Milawa, on the evening of the ploughing match.*

Speaking out about Detective Ward

14641. We come to a later letter dated 19th September 1879: – 'Since writing the rest I met Doig.' Who was he? – *James Doig, a farmer.*

14642. 'He says that Ward publicly stated that I was a detective in Gardner's hotel, Milawa, in the presence of Colin Gardner, J.P.; James Kelly, teacher; John Barry, farmer; A. McCormick, farmer and others.' That is what you refer to? – *Yes.*

14643. Did you consider that Ward was attempting to destroy your usefulness to the police for the purpose? – *I did certainly. What other effect could it have?*

14644. And you informed Mr. Nicolson that? – *I did.*

14645. For that purpose? – *For that purpose.*

14646. In this letter of the 19th September you say: – 'Since coming home I have met a large number of people who were at the ploughing match on the 16th. If there had been such a rumor current as you told me of, I would be sure to have heard it by this time. Rumors of that kind soon travel. I do not believe that Ward heard anything of the kind'? – *That refers to a conversation I had with Mr. Nicolson. Mr. Nicolson stated that he had heard through Ward that I had gone down on a mission to Melbourne to endeavor to obtain Byrne's pardon. I think it was some tale of that sort.*

14647. 'If he did, he alone is responsible for it. It has turned out as I feared. I knew well that if he found out what relations existed between you and me, he would do his best to spoil my chance of being useful to you.' That refers to Mr. Ward? – *Yes.*

14648. How did you come to know all those things. 'I have it on the very best authority from two different sources that he stated at the ploughing match that I 'was a detective,' that he 'was certain of it,' that he 'had seen my name on the list,'' and so on—that was your letter? – *Yes.*

14649. What led you to suppose Ward had that feeling towards you? – *Well, just from my personal impression of the man and conversations that have been reported to me—expressions he had uttered in Beechworth and elsewhere conveyed to me by others.*

14650. That he was attempting by all means in his power to destroy your usefulness in the attempt to catch the Kellys? – *I will not say all means in his power, but he was trying to do it in various ways.*

14651. The object, according to your view, is that he was trying to let it be known that you were so in order that you could not carry out your wishes to find out the outlaws? – *That was my impression.*

14652. What object would he have? – *Jealousy of his position, I suppose; that he, being the detective in charge, should effect the capture himself—esprit de corps I suppose you would call it.*

14653. You would not attribute it to any desire on his part to capture the Kellys through your means or any other? – *No.*

14654. But the opposite? – *I believe he was earnest in his desire to capture them, but he wanted to do it himself.*

14655. We have your letters here continually speaking against Ward. What object could he have in giving this information to others other than to prevent you getting information? – *That was the only object he could have had.*

14656. To turn all those who could possibly give you information against you? – *Yes.*

14657. To make them suspicious of you if you spoke? – *Yes, exactly.*

14658. We will pass on to the 12th November 1879. There are a lot of letters between, but there is really nothing that I can see of importance in them. On 12th November 1879 there is this: – 'On last Sunday week I met Aaron Sherritt on the Woolshed, and had a long conversation with him. He said the police were going to have another mustering match, and run in all the Sympathisers again, he taxed me with having let out something about Kennedy's watch, and said that you had been persecuting him about it.' What was the nature of the information that he gave you then about Kennedy's watch? – *The information already referred to—he stated that he had it, and in reference to the inscription.*

14659. Did he say Mr. Nicolson had been enquiring about it? – *Yes; he said he had been enquiring about it frequently and persistently.*

14660. 'He remarked that Ward and he were on bad terms, and that you negotiated with him personally now'? – *Yes, he made that remark to me.*

14661. And that he had no intercourse at that time at all with Ward? – *That is what I understood him to say. The negotiation was carried on through Mr. Nicolson personally.*

14662. Then from that we would understand that he and Ward had quarrelled? – *Yes.*

14663. Did he ever make any statement to you that he would drop you a few hundred notes? – *No; he made some offer with regard to money, which I declined; I think it was £50—a loan of some money, that was it. He knew I was in financial difficulties; that was the reason he made the offer, I suppose.*

14664. Would you tell the circumstances under which such an offer as that was made? – *No, I could not; I have only a hazy recollection of it; he said he had plenty of money, and if I were short he could lend me some.*

14665. This is a long letter you wrote about Tom Burke and his application for land? – *Yes.*

14666. Have you still the same opinion of Tom Burke that you expressed there? – *I have still.*

14667. And of the other members of the family? – *Ned Burke I considered certainly find tendencies in the way of sympathizing, but not the others.*

14668. 'He wished me to write to Graves, Gaunson, and Cooper, Ms.L.A., and to Reid, Wallace, and Wilson, Ms.L.C., and also to draw out a petition to Parliament'? – *That is perfectly correct.*

14669. You mention in this letter, 'Barry said that if he was Byrne—I interviewed Jack Barry, of Hedi, last night. Had a conversation in re the outlaws; he was rather more reticent than he usually is, and would let out nothing tangible. I am sure he knows something about them, but I think it is indirectly through Ned Burke. Barry said that if he was Byrne, he would ride into Beechworth and shoot Ward at the first opportunity. I asked him why? What reason had Byrne to dislike Ward more than another? He replied that Ward had seduced Byrne's sister Kate. I asked him how he (Barry) knew. He said he knew all about it, that the information had come through Byrne himself, and that he got to know it indirectly.' Was there anything of that going about with reference to the police or detectives in the district? – *Only that solitary instance which I mention.*

14670. And he actually made that statement to you? – *Yes.*

14671. You appear to have carefully reported to Mr. Nicolson all that you heard about Ward? – *Yes.*

14672. Was there a special kindly feeling existing between you? – *No, I think not.*

14673. On the 26th of November 1879 you say, 'Rode down through the Woolshed,' past Aaron Sherritt's house. 'Met John Sherritt, junior, and Pat Byrne (Joe's brother). I had a long and interesting conversation with these worthies, who manifested much pleasure in meeting me. I wondered at the marked change in Jack's manner towards me, as, on two or three previous occasions, he had carefully avoided me. I soon ascertained the reason. It appears, by their account, that the virtuous detective who is standing the season at Beechworth had stated, a day or two previously, that my 'name had been added to the blacklist at the office; that he believed that bloody Wallace was in constant communication with the outlaws." What do you mean by that about the detective?[178] – *That was simply a report of what actually occurred; a conversation between Byrne, Sherritt, and myself that Ward had spread that report in Beechworth, that I was on the blacklist at the office. That was meant to put Mr. Nicolson on his guard not to let Ward know that he had a bad feeling against me. These things were being frequently told me.*

14674. You simply meant by that that you and they were talking about Ward as being a man of very bad character; did you mean by that insinuation that Ward was engaged in immoral practices? – *There is no insinuation; there is simply a statement of conversation.*

14675. What did you mean by that? – *Will you read it?*

14676. 'The virtuous detective who is standing the season at Beechworth'? – *That is exactly what I meant. He had the reputation of acting immorally, putting it in a mild form.*

14677. Have you any knowledge within your own experience of his having done so that would justify you in saying that? – *No; not directly.*

14678. While you were pretending to give information to the police force, you were attempting to damn the character of a public officer without positive proof of facts? – *The expressions were strong, I admit.*

14679. What justification had you? – *The repeated attempts of Ward to report me, and reports of Ward's immorality.*

14680. Was it not your personal animus? – *No; I had no animus whatever.*

14681. Was there anything to justify you? – *I think it was too strong.*

14682. Was it untrue? – *No; I have still the opinion that he was not a man of moral character.*

---

178 - .

14683. Was there anything to justify you making such a statement in writing? – *Only the current reports.*

14684. You were occupying the position of a teacher of the youth of this colony? – *Yes.*

14685. Without having any proof positive, you did not hesitate to pen a sentence which involved the slander of a man's character, sufficient, probably, to cause him the loss of his situation in the public service, and without any positive proof? – *Without any positive proof any more than current reports.*

14686. And yet you thought yourself justified in slandering a man's character without having any proof? – *I did.*

14687. Were you not actuated by mere animus and nothing else? – *I do not think so.*

14688. I think it would be difficult to make us believe so – did you think at that time that Jack Sherritt was a Sympathiser with the outlaws? – *I did.*

14689. Is all the rest of your valuable information supplied to Mr. Nicolson of equal importance to that paragraph in your letter, in your opinion, after due consideration? – *Well, I admit that was unjustifiable and wrong.*

14690. Do you think that all the rest of all your writing is of equal importance, in the interests of the public, to that statement contained in your letter obtained from Jack Sherritt? – *I say the whole of that information was important to the public.*

14691. You think the whole of your information was of equal value? – *I am not talking about the equality —I say that may have been too strong, but the information I supplied was of use.*

14692. Were you aware, at the time you wrote this paragraph against Ward, that Ward knew you were in communication with Mr. Nicolson? – *He stated that I was publicly.*

14693. Did you know from Mr. Nicolson whether Ward knew? – *I did not.*

14694. Did you ask Mr. Nicolson? – *I reported the circumstance of Ward speaking about me in that way, and asked him to prevent Ward doing so.*

14695. Did you ask Mr. Nicolson whether he had informed Ward that you were in correspondence with him? – *I cannot recollect that point for certain.*

14696. To Mr. Nicolson.— Had you made Ward acquainted with the fact? – *No, Detective Ward was not aware of it till the Commission sat, to my knowledge.*

Playing the double game – Sherritt or Wallace?

14697. To the Witness.— Did Sherritt know you were in correspondence with Mr. Nicolson? – *He did not, that I was aware of.*

14698. Did you know that Sherritt was engaged in the confidence of the police? – *Yes, I believe I did.*

14699. You knew all through at this time that you were speaking of Aaron Sherritt? – *That he was in communication with the police.*

14700. Did you know it officially? – *Yes, from Mr. Nicolson.*

14701. Were you desirous of placing Aaron Sherritt upon the best possible terms of confidence with the police authorities? – *No, rather the reverse, if I understand your question. My impression all through was that Aaron was playing the double game, all through up to the time I left.*

14702. It may be the impression that you were playing a double game. We do not want impressions. Were not you actuated with a desire to represent to Mr. Nicolson that Aaron was playing double? – *I did so because I honestly thought so.*

14703. Will you now speak positively that Aaron ever admitted he had that watch? – *I will—he did several times.*

14704. Will you, if Jack Sherritt comes in and swears he did not, contradict him on oath? – *I will if he says so.*

14705. What were you at the time you were the correspondent of the police? – *I was following my usual occupation of State school teacher.*

14706. What salary had you at that time? – *I could not say; about £200 a year.*

14707. What are you doing now? – *The same.*

14708. At what salary? – *About the same.*

14709. You know what you are getting; what are you getting? – *About £15 17s. 6d., including maintenance allowance.*

14710. Do you mean to tell me you are still in the service of the State as a school teacher? – *Yes.*

14711. Were you aware that Sherritt was a paid agent of the police? – *From his own statements.*

14712. Not from Mr. Nicolson? – *I cannot say. I knew that Mr. Nicolson had seen him. I knew that he was frequently in Benalla, but that was all.*

14713. You knew he was recognized as a paid agent of the police at this time? – *I believed so.*

14714. And he was one of the men you swore this morning you relied on for obtaining information? – *Yes, one of them.*

14715. And you were at the same time ndeavouring to damage the man's character? – *For the simple reason that I believed he was playing double. While I could use very often information I obtained from the man, I had no confidence in him.*

14716. And you were obtaining money for doing that? – *I received no money except for my actual expenses.*

14717. Was the position you assumed with the police known to the Education Department? – *I believe it was, through Captain Standish.*

14718. Did you of your own free will, before entering into any engagement with the police, communicate with the department of which you were an officer, and get their permission? – *No, I do not think so. It did not interfere with my duties as teacher.*

14719. You never had any written permission to act in the capacity you then assumed? – *Never; because it was intended to be kept as private as possible.*

14720. That would not have interfered with the effectiveness of the service you were going to render? – *I think Captain Standish applied to the office; I never did directly.*

14721. Were any of the Kelly Gang at your school at any time? – *Not that I know of.*

14722. You were a schoolmate of Joe Byrne? – *For years, and playmate.*

14723. Did you make any arrangement with Aaron Sherritt for Joe Byrne to betray the other three? – *I did, at the request of Captain Standish. I used him as one of the means of communication.*

14724. Did you ever have any communication with Joe Byrne on the subject? – *Never.*

14725. At no time? – *At no time.*

14726. You only saw him on the road as you speak of? – *Only that.*

Book writing as a pretext for collecting information

14727. Were you writing a book about this time? – *I was doing something in that line, but I abandoned that idea.*

14728. What was the nature of the book? – *That has nothing to do with the Commission. I decline to say.*

14729. Was it any reference to the Kellys? – *It was simply a romance based on the country there, and it was in the interests of law and order.*

14730. In connection with outrages of a similar character to the Kellys'? – *The same.*

14731. We have it in evidence that you were often at Sherritt's house? – *Yes, I was.*

14732. Asking for information, because you were writing a book? – *I had to give some reason for wishing to know, and I conveyed that impression. I do not know that I actually told them.*

14733. Were those outlaws and their associates the heroes of the tale? – *They were not.*

14734. You are quite sure of that? – *I am sure of that. How could I possibly make them the heroes of a tale? I might make them the villains of a tale.*

14735. How far did you get with the book? – *Nothing more than notes. I did not stick to that idea long.*

14736. You wrote some? – *I did nothing of the kind.*

14737. You obtained information that would guide you? – *It was necessary to make some excuse, apart from the right one, for showing interest in the affair.*

14738. Have you destroyed those notes? – *Yes. Would you like to read them?*

14739. I think I can read you pretty well? – *Yes.*

Christmas in Kelly Land

14740. Did you write a series of articles in the Wangaratta paper against the police? – *No, I cannot say that I did.*

14741. There was a series of articles came out in the Wangaratta paper—you were not the author? – *I was in the habit of writing for the Wangaratta Despatch. I do not know what articles you refer to.*

14742. Were you in the habit of supplying this journal with information bearing on the pursuit of the Kellys and the conduct of the police? – *Certainly not. I have written various articles for the paper.*

14743. You never wrote on this particular question, the pursuit of the Kellys? – *Yes, certainly I have done so. There have been so many articles in the Wangaratta Despatch bearing on the Kellys, I cannot say which you refer to.*

14744. How many did you write bearing on this subject? – *I remember writing one leading article for them and a series of romance entitled 'Christmas in Kelly Land.' That was all I had to do with it.*

14745. Those were in no way reflections on the conduct of the police? – *I do not think it could be construed in any way into reflections on the police—certainly one article reflected on the backwardness of the rank and file in not carrying the pursuit to a successful termination sooner.*

14746. Did you write that article after you had seen Joe Byrne on the road, or before? – *I think before.*

14747. You carried that out by giving information so long after? – *I was not a policeman.*

You were in the pay of the police?

14748. You were in the pay of the police? – *I was not; I was only paid expenses.*

14749. You received a consideration for your services? – *No; I only got my expenses.*

14750. Did you render an account of every particular? – *No; it was not asked for.*

14751. How did you render the account? – *I was put to considerable expense travelling about.*

14752. Will your books show that? – *I have no books.*

14753. Could you give us any idea how you incurred this expense? – *Horse-flesh and horse-feed.*

14754. You had your own horse there? – *But still it would require horse-feed, and horse-feed was expensive, and travelling about from one place to another, and meeting Sympathisers and drinking with them, would soon melt the money. Of course, you all being teetotallers, cannot see that.*

14755. What time were you engaged in those services? – *Seven or eight months, or perhaps before.*

14756. What time were you engaged in this work? – *Evenings and nights, Saturdays and Sundays.*

14757. Never during school hours? – *No, that would not have done.*

14758. How much did you receive altogether? – *£80.*

14759. Did not you receive nearly £180? – *I cannot say.*

14760. Would you be surprised if it was £180? – *I would, indeed, be surprised if it was over £100.*

14761. Your first letter is August 1879, and your last letter is dated in March 1880; it must be a pretty good drinking outlay to spend all this £180. You commenced in August 1879, your first letter to Mr. Nicolson, and your last letter is 18th March 1880; that is about seven months; that is about £20 a month? – *I did not receive £100 altogether, I am sure.*

14762. Did Mr. Nicolson always express himself satisfied with your efforts? – *He did not.*

14763. When did he first begin to show dissatisfaction? – *I could not tell you exactly.*

14764. I have a letter here before me, January 26th 1880, from you?[179] – *It would be about that time.*

14765. In which evidently, from the tone of it, Mr. Nicolson has been declining to pay the sums you demanded; was that so? – *He did not decline, but he said he would have to consult his superiors; he thought I had gone to too much expense.*

14766. As a matter of fact, did he pay you at that time the amount you asked? – *I do not exactly remember.*

14767. 'The information I referred to I gave you at Benalla on the 12th. My expenses, which I positively understated at £25, you said you were not in a position to pay in full until you had consulted with your chief. You stated that you would write to him on the next day (13th), that you would probably receive his reply by return post, and that you would communicate with me at once. You did not do so. Beyond remitting the £6, you said nothing as to the balance of my expenses, nor do you in the letter I have just received.' That would be the 12th of January that he objected to pay any more apparently? – *Yes, about that time.*

14768. And you stopped supplying any intelligence from that period? – *No, I met him after at Wangaratta, and he paid me the balance; and on another occasion I met him in Benalla.*

14769. You say—'As to your hints re my intelligence being 'manufactured to raise money upon,' I do not believe that you think so. For this reason, that you know that I do not receive a penny for my information, and therefore have no inducement to stoop to such an infamous imposture.' Did Mr. Nicolson hint to you that he was not satisfied with the way your information was coming? – *He did on that occasion. He said it raised unpleasant suspicions when I was so slow in coming down, after returning from the bush after my Christmas holidays.*

---

179 - This letter referred to in 14764 is missing from the Wallace file held by the PROV.

A perfect deluge of writing

14770. There is one question I think you ought to answer candidly—have you supplied to the police one particle of information that you think upon mature consideration helped to catch the outlaws? – *I think so.*

14771. At what date did you supply it after receiving it? – *All through.*

14772. I have read your correspondence over, and I confess I cannot find any information. I have read until I am weary. It is a perfect deluge of writing, with not a particle of information in it. I may tell you that the members of the Commission are strongly of opinion that the information in no way contributed to the success of the capture, and was from the first unreliable? – *(No answer.)*

Report by Detective Ward, which Wallace says is concocted

14773. Here is a report from Detective Ward of 26th August 1879:—'North-Eastern District, Beechworth Police Station, August 26th 1879.—Memo.—I have the honor to report, for the information of the Assistant Commissioner, James Wallace, schoolmaster, Hurdle Creek, came into Beechworth on Saturday, 23rd instant. He had a horse and buggy with him. He purchased a bag of bread and a case of brandy, half a dozen of pocket handkerchiefs, one bottle of scent, and a package of arsenical soap. Tommy met him by appointment from the Saturday previous. When he was in Beechworth also he told Tommy he came to see him to go to Melbourne with him, to try and get Graham Berry and the Marquis of Normanby to sign a reprieve for Joe Byrne by giving information to the police where the other three could be caught. He said he would arrange everything if Tommy would go with the police, but he should get £2,000 out of the reward, and cautioned Aaron if it could be arranged that he should take good care not to go as a target to the front. He said Constable Slater was the best friend the Kellys had; he told his friends the movements of the police, and the Kellys heard it shortly after. He also said that Sergeant Harkins, of Wodonga, heard something about a shanty four miles from Wodonga; that the Kellys heard it and changed their quarters. He said Byrne is treasurer and confidential for the gang; that their money is running short; they have only £500 and the gold. He wanted Aaron to go to Chiltern or Wodonga to sell the gold for him, and he would be well paid for it. Aaron refused, and said he was too well known to Sergeant Lynch, of Chiltern. He said he had 50 or 80 ozs.; that it would be melted down into 20-oz. pieces. He suggested to get a man with Aaron to go digging in the Stony Creek, near Beechworth, for a week or so, and then they could sell the gold. He made arrangements for Aaron to go to Hurdle Creek to his place on Friday evening (but not to cross the river before dark), when some arrangement would be made for the sale of the gold and the trip to Melbourne. He said Joe Byrne came to his place on Thursday night the 21st instant; that he wanted him to see Aaron and find out if he (Aaron) was after them yet; if so, to tell him he would know the consequences. He said Joe is frightened that Ned will sell himself and Hart through some of his friends. He said unless Byrne could be got free they would shortly stick up a bank, and the first thing they would stick up is Oxley, as there is whip of money there. He said he wanted to have a conversation with Detective Ward, to try and find out what was the opinion of the police as to whether the Kellys were in the country or not, he wanted Aaron to shoot Ward, and it would be left on the Byrnes. Tommy states that he had about nineteen or twenty National Bank notes on him; that he spent about seven or eight pounds on Saturday night. On Saturday the 16th instant I met Mr. Wallace on the Beechworth road, near the Golden Ball. He was going to Beechworth. He said he would see me in Beechworth on that night, but failed to do so. I found on Sunday the 17th he spent a good part of the day at Sherritt's. On Saturday the 23rd I met him in Beechworth. We went into a public-house, and had several drinks. In course of conversation he asked me if I thought the Kellys were in the country. I said I thought they were. He said, 'Why do you not catch them?' In conversation it came down to this—the pardon of one to catch the other three. He said 'That is worked out; it can't be done.' In payment for a round of drinks he pulled out a National Bank note, and passed it to me and remarked, 'It is a pity you have not got the numbers now,' and 'You could do good.' I replied and said, 'Not at all, you are a friend of mine, I would take no action.' He left me and spent money very freely during the night. Tommy slept with him at the Imperial hotel, High street that night. They left at about seven am, for Mrs. Sherritt's, where he remained until about twelve o'clock noon, when he left for home. Tommy accompanied him as far as the Golden Ball. There is no doubt of him being a warm supporter of the gang. Strict watch will be kept on him in Beechworth when he comes in.—M. E. WARD, Dect. 2358. I have been to Sheepstation Creek on yesterday. After coming back, saw Mrs. Sherritt, who is of the opinion that they will shortly give a call at her place. If they do, she will immediately let me know.—M. E. WARD Det. 2358.' Had you any conversation of that sort with Aaron Sherritt? – *None whatever. It is a concocted report all through. It is a fact I bought things, though not all the things mentioned there. I got bread.*

14774. Is it the fact that you stopped there for the night? – *Yes.*

14775. Were you in company with Sherritt? – *Yes.*

14776. Can you tell us in what respects you say this report is concocted? – *In respect to the conversation at least. It is stated Sherritt made this report to Ward. I state that is altogether untrue; I never had any such conversation with him.*

14777. Sherritt might make those statements to Ward? – *Well, it is untrue that that conversation occurred between Ward and me.*

14778. Might not that occur between Sherritt and Ward? – *That might occur, because on that evening Sherritt was sent for by Ward. It is a fact that I was with Sherritt there, and I drove home and called at the Sherritts'.*

14779. Had you any conversation with him then? – *I did, but not like that.*

14780. In what are the circumstances incorrect? – *That part which states that I wanted him to do certain things for the outlaws, and that I was a friend of the outlaws, and other things. Of course I had to assume the role of Sympathiser, and was advised to do so by Mr. Nicolson, in order to carry it out.*

14781. Did you ever say that Byrne was in your place? – *I never did.*

14782. Was he, as a matter of fact, ever there? – *Not since they were outlaws; previously he was.*

14783. Can you inform the Commission on or about the date of the last conversation you had with Byrne? – *I cannot, it is so very long ago. It was shortly after his release from Beechworth prison, where he had been for some sentence or other.*

14784. Do you swear that you never saw Byrne or never spoke to him after the date of the committal of the murders? – *Only on that one occasion I have mentioned I never had any conversation with him.*

14785. By Mr. Nicolson (to the Commission).—You asked did he ever say to anyone that Byrne had been in his house, and he said no. (To the witness.) – Did you ever say that to the Sherritts? – *I may have done. I was instructed by Mr. Nicolson to lead them to believe I was a friend of the outlaws, and in communication with them. I may have made that statement to Sherritt.*

14786. By the Commission.—The fact is, you wish us to understand that you, as a schoolmaster occupied in the Government service at this time, were willing to engage in a position of this kind, regardless of truth or anything else, to assist in capturing those men? – *To a certain extent truth had to be sacrificed.*

14787. It was merely a question of degree then? – *Merely a question of degree.*

14788. Do you mean to say you were prepared to lie? – *I do not.*

14789. If you made this statement to Sherritt, would that not be untrue after the statement you have now made? – *It would be untrue, but I do not think I would have made that statement. I may have led him to believe it to a certain degree; but I am almost sure I never made that statement.*

14790. Did you not make the same statement to Captain Standish? – *Not that I remember; no, I am positive I did not. He was not misled by me in any way.*

Mr. Nicolson.—When I went to see this witness first in July, he denied that they had ever been at his house.

The Witness. – *I deny it still.*

14791. By the Commission.—This is a report of Detective Ward's, a month later, dated September 4th 1879.—[The same was read, as follows]:—'North-Eastern District, Beechworth Police Station, September 4th 1879.—Memo.—*Confidential.—I have the honor to report, for the information of the Assistant Commissioner of Police, I have seen Tommy this morning, and he has very little news. He gives his reasons for stopping so long at Wallace's is to try if Joe would call there, as he was expected but he did not call; but he states that he is certain Wallace knows their whereabouts, and can find them when he likes, but he will not sell Joe Byrne. Wallace and Tommy have made an appointment to go to Chiltern on Friday evening to try to meet a person who knows where Joe can be seen. I asked him if he would have any objection for me to be in Chiltern to see if Wallace would be there. He said, 'No you can come, and you might then get the gold when we are in the act of selling it.' Tommy states that the gang told Wallace they would not try the Oxley bank now, as there is too many police there—two troopers every morning when the bank opens; and another drawback, the ground is too soft. They are not going to do anything until the ground gets harder; they are frightened of the black boys. The gang were at Richardson's shanty, on the Chiltern and Wodonga road, about three weeks ago. Joe Byrne told Wallace that Grace Quinn had Sergeant Kennedy's watch and chain, as Byrne wanted to get the watch to return it to Mrs. Kennedy. They are very sorry for the shooting of Kennedy. Tommy says by the description of the person who gave him the threatening letter it must be a man named Jack Fox, a particular friend of the Byrnes. He received a sentence of nine months, some six years ago, for stealing a horse from Mr. Kennedy, of the Woolshed. I am not at all satisfied with Tommy's tale. I am of opinion that he has seen Joe Byrne himself; and most likely he is the identical person who gave the letter to Jack to post, and kept out of the way until yesterday himself. However, he assures me that we will get them, and that before long. I am giving him money to go to Chiltern to keep the appointment with Wallace. If you Would advise, I would like to go and be somewhere concealed, and watch the movements of those two, as, if they are there, there is some move on the board.—M. E. WARD, Det. 2358.'*—You have heard that report read? – *I say it is totally untrue so far as I am connected with it.*

14792. Did you never make any appointment with Sherritt? – *Yes, but not of that nature. On one occasion I was out in the Chiltern direction, when my horses got away, and I made an appointment to go out the following Saturday if they did not come home. The rest has all been built up on that. Sherritt was to look for the horses on the Woolshed Ranges, and of course all these circumstances were reported to Mr. Nicolson.*

Detective Ward's examination of Wallace, including Wallace's insinuations against him

14793. To Detective Ward.—Do you desire to ask any questions of Mr. Wallace?

14794. By Detective Ward.—The only question I would ask, with your kindness, is—have you and I been on friendly terms all this time you were writing? – *The reverse, I should say.*

14795. Did you always speak and shake hands with me? – *We have always done that certainly, but I have been told by every one that you ran me down behind my back, and so on; and said I was in the pay of the police, and a Sympathiser at another time.*

14796. You referred in your letters a deal as to my immoral habits—can you point out one instance of your own knowledge during the time that you knew me. On your oath, is there a man in the North Eastern District more highly respected amongst the respectable citizens of Oxley and Beechworth than I am? – *The Commission.—It is no use asking that question.*

14797. By Detective Ward.—Do you know anything personally about it? – *I know no one in the North-Eastern District who bore a more unenviable character for immorality than you yourself.*

14798. Can you give any instances? – *Tampering with the pupil-teachers—the girls—in the Beechworth State school.*

14799. Give the name? – *I cannot.*

14800. By the Commission.—Was there any stir made about that at the time? – *I believe so—only from report and through others. I believe Captain Standish made an enquiry into the matter, and it was hushed up.*

14801. Did you hear anything of the result of that enquiry? – *I did not.*

14802. By Detective Ward.—Any other person? – *I have heard you are the father of several illegitimate children.*

14803. Will you just give one if you can. To a man like you, with such a knowledge of the world, one is nothing—give half a dozen? – *It was currently reported in the North-Eastern District that you were the father of the illegitimate child of Miss Mason of Tarrawingee.*

14804. Who told you that; I want an oath on that; what year was it? – *I cannot give the year.*

14805. Was it seven years or ten years ago? – *Within two or three years ago.*

14806. Are you aware where I was the last three years? – *Knocking about the North-Eastern District.*

14807. When did I go there? – *I cannot say.*

14808. Did Miss Mason tell you? – *No, it was currently reported—that was all.*

14809. Can you give me the name of someone? – *I cannot.*

Detective Ward.—I have no more questions. I defy Mr. Wallace or any other person, as far as I am concerned: and another thing I most distinctly say, that I had no knowledge of this man being employed in any way till the Commission sat.

14810. By the Commission (to Detective Ward).—Did you say in the presence of anyone that he was employed? – No, I could not.

14811. By Mr. Wallace (to Detective Ward). – *You did not say so in the presence of James Doig and this witness?* – No.

Nicolson's questions to Wallace

14812. By Mr. Nicolson (to the witness).—There is one question I would ask—was it not currently reported that Joe Byrne was the scribe of the gang? – *Yes.*

14813. When you offered your services, was it one of your designs to volunteer to reduce this collection of writing of Byrne's into shape for him—was that not the arrangement with myself? – *That I should endeavor to get hold of this diary.*

14814. And get the confidence of the gang through that? – *Yes, that was the point I went into the bush for, to receive this diary, and I missed them some way or other.*

14815. By the Commission.—Did you ever get the diary? – *No; I left the district, and I would not know whom to apply to. There is one point I should like to mention—I was asked if I received payment from any member of the police but Mr. Nicolson. On one occasion, in visiting Mr. Nicolson, I received a sum of money from Captain Standish. Of course I regard that as coming from Mr.*

Nicolson, as it was with him I had all the communications; and along with the money I received a message to the telegraph operator, in case I wished to communicate any hour of the night.

14816. By Mr. Nicolson.—Was there any person present in the room? – *Captain Standish and yourself; that is all I think.*

14817. Do you remember the amount? – *£25; and it was Captain Standish fixed that amount himself. I asked for an advance of money for expenses to do certain work, and I required a horse, and that contained sufficient money to procure a horse.*

14818. Do you remember the note he gave you to the telegraph office? – *Yes.*

14819. To convey the information to whom? – *To Captain Standish himself. I think it was, if I remember rightly, to the telegraph operator – 'Please forward telegram to me at once to Beechworth. Most important. The office at Beechworth is open all night.—F. C. STANDISH, Chief Commissioner of Police.'*

14820. Was not the description of the late Sergeant Kennedy's watch publicly known? – *I did not know it.*

14821. Were you not aware it was known publicly? – *No more than speaking to you in conversation about the stains; you remarked you believed it was a presentation to him.*

14822. You remember on that concluding correspondence with me. You say you have got the balance of your money—the £19? – *Yes.*

14823. That concluded the matter? – *No, that did not conclude our relations.*

14824. As regards money? – *No, there were some expenses after, £5 13s. I claimed, and it was decided to let the horse stand for that.*

14825. Do you remember meeting me afterwards? – *Yes, on the Benalla platform.*

14826. Do you remember the 17th April, a Saturday? – *I do not remember the date.*

14827. When you reached that platform at Benalla, do you remember speaking to anyone besides a few words to myself? – *Mr. Graves, I think, was on the platform. I went down in the train with him the greater part of the way to Melbourne to Seymour.*

14828. You saw me on that day? – *Yes.*

14829. And you saw me at Wangaratta as well? – *I did.*

The Connor letter

Mr Nicolson asked for a letter to be read. The letter concerned was the Connor letter. The letter was read in full, except for the signature (Connor). The letter is discussed in Chapter 16, with a full transcript of the letter at Appendix 7.

14830. Mr. Nicolson.—Do you recognize any portion of that as your own composition? – *None whatever.*

14831. If anyone stated that they saw the original of that in your handwriting, would that be untrue? – *No, because the original of that was in my hand, after it had been sent to Mr. Graves.*

14832. Where was that? – *Graves was in correspondence with me about something and enclosed that, and asked my opinion about that.*

14833. Was that before I saw you that day in the train? – *I cannot say; I think it must have been afterwards. The letter was not anonymous; the signature had been evidently cut out in the copy that was sent to me by Mr. Graves, and I think that is the whole of the letter that was sent to me by Mr. Graves asking my opinion about it. I said I thought it had been concocted by someone on the Woolshed.*

14834. Was that before or after you went down to Melbourne? – *I cannot say.*

14835. You remember seeing me on the train as far as Benalla, and then you went on to Melbourne? – *Yes.*

14836. Did this come into your possession before or after? – *I could not say; it must have been after.*

14837. By the Commission.—Did you see the letter before it was sent to Mr. Graves? – *Never.*

14838. Did you know the writing? – *I did not.*

14839. You did not know the party who wrote it? – *I am positive I did not know. I had an impression, from the style, that it was written by a man named Murphy, on the Woolshed, from hearing Sherritt say that Murphy had written some articles that appeared in the Age on the same subject.*

14840. When Mr. Graves asked your opinion on that, what answer did you give? – *Generally, I think I said there was not much in it; there was some truth, but it was not altogether true. I do not recollect exactly, it is so long ago.*

14841. By Mr. Nicolson.—You state on your oath that you did not see that document before it reached Mr. Graves? – *I do. I did not see it or any part of it.*

The first time I saw it was when it was sent to me by Mr. Graves with some correspondence apart altogether from the Kelly affair.

* * *

The questions about the Connor letter completed the examination of James Wallace. The witness then withdrew.

After two days of questioning, the people of Yea would have been surprised to learn that Wallace was being treated as a suspected lawbreaker and not merely a witness to recent events in the North East. The questions directed at him had become progressively more aggressive over the course of the two days, while Wallace's answers were consistently evasive and sometimes contradictory. This, along with his 'flippant manner and reprehensible conduct', only served to antagonize the Commissioners.

Wallace would not admit any sympathy for the Kelly Gang or acknowledge assisting them in any way. He denied ever having had any of the gang at his house, but clearly failed to convince the Commissioners on this point. He had failed to report having seen Joe Byrne one night on the road between Bobinawarrah and Sebastopol. And he denied being the author of the Connor letter received by Mr Graves MP.

In frustration at his evasiveness, Wallace was asked, 'Have you supplied the police one particle of information that you think upon mature consideration helped catch the outlaws?' When he answered that he thought he had, one of the Commissioners rendered Wallace speechless by responding, 'I have read your correspondence over, and I confess I cannot find any information. I have read until I am weary. It is a perfect deluge of writing, with not a particle of information in it. I may tell you that the members of the Commission are strongly of the opinion that the information in no way contributed to the success of the capture, and was from the first unreliable.'

The Commissioners had failed to glean any admission or evidence of guilt from James Wallace. However, circumstantial evidence given by others prior to Wallace's appearance, and which would be given after his appearance, was damning.

Evidence given after Wallace's evidence

John Sherritt, Thomas Bolam (Inspector-General of Schools), JH Graves MP (who had just stepped down as one of the Commissioners), Captain Standish and Superintendent Hare were all questioned about James Wallace.

John Sherritt

John Sherritt was called to give evidence immediately after the Commissioners had finished their cross-examination of Wallace.[180] He answered numerous questions about his dealings with Wallace. Whilst he did not provide any evidence of Wallace's complicity with the Kelly Gang, he nevertheless contributed to the growing image of Wallace's dual character with a story about a cow that Wallace had stolen from the Sherritt herd and had then butchered for meat.

The Commissioners started their questioning of Sherritt by asking him about his occupation, to which he responded that he used to take contracts for fencing before he was sworn in as a member of the police force.[181] They then immediately got down to business with a series of questions relating to Kennedy's watch, which they obviously asked in light of the answers given by Wallace about this matter, and to the implication Wallace gave in his letters to Nicolson that the Sherritts were at some point in possession of the watch.[182] Sherritt denied that he or anyone he knew had ever possessed or seen the watch, or that he had ever told anyone that it had ever been in his possession. He told, though, that he had heard another party asking his brother if he could get the watch from Mrs Byrne. When asked who that person was, he replied that it was James Wallace, the schoolmaster.[183]

---

180 - Minutes of Evidence, evidence given by John Sherritt, Q14842–Q15039.

181 - Minutes of Evidence, Q14842–Q14843.

182 - Minutes of Evidence, Q14844–Q14850.

183 - Minutes of Evidence, Q14849.

John Sherritt told the Commissioners that there was a lot of information he could give that he wished would not be published. He had a lot to say, if he was allowed. At this point the press was requested to clear the room, and Sherritt's remaining evidence was heard in private. He told the Commissioners that he used to go to school with Wallace and had been at Wallace's house once or twice during the 20 months the Kellys were at large after Stringybark Creek.

In response to the Commission's questions, John said he was not aware that Wallace worked for the police, but that he had been warned about Wallace by Mr Nicolson, and also warned to be careful about what he said to him about the outlaws.[184] It is interesting to speculate about why Nicolson would have given this warning about Wallace – was he keeping an open mind about where Wallace's loyalties really lay?

When asked if he had supplied Wallace with any information on Ward, Sherritt answered, 'No; I knew what kind of character he was myself, if I had never been warned of him.' He then told of an incident where Wallace had stolen and killed one of the cattle that he kept in Wallace's paddock. The cattle had been placed there because Wallace had nothing to eat the grass – the arrangement being that Sherritt would remunerate him when he took the cattle out. Wallace told him that one of the cows had died, but then acknowledged that he had killed it himself. When the Commissioners put it to him that it was a serious allegation to bring against Wallace, Sherritt said he would not have said it unless he could bring witnesses to prove what had happened.

When asked what Wallace did with the carcase, Sherritt replied that he, 'Kept a quarter himself, sent a quarter to his father-in-law, and some more to his own people.'[185] (The historian Arthur Hall in *The Headmaster of Hurdle Creek* speculated that part of the slaughtered beast was likely enjoyed by the Kelly Gang camped in nearby Sawpit Gully.)

---

184 - Minutes of Evidence, Q14859–Q14876.

185 - Minutes of Evidence, Q14876.

Thomas Bolam, Inspector-General and Acting Secretary of the Education Department

Thomas Bolam gave evidence on 4 August 1881.[186] The Commissioners asked him whether he knew James Wallace, teacher, who was at Hurdle Creek. Bolam answered that he didn't know him personally but knew him professionally. He admitted that Wallace had always 'stood well' with the Education Department as a 'man of good character and a zealous teacher'. However, when asked about the reasons for Wallace's removal from the North East, Bolam answered as follows:

> *Rumours reached me that he was showing very friendly relations to the outlaws. I also heard that he was a schoolfellow of one of them. I at once examined old reports in the Education Department, and from those learned that he had attended the same school with Joseph Byrne, and that he had been in the same class with him for some considerable time. I saw that he had great facilities for assisting the outlaws – that his position as teacher of half-time schools enabled him to be constantly moving about, and in that way that he had opportunities of seeing them. I also saw that his position as postmaster gave him very great facilities for rendering them assistance: and taking all this in together I called upon Captain Standish, and pointed out to him that I was under the impression that the facilities which Wallace had for assisting the outlaws were so great as to induce him to render them some assistance, and the fact of his being a schoolmate, and evidently an old friend of one of the outlaws, would be likely to lead him to help them if it was in his power.*[187]

Standish agreed with Bolam's assessment and it was at this point that plans were made to remove Wallace from the North East.

---

186 - Minutes of Evidence, Evidence of Thomas Bolam, Q15040–Q15102.

187 - Minutes of Evidence, Q15056.

Of Wallace's endeavours to secure his former Hurdle Creek appointment for his brother, Bolam said:

> Mr James Wallace strained every nerve to secure that appointment for himself [Benalla East] but in his correspondence he showed a very great anxiety for us to put his brother into his place at Hurdle Creek. I thought that was unusual, and that there must be some ground for his showing this great anxiety, and my mind seemed to be satisfied that he was anxious to be in a position like Benalla, where he could get constant information and assist the outlaws still further, and at the same time he was able to communicate with them through Hurdle Creek and Bobinawarrah schools. His letters applying for the Benalla East school were of such a character as to lead me to be very suspicious that he had some ulterior object in view.[188]

Bolam told the Commissioners that it was his private impression that Wallace, although ostensibly assisting the police (something which he had only found out about during the previous day's proceedings), had not acted fairly by them. He added:

> I have heard all sorts of rumours, and I am quite satisfied in my own mind that he has been at heart ready at all times to assist the outlaws.[189]

When asked whether he thought Wallace was a desirable man to be retained in the Education department, Bolam replied:

> *I do not think it is desirable that we should retain in the service a man who would render assistance to those outlaws, but I feel there is a difficulty in our way in dealing with a case like this without proof.*[190]

---

188 - Minutes of Evidence, Q15083.

189 - Minutes of Evidence, Q15087.

190 - Minutes of Evidence, Q15088.

The Commissioners concluded their questioning of Bolam by asking if he had heard 'of any man being stuck up in the Beechworth district about Christmas 1878?' The robbery had been attributed to the Kelly gang, in company with a fifth man. Bolam answered:

> *Yes, I read accounts in the newspapers of the sticking up of the hawkers by the Kelly gang, and I was under the impression, from the accounts which I read (I have not kept them to refer to), that the stranger who was with the outlaws at the time very possibly was Wallace. This, I believe, was during the Christmas holidays, and I thought it was quite possible that Wallace would be with the outlaws at that time; but this is only a supposition of mine.[191]*

Bolam could not recollect whether he had read the account of the 'sticking-up case' in newspapers of the time, or later around the time when Ned Kelly was committed for trail at Beechworth.

The Hon. James H Graves MLA

On the same day he advised his fellow Commissioners that he had resigned from the Commission, Graves was sworn and examined as a witness.[192] In his introductory comments to his 'late brother Commissioners', he gave an overview of the Kelly family members and the men connected to them by marriage, and of how the removal of Constable Flood from the Greta district resulted in the Kellys and their friends and connections getting ahead. He also expressed the view that there had been missed opportunities to capture the men.

In relation to the Connor letter, Graves said he had made enquiries into the allegations made therein, and was satisfied that the greater number of statements were accurate. He subsequently passed the letter on to Captain Standish in the expectation that he would endeavour to remedy any defects.

---

191 - Minutes of Evidence, Q15089.
192 - Minutes of Evidence, Evidence of The Honourable JH Graves MLA, Q15488–Q15572.

The Commissioners asked him many questions about the Connor letter. They asked him if he had forwarded the letter to Wallace the schoolmaster. Graves answered that he wasn't sure. When it was put to him that Wallace swore that he did, he replied that he would not swear that he did not, but knew that he (Wallace) had seen it, because he remembered asking him about several particulars in it. Graves said he had shown the letter to half a dozen people for the purpose of ascertaining whether they believed the statements therein to be true.

Graves thought that Wallace might have known something about the letter 'because Wallace knew more about the Kellys than anyone else'. His impression was that Wallace could have told him who wrote it. When asked if he was still under that impression, Graves replied that he thought it was written by a constable of police. He was also satisfied that Wallace did not know anything about the letter prior to his receiving it. 'He might know many of the facts in it, but my own impression is, from my conversation with him, that he did not know of some of the contents of that letter.'

Graves was asked how long it had been before Wallace received the letter from him that he had last seen Wallace. He thought he had seen him about a month before the letter was written. He couldn't be entirely sure, though, because of the passage of time, but added that 'Wallace was the schoolmaster near Oxley, and I was constantly going by the train to Wangaratta, and I do not think I ever went there without seeing Wallace.' When asked if he might have perhaps seen him a few days before he (Graves) received the letter, he answered that he might have, but did not think that he did. 'I was constantly in the habit of seeing him, and I knew he was a schoolfellow of Byrne.'

It would seem that Graves was trying to downplay his relationship with Wallace. When the Commissioners pointed out to him that the letter was dated the 19th (April) and that Wallace swore he had an interview with him on the 17th, Graves answered that he had no recollection of such an interview. When the Commissioners told Graves that they thought Wallace had said he had travelled in the train with him on the 17th, or had seen him on the station, Graves didn't answer the question, alluding instead to Wallace's knowledge of the Kellys:

> *My impression was from the first, about this year 1880, that Wallace knew more about them than anyone else in my district, but I have no actual grounds for that except my own supposition. My own belief was that the principal time that the Kellys were out (this is a matter of mere belief) they kept in the immediate neighbourhood between Greta and Moyhu. Either at Glenmore Station, or on the Hedi Station...[193]*

Graves was then questioned by Mr Nicolson. The Connor letter had made certain statements about men under Nicolson's command not being allowed out of their barracks. The implication was that the men were not being effectively used in the way that Superintendent Hare had used them. Graves said that the statements in the letter were so extraordinary that he made a point of going to the district to ascertain the facts before he would communicate with Captain Standish about the letter, or bring the matter before Parliament. Having gone to the district, he found that men had been 'shut up in the barracks, and not employed'.

Turning his mind back to his meetings with Wallace, Graves thought that all he had spoken to him about was the matter of Ward's general conduct, and also about the probability of Aaron Sherritt being true or false.[194]

Nicolson asked Graves if he remembered telling Captain Standish at the time he handed him the Connor that he had not seen Wallace for several months.[195] Nicolson then referred Graves to a letter written by Captain Standish and dated 5 May 1880 in which Standish wrote:[196]

> *I saw Mr. Graves this morning. You are quite wrong in your surmises about the anonymous letter which I forwarded to you, as Mr. Graves assures me that Wallace had nothing to do with the writing of it, and that he (Mr. Graves) has neither seen nor held communication of any kind with Wallace for many months.*

---

193 - Minutes of Evidence, Q15506.

194 - Ward's conduct and the trustworthiness of Aaron Sherritt were, of course, two matters that Wallace constantly harped on about in his letters to Nicolson.

195 - Minutes of Evidence, Q15539.

196 - Minutes of Evidence, Q15540.

Graves answered that that would simply be untrue, for he had seen Wallace. He confirmed he had asked Wallace about statements in the Connor letter, and that he had done so because he believed Wallace knew so much about the Kellys. The only recollection he had of his discussions with Wallace was that they spoke about whether Detective Ward was a capable man and whether it was likely that Sherritt was selling the police. That was principally what he knew Wallace would know, from his having been a schoolfellow of Byrne's and knowing his private character.

Captain Standish

After Graves's evidence, Captain Standish was recalled for further examination on 30 and 31 August 1881.[197]

The Commissioners grilled Standish mercilessly about his condemnation of Nicolson.[198] As regards Nicolson's use of agents, he was asked if he did not think it was right after eight months lack of success (by Superintendent Hare) that another officer might try another system. The Commissioners were talking here about Nicolson's secret agency system. Standish replied that Nicolson had employed some agents who were in communication with the Kellys, whereas he himself had been very cautious, knowing so many were sympathisers. Out of the blue, though, the Commissioners asked him if he had had anything at all to do with Wallace the school teacher. Standish confirmed that he had.

After a series of questions about the Sherritts (John and Aaron), the Commissioners returned to Wallace, asking Standish if he had ever spoken with him.[199] Standish replied that Wallace had come in to see him shortly after he (Standish) had arrived at Benalla, when Wallace offered his services during the Christmas holidays. Standish said, though, that before employing a man of this kind, it would be necessary to make enquiries. He told the Commissioners, 'I found out shortly after that there were reasons why I should not employ him.' He

---

197 - Minutes of Evidence, further examination of Captain Standish, Q15774–Q15959.

198 - Minutes of Evidence, Q16014–Q16017.

199 - Minutes of Evidence, Q16033.

painted Wallace as unreliable from the beginning, putting great weight on an incident that occurred early in their association.[200] He described how he and a constable went to the Hurdle Creek School early one morning (not long after the Stringybark Creek murders). He told Wallace he was there to meet an informant. There was no informant, but he told Wallace there was to mislead him. On Wallace's invitation, the two men went into Wallace's house for breakfast. Standish said he was there for two hours and that Wallace told him that Joe Byrne was in the habit of visiting, but had not been there for some time. He then asked if Aaron Sherritt had been there recently, to which Wallace replied not for six weeks. However, on returning to Benalla, Standish said he found Aaron Sherritt was waiting to see him. Sherritt told him that he had just spent two days with James Wallace. This, Standish told the Commissioners, showed him that Wallace was unreliable.

Standish told the Commissioners that in his discussion with Aaron, Aaron told him that he had seen Byrne and had a long talk with him. Byrne had told Aaron that he was not disinclined to throw his mates overboard, provided that it was guaranteed he was not taken up by the police, and that the sum of £100 or £200 was paid to him to get out of the country.[201] Standish went on to say that Wallace came in to see him at Benalla very shortly afterwards, and that they had a long talk during which Wallace told him that Byrne had evidently decided he would not throw up his mates. He subsequently corrected himself by saying that Wallace's communication about Byrne was probably made in writing.[202]

Nicolson then had the opportunity to question Standish.[203] He asked him if he remembered Mr Graves showing him (Standish) the letter

---

200 - Minutes of Evidence, Q16034.

201 - Minutes of Evidence, Q16034.

202 - Minutes of Evidence. In Q16035, the Commissioners referred Standish to a letter from Wallace dated 29 August 1881. It is not known to whom this letter was addressed (perhaps the Commissioners?) as enquiries at the PROV and a Trove search has not uncovered the letter. It would seem, though, from the line of questioning put to Standish by the Commissioners that the letter included an account by Wallace of his interview with Standish at Hurdle Creek, in addition to other matters. Wallace must have said in the letter that he had written to Standish to the effect that Byrne would not give up his mates.

203 - Minutes of Evidence, Nicolson questioning of Standish, Q15894–Q15932.

signed Connor, to which Standish replied that he did. Standish added that he also recollected him (Nicolson) saying that he believed the letter had been written by Wallace.

Nicolson referred Standish to his letter dated 5 May 1880, in which he had referred to the meeting he had had that morning with Graves. Standish said that he recollected his conversation with Graves perfectly. Nicolson replied, 'Well, I do not wish to pay you a compliment, but I believe your evidence to be correct in preference to believing Mr Grave's contradiction.'[204]

The contradiction Nicolson was referring to was that Graves had (on the one hand) told Captain Standish on 5 May 1880 that he had neither seen nor held communication of any kind with Wallace for many months, only to admit under cross-examination that this was untrue.

Francis A Hare

Superintendent Hare was questioned about the evidence given the previous day by Captain Standish.[205] He was asked about the interview that had taken place between Standish and Wallace. Hare said he remembered advising Standish not to proceed with the interview, but that the interview took place after he (Hare) had left the district. When asked by the Commissioners if he been informed about what had taken place at the interview, he answered that it was about making an appointment to meet Joe Byrne in the bush (presumably for Wallace to meet with Byrne).

The Commissioners asked Hare about his use of agents. He was asked how many agents he had employed after he replaced Nicolson prior to Glenrowan. Hare answered that 'Diseased Stock' brought him information, and that he also had Aaron Sherritt, a man named Stevens, and another man whom he had sent out to Glenrowan two or three days before the Kellys were captured. After being prompted

---

204 - Minutes of Evidence, Q15931–Q15932.

205 - Minutes of Evidence, Evidence of Francis A Hare as relates to Wallace and his use of agents, Q16442–Q16657.

by the Commissioners, he had to admit that all these agents had, in fact, been formally employed by Nicolson, with one exception. That exception was Tommy (Aaron Sherritt) who Nicolson had dismissed ('No more payments for Tommy'), and who Hare therefore had to take on himself.

Nicolson had discharged most of his agents prior to Hare taking over from him in the week prior to Glenrowan. Hare couldn't recall how many agents Nicolson had discharged. He said he had heard Superintendent Sadleir say in evidence that there were certain agents that Nicolson did not feel right about handing over to him (Hare) without first consulting with them. Wallace would have been one such agent, although the reality was that by this time Nicolson had already dispensed with Wallace's services.

Nicolson then asked Hare a series of questions about Detective Ward.[206] He asked if he (Hare) had received any complaints about misconduct by Ward. Hare replied that he had received no complaints and that the inference of misconduct was due to Wallace. He added, 'I know he was always speaking against Detective Ward. I knew what kind of man Wallace was. I can read all those men, and I knew what he meant by his attacks on Detective Ward.'

Nicolson asked if, as far as he knew, there was any justification for Wallace's complaints? Hare replied:

> *No. Detective Ward was a most hardworking sober steady man, and he was a most valuable man in this way, that he could find any person I wanted in that part of the country of whatever description. He would bring him on the very shortest notice.*

On the final day of the Commission hearing evidence (20 September 1881), Mr Hare handed in three declarations (affidavits). Two were from police constables (Constable Phillips from the Police Station at Goornong, and Constable Fitzgerald from Yea), and the third was from a Yea grazier (James Webster). The declarations all cast Hare in a favourable light compared to Nicolson.

---

206 - Minutes of Evidence, Q17243–Q17246.

Constable Phillips's declaration also detailed a conversation he heard between Ned Kelly and Joe Byrne when they were inside Mrs Jones's hotel some 10 minutes after the first encounter. The conversation is of interest because it included Ned saying to Joe, 'I always said this bloody armour would bring us to grief.'

Before tendering the next two declarations, Hare told the Commissioners that he was handing them in as a result of Wallace having spoken about who he believed had been the writer of the anonymous letter (the Connor letter), in which certain things had been stated about Mr Nicolson and in which it was put that Nicolson should be removed from the district. He then handed in the two declarations.

The first declaration from James Daniel Webster read as follows:

> *I, James Daniel Webster, of Yea, in the colony of Victoria, grazier, do solemnly and sincerely declare that previous to Superintendent Hare giving evidence before the Police Commission, as follows, viz.:—'That a schoolmaster in the North-Eastern district had been acting as an agent for the police, and identifying him as a school-fellow of Joe Byrne,' I had several conversations with 'Wallace' at Yea (where he is now stationed) on the subject of the Kelly business, and he frequently stated that the outlaws were much harassed by the tactics adopted by Mr. Hare, and were afraid of him, as he constantly kept them on the move. He further stated that they (the outlaws) had great contempt for Mr. Nicolson for the mode he used for capturing them. He (Wallace) not only made this statement to me, but I am informed he has also made the same statement to other persons residing at Yea. And I make this solemn declaration conscientiously believing the same to be true, and by virtue of the provisions of an Act of the Parliament of Victoria rendering persons making a false declaration punishable for wilful and corrupt perjury.—J. D. WEBSTER. Declared before me, at Melbourne, in the colony aforesaid, this 18th day of September, in the year of our Lord One thousand eight hundred and eighty-one—J. B. Motherwell, J.P.*

The second declaration from Constable Fitzgerald read as follows:

> *Yea, 19th September 1881.—I, James Fitzgerald, of Yea, make affidavit that soon after the destruction of the Kelly Gang of bushrangers at Glenrowan, James Wallace, State school teacher, stated to me that the gang were in terror of the means of pursuit adopted by Mr. Hare—that he always kept them moving about, whereas under Mr. Nicolson's mode of pursuit they felt content and safer. Wallace also stated that the hired agents worked better and were more faithful to Mr. Hare than any other of the police officers, and that was an additional reason the outlaws had of fearing Mr. Hare.—J. FITZGERALD. Signed and swore before me at Yea this 19th September 1881—J. D. Webster, a Commissioner of the Supreme Court of Victoria for taking affidavits.*

Hare also submitted his own affidavit, in which he downplayed the reliability of the information provided to him prior to Glenrowan by the agent known as the 'Diseased Stock Agent' (DSA). Nicolson had stated that a few days before Aaron Sherritt was shot, DSA had given reliable information that the outlaws were out and intended to make a raid. However, Hare declared in his affidavit that the only information furnished to him was simply that the outlaws would soon make a raid on some bank, as they were short of money. He stated that he had been told by Mr Sadleir, in the presence of the informant, that the agent had constantly been giving similar information for many months past.

The Commissions' recommendations re Wallace

The Second Progress Report of the Royal Commission was issued on 12 October 1881. The recommendations as they related to James Wallace were damning.

> *That in consequence of the reprehensible conduct of Mr. James Wallace, the State school teacher of Hurdle Creek, during the Kelly pursuit, and his alleged sympathy with the outlaws, together with the unsatisfactory character of his evidence before the Commission, your Commissioners think it very undesirable*

> *that Mr. Wallace should be retained in any department of the public service. We therefore recommend his immediate dismissal from the Education Department.*

The report included a concisely written sketch (summary) of the events that led to the destruction of the Kelly Gang.[207] At page xxii, the Commissioners referred to the anonymous letter sent to the Honourable JH Graves MP that unsparingly criticised Mr Nicolson's character and conduct throughout the pursuit. The Commissioners noted that the letter had been signed by 'Connor' but that this was evidently a fictitious name. The Commissioners stated that:

> *The witness Wallace, a State-school teacher, and an alleged Sympathiser with the gang, was the putative writer of the document, but he denies the allegation, and subsequently, in a communication addressed to your Commission, he declares that it was the joint concoction of Jack Sherritt and the outlaws, in order to have Mr Nicolson removed from the district. But Wallace's bona fides and veracity are open to grave suspicion, and his flippancy of manner, when before your Commission, apart from his evidence respecting his equivocal relations with the gang, mark his statements as wholly unreliable.*[208]

---

207 - The sketch comprised the following chapters: I – The Kelly Family; II – The Kelly Country: III – Causes of the Outbreak; IV – The Wombat Murders; V – After the Murders; VI – The Sebastopol Raid; VII – Inspector Brook Smith in Pursuit; VIII – Provisioning the Outlaws; IX – The Euroa Bank Robbery; X – Captain Standish and Supt. Hare in Charge of the Pursuit; XI – The Queensland Trackers; XII – Mr Nicolson Resumes Charge of the Pursuit; XIII – Mr Nicolson's Recall; XIV – Superintendent Hare Supersedes Mr Nicolson; XV – Glenrowan.

208 - The communication from Wallace to the Commissioners referred to in this paragraph is not included in the Appendices to the Second Progress Report.

20
The fallout from the Royal Commission

Within a month of the release of the Commission's Second Progress Report, Wallace was suspended as head teacher at Yea State School. He would remain on full pay, however, until 10 May 1882 when his employment with the department was finally terminated.

James and Barbara were devastated by this turn of events. Wallace had lost his professional reputation and doubt had been cast on his integrity. If he could no longer work as a teacher, how could he continue to provide for his steadily growing family?

Wallace visited Thomas Bolam at the Education Department, asking to see the evidence against him and requesting a board of enquiry. He wrote letter after letter to the Education Department, the newspapers, and to politicians asking to be reinstated. He began to realise that all doors were closed to him.

Throughout the latter months of 1881 and early 1882, the political fallout from the Kelly saga continued. The Royal Commission report was damning in its assessment of James Wallace, but did not spare the leading lights of the police investigation, either. The recently retired Captain Standish, Chief Commissioner of Police, was severely criticised for his lack of leadership and judgement and for the difficulties this caused his officers. Assistant Commissioner Nicolson and Superintendent Hare were both recommended for retirement from the police force (both would become police magistrates). Detective Ward, whilst found to have rendered active and efficient service during the pursuit of the gang, was also found guilty of misleading his superior officers on several occasions, and was censured and reduced a grade. And Sergeant Steele was censured for his actions at Glenrowan.

Wallace took steps through his acquaintance with a member of parliament to obtain access to the Royal Commission's report. Not only did he get to read the report, but he also tore out and souvenired a page (page 583) containing Captain Standish's answers to questions relating to his dealings with Wallace.[209] A Wallace descendant still holds the souvenired page, which contains annotations by Wallace where he has tried to pick apart Standish's answers. At the bottom of the souvenired page, he wrote:

> *In this page Captain Standish admits himself to an untruth on his own part. Where Aaron Sherritt's version does not correspond with mine he prefers to believe the evidence of a convicted criminal who had been mixed up in all the horse stealing crimes of the Kellys for years. He says in par. 16033 that he found out there were reasons why he should not employ me. Yet he afterwards not only advanced me £25 for a horse & other expenses, but lent me a revolver & ammunition and gave me a written order on the telegraph service. Then he admits (par. 16036) that on the whole my statements are true.*

Wallace was looking for a way out of his predicament and picking apart the evidence of the Chief Commissioner was a good start. Wallace makes some good points – the evidence showed that he had received £25 from Standish, and his claim when giving evidence that Standish had loaned him a revolver went unchallenged. Wallace would later incorporate these points into a letter he would write to *The Age* newspaper in response to a damning article it published about him, titled 'Wallace, the Schoolmaster'.

Wallace was an avid reader of newspapers. A Wallace family member possesses copies of articles and letters that appeared in various newspapers, all carefully copied by hand by James for his future reference, as well as notes he wrote for himself and drafts of letters

---

209 - Minutes of Evidence, questions 16033 to 16036 relate.

that he sent to the Education Department, Nicolson and others.[210] Wallace took particular interest in editorials and letters to editors that questioned the fitness of the Royal Commissioners and the legality of the Commission's recommendations.

One article copied by Wallace appeared in *The Argus* of 19 October 1881. *The Argus* reminded its readers that when the Commissioners were appointed, the newspaper had drawn attention to the unfitness of some of the gentlemen selected. Speaking of the Chairman, they had said at the time, 'For this post a man of good judgement & with a clear head is necessary, and the Ministry has selected the most wrongheaded and prejudiced man in the Assembly.' *The Argus* considered some of the other Commissioners to have been little, if any, better. The editors concluded that the Commission had made illogical findings that bore distinct traces of strong animus and petty spite. They considered that recommendations based upon an enquiry that was conducted so unfairly were not worth the paper on which they were recorded.

Another article titled 'Opinion of the Press', which appeared in *The Australian* on 22 October 1881, was also of interest to Wallace. It expressed the view that discussion of the merits or demerits of the Police Commission was rendered superfluous by the fact that the greater part of the recommendations were *ultra vires*. Further, that the evidence the Commission allowed itself to listen to day after day made it the laughing stock of the community and showed its total unfitness for the judicial duties it had assumed. Nothing was said in this article, though, about how the press had come to this opinion.

The Seymour Express in its 4 November 1881 edition noted reports that Mr James Wallace the state school teacher at Yea had been suspended in consequence of his alleged sympathy with the late Kelly Gang. In the name of British fair play, it called for a protest against such highhanded conduct:

---

210 - These documents are held by a Wallace family member who has requested to remain anonymous. The notes and draft letters cover a period immediately after the Royal Commission, continuing to the time Wallace was in Queensland. The author was allowed to photograph all of the documents.

> *To convict a man before he has had an opportunity of making his defence is contrary to all rules of equity and law. No doubt at the proper time Mr Wallace will be able to give a satisfactory explanation of his part in the affair.*

Wallace would use this denial of natural justice argument the following year in a letter to the editor of *The Age* in response to its 'Wallace, the Schoolmaster' article.

The Argus of 20 November 1881 reported that Wallace had applied to the Minister for Education for a full enquiry into his case. It expressed the view, though, that it would be inadvisable to appoint a board to review the action of a commission. Wallace disagreed and wrote (underlining his words for emphasis) beneath his handwritten transcript of this *Argus* article:

> *It would be most unjust in the absence of direct proof to maintain that Wallace personally knew anything of, or had any complicity in the doings of the gang immediately prior to Glenrowan, or, indeed, at any period during which he was acting for the police. The most that can be urged is suspicion.'*

In contrast with the *Argus* article, Wallace was in full support of a single sentence letter that appeared in the *Evening Mail* on 25 November 1881 that read, 'No doubt Mr Wallace is entitled to a full opportunity to defend himself from the allegations made to his detriment.'

Wallace also liked the 3 and 10 December editions of *The Town Talk*.

The Town Talk of 3 December 1881 complained that Wallace had been singled out for special attention and suspended from the Education Department for his alleged sympathy with the outlaws, while others (albeit policemen like Messrs Nicolson and Hare) who the Commission had found against were still in employment:

> *Even-handed justice is not always the law of the land, although we boast of a remarkably clever jurisprudence, both legislatively and judiciously. There seems to be some strange hitch, to say the least of it, or malversation of justice, to say the worst of it,*

> in regard to the case of Mr Wallace, state-schoolmaster at Yea, recently suspended for alleged sympathy with the late members of the Kelly Gang. As we are aware, the report of the board has been treated in most quarters as so much waste paper, but Mr Wallace has been quietly suspended. If the report is worth the paper on which it is written, why, we would ask, has not every other 'suspect' been treated in the same way? The board proposes to do away with the services of Messrs. Nicolson, Hare, and others, and to reduce a dozen. The Government have done nothing in this most important direction, but they have succeeded in only temporarily dealing with a country schoolmaster – and that to his injury. It seems monstrous that he should be singled out for absolute persecution, and loss of temporary employment at least, while other men, according to the remarkable report of the board, are able to enjoy all the emoluments of their position. The matter certainly should be dealt with promptly, and Mr Wallace should no longer be left in doubt as to his ultimate fate. If he is to be judicially hung, well and good; if acquitted, the sooner the better.

The Town Talk of 10 December 1881 sarcastically reported on how Wallace's case was now being considered by the Education Department:

> State-school teacher Wallace, discharged from his employ by the recommendation of the Police Commission, but only suspended by a more merciful (?) Government, has had a supreme satisfaction. After strenuous protests against the maltreatment he received at the hands of the commission in being brow-beaten, dazed almost to death by a volley of questions (some most purposeful in a certain direction, as the context may yet show; others, purposeless altogether), in evidence being given against him in his absence, without his having permission to be present; in his being denied not once, but repeatedly, a copy of that evidence after the decision of the commission was given – after all, he has received his reward indeed. His case 'is being considered by the department?'

> *Now, do our readers know what that means in any Government office, and most of all in the Education department? We do. It means a wearisome struggling with bungling administration and red-tape clerkism which may end perhaps on this side of the grave perhaps not. Pause, Mr Wallace; do not attempt to get justice, but borrow a copy of 'Bleak House', and ponder over the mysteries of Jarndyce and Jarndyce, the fate of Miss Flite, and other minutia of the Court of Chancery. If, however, you manfully determine on proceeding, do so with boldness, and demand your rights, even at the foot of the Speaker's chair.*

Wallace must have been buoyed by all these reports condemning the way he had been treated by the authorities. Towards the end of the year, he wrote a report of his own responding to the Commission's findings against him, which he sent to Thomas Hunt, Member of the Legislative Council for Kilmore and Anglesey.[211]

Mr Hunt tabled Wallace's report in the Legislative Assembly on 14 December 1881.[212] He moved, 'That there be laid before this House the report of James Wallace, formerly State school teacher at Yea, in reply to the finding of the Police Commission.' His motion was agreed to after being seconded by Alfred Deakin.[213] It would be fascinating to read what Wallace had to say in his report, but the report cannot be found in either the PROV or the Victorian Parliamentary Library archives.

---

211 - Thomas Hunt was an Irish Catholic who settled in Kilmore after arriving in Victoria in 1858. He became a journalist and in 1865 founded the *Kilmore Free Press* and then went on to acquire or establish several other country papers. He became a member of the Legislative Assembly in 1874 and held the seat of Kilmore and Anglesey between 1877 and 1888. He was an early supporter of Sir Graham Berry and the ideal of a 'yeomanry' of smallholders. His association with Irish and Catholic affairs and public figures was close and continuous and he attained the status of a leading voice in the Irish community before the end of the 1860s. (This Information about Thomas Hunt MLA is sourced from the *Australian Dictionary of Biography Vol. 4* and Thomson K & Serle G, *A Biographical Register of the Victorian Legislature 1851–1900*, ANU Press, 1972)

212 - Hansard, 11th Parliament, Vol. 38 (Nov–Dec 1881), page 1178.

213 - Alfred Deakin – refer *Australian Dictionary of Biography, Vol. 8*. https://adb.anu.edu.au/biography/deakin-alfred-5927 Deakin would one day become Australia's second Prime Minister.

In March 1882, *The Age*, *The Argus* and *The Daily Telegraph* reported on how Sergeant Steele, against whom the Commission had made adverse findings regarding his conduct at Glenrowan, had been exonerated in a subsequent Board of Inquiry. Wallace underlined those parts of the articles that he considered might be helpful to him in any future appeal.

The Age article of 15 March 1882 had reported that Sergeant Steele, who had protested against the findings of the Police Commission and had asked for a board of inquiry, had had his request granted. It reported that three stipendiary magistrates had been appointed to enquire into the charge of reckless shooting at Glenrowan of which Steele had been accused. The Board of Inquiry did not take long to consider the matter – *The Argus* on 31 March 1882 reported that it had not only exonerated Sergeant Steele of the charges against him, but had also complemented him. *The Argus* reported:

> *The board commenced by saying that they 'took steps to insure the attendance of all witnesses who gave evidence against Sergeant Steele and whom he had no opportunity of cross-examining.'*

> *Here we have a picture given of that burlesque of justice which delighted Mr Longmore and Mr G. W. Hall and against which we felt called upon to protest in the interests of society. Not only in the case of Sergeant Steele but in many other instances evidence was taken behind a man's back, and the first the accused knew of a charge being seriously entertained against him was the intimation that he had been found guilty and sentenced.*

The Daily Telegraph of the same date also reported upon Sergeant Steele's acquittal:

> *The results of the inquiry affords evidence of the hasty manner in which conclusions were jumped at by the majority of the police commissioners and gives another proof of the necessity of pausing before carrying out their recommendations.*

> *Fortunately the suggestions of the commission were not acted upon or gross injustice would have ensued.*

The newspaper reporting on the conduct and conclusions of the Royal Commission would lead you to think that major errors of judgement had been made. Much was said about evidence being taken behind people's backs with no right of reply, with that certainly being an issue with respect to James Wallace and Sergeant Steele. It has to be remembered, though, that the Commission was not a court of law. The purpose of the Commission was to inquire into the conduct of the Police Force of Victoria and to try to determine the reasons why the Kelly Gang was able to remain at large for so long, with the Commission successfully identifying dysfunction at the top of police command as the primary reason.

Many citizens in Kelly country were shocked at the Commission's criticism and censures of the police and rallied to support the district's police officers. The adverse findings against Sergeant Steele, who the Commission had recommended be demoted, was a particular concern of people in Wangaratta, who had in October 1881 held a public meeting to generate support for Steele. Ultimately, the Board of Inquiry corrected the record and Sergeant Steele succeeded in having his demotion overturned. The Board found that the adverse findings against him had come about as a result of false information being given against him in evidence by another officer.

Wallace took a particular interest in the reports about the Commission's findings against Sergeant Steele being overturned on appeal. He underlined the sentences in *The Argus* and *The Daily Telegraph* reports about the charge against Steele coming about as a result of evidence having been taken behind his back, which he was never given the opportunity to challenge. In Wallace's mind, the same thing had happened to him! Wallace was unsuccessful, though, in having a board of inquiry appointed to consider his case. Had he been successful, he might well have found himself in even more trouble.

From the time he was relieved of his duties in November 1881, Wallace started collecting references from people who would vouch for his good character. One reference was from a missionary named Archibald Mills, who resided in Yea. He wrote on 7 January 1882:

> *I have known James Wallace for the last 18 months during his residence in Yea as the state school teacher, and have found him to be both honourable and respectable in all his dealings, and as a teacher has attended to his duties, and performed them with diligence and punctuality, and has given great satisfaction to the parents for the progress the children have made under his training.*

Another reference was from Alexander Lang JP who was a member of the Board of Advice at the time Wallace was teaching at Hurdle Creek. He said, 'I have known Mr J Wallace late of Hurdle Creek for a number of years and have always found him to be honest and upright and well-spoken of.' He went on, 'I consider him to be a good teacher, kind and gentle with the children and attentive to his duties.'

There was also a reference from John Loch JP who wrote that he had known Wallace for 15 years, going back to his time as a teacher at the El Dorado school. Similarly, the four members of the Education Board of Advice for Central Riding of Oxley (at the time Wallace was at Hurdle Creek) wrote a letter where they concluded that if Wallace had committed an error (then) 'it was an error of judgement and not of inclination to do wrong'.[214]

The references were obtained by James in the hope he could use them to persuade the Education Department that he should be retained as a teacher. However, he was misreading the situation entirely. His worth as a teacher was not what was in question.

At the same time that he was arguing his case and collecting references, Wallace was also taking steps to liquidate his assets. He very quickly sold his selection at Bobinawarrah to his neighbour Charles Lloyd, who owned the land immediately to the north of Wallace's land. Charles was the Oxley Shire engineer and was not related in any way to the Lloyds at Greta who were well-known Kelly sympathisers. Wallace would have needed to use part of the proceeds from the sale of his property to repay the £125 mortgage he had taken out several months prior to the siege at Glenrowan.

---

214 - Robert Wood, JP Chairman; Daniel Cozens, Correspondent; Alex Simpson, Member; and GH Brown, Member.

Wallace also sold his goods and chattels to his brother Andrew, who was the proprietor of the Yea Coffee Palace. The sale contract was dated 28 December 1881. For the sum of £30, James sold Andrew his 'goods and chattels as standing in or upon his messuage or tenement situate at Hastings Cottage and depasturing on the Yea Town Common'. The sold items comprised:

> *(In Hastings Cottage) one chest of drawers, two mirrors, kitchen furniture including cooking utensils, crockery and glass wear, two pair of single lamps, one eight-day clock, twelve volumes of books including family bible and album; and (Depasturing on Yea Town Common) one grey horse branded W on shoulder, two red and white cows one branded OM (and) the other unbranded.*

James then entered into a Memorandum of Agreement with Andrew whereby he would pay him one shilling and sixpence each week to hire back the very goods and chattels he had just sold him. The agreement states that the goods had been absolutely sold and that there was no verbal or other understanding between the parties that after the payment of a certain amount of rent the goods shall again become the vendor's property.

The contract with his brother shows that Wallace was in quite a desperate financial predicament. With the impending loss of his teaching job, he needed all the money he could get his hands on. He may also have been preparing for possible flight, knowing that the police detectives were conducting investigations into his role in keeping the Kelly Gang at large.

The sale contract between Wallace and his brother Andrew was witnessed by James Webster, the father of Charlotte Webster who worked with Wallace at the Yea State School. James Webster was a Yea landowner who was also a Commissioner of the Victorian Supreme Court for the taking of affidavits. Webster had himself prepared an affidavit, which was one of the three affidavits tendered to the Royal Commission by Superintendent Hare. In that particular affidavit, Webster described how Wallace had stated in conversations with him that the tactics adopted by Mr Hare in pursuit of the Kellys were more effective than those adopted by Nicolson.

Interestingly, the comments attributed to Wallace by James Webster had many parallels with statements that had been made in the Connor letter. Wallace sometimes just didn't know when to shut up!

21
The search for evidence of Wallace guilt

Within a month of Glenrowan, the police were seeking information that might bring people who had assisted the gang to justice. A strictly confidential memo dated 1 July 1880 from Frank Secretan, Inspector-in-charge of the Police Department Detective Office stated:

> *The Government are extremely anxious to obtain evidence against the persons who made the armour for the gang, and also against any other persons who have aided and abetted them since the first police murders. Any action that may be taken will be under the criminal law and practice statutes.*

Police investigations continued into 1881 and overlapped the sittings of the Royal Commission. The nature of the questions put to Wallace at the Commission shows that he was suspected of being an active sympathiser, and his answers reinforced that suspicion. The Detective Department did not wait for the Commission's report to be handed down before they started investigating him. Wallace would have been well aware of the police investigations as word would have filtered back to him from various sources.

A considerable number of reports on the 'Special enquiry re James Wallace' were prepared by Detectives Considine and Ward.[215] A transcription of all the reports is included at Appendix 8.

---

215 - The Kelly Historical Collection at PROV (VPRS 4966).

22 December 1881 report by Detectives Considine and Ward

This first report by the detectives ran to 16 pages and highlighted the methodical nature of their investigations. It starts with them reporting that they had first proceeded to Beechworth on 8 December where they saw James Francis Kelly (unrelated to the Kellys of the Kelly Gang), a schoolmaster near Beechworth, who they knew had an intimate knowledge of Wallace's friends both in the neighbourhood of Beechworth, Hurdle Creek and the King (Valley).

Mr Kelly was the head teacher at State School 1740, located on the Beechworth–Melbourne Road. He had a record of trouble with parents, the School Board of Advice and the police at Benalla and Beechworth. The end came when he started daily pub crawls 'flying from one public house to another'. In August 1883, at the age of 30 years, he was dismissed by the Education Department 'for conduct unbecoming of a teacher'.[216] However, there is nothing in the detectives' report to indicate that Mr Kelly provided them with any helpful information.

The day after visiting Beechworth (9 December) the detectives proceeded to Oxley and Milawa, where they made some cautious inquiries about purchases that Wallace had made from some of the stores there. They had heard that he had purchased a greater quantity of tinned fish (and other provisions) than he or his family could consume.

They also heard that one night during the time the Kellys were at large, Wallace had asked a man named James O'Neil if he would go to the Whorouly property of a Mrs Connors, an aunt of Joe Byrne's, to warn her of an impending police raid on her property.[217] The Kellys were supposedly at the property on the night concerned. Wallace had apparently been told of the proposed raid by Captain Standish and wanted to send a warning, but O'Neil refused.[218] Wallace then sought out a man named Dwyer to see if he would go instead, but he also

---

216 - This information about James Francis Kelly has been taken from *Pioneer Teachers of the Kelly Country*, chapter 6, 'Problem Teachers'.

217 - One wonders if this Connors family, related by marriage to Joe Byrne, might have been the inspiration for Wallace's signing off the letter to Mr Graves as being from 'Connor'.

218 - It is unclear when or how (or why) Captain Standish might have informed Wallace of this pending visit by troopers to the Connor residence.

refused. The detectives said they did not consider it advisable (perhaps 'necessary at this stage' would have been a better reason) at that stage to question either O'Neil or Dwyer, but reported that as the information had come from a reliable source, they had no doubt of its truth.[219]

The detectives also reported that they had been informed that towards the end of 1879, a youth named (Alexander) McGreggor, who was about 17 years of age and attending Ballarat Grammar School, had received a letter from Wallace (to whom he was personally known). Enclosed within Wallace's letter was another letter addressed to Miss Kate Byrne care of Beechworth Post Office, which Wallace instructed McGreggor to post. McGreggor did as instructed, but had first shown Wallace's letter to a school mate named Munro (who was by this time the assistant clerk at the Court of Petty Sessions in Wangaratta).

The detectives had also heard about and then visited what would later become known as the 'hut behind the school':

> *Having heard of the discovery of a hut in the bush near Hurdle Creek we proceeded there and found that a bushfire had destroyed the hut 15 x 11 feet situate at the foot of One Tree Hill, opposite a gap leading into Saw Mill gully through which there is a direct track leading to Wallace's late school Bobinawarrah at a distance of about four (4) miles, through an unsettled district. The hut we were informed was built some six or seven ago by some splitters and fencers who occupied it at that time, but since then we failed to find out any person who occupied or heard of its being inhabited…*

> *… the neighbourhood appears a most isolated one the nearest house being about three (3) miles where the herdsman David McCallum resides, he it was in company with a neighbour named Doig discovered the recent occupation of the hut. They state it contains three (3) bunks, two (2) large and the (1) double over which attached to the roof were grab rope loops as if used for hanging up guns.*

---

219 - The detectives did not divulge the source in their report.

> There was a quantity of empty bottles both inside and outside the hut, none of which had any labels. (We ourselves saw a number outside the hut). There were also a few tins but not many. There is a spring of fresh water close to the hut, the only one within miles. Both McCallum and Doig have no hesitation in saying that the hut had the appearance of having been occupied within the last two (2) years, though by whom they cannot say, but on being questioned as to their opinion on the subject they said there could be but little doubt but that it was occupied by the outlaws as had anyone been working such as splitters etc in that neighbourhood they could not help knowing it.

The detectives worked their way back to Beechworth but failed to find anything important, other than that it was the opinion of several respectable residents that Wallace was an active sympathiser of the outlaws. They then called upon Mrs John Sherritt (at Sheep Station Creek), who told them of various visits they had received from Wallace. She said that Wallace had called at her place in August or thereabouts and borrowed an old saddle that he failed to return and subsequently paid her £3 for. Not long after that he called by again, this time in a buggy, and asked her – in her daughter Mary Jane's presence – whether she had any mouldboards for sale.

Mrs Sherritt also remembered Wallace, once again with his buggy, calling at her place on or about 23 August 1879. She saw that he had a quantity of stores in his buggy, including bread and a case of brandy. He had dinner at her house and left in company with Aaron. The detectives reported that:

> Mary Jane Sherritt can corroborate her mother's statement with regard to Wallace borrowing the saddle and wanting to purchase mouldboards etc and adds that she frequently saw Wallace at Mrs Byrne's (mother of Joe Byrnes outlaw) house, where he (Wallace) had various meals and usually slept on the sofa, this was during the time the outlaws were at large, viz. 1879.

It would transpire that James O'Neill and Dwyer – who Wallace had tried to send off to warn the Kellys of a pending police raid – had both been working at the time at the property of Mrs McGreggor, whose son was the young man who Wallace had asked to post the letter addressed to Miss Kate Byrne.

After a short break in their investigations due to Detective Ward having to attend court in Melbourne, the detectives travelled to John Dwyer's selection on the King River. They questioned him about what they had heard had passed between him and Wallace. Dwyer admitted that Wallace had asked him to do a certain thing for him, but refused to tell them anything more. That refusal was taken by the detectives to be a sign that the information they had previously obtained was correct.

Fearing that Dwyer would try to communicate with O'Neil, the detectives proceeded that evening to Hurdle Creek to interview him. After a good deal of pressure, O'Neil told them that he had called at Wallace's house sometime in 1879 and that Wallace had asked him if he would do him a favour. He had told him he had heard that the Kellys were at Mrs Connors' house, and asked if he would go and warn them that a body of police were to be sent there. O'Neil said he refused, whereupon Wallace turned to his wife (Barbara Wallace) and said he would go himself. His wife started crying and told him that if he persisted in going, she would not be there when he returned. Wallace then asked him who else might go and that was when Dwyer's name came up. Wallace then went with O'Neil to call on Dwyer. O'Neil said he did not hear their conversation, but knew that Dwyer did not go to warn the Connors.

The detectives interviewed Mrs McGreggor, who they said was a most respectable person. She confirmed that O'Neil had called Dwyer out of her house one night during the time the Kellys were at large. She told them that mysterious hints as to the speedy capture of the Kelly Gang were thrown out by O'Neil at the breakfast table the following morning.

Alexander McGreggor was also questioned about the letter he received from Wallace while he was at school in Ballarat. He confirmed what the detectives had heard, and added that after he returned home Wallace had asked him if he had received his letter and whether he had posted the enclosed letter as he had asked. Alex said he told Wallace that he had done as asked, and described how Wallace had laughed the matter off.

The detectives next headed to Hedi to interview Edward Burke who Wallace had referred to in his evidence at the Royal Commission as a sympathiser:

> *After making these enquiries at Hurdle Creek we on the following day returned to Hedi and on the day after saw Edward Burke referred to in Wallace's evidence given before the Police Commission. He (Burke) of course denies in toto Wallace's allegation that he was in communication with the late outlaws and states that he had no conversation with Wallace relative to them at all. He admits going on a trip with Wallace about Xmas 1879 but says they only went to the Wonnangatta River Gippsland, calling at the township of Hawksdale. They took a pack horse with them.*[220]

> *At the outset we had little or no hope of obtaining any information from the man Burke as from our knowledge of*

---

220 - A Christmas trip to the Wonnangatta River would have been quite an undertaking, requiring in the order of 10 days. A bridle trail ran between Wangaratta and the Wonnangatta, and it is likely that Wallace and Burke would have accessed this track near the headwaters of the Rose River. The reference by the detectives to Wallace and Burke having called at the township of Hawkesdale is a mystery though, as there was never a township by this name in the Wonnangatta River area. However, there was a pastoral run known as Eaglevale Station at that time and it is possible that when the detectives came to write their report, they mistakenly wrote Hawkesdale instead of Eaglevale. Alternatively, another 15 miles or so down the Wonnangatta River there was an old gold mining place called Hawkhurst, so perhaps the detectives had mistakenly written Hawkesdale instead of Hawkhurst. The handwriting in the detective's report is very clear and the report definitely says Hawkesdale, but as noted above there was no township or locality by that name at the time (or even now). Given the lengthy nature of a pack horse trip to the Wonnangatta River, one wonders if there was a purpose to the trip. Undertaking a trip like this simply for enjoyment would have been unusual in those days and while Wallace may have had the luxury of Christmas holiday break from school, a selector like Burke certainly didn't have such a luxury.

> his character he being a reported cattle duffer and an associate
> of criminal class in this district, but his name having been
> mentioned by Wallace in his evidence before the Commission we
> deemed it advisable to see him.

The detectives report then turned again to Wallace's purchase of stores at Oxley and Milawa. They found that between 24 June and 11 September 1879, Wallace had purchased tea and sugar at Dunlop's store, Oxley, that was largely in excess of what he would require for his own private use, and that he had subsequently made various cash purchases, one of which Mr Dunlop remembered particularly being for about £2 worth of tinned fish.

As the destruction by fire of the 'hut behind the school' also destroyed the tins and other material around the hut, the detectives decided not to push their inquiry into Wallace's purchase of the tinned fish, as they felt word would have got back to him and put him on his guard. They felt their inquiries had up to this time been made in such a manner that no one would suspect their true object (being the establishment of a link between the tinned fish sold by Mr Dunlop, and the burnt-out tins at the hut site).

The detectives then turned to Wallace's relationship with the Byrne family. They referred to his statement (at the Royal Commission) where he said, 'That I can solemnly swear and am prepared to swear that it is over fifteen years as far as I can recollect since I spoke to Mrs Byrne on any subject whatsoever.' This they said was distinctly contradicted by the statement made by Miss Sherritt (Mary Jane Sherritt). To catch Wallace out, they proposed that the saddles the police took possession of at Glenrowan after the capture of the Kelly Gang be sent from Benalla to Beechworth so they could be shown to Mrs Sherritt and her daughter, to see if they could identify any of them as the saddle Wallace purchased from her (Mrs Sherritt).

The report ended as follows:

> In conclusion we would beg to state that if the object of this
> inquiry is to prosecute Wallace, we do not think that sufficient

evidence can be obtained to sustain a conviction for the following reasons. 1ˢᵗ owing to the length of time that has elapsed and the inability of people to fix or remember dates. 2ⁿᵈ the unwillingness of persons to come forward and give evidence in a public court.

That in the present state of feeling on the matter in this District, such a prosecution would be anything but advisable. If on the other hand the result of this inquiry is to justify the findings of the Commission and action taken by the Government in Wallace's case, sufficient evidence can be obtained to prove beyond a doubt that Wallace was an active sympathiser of the late Kelly Gang.

29 December 1881 report by Detective Ward

This report from Detective Ward describes his enquiries in Yea, and his efforts to identify the saddle that Wallace acquired from the Sherritts.

Ward reported that he proceeded to Yea on Friday 23 December. He made careful enquiries, but could obtain no information. He reported that James Wallace and his three brothers were in town and carefully watched his movements.[221]

Ward reported that he left Yea on the Saturday having given instructions to the local constable (Constable Fitzgerald) to try to elicit information from a publican there named Purdy. Ward had heard that Wallace had told Purdy that he had often carried tinned fish and preserved meat to the outlaws. Constable Fitzgerald reported back that although Purdy would say nothing at the present time, he was of the opinion that he

---

221 - Andrew and William would have been two of those brothers: Andrew Wallace, the next eldest after James, was the proprietor of the Yea Coffee Palace; William Wallace was teaching at Boundary Creek State School while boarding with James and Barbara at Yea. The third brother was most likely 19-year-old John Wallace, whose movements later seemed to shadow James's. The Wallace brothers were close. William was certainly a Kelly Gang sympathiser like his older brother. Andrew and John may not have been active sympathisers like James and Andrew, but would have rallied around James in his hour of need.

would speak the truth and give good evidence for the prosecution if he was subpoenaed.[222]

After leaving Yea, Ward returned to Beechworth from where he and Senior Constable Mullane rode down to Sheep Station Creek to contact the members of the Sherritt family who could identify the saddle bought from them by James Wallace, and which was afterwards found in the possession of the Kelly Gang at Glenrowan. John Sherritt subsequently called at Mullane's private residence in Beechworth where he was shown three saddles, one of which he was able to pick out as his. His daughter Anne Jane Sherritt also called at Mullane's residence later that day and also picked out the same saddle, which she said Wallace had taken away from her father's place in July or August 1879.

Ward made inquiries in and about Beechworth, Black Springs, Woolshed and Sebastopol, but reported that he was unable to obtain any further information. He reported that Constable Mullane would investigate further, he being on very friendly terms with Mrs Byrnes and various other persons, including Cornelius O'Donaghue who he thought might be able to give further information about Wallace's movements – unless they had been 'got at' by Wallace or his brothers.

In January 1882, under instruction from the Crown Law Department, Detectives Ward and Considine undertook further investigations into Wallace's activities. They sought out associates of Wallace and any piece of evidence that might link him conclusively to the Kelly Gang.

17 January 1882 report by Detectives Considine and Ward

The detectives' first report after receiving the Crown Law Department instruction was undated. However, the report contains a chronological summary of the detectives' travels commencing on Saturday 7 January,

---

222 - It seems Wallace was unable to keep his mouth shut, particularly when drinking. As when he flashed the National Australia banknote in front of Detective Ward at that hotel in Beechworth, telling a publican at Yea that he had supported the outlaws was another example of reckless behaviour. It possibly also reveals that a certain type or class of person might not have been outraged at such an allegation, and that Wallace might have confided in Purdy on the assumption that he was of such a class.

which enables us to work out that it was written on 17 January 1882 at Glenrowan. This is reinforced by a letter the detectives wrote on 27 January 1882 that details their subsequent travels, starting with them being at Glenrowan on 17 January.

The report includes details of enquiries the detectives had made into whether Wallace's father had ever been a dealer in old metals; into Wallace's purchase of several pairs of mole-skin trousers of a larger size than he would wear himself; into statements Wallace was reported as having made at Bobinawarrah about seeing Joe Byrne; into the relationship Wallace had with the Woolshed blacksmith named Straughair who was suspected by the people there of making Joe Byrne's armour; and into the chain of possession of the saddle that Wallace had purportedly purchased from the Sherritts and which was found in the aftermath of Glenrowan.

The following table summarises the enquiries the detectives made over the 10 day period, as documented in the letter:

Date	Nature of enquiries
Saturday 7 January 1882 El Dorado	The detectives enquired into whether Wallace Snr had ever been a dealer in old metal. Wallace Snr was visiting Yea at the time of their visit, but they learned that he only dealt in butter, eggs and the like, and was not known to deal in old metals. The detectives instructed a local constable, who knew nothing of the nature of their enquiry, to visit Wallace Snr on his return and ask him if he had ever dealt in old metals in the previous three years. The pretext for making enquiries was that they were investigating copper plates that were stolen sometime before, and were making enquiries pursuant to the Metal Dealers Act.
Sunday 8 January 1882 Hurdle Flat & Stanley	The detectives interviewed a state schoolmaster named McAlice [sic] whose friends resided in Oxley near Hurdle Creek.[223] He informed them that Wallace had apparently purchased several pairs of moleskin trousers of a larger size than he could wear himself from a storekeeper in Wangaratta. However, he had no specific knowledge of this – it was just information that had been commonly reported since Wallace's suspension.

---

223 - McAlice was the schoolmaster Crawford McAliece, who had been James's best man when he married Barbara Allan in 1874.

Monday 9 January 1882 Black Springs & Newtown	The detectives interviewed Mr Vale, the schoolmaster at Hillsborough (a town to the south-east of Beechworth). Mr Vale informed them that a Mr Hugh Ferguson of Hurdle Creek had told him of a day when Hugh, in company with others, was at the Bobinawarrah Post Office at a time it was reported that Joe Byrne was sick. They were speaking about Byrne when Wallace came out of the post office and said it could not be true as he had seen Joe the night before and he was all right then.
Tuesday 10 January 1882 Woolshed	The detectives interviewed Mrs Sherritt Junior, who informed them that Wallace was very friendly with a blacksmith named Straughair in Woolshed who was suspected by the people there of making Joe Byrne's armour. Straughair was also particularly intimate with Mrs Byrne.
Wednesday 11 January 1882 Wooragee	The detectives proceeded to Wooragee where John Sherritt Senior was employed working in the bush. However, they were unable to see him.
Thursday 12 January Wooragee	The detectives met with John Sherritt Senior and obtained his statement.
Friday 13 January 1882 Woolshed	The detectives interviewed a confidential person at Woolshed about the connection between Wallace and Straughair. They ascertained Wallace was on very intimate terms with Straughair and used to leave his horse there when visiting the Sherritts or Byrnes, and also that Straughair used to work late at night. The detectives reported that they had very little doubt that Straughair made Joe Byrne's armour, but due to the length of time that had elapsed there was no feasible chance of obtaining any proof.

Saturday 14 January 1882 Wangaratta & Milawa	The detectives tried (but failed) to obtain any corroboration regarding Wallace's purchase of trousers (moleskins) in Wangaratta. They then proceeded to Milawa where they saw the storekeepers there, namely a Mr Colin Gardiner and a Mr Warren. They learned from Mr Gardiner that Wallace was a credit customer with a running account, whose supplies were entered into a book. While there did not appear to be any suspicious items booked to Wallace's account, Mr Gardiner and his daughter Isabelle told them that Wallace had also made frequent cash purchases of tinned fish, as well as bread and sometimes a bottle of brandy. He made those cash purchases at night after the store was closed, during the time the time the Kelly Gang was at large, but they could not give dates. Mr Warren allowed the detectives to see his books, which showed nothing suspicious with Wallace's purchases, with the exception that on 11, 16 and 18 of August 1879 he had purchased 29 loaves of bread, which seemed largely in excess of what he required for his own use. None of those purchases were cash purchases, however.
Sunday 15 January 1882 Oxley, Moyhu & Hurdle Creek	The detectives proceeded to Moyhu. Wallace did not appear to have dealt with the storekeepers there, despite frequently visiting the hotel and store.[224] However, they learned from a storekeeper named Mr Lewis of a suspicious transaction by a young man named McAuliffe (a well-known sympathiser) who had paid for some purchases with a Bank of New South Wales £5 note that was doubtless one of the Jerilderie bank notes. The detectives next visited Mr Ferguson of Hurdle Creek, who admitted to having had a conversation with the schoolmaster McAlice [sic] relative to Wallace having said something about the outlaw Joe Byrne. He had not himself heard Wallace say it, but had only repeated what he had heard from others. However, he could give no information about how he had come to hear the information, or the names of anyone who had heard or taken part in the alleged conversation. The detectives therefore put the matter down to being an idle rumour upon which no reliance could be placed.

---

224 - It seems the 'store' visited by Wallace was different to the premises operated by the storekeepers, but it is not clear what the difference is.

Monday 16 January 1882 Returned to Wangaratta enroute to Benalla	In Wangaratta, the detectives saw Mr Munro. He denied that Mr McGreggor had ever shown him the letter the detectives had referred to in their previous report (the letter that Wallace had asked McGreggor to post from Ballarat). He stated, however, that he had had a conversation with McGreggor at Hurdle Creek on the subject, but that this was after they both left school. The detectives considered that McGreggor must have been mistaken in his statement to them about the matter, and that the information would not be admissible as evidence.
	On reaching Benalla, the detectives set to work to trace the saddle identified by Mrs Sherritt. They thought it very doubtful that the saddle could be traced to the possession of the Kelly Gang (because it had not actually been found in the Kelly's possession, but rather in the stable at the McDonalds Railway Hotel).
Tuesday 17 January 1882 Glenrowan	The detectives obtained the names of all the constables who were stationed at Glenrowan with a view to ascertaining who took possession of the saddles and other property brought there by the Kelly Gang. Eight saddles had been taken into possession, of which two had been given up to Mrs Skillion (Ned Kelly's sister). The remaining six saddles were still in the possession of the Benalla Police.
	The constables through whose hands the saddles were supposed to have passed were scattered throughout various districts, but would all be contacted in an effort to trace the chain of possession of the saddles. Particular attention was to be given to tracing the saddle that had been identified by Mrs Sherritt (the one that had been purchased by Wallace), with a view to tracing it to the possession of the Kelly Gang. As two of the saddles recovered at Glenrowan had belonged to the murdered police, it was hoped that if the saddle identified by Mrs Sherritt had been found at the same time and place as those two saddles, it would prove conclusively that they were one and all brought there by the Kelly Gang.

The letter ends with the detectives reporting that they would proceed to Shepparton the following day (which would be Wednesday 18 August) to make enquiries there. Detective Ward would then proceed to Wallan Wallan and return to Melbourne with a file of the Wangaratta Despatch 1880 containing the serial 'Christmas in Kelly Land' of which Wallace was the author.

18 January 1882 – statement taken by Detective Considine

While at Katamatite (a small settlement to the north-east of Shepparton), Detective Considine took a statement from Mrs Fanny Cox on 18 January 1882. Mrs Cox's statement is as follows:

CONFIDENTIAL

Forward to Mr Harriman and Mr Chamley, ACCP Witness
FANNY MARY GRACE COX, states,

I am a married woman and reside with my husband who is a police constable at Katamatite. In September 1879 I was single: my maiden name was Rogers. My father kept an hotel at Beechworth and I managed a shop there for him. I know James Wallace, late school teacher at Bobinawarrah. He used frequently to stay at my father's hotel whilst in Beechworth, and he has purchased tinned fish from me on several occasions, I cannot now recollect how much. He generally used to leave the Hotel at Beechworth either very late at night or early in the morning. How I know this is that he used to ask me to leave the back door open, saying that he would be off early. In September, previously mentioned, I was staying at Mr Allans at Oxley[225]: whilst there I went on a Saturday to have tea at James Wallace's house at Bobinawarrah. Wallace was there whilst at tea. Wallaces have a boy, a child about six years old, who was sitting next to me at the table. While playing with my watch chain, he whispered to me 'Ned Kelly has not got a watch and chain like you,' and added, 'do you know Ned Kelly?' I said to the child, 'No, I don't know him.' He said 'he was here the other day and gave me a shilling.' I think Wallace must have overheard what the child said, as he, Wallace, asked me, 'what has the child been saying to you Miss Rogers?' I said 'he has been telling me that the Kelly's have been paying you a visit.' Wallace then said, 'don't take any notice of

---

225 - Mr Allan at Oxley was Wallace's father-in-law.

> *what the child has been saying.' He appeared very much annoyed and told Mrs Wallace to put the child to bed, and I heard him being slapped afterwards.*

Mrs Cox's statement was sent to the Acting Chief Commissioner with a separate cover letter dated 21 January 1882 requesting it be forwarded to Mr Harriman of the Crown Law Office.[226] The cover letter was headed 'Re James Wallace, suspected of aiding and abetting the Kelly Gang'.

27 January 1882 report by Detectives Considine and Ward

On 27 January 1882, the two detectives sent their next report. A good portion of this report is irrelevant to the investigations into Wallace, but what is relevant is the further investigations they conducted into the chain of possession of Mrs Sherritt's saddle.

On Tuesday 17 January, they had interviewed Mounted Constable Alexander at Glenrowan. On Wednesday 18 January, they had interviewed Constable Bracken at Wallan Wallan and Constable Shellard at Shepparton. This was the same day that Detective Considine took the statement from Mrs Fanny Cox that was of such importance that it had already been separately sent to the Acting Chief Commissioner. On Friday 20 January, the detectives interviewed Constable Major at Colac, and on Tuesday 24 January, they interviewed John Sherritt, presumably at Woolshed. The interview with John Sherritt produced the following statement, which was included in the detective's report:

> *I known James Wallace for many years we were school mates*
>
> *I remember 1878 when the police were murdered at Stringy Bark Creek by the Kelly Gang. I knew the Kelly Gang as Byrne was a school mate of Wallace's and mine. I remember all the time the Kellys were at large, and I know James Wallace was an*

---

226 - VRPS 6888 Reel 2.

active sympathiser of the gang. I had a very good opportunity of judging it as Wallace frequently came to me and my brothers William and Aaron and wanting us to go out into the bush with him on horseback to make tracks to deceive the police and to try what the black trackers were made of but on all occasions I declined to have anything to do with him.

I remember Wallace borrowing a saddle from my mother in the month of August 1879 he promised to return it but he failed to do so. About a fortnight after this he paid my mother £3 for the saddle and said he could not return it.

I also saw Wallace at our place on a Sunday in August 1879 he came from the direction of Beechworth he had a horse and buggy with him in the buggy he had a bag of bread and meats and tinned fish. He had dinner at our place on that day and left going in the direction of Hurdle Creek.

Wallace was constantly annoying me with questions, viz. if I could tell him the movements of the police, to try to ascertain for him how many were stationed in Beechworth and what was their opinion as to whether the Kellys had left the country or not.

Wallace told me that Joe Byrne was in the habit of calling at his place that he was a good fellow and would do him no harm. On the occasion when annoyed by Wallace as to the movements of the police, I told him that I saw four (4) mounted men going down the old El Dorado road, he (Wallace) immediately went to Mrs Byrnes and informed her of what I had told him. This I am certain of for Patsy Byrne told me immediately. Wallace was on the most intimate terms with Mrs Byrne and all her family and was a frequent visitor during the time the Kelly Gang were at large.

This report by Detectives Ward and Considine highlights the exhaustive efforts they made to obtain the evidence that would be required to secure a conviction against Wallace. In relation to the Sherritt saddle, it was not enough for them to know that Wallace had provided this to the gang – it had to be provable in a court of law. The detectives were playing it fair.

30 January 1882 report by Detectives Considine and Ward

This was the detective's final report. They had done all that they could to compile evidence against Wallace, but had not been able to obtain any fresh information with the exception of Mrs Cox's statement, which they hoped would be of some value. As regards the saddle that Wallace had purchased from the Sherritts, they concluded that the evidence connecting this to the Kellys was weak as it had not actually been found in the Kelly's possession, but rather in the stable at the McDonalds Railway Hotel.

* * *

One wonders what information about Wallace's activities might have been uncovered had his wife Barbara been called upon to give evidence at the Royal Commission. As the Royal Commission was not a court of law, there would have been no reason not to call her (and every reason to have done so!). However, as Detectives Ward and Considine were undertaking investigations with a view to a possible prosecution of Wallace, they would have been disinclined to interview Barbara Wallace due to the convention that spouses may be exempted from testifying against their spouse.

22
The Crown Law Office calls for the Wallace file

Inspector William Montfort, the Police Superintendent in Benalla, had been sent a confidential note by Mr Harriman of the Crown Law Office, asking his opinion about the case against Wallace. Montfort replied by letter dated 13 January 1882 that the investigations had been undertaken (they were, in fact, still in progress) by the detectives without his involvement and that he was therefore not in a position to enter into the merits of the case against Wallace.[227] He did, however, express the view that:

> ... it would be highly impolitic from my point of view to bring him before a court, not from any tenderness towards him or the witnesses, but because of the effect such a course will in my opinion, produce amongst the people in the Kelly country, so far as giving us information in future.

Montfort added, however, that if Mr Harriman was determined to proceed with the case, he would assist to the best of his ability. He also offered to meet with Mr Harriman in relation to the matter. And just in case Mr Harriman might have thought he was insincere in his efforts to help bring Wallace to trial, Montford ended his letter by saying:

> I regret that you should be under the impression that sentiment would lead me to wink at crime, in any shape or form, and no-one can undeceive you upon that point better than the Attorney General who has known me personally for many years.

---

227 - This letter by William Montfort is one of six letters – all that remains of the formerly more comprehensive Wallace File from the Kelly papers held by the Public Record Office, Melbourne.

By the end of January 1882, Mr Harriman had become impatient. On 31 January he shot off a memo in his inimitable, hard-to-read scrawl to the Chief Commissioner of Police asking if he would be so kind as to send the Wallace file to his office. The file was sent to him that same day.

On 4 February 1882, Mr Harriman sent off another memo: 'Please allow L.O. (Law Office) of Melbourne to pursue enquiries, re having papers for further investigation. All facilities to be approved.'

On 14 April 1882, he sent a follow-up note: 'What have you to report? We are getting tired of delay and want some information at any rate, as the matter cannot be delayed any longer.'

In the end, the lack of concrete evidence combined with concerns about inflaming the people in Kelly country, resulted in the case against Wallace being dropped.

Wallace, of course, was unaware that charges against him would not be forthcoming. Later in the year (1882) he would leave the state and stay away until the heat had well and truly abated.

23
Wallace appeals his dismissal

On 10 May 1882, James Wallace was officially dismissed from the public service when his salary was finally terminated. He had been on suspension on full pay since October.

Mr Bolam, Secretary of the Education Department, wrote to Wallace on 12 May 1882 to tell him that his case had received full consideration and that the Department's decision was final.

Wallace was not a man to give up easily, though. On 18 May, a few days after receiving Bolam's letter, he wrote to The Hon. JM Grant JP, Chief Secretary and Minister for Education, complaining that Bolam had given him no reason for his dismissal. Unless he was told what he had been charged with, he was unable to produce rebutting evidence in his defence. He suggested some mistake had evidently occurred, or perhaps the pressure of more important business had prevented Grant from considering the case himself. He could only infer from the newspapers that his suspension had been due to the Commission having considered him a Kelly sympathiser, which he could prove to be erroneous.

Always one to add a bit of colour to his letters, Wallace said that after he had been informed that the Minister (Grant) was considering his case, he had waited for the outcome while his wife and children starved. That was a rather dramatic statement, considering he had been kept on full pay for more than six months!

Wallace solemnly and sincerely declared:

> 1. *That the contract entered into by me with the Victorian Government through their representative the Asst. Comr. of Police has been duly and religiously carried out on my part.*

2. *That I gave more genuine, immediate, and useful information to the Police than any other person did – information that should have led to their capture long before.*

3. *That I never in any way assisted or countenanced the outlaws and never entertained the slightest sympathy with them.*

4. *That I never to my positive knowledge met, or had any conversation with them.*

5. *That I never visited them, and that they never visited me during the term of their outlawry.*

6. *That beyond a simple salutation in passing, I never at any time spoke to a member of the Kelly family.*

7. *That since leaving school on the Woolshed Creek I did not meet with the outlaw Byrne more than half a dozen times altogether during a period of 14 or 15 years preceding his outlawry.*

Wallace's appeal to Grant was as verbose as his letters to Nicolson had been. He complained that he had been 'gratuitously impugned by the Commission on the strength of the malevolent imagination of certain witnesses whose evidence was taken in (his) absence'. He complained that 'much stress had been laid upon the fact that (he) did not immediately report his meeting one night with the person who might have been Joe Byrne'. While he was 'well aware that certain portions of the printed evidence read very badly, that was the Commissioner's fault', not his.

'There was not a single point that could not be clearly and thoroughly explained to everyone's satisfaction.' He had 'been maltreated and insulted most grossly, and all the rules of evidence had been entirely ignored.' He could prove the evidence taken in his absence was false. 'Too much of the evidence was taken for granted.' The prejudice the Commissioners had towards him 'was due to them being carefully educated against (him) beforehand,' which, together with his own reticence and the false assertions of witnesses, led them to form a bad opinion.

He complained that Bolam's assertion that something he had said in one of his letters to Nicolson was untrue and had made a bad impression on the mind of the Commission. He could prove it to be true!

He acknowledged that what he had said in his letter about Detective Ward read badly, but he was not responsible for that. He claimed that the Commissioners had selected a sentence in his correspondence and had twisted it so it appeared to be an attempt on his part to slander that officer. He had been fully prepared to explain his comments at the time, but did not think the Commissioners were authorised to investigate the private life of the detective!

Wallace wasn't finished. The fact that his evidence did not please the Commission was not his fault. Had they gone the right way about it, they should have had a full, straight, and correct account of all he knew of the business. He could easily and clearly disprove that he entertained sympathy for the outlaws. And as to the Commission's vague, indefinite charge of reprehensible conduct, he could 'appeal to the testimony of all those best qualified to judge (his) conduct.'

It should also be borne in mind, Wallace said, that the testimonials (references) he had obtained 'were written at a time when (his) reputation had already been blasted by the Commission' and 'while the flying rumours gathered as they rolled'. 'If such favourable testimony could be obtained under adverse circumstances, then imagine what (he) could have obtained previously!'

Despite his now strained relationship with Nicolson, Wallace even had the gall to say that Nicolson was reported to have said that he was 'the straightest man he ever had dealing with'; that Mr Sadleir 'knew nothing against (him)'; and that Mr Bolam (the very man whose suspicions resulted in Wallace being removed from Hurdle Creek) 'swore that (he) was a man of good character and a zealous teacher who had always stood well with the Department!'

Wallace went on to say that had he been in the least degree guilty, then surely he would not have remained in the colony or in the service (of the Education Department), and he would not have applied for a board of enquiry and challenged a criminal prosecution. In light of all that, he was confident that Mr Grant (the recipient of this letter) would ultimately give him an opportunity of bringing forward evidence for his defence to rebut the evidence given against him. He was certain he could clear his name. He had from 40 to 50 witnesses to call, and a vast amount of conclusive documentary evidence.

Still Wallace went on. He was 'surprised and grieved on receiving the news that Grant had decided to dismiss (him) without granting (him) an interview or giving (him) a chance of defence.' He could quite fully appreciate the necessity that existed for the strict maintenance of discipline and purity in the Education Department – indeed, no one had a higher respect for his superior officers than he did. But, he said, he 'could not afford to be wrongfully defrauded of (his) reputation and position and was quite able to prove his absolute and entire innocence if (he) was given the opportunity to do so. The government was bound by contract to protect (him) and afford (him) justice'.

Wallace then brought up the recent Phoenix Park murders in Dublin, which he said had shocked the civilized world by its horrible atrocity.[228] 'Suppose,' he wrote, 'that some respectable person had given information in confidence to the British Government that would have led to the prevention of that crime or to the identification and punishment of the murderers. Would the British Government have not felt bound to protect such a person who had assisted the authorities at the risk of his own life?' The parallel with his own case was that he had given information to the police that the Kellys' outrages were being contemplated long before they were committed. The information he provided should have led to their immediate capture.

Wallace wrote, though, that he was of a 'forgiving nature and incapable of animosity'. He had 'no desire to reopen something that had caused so much bad feeling, and would be quite content if exonerated of the charge against (him)'. However, if he was not exonerated, he 'would need to use all the means available to (him) under British law to vindicate (his) innocence.' He 'could not afford to wrongfully lose (his) reputation, or to have (his) children branded as the offspring of a felon, without cause.' He said he 'should have taken the initiative long ago and

---

228 - The Phoenix Park murders occurred on 6 May 1882 when an Irish rebel group called the Invincibles assassinated Lord Frederick Cavendish and Thomas Henry Burke in Phoenix Park, Dublin. The murders happened only 12 days before Wallace wrote his letter to Grant.

prosecuted (his) detractors in the law courts, were it not that (he) was restrained by a sense of discipline and duty as a government servant.' The facts, he said, happened to be on his side, and he respectfully submitted that he should not be subjected to the necessity of going to law to clear his character. He 'was quite willing to accept the decision (to terminate his employment) and accept dismissal on a minor point if accompanied with the usual retiring allowance.' He humbly prayed, though, that his dismissal from service would not be recommended on the ground of sympathy with criminals, as he was entirely innocent and always had been. And on that note, he ended his letter by appealing to Grant's favourable consideration and well-known sense of justice. He signed off as, 'Your obedient servant, James Wallace.'

Wallace was in dire straits when he wrote his letter to Mr Grant. He was now unemployed with no prospects of any further employment with the Victorian public service. He had a family to support and would say whatever he had to in order to keep his job. He would say that he was not, and had never been, a Kelly sympathiser until he was blue in the face, but it was all in vain. Saying he would fight his case in the courts and actually doing so were two different matters. All he had said at the Royal Commission and in his letter to Grant was contradicted by the evidence Considine and Ward had collected from people like the shopkeeper at Milawa and the housewife who recounted what she had been told by Wallace's young son. The Minister's decision would not be reconsidered and Wallace was probably lucky that he did not get to have his day in court.

24
Unwanted publicity

A month after his dismissal, Wallace left Yea and moved to Melbourne.[229] It is not known where he lived whilst in Melbourne, or whether he was accompanied by his family. It is possible his wife and children remained behind in Yea, given his brother William was still teaching at Boundary Creek School at this stage.

Wallace immediately found himself a part-time job teaching at the Yarra Park Night School, where he taught for five months until 31 October 1882.[230] Although the night school was run out of a state school building (the new Yarra Park State School No. 1406 at the corner of Punt Road and Wellington Parade, Richmond), night school was not subject to the oversight of the Education Department. During his time teaching at Yarra Park Night School, Wallace may have authored two articles on education that were published in *The Age* newspaper on 10 June 1882 (titled 'The Education Department') and 26 August 1882 (titled 'State Night Schools'). The articles, which Wallace would later submit with a future employment application as examples of his writing, were published in one instance (the State Night School article) as being 'from a correspondent' and in the other instance without being accredited to anyone.

Wallace was lucky to obtain his part-time teaching role in the first place, but was luckier still to retain the role following the publication in the 10 June 1882 edition of *The Age* newspaper (the same edition in which the above-mentioned article on 'The Education Department' was published) of a full-page supplement headed 'Wallace, the Schoolmaster' setting out all the allegations against him.

---

229 - Pioneer Teachers of the Kelly Country, page 190.

230 - Yarra Park State School No. 1406 opened in 1874. The school closed in 1992 after which the heritage-listed building was converted into prestige apartments.

WALLACE, THE SCHOOLMASTER.

A CHAPTER IN THE HISTORY OF THE KELLY GANG.

The case of James Wallace, State school teacher, whose dismissal from the public service was recently announced, forms a curious and not uninstructive chapter in the history of Ned Kelly, the outlaw, and his companions in crime. The circumstances connected with his alleged sympathy, if not complicity, with the gang are surrounded with uncertainty and mystery, the unravelling of which has totally baffled all the exertions of the police.

Wallace was a State school teacher in the North-eastern District when Sergeant Kennedy and his comrades were murdered near Mansfield. He conducted two half-time schools, one at Hurdle Creek and the other at Bobinawarra, about ten miles distant from each other. The former was his head-quarters, and there he also acted as postmaster.

Having been a schoolmate of Joe Byrne, a strong friendship had grown up between him and the outlaw, and from his position and long residence in the district he was intimately acquainted with the peculiarities of the country, the haunts of the gang, their relatives and sympathisers. When therefore he applied to Captain Standish, early in 1879, to be employed as a secret agent, the Chief Commissioner, although inundated with similar offers, felt personally disposed to avail himself of his services, and that he did not do so was simply owing to Wallace's apparent untrustworthiness.

The Chief Commissioner was led to this conclusion owing to a very peculiar circumstance. Negotiations had been secretly opened with Captain Standish by a well known spy with a view to inducing Joe Byrne to betray his mates. Acting upon an understanding with this Agent, the Chief Commissioner, accompanied only by an orderly, left Benalla one night without allowing his destination or departure to be known. He rode through the bush straight towards Hurdle Creek, but he failed to meet his informant. About eight o'clock in the morning he found himself near the schoolhouse. Wallace observed him and having previously been in communication with the Chief Commissioner in relation to the Kellys he at once invited him to breakfast. In the course of the conversation that ensued the schoolmaster stated that he had long been on terms of friendship with Byrne and Aaron Sherritt, but neither of them had been near his place since the murders. The Chief Commissioner rode back to Benalla, where he found Aaron Sherritt awaiting his return. In the interview which followed Sherritt stated that he had been staying some time at Wallace's house, and had only left it the day previously. This incident led the Chief Commissioner to think that Mr. Wallace was not very reliable. The facts connected with the bootless errand of the Chief Commissioner are variously recounted, one version being that Captain Standish was led to expect that Joe Byrne would meet him, but that he refused to do so at the last moment. Further, that at the very time he was partaking of breakfast the outlaw was in the room adjoining. This, however, was stoutly denied by Wallace.

Some six months later, Mr. Nicolson, who had succeeded to the command of the pursuit, visited Wallace, and, thinking that his services might be useful, undertook to employ him as a secret agent. Wallace shaped splendidly at the start. He was a very prolific correspondent, and if his other exertions bore any proportion to his epistolary zeal the Kellys must have soon been run to earth. He furnished elaborate accounts respecting his adventures in search of the outlaws' lair, that read like extracts from the romance of Robin Hood and his Merrie Men. He described with great circumstantiality the physical peculiarities of the ranges he had crossed over, the creeks and ravines he had crossed, the individuals he had met and conversed with, and drew a lively picture of the outlaws holding a sort of rifle tourney in the depths of the forest and otherwise spending the leisure and tranquil hours in their mountain home.

After a time a game of cross-purposes arose between Wallace and Detective Ward. While they outwardly expressed the utmost friendship they were secretly writing to Mr. Nicolson denouncing each other in emphatic terms. Wallace charged Ward with revealing police secrets to the sympathisers, and with being guilty of conduct which, on moral grounds, was highly reprehensible. Ward, on the other hand, repeatedly furnished reports directly implying that Wallace was in secret league with the outlaws, selling their gold, changing their notes and supplying them with provisions and clothing. The detective had not been in-formed of the fact that Wallace was employed by the police, and he naturally kept a watchful and perhaps a jaundiced eye upon that gentleman's movements.

Wallace was consistent in one particular – namely, that notwithstanding the voluminous nature of his correspondence he avoided communicating anything of importance to the police. That he could have otherwise acted there seems little doubt, inasmuch as upon his own admission when under examination he had met Joe Byrne on one occasion and Ned Kelly on another, but failed to inform Mr. Nicolson of the fact until the matter was mentioned to him some weeks afterwards. The reasons he assigned for this singular reticence were the distance he was from Benalla, the utter uselessness, as he considered, of giving the information, and the probability of Detective Ward communicating the intelligence to some of the sympathisers, and thus directly compromising him.

At length Mr. Nicolson began to think Wallace's letters, unaccompanied by a more satisfactory outcome of his supposed efforts, somewhat monotonous. He expostulated with Wallace, and threatened to dispense with his services. He had received various sums of money, and in his letters frequently applied for payment of certain amounts. On one occasion he had hinted that owing to the time he devoted to the Kelly business he was likely to lose £10 by way of results from his schools, but it was subsequently proved that he had a fixed salary, and did not depend upon results for any portion of his remuneration. When the Assistant-Commissioner wrote on the subject of paying him for his services, Wallace repudiated the insinuation that he had ever been a paid agent. He only required and demanded actual expenses incurred in prosecuting his inquiries.

Finding apparently that nothing was likely to be gained from a further retention of his services, Wallace ceased to be employed by Mr. Nicolson some time prior to the destruction of the gang. There seems good ground for believing that Wallace was cognisant of the haunts and doings of the gang to a much greater extent than he has ever acknowledged. In one of his letters the following significant passage occurs:— 'When time shall have dissolved the obligation of secrecy I shall be able perhaps to state more fully,' &c., &c. Again, in his late letters he takes credit for his efforts in assisting to save life; and he darkly hints at being, in some way not stated, instrumental in bringing about the capture and destruction of the outlaws. His testimony and correspondence, however, are characterised by great caution, and are more specious than satisfactory or convincing- He writes a readable letter, and has a literary and somewhat cultivated style; but from a police point of view their principal feature indicated more than ordinary powers of imagination.

Wallace's proceedings became known to the officers of the Education department some months prior to the destruction of the gang. Despite strenuous efforts to be removed from Hurdle Creek to Benalla, and his expressed desire that his brother should succeed him in the position which he then held, in consequence of certain representations made to the department arrangements were privately made to remove him. This was determined upon about a week before the affray at Glenrowan. Without any previous notification his successor was sent up to Hurdle Creek, bringing with him his authority to take immediate charge of the school, and instructions to Wallace to at once proceed to Yea to take over the local school. Owing, however, to Wallace's connection with the Post Office department he could not leave as soon as directed. Some days are said to have elapsed before he proceeded to his destination.

It would be most unjust, in the absence of direct proof, to maintain that Wallace personally knew anything of, or had any complicity in, the doings of the gang immediately prior to Glenrowan, or, indeed, at any period during which he was acting for the police. The most that can be urged is suspicion. Immediately upon his suspension his case was entrusted to one of the ablest and most experienced officers in the Government service for investigation, and he, together with a prominent official in the Education department, went into the matter most carefully, and though there were many things inexplicable, and surrounded with suspicion, nothing was discovered that when duly weighed and regarded from a legal point of view could be construed into an absolute charge against Wallace of any participation in the proceedings of the gang.

A remarkable discovery was, however, made by the police about six months sub-sequent to the extermination of the outlaws. While scouring the country in the vicinity of Hurdle Creek a solitary hut was found in the bush. It presented the appearance of having some time previously been in permanent occupation. It was fitted up with four bunks, and the place was strewn with empty tins, such as those used for preserved fish and meat, an immense quantity of bottles, and similar indications of good living. Now, it has always been a mystery where the gang concealed themselves for the six or eight months that preceded their final exploit. It has been stated that they were located at Wilson's paddock, near Greta, also in a paddock near Sebastopol, where they are said to have been frequently seen by the owner of the land. They have also been described as travelling constantly from one portion of the district to another. But there is no evidence to support those statements. It must be obvious that, in order to ensure an uninterrupted supply of provisions and secure themselves against the inclemency of the weather, they must have had a fixed abode of some sort – one of easy access, and removed from the general surveillance or suspicion of the police authorities. The hut found near Hurdle Creek would have answered every purpose. From the inquiries made in the neighbourhood sufficient information was gleaned to lead the authorities to conclude that the outlaws for a time lay concealed in this hut.

The police at the time were averse to reopening the Kelly business, and no action was taken in relation to the discovery for some months. Then, however, the matter was taken up and strict search instituted. The officials who had undertaken to investigate the matter despatched two detectives to the scene, but their mission proved fruitless. Their visit had been apparently forestalled. On reaching the spot they found the hut burned to the ground, and the tins, bottles and similar debris totally destroyed so as to prevent a possibility of identification. The destruction had been caused, the detectives thought, by a bush fire; but an examination of the place showed that the fire had commenced a little below the hut on the rise, and the flames having done their work soon died out after passing over the spot where the hut stood. Regret was ex-pressed by several upon becoming acquainted with the fact that the police in the first instance had not taken the precaution to preserve the empty tins and bottles seen in and around the hut, inasmuch as the identity of the purchasers might thereby have been traced.

> *Other circumstances of a suspicious nature were discovered that strengthened the supposition that Wallace was cognisant of the whereabouts of the outlaws, but there was only one witness who could give decisive evidence upon the point. That witness, when sought, had disappeared, from no other motive seemingly than to defeat further inquiry. After a close scrutiny of all the facts connected with Wallace's case, the most that can be said is that his conduct was inexplicable, mysterious and unsatisfactory. The evidence against him is purely circumstantial. At the same time it must be remembered that he had the power in his hands to remove any doubts as to his bona fides, and if he, as he states, has allowed certain obligations to seal his lips he cannot blame the department for putting the very worst construction upon his silence. If guilty, he has been but lightly punished; if innocent, he has only his own reticence to thank for his dismissal. Of this there cannot be a reasonable doubt; that under the circumstances the Government was left no other alternative than to dispense with his services as a State school teacher, in accordance with the recommendation of the Royal Commission on Police.*

The publication of this article must have surely stimulated some interesting discussion among Wallace's night school pupils!

Any hope Wallace might have had of keeping things quiet was gone, and the stigma of his involvement with the Kellys engulfed the family. He refused to be beaten, though, as there was too much at stake. As usual, his weapon of choice was his pen and he sent a reply to *The Age* that was published four days later. Wallace's reply is a great example of his literary style, and unashamedly presents his own preferred version of the truth:

> **To the Editor of The Age.**
>
> *SIR – On reading the article with above heading in your issue of this morning, I begin to doubt that I am myself. In*

common fairness, I trust you will permit me to contradict the misrepresentations it contains, as if allowed to pass, they may work me serious injury. In the first place, I deny emphatically that there are, or ever were, any just or reasonable grounds for suspicion that I entertained or expressed any sympathy for the outlawed Kelly Gang. The alleged strong friendship said to have existed between Byrne and myself, is purely mythical. The extent of our mutual relations may be judged from the fact that during the fifteen years preceding his death, I did not meet with him more than half-a-dozen times altogether, and then only casually. No application was ever made by me to Captain Standish for employment as a secret agent, and until I read your paper this morning, I was not aware that I ever had the honour of that gentleman's company to breakfast. No outlaw ever visited my house.

The references to the alleged strained relations between Detective Ward and myself are untrue, uncalled for, and unfair both to that officer and myself. No assertion was ever made by me in connection with that business, that cannot be absolutely proven to be true. The circumstances of my transfer from Hurdle Creek to Yea, are shamefully misrepresented. The insinuation that I was unreliable is a cowardly and gratuitous one. I do not know of anything in my conduct that was mysterious, inexplicable, or unsatisfactory. What earthly connection has the discovery of a hut in the ranges with me? How very conveniently the aforesaid hut and debris, together with some unnamed witness, are made to disappear. The charge of reticence made against me, does not hold good, when viewed in the full light of the facts of the case. I did not shrink from the inquiry, I courted the fullest investigation. I asked, as a matter of justice, that I should be allowed a Board of Inquiry. This request was refused, and dark and covert threats of probable action on the part of the law officers of the Crown were made, upon which I directly and fearlessly challenged a prosecution. When I was informed that the 'prominent official' referred to, was making frantic efforts to get up a case against me, I acted as any honourable man would have done.

I promptly wrote offering all the assistance in my power towards getting up the case, and tendered all information, books, and papers in my possession on the subject. My offer was not acknowledged. Surely I was better able than anyone else to assist in unravelling the so-called mystery, which is alleged to have baffled the police. I was suspended, without reason being given. After six months suspension, I was dismissed without any official reason. My applications for a Board of Inquiry were not acknowledged for months, but through the press I was informed that the Minister had refused me that privilege, and had referred my case to the Cabinet. I am at a loss to understand why the question of my innocence or otherwise, should be trammelled by party interests. On personal application to Mr Grant, in company with a well-known Melbourne pressman, I was refused an interview.

On waiting on Mr. Brown, the Secretary, I was informed that I was dismissed on the recommendation of the police board, but he did not say why. The writer of the article in your column goes on to say, 'It would be most unjust, in the absence of direct proof to maintain that Wallace personally knew anything of, or had any complicity in, the doings of the gang immediately prior to Glenrowan, or indeed at any period during which he was acting for the police. The most that can be urged is suspicion.' If these be his real sentiments, what object can he have in dishing up these defamatory insinuations? In concluding his remarks, he says:- 'Under the circumstances the Government was left no alternative than to dispense with his services as a State School Teacher. 'I differ with him. I think the Government should have allowed me an opportunity of knowing why I was thus summarily rubbed out. They should have allowed me an opportunity of bringing forward rebutting evidence in my own defence. Having been cruelly denied one of the commonest privileges of British citizenship, I have no other alternative but to endeavour to have the whole facts of the case thoroughly sifted in the Law Courts, in an action for libel against my detractors. And until that is done, I must request your readers to postpone their decision against my case.

Yours, & C.,

James Wallace, 10th June, 1882.

Wallace's letter contains a great deal of falsehood. He did approach Captain Standish with an offer of help, and Standish's statement at the Royal Commission about enjoying breakfast at Wallace's residence was not disputed and was in fact strengthened by his recounting of the meeting he subsequently had in Benalla with Aaron Sherritt. Unfortunately for Wallace, other evidence given at the Commission pointed to him having been on intimate terms with at least some of the Kelly Gang, and to him harbouring great animosity towards Detective Ward. Not surprisingly, Wallace's threat of a libel action came to nothing.

25
Flight to Queensland

Towards the end of 1882, with pressures mounting upon him, Wallace left his family and headed to Sydney. From there he worked his way through northern New South Wales and into Queensland, 'navvying' (undertaking unskilled work) for a short time for the railways. By January 1883, he was based at Talgai Station on the Darling Downs.

Talgai Station was an immense pastoral property owned by two brothers named George and Charles Clark. The Clarks were squatters and during the 1860s and 1870s had developed Talgai Station as arguably the most successful sheep stud in Queensland, producing immense amounts of quality merino wool and trading in high-quality rams. Talgai Station was so large that it had its own self-contained community that included employee's cottages, a smithy, stables, barn, woolshed, slaughterhouse, dairy and a school.

The Wallace family say that James found work at Talgai Station as a tutor for the owner's children, although there is no official record of this. A member of the Wallace family also says that he became involved with another woman during this period of enforced separation from his family, although that is also unverified.[231]

It is ironic to think that a man like Wallace who was supposedly a champion of the selector cause would end up working for squatters like the Clarks. Whatever was the nature of the work he was doing at Talgai Station, he was soon hankering to be employed as a teacher once again. On 13 January 1883, he wrote to the Queensland Department of Education saying that he would be pleased to take any position they might offer him. His return address was given as c/- Charles Clark Esq., Talgai Station, Hendon, near Toowoomba.

---

231 - The story is unverified, but in light of Wallace's character and the duration of the separation from his wife and family, it would not be surprising if it were true.

In his application to the Queensland Education Department, Wallace described himself as being twenty-eight years of age, strong, healthy and energetic, married with a family of five children, three of which were school age. He also described his qualifications and his 12 years of teaching experience, first as an apprentice teacher at the El Dorado State School No. 246 and then as the head teacher at Hurdle Creek State School No. 1046 and later at Yea State School No. 699. He also falsely stated that he had resigned from the Victorian Education Department to take up the business of travelling insurance agent.

With his application to the Queensland Education Department, Wallace included the following copies of some of his 'contributions to the Victorian Press':

- His article published in *The Age* newspaper on 20 November 1880 as part of an editorial critical of the police efforts to capture Ned Kelly and his gang.

- The article 'The Education Department' published in *The Age* on 10 June 1882.

- The article 'State Night Schools' published in *The Age* on 26 August 1882.

- Another article titled 'Employes in Shops Bill' (publication details of this article have not been found).

The first of the above articles was undoubtedly written by Wallace. Whether he was indeed the author of the other articles is not known, given they were published without accreditation. It is possible that Wallace simply included these articles with his application to impress those who would be assessing his application.

Wallace's application was successful and resulted in him obtaining a teaching position at Ipswich West, some 20 miles south-west of Brisbane. Ipswich was then a fairly primitive township that served a wider farming community, but having grown up in the Woolshed Valley and El Dorado, and having taught at Hurdle Creek, Wallace would have been accustomed to such conditions. He commenced work in February 1883 and sent for Barbara and the children to join him.

It would have been a long and tiring journey, travelling by train to Sydney, then by sea to Brisbane, and lastly by stage coach to Ipswich.

Two months into Wallace's new teaching role, the Queensland Education Department learned the truth about his dismissal as a teacher in Victoria. John Anderson, the Under Secretary of the Queensland Education Department, had written to his counterpart in Victoria upon receiving Wallace's application, and it was only now that he received a response. The reply was brief and to the point, drawing attention to the terse note that had been written at the foot of Wallace's record sheet: 'Was removed upon recommendation of the Police Commission on account of supposed complicity with the Kelly Gang.' A copy of the Royal Commission's report and of the Minutes of Evidence was also forwarded to Mr Anderson.

In response to a threat of dismissal, Wallace submitted an eloquent appeal in which he stated that 'having already paid the penalty for any indiscretions I may have committed in Victoria, it is unfair that I should be again punished here. Earthly punishment should not be eternal.'[232] He finished his letter with a reference to some words from the poet Longfellow and an appeal for favourable consideration:

> *'Act, act in the Living Present,*
>
> *Heart within and God o'erhead.'*
>
> *Respectfully asking your favourable*
>
> *Consideration of the above*
>
> *I have the honor to be,*
>
> *Sir,*
>
> *Your most obedient Servant,*
>
> *James Wallace*

---

232 - Wallace's appeal was dated 29 March 1883.

Wallace's literary skills and persistence greatly impressed John Anderson, who prepared a detailed memorandum for the Education Minister's consideration in which he recommended that Wallace be given probation.[233] Owing to the voluminous nature of the Minutes of Evidence, Anderson reported that he had only had time to read the evidence given by Wallace himself, together with that of General Inspector Bolam and John Sherritt. He mistakenly noted that as far as he was aware, Wallace's name did not appear in any other part of the evidence.

Anderson considered that the Commissioners had regarded Wallace's relations with the outlaws as equivocal. He noted that they had accused Wallace of flippancy in giving his evidence, but considered that the Commission's questions appeared to have been calculated to elicit impertinent replies. As far as Wallace's evidence was concerned, he thought it read like the evidence of a man who had nothing to conceal, and that it was notable for the maintenance of consistency throughout, under questioning that at times was evidently unfriendly.

In respect of John Sherritt's evidence, Anderson thought it did little to convict Wallace for active sympathy with the gang. In fact, Anderson seemed to be affronted that Sherritt had professed friendship to Byrne whilst acting as a police spy and contriving for his arrest. He felt that Sherritt's role in the Commission was to blacken Wallace.

Anderson considered Thomas Bolam's evidence to be the most important. He noted that Wallace's character both as a man and as a teacher stood high with the Department, which had not known of his connection with the police. He noted that Bolam had reported that Wallace appeared to be deserving of promotion, that he had always stood well with the Department, and that he was a man of good character and a zealous teacher. He also noted that whilst Bolam had recognised the facilities Wallace had at his disposal to assist the outlaws, he had pointed out to Mr Ramsay (the Chief Secretary) that 'he was not in a position to make any charge against Wallace'.

---

233 - The memorandum was prepared by John Anderson, Under Secretary for the Queensland Department of Education, and dated 8 March 1883.

Anderson had some concerns that Wallace had not alerted the Education Department to the fact that he had offered assistance to the police and that for seven months had worked as a police spy for which he received £80 for his services. He was also concerned that Wallace had dishonestly represented to the police (Nicolson) that his police work would cause him to lose from £5 to £10 in 'results' at the approaching examinations when his salary was in fact fixed and not liable to be affected by results.

To what extent Wallace was playing a double game, if at all, Anderson admitted that he was in doubt. He had a faint impression that he had wished to save Byrne, his old school mate, by inducing him to contrive the betrayal of Hart and the two Kellys. It was clear, he thought, that Wallace had been playing with pitch, and that the usual consequences had followed.

However, as far as Wallace's suitability for employment with the Queensland Department of Education was concerned, Anderson concluded:

> ... He is a man of good ability, well trained as a teacher, & the type this service requires. His character was blameless and his reports as a man and a teacher and in the eyes of the department he served to within a few weeks of the Glenrowan affair. The district inspector recommended him for promotion, & it may be inferred that his character in the district was good, & that he gave satisfaction to the School Committee and the parents generally. Mr Bolam certainly came to form a strong opinion of his collusion with the gang, but apparently without any evidence – he perceived that Wallace had facilities for doing what he was suspected of doing, & seems to have drawn from that fact an inference of guilt. A transfer to Benalla would probably have been a promotion to Wallace, & would certainly have kept him in the district where he had old ties, while his brother's transfer to be his successor at Hurdle Creek & Bobinawarrah would have meant promotion to the young man, as Mr Bolam admits. Are

> *those facts a sufficient and natural explanation can be found for Wallace's urgency viz the school appointments without supposing that his anxiety to assist the outlaws was his motive.*
>
> *One is struck by the absence of all overt act in confirmation of the suspicions attaching to Wallace. Bad as Mr Bolam's impressions were, he did not, even when the Commission sat, consider Wallace unfit for employment. That Wallace was much respected in his new district is abundantly testified by a magistrate, a clergyman of the Church of England, the Chairman of the Shire Council, and the school board (see papers attached to his application). There is no reason to doubt that if the Royal Commission had not made a strong representation on the subject Wallace would have been undisturbed by the Department of Education, & would still be in its service.*
>
> *His personal appearance rather recommends him; he is young, healthy, intelligent & courageous; recognises that he has had a lesson; is willing to work for his wife and children. I believe him to be able to do good work for this country, and that, if employed, there would be little danger of his resorting to that of which he has been suspected.*

Anderson suggested that Wallace be retained for the time being on the same terms as he was then engaged, and that he should be made aware that the evidence taken by the Royal Commission in Victoria, together with its report thereon, has been under consideration. Furthermore, that he should be advised that his admission into service as a classified teacher could only be approved after probation. Anderson's suggestion was duly adopted by the Minister.

While at Ipswich, Wallace continued to monitor the news from Victoria. He took great interest in a case regarding the impropriety of the head teacher at Beechworth State School (a man named Edward Samuel Harris), and in a scandalous divorce case involving Thomas Bolam. He made contemporaneous notes (held by the Wallace family) of both cases.

Edward Harris was suspended from his role at Beechworth State School on 15 January 1883 on the charge of highly unbecoming conduct with some of the female students, two of whom were sent to Melbourne for an abortion, one of whom died as a result of the operation. It was reported that the school house was devoted to assignations at night, not only by Harris, but also by others who had been seen entering and leaving the building.

In an earlier chapter dealing with Wallace's letters to Nicolson during the Kelly years, it was noted that he had, in one of those letters, cast aspersions on the morality of Detective Ward. When Wallace appeared at the Royal Commission, he was asked if he could give an example and answered with an insinuation that Ward had tampered with girls (pupil teachers) at the Beechworth State School.[234]

Wallace seemingly knew that something untoward was going on at Beechworth State School when he made his accusations against Detective Ward. What did he know? Why would he have thought that Ward was involved? Or was he just making mischief by implicating his enemy Ward in a scandal that he knew about but for which there was no reason to believe Ward was actually involved? Perhaps it was Wallace's flippant accusations against Detective Ward that actually sparked the investigation into Mr Harris, rather ironically led by the very man he had cast aspersions against.

Harris refused to attend a board of inquiry that was convened at Beechworth on 22 January 1883 to hear the charges against him. Instead, he left for Melbourne from where he wrote a letter to Mr Bolam (Inspector-General of the Education Department) in which he took exception to one of the members of the school advisory board sitting and hearing the charges against him on the grounds that the person concerned had himself used the schoolroom for immoral

---

234 - Minutes of Evidence, Q14798.

purposes.[235] He also proffered charges against several leading citizens of Beechworth who he expected would give evidence against him. A copy of that letter has not been located and hence the names of those he accused are unknown. Harris's body was found in the Yarra River two days later (on 24 January 1883).[236]

In a newspaper report on the Harris case, it was noted that Mr Bolam had applied for leave of absence due to his months-long efforts to collect the evidence necessary to support the charges against Harris. The report concluded by reminding readers that it was owing in the main to Mr Bolam's exertions that the Department had been able to obtain the information regarding the conduct of the school teacher Wallace, which enabled the government to dismiss him from public service in accordance with the recommendation of the Royal Commission.[237]

In respect of Mr Bolam, Wallace made a note headed with a Latin phase *Re morthius nil nisi bouam* (which roughly translates as 'Death or nothing but honor'), which reads as follows:

> *Mr Bolan seems all through to have taken a leading part against me. This is borne out by experience. What his motive was I cannot imagine unless he was actuated by friendship for Captain Standish and espoused the latter's cause in his quarrel with Mr Nicolson. Mr Bolam was a freemason. Captain Standish*

---

235 - School districts containing one or more schools were managed by a Board of Advice. Membership of each board comprised no less than five or more than seven members. Members were elected by ratepayers and served without payment or other incentive. Clause 15 of the Education Act 1872 specified the duties required of the Boards of Advice. Those duties were to: (i) stipulate the use that could be made of school buildings after children were dismissed at the end of the school day or on days when no school was in session, and suspend any school teacher for misconduct and report the cause of such suspension to the Minister; (ii) report on the condition of the schools with respect to the premises and their condition and whether new schools were required; (iii) visit schools from time to time, and record the number of children present, and offer an opinion as to the general condition, and management of the school/s and (iv) use every endeavour to induce parents to send their children regularly to school, to compare the attendance of children at school with the roll for the school district, and to report the names of parents who failed or refused to educate their children or to send them to school. However, the Department of Education kept central control at all times, choosing to take advice from local Boards or not as it saw fit.

236 - A report on the inquest into Harris's death appeared in *The Age* newspaper on 27 January 1883, and in *The Argus* on 29 January 1883.

237 - *The Argus*, 29 January 1883.

was chief of that mystic brotherhood. That there was a strong intimacy between them was shown in the evidence taken in the Bolam divorce case in September 1883. In the report of the inquest of the body of Harris the schoolmaster (Herald, Jan 26, 1883) it is shown in evidence that Mr Bolam and Detective Ward were working together.

In the aforesaid divorce case, it is clearly shown that Mr Bolam 'lost his head' occasionally and made mistakes. In a reference to that case the Argus of October 1883 says 'During the hearing of the case the petitioner had to admit to a number of improprieties which proved him peculiarly unfit to hold the office of inspector general of schools; and it has been decided by the Government that he shall be relieved of his office.'

It was as if Wallace had convinced himself that he was innocent and that Bolam had taken action against him for other reasons. There was, of course, no reason why Bolam and Standish should not have been friends, and as for Bolam and Ward working together, there was no reason why they shouldn't have been, given they were investigating a schoolmaster who was suspected of interfering with the female pupil teachers.

Resignation from the Queensland Education Department

After two years at Ipswich, and despite all he had gone through to keep his job with the Queensland Education Department, Wallace surprised his employer by resigning in February 1885 to take up a job in Brisbane selling insurance for the National Mutual Assurance Company.

A brief reference ('Career of Mr James Wallace') from the Department of Public Instruction and dated 27 July 1888 states as follows:

Career of Mr James Wallace

Mr James Wallace was Head Teacher of the small State School at Ipswich Reserve from the 19th February 1883 till the 20th February 1885.

> *The Inspectors reported favourably on his work. His resignation, spontaneously tendered, was accepted by the Minister from the 20th February 1885.*

The Wallace family remained in Brisbane for a little less than three years before returning to Victoria. Little is known of their life during these years, other than that they rented a house in the Brisbane suburb of Lutwyche, and continued to grow their family with two new additions.[238] They were probably quite content to be enjoying a quiet life after the trials and tribulations of the years before.

---

238 - Lillian Violet Wallace was born during 1885. Hubert Wallace was born the following year.

26
The Band of Brothers

James Wallace was not the only sympathiser in his family. His brothers Andrew and William were also sympathisers, perhaps for no other reason than a sense of loyalty to their older brother and a desire to protect his friend Joe Byrne.

Both Andrew and William were working as pupil teachers at the El Dorado State School in 1879. Andrew had been there since 1872, having taken over James's position after his appointment to Hurdle Creek. Neither had had any issues with the school until William inexplicably left the school grounds without permission on 27 August 1879, telling the school's head teacher Thomas Trembath that evening that he was tired of teaching and wanted to give it up.[239] This was the same day that James wrote a letter to Nicolson in which he gave his version of the meeting he had had a few days earlier at the Imperial Hotel in Beechworth with Aaron and Detective Ward.

In the week prior to the hotel meeting, there had been a fundamental change in James's attitude, and presumably in the other members of the Wallace family, towards Aaron. One wonders if there might have been more to William's abrupt disappearance from the school on 27 August than him simply being tired of teaching.

On 15 September 1879, Thomas Trembath sent a telegram to Mr G Brown, Secretary of the Education Department informing him that Andrew Wallace was in a melancholy state and that his mother wanted to send him away for a change. He requested that William Wallace should relieve his brother James at Hurdle Creek so that James could

---

239 - Trembath wrote to the Education Department to inform them of this, adding that William returned the next afternoon with his father Charles who told him that his son would like to continue teaching after all. Whatever was wrong with William, he obviously got over it because two months later Trembath asked the Education Department for a bonus for having promoted William from the third to second class (on the teacher grading scale). Head teachers received a bonus as their pupil teachers advanced through the teaching grades.

accompany Andrew for whatever treatments he required. James also sent a telegram to the Secretary that same day requesting one week's leave so he could take Andrew for treatment.[240]

There was no ulterior motive for Andrew taking time off, as it turned out that he had an epilepsy condition. Whatever treatment he required did not take long to get, as James wrote a letter to Nicolson from Bobinawarrah on 19 September. His reference in that letter to having met a large number of people 'since coming home' who had been at the ploughing match on the 16th, indicates that he and Andrew had only been away for several days, which would have been enough time for them to have visited Melbourne for treatment had that been necessary. It is not known if Andrew returned to his teaching job, but if he did it was only for a short time, as by the end of 1879 it is believed that he was in Yea running the Yea Coffee Palace.[241]

James made three attempts to have his brother William take over his schools at Hurdle Creek – first when he (James) tried to be transferred to a State School near Beechworth, secondly when he tried to be posted to a new school due to be opened in Benalla, and finally as a condition of his being transferred to Yea. These attempts, which may have been (as thought possible by James Anderson at the Queensland Education Department) no more than a desire to secure improved employment for his brother, gave rise at the time to a suspicion that he had an ulterior motive. His attempts were unsuccessful because the Education Department had become suspicious of Wallace for all the reasons Thomas Bolam expressed to the Royal Commission.

Instead of Hurdle Creek, the Department transferred William first to the Peechelba State School for a short-term assignment, and then

---

240 - Mental illness was a common trait in the Wallace family – 'melancholy' was something that would ultimately see William committed to the Beechworth Asylum. It appears, based on Trembath's telegram, that Andrew might also have suffered from melancholy, as well as well as the epilepsy that would cut short his teaching career.

241 - The specific date that Andrew Wallace went to Yea is not known, but it is believed to have been in 1879. We know for sure that he was running the Yea Coffee Palace in 1881, because this is referenced in legal documents signed by him and James at the time. It is not known how long he lived at Yea, but in 1887 he married a woman named Catherine Beatty at Botharambo (near Chiltern) and was described at that time as being a store assistant in Wangaratta. Andrew died on 1 December 1908 in Rutherglen, aged 52 years. His death certificate records his profession as being a 'carrier' (someone who transports goods). He is buried in Wahgunyah (Carlyle) Cemetery – grave no. 591A; burial no. 1821.

to the Boundary Creek State School to the west of Yea where he commenced his duties on 1 August 1880 – about a month after James's own transfer to Yea.

In 1882, when Detective Ward was in Yea to investigate James, Ward was kept under close watch by the Wallace brothers. That indicates that Andrew and William were looking out for James's interests. Later that year, Andrew would also purchase James's chattels after his dismissal from the Education Department and before he took flight to Queensland.

There is reason to believe that William was under considerable stress due to the whole Kelly business. Having moved James away from Kelly country, the Education Department wasted no time in moving William out as well. Compared to his situation at El Dorado where he was still living at home with his parents and teaching at the local school, it is likely that William would have found living with James and his family at Yea and teaching at Boundary Creek somewhat challenging.

In 1882, a charge was brought against William for using bad language to his pupils. William wrote to the Department from Yea on 7 August 1882 saying that he did not remember doing any such thing and the charge was ultimately not sustained, according to a report in the *Alexandra and Yea Standard* on 22 September 1882. However, the Department decided to transfer him to another school at Kanyapella (near Echuca).[242] William refused the transfer and was therefore dismissed from service.

Towards the end of 1882, both James and William had left the Yea district. Both moved to Melbourne, where James taught for a time at the Yarra Park night school. Believing he could be arrested and charged at any time, he eventually made his way alone to Queensland.

William's life was lurching from one calamity to another. On 2 October 1882, he went out drinking at the Hokitiki Hotel at Emerald Hill (Melbourne) with a man named Walter Stewart – a Kelly sympathiser from Rutherglen. Their drinking session came to an abrupt end, however, when Walter's estranged wife suddenly burst through the

---

242 - Kanyapella South No. 2490.

door and attempted to shoot her former husband. Although Walter was only standing about nine feet away, the shot missed and William took the revolver from the woman and handed it to the publican.[243]

A newspaper report of the shooting incident described how William and Walter had been talking together about a court case involving Thomas Bolam (the nemesis of the Wallace brothers). The case was very newsworthy at the time, being a divorce case, which saw a great deal of dirty linen about Bolam and his wife becoming public knowledge. Bolam's misfortunes must have been very satisfying to the Wallace brothers given their dealings with him.

The next we know of William is that on 2 December 1884 he was admitted to the Beechworth Insane Asylum. He was 25 years old at the time of his admission and his place of abode was recorded as being El Dorado (probably with his parents). The recorded cause of his admission was 'over study and confinement' (essentially a combination of mental exhaustion and the adverse effects of limited social interaction or being confined in one place for too long). It was also recorded that he had suffered one previous attack. He would remain at the asylum for one and a half years.

Elaine Wallace, a granddaughter of James and Barbara, recalls her father (Hugh Wallace – the eighth child of James and Barbara) often speaking of the Wallace boys as being a 'band of brothers', with James being very much the dominant sibling. His brothers tended to follow in his footsteps, which partly explains how William came to join him in Yea, and how John and Gilbert and their families would later follow him to a new life in Kerang.[244] Only brother Hugh, the gentle giant as they called him, would ultimately remain in the North East, supporting his parents on their farm at Chiltern.

---

243 - The shooting was reported in the *Mount Alexander Mail* on 11 October 1882.

244 - John (Jack) Wallace, the fourth son of Charles and Marion, was born in El Dorado in 1863. He would marry Harriet Grigg, the daughter of a pioneer family from the Corryong, in April 1890. The couple was always known to the family as Jack and Hetty.
Gilbert Wallace was born in El Dorado in 1869.

27
Animosity towards Mr Bolam

As previously stated, while living and working in Ipswich, Wallace continued to take a strong interest in what was going on in Victoria. The Samuel Harris case and Mr Bolam's role in it was of particular interest to him, as was Bolam's divorce case.

Among the papers held by Wallace family members is a draft of a letter Wallace was proposing to send to one of the Victorian newspapers. The draft letter was written sometime after 1883 and makes reference, among other things, to the inquest into Harris's death and the Bolam divorce case. It seems the letter was never sent, but it gives an insight into his feelings about Bolam, who he seemed to blame for the 'miserable plight' he found himself in as a result of having to leave Victoria to find work.

In his draft, Wallace took great interest in the fact that Bolam and Detective Ward had worked together in getting up the case against Harris, and drew comparisons to the strong intimacy that existed between Bolam and Captain Standish, which he put down to them both being freemasons (Captain Standish, in fact, being the 'chief of that brotherhood'). He also took great delight in the fact that Bolam had to admit during his divorce case to a number of improprieties that made him unfit to hold his position within the Education Department, and that as a result the government decided to relieve him of his office.

As far as his own dealings with Bolam, Wallace complained as follows:

> *I waited on Mr Bolan not once but often during my suspension, asked him to provide me a copy of the evidence given against me. I asked for a board of enquiry. He said he would consider my request. I then obtained through the courtesy of a member of Parliament permission to see the minutes of evidence of the Police Commission. I waited again on Mr Bolam and in a lengthy*

interview went through the whole matter and produced strong documentary evidence in support of my assertions. Mr Bolam admitted my explanations were very plausible and said further enquiries would be made.

I wrote again a formal application to Mr Bolam Acting Secretary, asking in the most respectful terms that as a matter of justice I should be allowed a board of enquiry, and as my former applications were not acknowledged I took the precaution to register the letter. About the same time the parents and residents of Hurdle Creek prepared a report on my behalf. I was then informed through the columns of the Argus that my application was refused.

I tried to see Mr Grant and for a friend to introduce me to him.[245] Mr Grant refused me an interview and referred me to Mr Bolam in whose hands he had left the case. On waiting on Mr Bolam again, he informed me that he was making enquiries and that I should hear from him later on. Indirectly I was informed that the police were going to make it very hot for me and shut my mouth with a criminal prosecution if I did not clear out. The next step was my summary dismissal without any reason being given. For months I did nothing else but strenuously endeavour to get justice. Then having no money and not being able to get employment, I was in a miserable plight. My wife was ill and within a few days of her confinement, I received a telegram that one of my children was dying of scarlet fever. I had to give up the struggle and go to nurse my child through its illness. Then leaving my wife & family dependent on the charity of relatives I sold my few remaining articles of furniture to pay my passage to Sydney. There I was refused employment as I had been in Melbourne. I worked my way through N.S.W. as a navvy on railway works and then on a station in southern

---

245 - James McPherson Grant MLA, Chief Secretary and Minister of Public Institutions.

Queensland to get enough money to carry me to Brisbane where I got employment from the Edu Dept here.

Mr Bolan seems all through to have taken a leading part against me. This is borne out by experience. What his motive was I cannot imagine unless he was actuated by friendship for Captain Standish and espoused the latter's cause in his quarrel with Mr Nicolson. Mr Bolam was a freemason. Captain Standish was chief of that mystic brotherhood. That there was a strong intimacy between them was shown in the evidence taken in the Bolam divorce case in September 1883. In the report of the inquest of the body of Harris the schoolmaster (Herald, Jan 26, 1883) it is shown in evidence that Mr Bolam and Detective Ward were working together.

Mr Bolam obviously had no interest in helping Wallace in any way. The decision to dismiss him had been made and would not be revisited.

28
Return to Victoria

In December 1888, after a six-year absence, James felt it was safe for him and his family to return to North-Eastern Victoria. The authorities had long ago decided not to prosecute him, adversaries like Captain Standish and Thomas Bolam were now dead,[246] Detective Ward was no longer in the district,[247] and most people in Kelly country were keen to put the past behind them and move on.[248] That said, there was still an element of risk associated with returning – the Sherritt family would certainly not have been happy about his return.

The Wallaces initially rented a house in Ford Street, Beechworth.[249] The family was still growing – another son they named Hugh Percy Wallace (James and Barbara's ninth child) was born there. The large purchases of bread and other supplies that piqued the interest of the detectives back in the Kelly years would now be easily explained away!

In 1889, James's parents moved from El Dorado to a 53-acre property called 'Barambogie' near Chiltern.[250] James and his family moved in with them later in the year. James was still working as an insurance agent at that time, but a recession was beginning to set in, sales were hard and he began to turn his mind to how he might return to his old profession. He needed to present a convincing case to the Education

---

246 - Captain Standish had died on 19 March 1883 at the Melbourne Club where he had lived for the previous 11 years. Thomas Bolam had died by suicide on 22 February 1884. Bolam's suicide was attributed to the stresses he was under as a result of his divorce and dismissal from the Education Department.

247 - Detective Ward had relocated to Melbourne in 1880.

248 - For many years, those who had sympathised with the Kellys went quiet. In light of what the gang had planned to do at Glenrowan, some were embarrassed at the fact that they had supported a man who today might be termed a terrorist.

249 - The address is not known.

250 - Barambogie (Lot 1 on Section J Parish of Chiltern County of Bogong). The property comprised 53 acres. Charles Wallace purchased the property in April 1889.

Department, and to that end he travelled to Melbourne in the hope of enlisting the support of Charles Nicolson, now a police magistrate.

Staying for a short time at the Essendon home of a teacher friend, James penned the following letter to Nicolson:

C H Nicolson Esq. PM

April 11th. 1889

Dear Sir,

I am going to make another supreme effort to have the order-in-council under which I was dismissed from the Education Department on the recommendation of the Police Commission cancelled; and have confident hopes of success. Mr. Bolam my then inveterate enemy, is no more; and others to whose interest it was to crush me at the time, are either no more, or no longer interested in injuring me.

You kindly stated, when I was called on to give evidence, that you considered I was under your protection. Now, after the lapse of years, may I ask whether I can depend on you for any support in the above attempt, or whether I may refer to you in any way as to my conduct at the time.

Apologising for troubling you, I have the honour to be Dear Sir, Yours very faithfully,

Signed, James Wallace.

After sending his letter, James managed to engineer a chance meeting with Nicolson at Melbourne's General Post Office in Bourke Street to further push his case. Just as he had in the Kelly years, he quickly followed up with another letter on 1 May:

Esperanza, Richardson Street

Essendon

May 1st 1889

C H Nicolson Esq. PM

Honourable Sir,

Referring to our conversation of the other day at the Post Office, Bourke Street, I have the honour to thank you sincerely for the kindly expressions you used to me on that occasion, viz. that you 'had no animus against me', that you 'would be pleased to hear of my success in obtaining re-employment for the Education Department', and that 'you did not think I was a Kelly sympathiser'.

I regret exceedingly, at the same time that you should, for one moment think that I 'had treated you badly'. Permit me to assert most emphatically that I never did in any way or at any time work or speak against you, but the contrary. It has been my misfortune all along to be blamed for the act of another; and I trust to be able to prove this to your complete satisfaction.

The Education department of Victoria are now in want of teachers with my qualifications. I was in that service for 12 years and my departmental record for that period for character, capacity and efficiency, I am proud to say, is surpassed by none, as the Inspector-General now testifies. I have reason to believe if now, after the lapse of seven years, you will be good enough to say 'that you do not think I was a Kelly sympathiser' I can easily obtain re-engagement in the Education service.

In charity to my wife and seven children, I would ask your favourable reply.

Apologising for troubling you, I have the honour to be Dear Sir, Yours very faithfully,

Honourable Sir, your obedient servant, James Wallace.

It is unlikely that Nicolson would have bothered replying to these letters. He was never going to give Wallace a reference. Even if he did believe that he had not been a Kelly sympathiser, he was certain that he had been the writer of the Connor letter that painted Nicolson himself in such a bad light and was probably the main reason for him being replaced by Hare in the final days of the Kelly hunt.

However, James Wallace was not a man to give up easily. On 3 May 1889, he went to see FC Mason, a local Justice of the Peace, to make a sworn statement about the meeting he had had with Nicolson in Melbourne. According to James, the two men had the following conversation:

> *Mr Nicolson received me in a friendly manner ... I asked him to be good enough to put in writing a statement he had used to me a few days previously in Bourke Street 'that he did not think I was a Kelly sympathiser.'*

According to James, Nicolson's reply was along the following lines:

> *Well, I did not think you were a Kelly sympathiser at the time you were working with me, and I did not think you were a Kelly sympathiser at the time the Police Commission were sitting; but in view of the serious allegations against you, and from the fact that I still think you wrote the anonymous letter which led to my recall, I don't see that I am called on to take responsibility of recommending you for employment as a schoolmaster.*

It seems Nicolson regarded James Wallace as a likeable rogue. Informally, he told him that he would be pleased to hear of his success in obtaining re-employment from the Education Department. But he refused to put anything in writing or to take a professional risk of any sort on his behalf.

James had collected numerous written references back in 1882 and with his usual tenacity he spent much of May 1889 adding to these. He solicited many statutory declarations from residents of the North East (family and friends, admittedly) denying he was ever a Kelly sympathiser or that he had ever rendered the outlaws any assistance. He also collected references from teaching colleagues, although interestingly none of these were teachers in the North East.

C W Lloyd JP,[251] who purchased Wallace's selection back in 1882, provided the following reference dated 25 May 1889:

> *To whom it may concern. During the time that Mr James Wallace was in charge of the 'Hurdle Creek' School, I resided & still reside on the farm next to the School; I knew Mr Wallace intimately and saw him almost daily. When he left I bought his Selection, which I now hold. I know his family and connections and always regarded them as honest, respectable people. I never had the slightest suspicion of him being a Kelly Sympathiser and from my knowledge of his character, position and surroundings, I do not think it possible that he could in any way be an accomplice or sympathiser with enemies to Society.*

James also obtained statutory declarations from his wife Barbara and brother Hugh. Barbara's declaration is as follows:

> *I, Barbara Allan Wallace of Barambogie, Chiltern in the Colony of Victoria, wife of James Wallace, do solemnly and sincerely declare THAT during the Kelly episode I resided with my husband at the Hurdle Creek State School No. 1046. I filled the position of sewing mistress in the aforesaid school and looked after the attached post office.*
>
> *I am quite certain that my husband never entertained the slightest sympathy for the outlaws, and equally certain that he never expressed any.*
>
> *I remember the visit of Captain Standish and Mr Nicolson to my husband during the Kelly pursuit. I was fully aware of my*

---

251 - C W Lloyd was an Oxley Shire Engineer who had owned the selection next door to Wallace's selection.

> *husband's relations with Mr Nicolson, which were perfectly loyal and straightforward.*
>
> *I remember seeing the confidential letters from Mr Nicolson to my husband; and that in one of his later letters Mr Nicolson thus wrote to my husband – 'I have every confidence in your faith and ability to perform what you undertake; and I wish to prove this to you particularly by exercising discretion even in verbal communications which might bring the names of others into question.'*
>
> *(Declared at Chiltern on the 26th May 1889 before John Lock J.P.)*

Hugh's statutory declaration reads as follows:

> *During the year 1879 and the first half of the year 1880 I resided with my brother James Wallace at the Hurdle Creek State School and looked after his selection and stock. During the whole of the aforesaid time I was on the most intimate and paternally confidential terms with my brother. I never once heard him express a single sentiment in favour of the outlaws or their crimes. I am positive he did not assist or shield them in any way. His sympathies were entirely on the side of law and order. I am sure the outlaws never visited either the school or the selection. They would not have visited the school without my seeing them and they would not have been on the selection without leaving traces which I would quickly notice. (Declared at Chiltern on the 26th May 1889 before John Lock J.P.)*

Hugh was a 'simpleton' who received inadequate education to have enabled him to have composed or to have written that reference. His reference (affidavit) was almost certainly written for him by James, and appears to be in James's handwriting. The affidavit was declared before John Lock JP, who was another of James's referees, having written the following reference for him the previous year:

Chiltern 19th Dec 1888

This is to certify that I have known Mr James Wallace from his youth. As a pupil, and afterwards as a pupil teacher, in State School No. 246 El Dorado he was a promising young man of an exemplary character of which I was well enabled to judge having been then a member and correspondent of the local Board of Advice.

I believe Mr Wallace to be a man of good moral character and an excellent teacher.

John Lock J.P.

Northern Bailiwick

Victoria

The Wallace family hold an undated and unsigned draft of a letter that James presumably sent to the Secretary of the Education Department respectfully requesting to have his job reinstated, a transcript of which appears below. The carefully handwritten draft has been heavily corrected with words crossed out and replaced as James tried to find the right tone. It is obvious that he spent considerable time labouring over this letter. The letter shows signs that he was very regretful for having sacrificed his position as head teacher, and that he was very desirous of regaining his old status. Interestingly, he admits to the 'indiscretion' of assisting the police, but of course there is no reference to any indiscretion in assisting the bushrangers.

The Secretary,

Education Dept.

Sir,

In reference to my application for reinstatement in your Department I would again most respectfully point out that my dismissal from the public service of this colony under such peculiar circumstances has virtually incapacitated and disqualified me from earning my bread by my profession or calling. This severe penalty under which I have existed for the last eight years cannot but be admitted as a very heavy punishment for any indiscretion on my part.

Now, after the lapse of these years, having undergone such a terribly severe penalty, I respectfully beg to say I regret that as a schoolteacher I was induced under the circumstances, of which the records are in your Department, to engage to such an extent in the assistance of another branch of the Govt. Service (the Police). I beg most respectfully to remind you that I was the only one singled out for such frightful punishment. I attach no blame to your Dept. in connection with this matter, but fully recognise the position in which the Government were circumstanced in dealing with the report of a Royal Commission.

I place myself unreservedly in your hands, and seek nothing further than reinstatement as a teacher in the Education Dept. in which for 12 years I have an unblemished record for conduct and efficiency.

James Wallace 1890,

(Dismissed in 1882).

In the end, all of James's efforts were to no avail. He would never work for the Education Department again. His teaching career was over, but he had a unique set of skills that would make him ideally suited for another career – journalism.

James had always been a dedicated and prolific writer of letters to the editor. During the Kelly years he wrote letters to, and articles for, the *Wangaratta Despatch*, including the much referenced (but now lost) controversial article titled 'Christmas in Kelly Land'. Later, he wrote a comprehensive rebuttal to *The Age* article 'Wallace, The Schoolteacher' and (according to him) a number of articles about the state of the education system in Victoria and the conditions endured by shop workers.

After his unsuccessful attempt to resurrect his teaching career, Wallace started writing for a newspaper called *The Kerang Times*. An editorial 'The Old and the New' published in the Tuesday 2 July 1889 edition of the paper is thought to have been written by Wallace, which, if true, gives an insight into his way of thinking.[252] The editorial reflects on the changes that had occurred in the Kerang district over the twelve years since the paper's inception, including the growth of the town of Kerang and the increase of settlement in the surrounding areas. The editorial ended with an unattributed quotation from part of a speech given two years earlier by Sir Henry Parkes about how this country might be governed:

> *In a young country like this it is difficult to find reasons to justify the formation and existence of a Conservative party. For what have we to conserve? With perfect freedom to govern Australia – in the manner we think best, we have chosen to frame our institutions upon British models. But we are by no means bound to adhere to them should they prove faulty, and just as we took upon ourselves to reconstruct the Upper House of Parliament, on account of its selfish obstructiveness, so in course of time it may be incumbent upon us to take drastic measures of a similar character*

---

252 - Research material held by Arthur Hall included a copy of this article (which was published with no details of its authorship), but which Mr Hall was confident had been written by Wallace.

for the better and more direct government of the country by the people, whose heritage it is. Nor can it be said with any truth that in this country, at all events, private property and its rights are endangered by the progress of democracy. In the first place our extreme liberals are neither socialists nor communists, and in the next nine-tenths of the population are possessed individually of a share of this world's goods, which fact renders it in the highest degree improbable that they will ever be despoiled by a lawless minority. [253]

If this editorial was written by Wallace, then it is clear that he was very much an 'Australian native' in outlook.

Wallace would eventually embark on a journalism career, but for now he was still a disenchanted insurance salesman living with his parents in Chiltern. The last day of 1889 saw him, Barbara and their children back in Beechworth where they attended an event organised for the entertainment of the old residents who had settled in the Ovens district prior to 1863. The event was organised by his Honour John A Wallace, a Beechworth-based mining entrepreneur and politician.[254] John A Wallace had no connection at all to James's family, but would have been well aware of who James was and the role he played in the events of a decade earlier. The two of them may have shared a common surname but their political outlooks were poles apart.

The Beechworth event included a formal dinner. The extensive list of invited guests was subsequently published in the *Ovens and Murray Advertiser* on 11 January 1890. Although Barbara Wallace (née Allan) had come from a family who had settled in the Ovens district prior to 1863, no member of the Allan family was on the list of invitees to the formal dinner. Nevertheless, James and his family attended the day's

---

253 - The author of this passage is Henry Parkes, an Australian politician and journalist who played a key role in the federation of the Australian colonies into a single nation, which became the Commonwealth of Australia in 1901. The passage is taken from a speech Parkes delivered in Sydney to the Australian Natives' Association on 27 May 1887. The speech was subsequently delivered again by Parkes on 24 October 1889 in the town of Tenterfield, NSW (after which it became known as the 'Tenterfield Oration'). The speech is regarded as a seminal moment in the movement for Australian federation.

254 - https://adb.anu.edu.au/biography/wallace-john-alston-4792

activities, with James describing in his diary how much they enjoyed mixing with old friends.

On the first day of the New Year (1890), his Honour John Wallace was busy again opening the new Wallace Memorial Ward at the Beechworth Benevolent Asylum (also known as the Insane Asylum). James Wallace also attended this opening – the family having had first-hand dealings with the asylum due to William Wallace being admitted there as a patient some six years earlier and having remained a patient there for one and a half years.

James continued his work as an insurance salesman, now for the Equitable Insurance Company. A few remaining pages from his diary provide an insight into his activities between December 1889 and January 1890 as he canvassed for sales in Beechworth, Spring Creek and Chiltern, in between spending time with his family.[255] It was becoming harder to find clients with cash to spare for the 'luxury' of insurance in the years leading up to what would be called the 1890s depression. Despite the frustrations of his work, his diary indicates that he enjoyed the opportunity it afforded to roam around the district, talking with old friends and 'partaking'.

Wallace's diary entries are all rather mundane compared to the polished, flowery style of his public letters and his letters to Nicolson. He recorded his attempts to canvass insurance business, with references to people putting him off for another time. An insight into his character is given in another entry about his payment of a small deposit for a sewing machine, the balance of which he didn't intend to pay a further farthing of. Perhaps for Barbara's benefit, his diary justified his expenditure at hotels as an investment that may lead to pounds of business.

James had by now given up all hope of returning to the teaching profession. The Education Department may have been in want of

---

255 - It would seem likely that an inveterate writer like Wallace would have kept a diary for much of his life. All that remains, however, are a few pages torn out of his diary from 1889–1890 (the pages concerned being held by a member of the Wallace family). It is likely that Wallace would have kept a diary over the years 1878 to 1880, but that he would have taken care to ensure it contained no entries relating to his dealings with any of the members of the Kelly Gang.

qualified teachers six months earlier when Wallace was seeking a reference from Nicolson, but with the onset of the depression, the Victorian Government was now actively retrenching teachers and reducing the salaries of others.

Selling insurance was also becoming all but impossible and James would give up his insurance job in the early part of 1890, saying in one of his letters that he had been reduced to 'snipping and dealing in wattle bark, and other things'.[256] This period in his life must have been particularly stressful – he was only 34 years old and had to support a wife and eight children on no regular income. For most of 1890 through to the end of 1891, he was essentially confined to his 'snipping and dealing' activities.

In early April 1890, James's brother John Wallace was married in Melbourne to Hettie Grigg.[257] However, the happy times associated with that event were short lived, with William Wallace being committed to the Beechworth Insane Asylum on 9 May, after suffering from melancholia for the two previous weeks.[258] This was second time William had been committed to this institution, where he would remain until his death on 26 September 1895. The asylum records for this second admission give no place of abode, but state that he was in good bodily health and condition.

The Wallace family was not alone in its hardship. Times were also very hard for the Byrne family – the year 1891 saw Joe's sister Catherine arrested in Carlton and sentenced to six months imprisonment for vagrancy.[259] Catherine had been living rough, possibly as a prostitute. Soon after her sentencing she was confined to the Kenmore asylum in Goulburn, where she died many years later.

---

256 - Letter held by the Wallace family.

257 - John Murray Wallace was the fifth son of Charles Moreland Wallace and Marion Murray. As John was born in 1863, it is unlikely that he would have played any role in the Kelly affair, although his wife Hettie was to later express relief when they left the North-Eastern Region for good. John and Hettie married in St Kilda on 7 April 1890.

258 - Melancholia is an outdated medical term, but was essentially a mental condition and especially a manic-depressive condition characterised by extreme depression, bodily complaints, and often hallucinations and delusions.

259 - *The Argus*, 27 October 1891 report on Catherine Byrne's sentencing on 26 October 1891.

29

The Kerang years

In 1892 the Wallace family had a change of fortune after James was appointed as a journalist for the *Kerang Times*.[260] They packed their bags and relocated to Kerang, which would become their home for the next decade. The family rented a house in Nolan Street, a short walk from the commercial centre and the newspaper's office in Scoresby Street, and a short walk to school for the children.

With James now having a regular income like he used to have back in his teaching days, the Kerang years were a relatively settled and secure time for the family, particularly for the children. The new job also enabled James to indulge in his passion for writing, although reporting on the local news was rather mundane.

James had a strong influence over his brothers. William had accompanied him to Yea all those years ago, and now John and his wife Hettie, and Gilbert followed him to Kerang.[261] The brothers obviously had some lively times when they got together, with John being charged on 18 March 1892 for being drunk and disorderly, and James being charged for that same offence on 15 September. So much for James's claims in his various job applications of being a teetotaller!

The year 1892 was quite eventful for the Wallace family. Apart from the move to Kerang and the drunk and disorderly escapades, August of that year saw Barbara's brother William Allan marry Esther Sherritt, sister of Aaron Sherritt – the man whose murder 12 years earlier James had had a hand in. We can be certain that James and Barbara were not invited.[262]

---

260 - *The Kerang Times* had a circulation covering Kerang, Swan Hill, Pyramid Hill, Koondrook, Durham Ox, Boort, Cohuna and Gunbower and throughout the shires of Swan Hill, Gordon, East Loddon and Echuca.

261 - The year 1892 ended on a sad note with the death of John and Harriet's six-month-old son Hugh Douglas Wallace (their second child) on 1 December 1892.

262 - Family history has it that after James and Barbara left for Kerang they were never heard of again in the North East.

The following year, James and Barbara welcomed their tenth child Barbara Eva into the world in September.[263] However, their happiness was short lived, with baby Barbara dying only four months later in January 1894. Child number eleven – Ruby – was born soon after.

1894 was also an eventful year. In July, James was promoted to the position of Manager and Editor of *The Kerang Times*.[264] And later that year, James and Barbara's 16-year-old son George took up a pupil teacher position at Kerang, thus continuing the Wallace family tradition of entering the teaching profession. Around this time, James's brother John transferred to a teaching post at a school in the Wimmera.

The Kerang years ticked by. In 1895, John and Hettie lost their first-born child, but welcomed another.[265] And, of course, 1895 also saw the death of James's brother William who died at the Beechworth Asylum.[266]

In June 1896, tragedy struck the Wallace family, with the death from rheumatoid fever of their son Arthur 'Prince' Wallace at the age of twenty.[267] Prince was a family favourite and his death hit James very hard. The family experienced further loss a month later with the death of Barbara's mother in Milawa, followed not long after by the death of James's mother in Rutherglen.[268] Over the period of all these deaths, Barbara was pregnant with their twelfth child, which would have been the cause of further stress.

As the Manager and Editor of the *Kerang Times*, James wrote an editorial for each edition of the paper under the pseudonym '*Olla*

---

263 - Barbara Eva Beatrice was born in Kerang on 28 September 1893.

264 - Notice of Wallace's appointment was given in *The Kerang Times*, 13 July 1894 (page 2).

265 - Hettie Muriel Wallace, first born child of John and Hettie Wallace, died on 3 March 1895 and was buried at Boorhaman Cemetery. John Dugald Wallace was born on 22 July 1895 in Boorhaman.

266 - Two of James's own children would come to be committed to asylums. It is said by Wallace family members that there is a history of mental illness within the family that balances a tendency for brilliance, noting that many Wallace descendants have gone on to become teachers, doctors and ministers of religion.

267 - The death of Arthur (Prince) Wallace was reported in the *Kerang Times* on 26 June 1897, which described him as a young man who was universally liked.

268 - Marion Wallace died at Boundary Road, Rutherglen on 5 November 1898. Cause of death was exhaustion and senile phthisis (duration 12 months). Her son Andrew Murray Wallace (one of the 'band of brothers') was the informant.

Podrida', which is a Spanish term for a mixed stew. The editorials were usually mundane musings about the various goings-on in the Kerang district. Occasionally though, his real feelings would poke through the dross, and you can get a feel for a belief system and line of thought that might explain some of his actions back in the Kelly years. His editorials for Friday 6 August 1897 and 9 June 1899 are good examples.

In his '*Olla Podrida*' of Friday 6 August 1897, written only a month on from Prince's death, Wallace wrote about a lecture delivered that week in Sydney by Mr Ben Tillett on the 'Wealth and Progress of the Empire'.[269] Tillett was a British socialist, trade union leader and politician, who was visiting Australia on a speaking tour. The lecture related to Tillett's views on the British Empire and its economic and political influence around the world, as well as his ideas on socialism and workers' rights. The editorial quoted Tillett as questioning how so much poverty and distress could exist in the world, given all the signs of wealth and progress. How could it be that out of a world population of 400 million people, 350 million of those were in a state of poverty? The answer, according to Tillett, was that 50 million of the population controlled the remainder, and that this was the grossest form of slavery the world had ever known. Wallace ended his editorial by quoting Tillett as saying that 'In England, if a person stole a turnip, he was punished by the man who stole the field.'[270]

The '*Olla Podrida*' editorial of 9 June 1899 is a classic example of Wallace writing. It commences showily, with Wallace displaying his intellectualism with quotations from four prominent philosophers and one 'boodler'.[271] The first four quotes are from men who used their brains, kept their eyes and ears open, and were thinkers. The last was from Jay Gould, an American railroad magnate and financial speculator who is generally identified as one of the 'robber barons' of the Gilded Age, who we are told used the public for his own advantage. The

---

269 - https://en.wikipedia.org/wiki/Ben_Tillett

270 - This quote is often attributed to Frederick Douglass, an American social reformer, abolitionist, orator, writer, and statesman. However, there is no solid evidence that Douglass actually said this. It is possible that this quote is a paraphrase or a misattribution. The origin of the quote remains unclear.

271 - Boodler (in the context in which it is used by Wallace) is defined in *Wiktionary* as, 'one, especially a politician, who seeks or receives boodle; a political grafter'.

sentiments in this editorial are the kind that might have been held by some of the selector class back in the Kelly days. Most of his grandiose statements were made by other people but were unacknowledged by the writer of '*Olla Podrida*'. He wrote:

- '*The time will come, is surely coming, when the public will be educated, will unite and pull together for the general good, each for all and all for each, in the brotherhood of humanity.*'[272]

- '*Instead of the combination of the few for the plunder of the many, the many will unite to see that none are plundered, that all have at least equal opportunities.*'[273]

- '*There are signs in evidence now of a better order of things.*'

- '*People are beginning to realise that the remedy is in their own hands, that by united action at the ballot box they can by degrees purify the moral atmosphere.*'[274]

- '*While the world was younger it was necessary to resort to physical force, and right existing wrongs by wholesale murder and wanton destruction of property. In our more enlightened times, such barbarous methods are unnecessary. It only requires now that a sufficient number of honest men shall sink petty individual differences and, agreeing on a few broad lines of common interest, use their privilege of the franchise to shift gently undesirable representatives, and return others with a cleaner record to take their places.*'[275]

For Wallace to have inserted these statements into his editorial shows that he was well read and knowledgeable of the writings of these

---

272 - This statement was made by Robert Owen, an influential early 19th-century advocate of utopian societies, who made the comment in his book *A New View of Society*, published in 1813. Owen was known for his advocacy of cooperative communities and social reform, and his ideas influenced the development of the cooperative movement in the 19th century.

273 - This statement is attributed to Henry George, a prominent American political economist and journalist, best known for his book *Progress and Poverty*, published in 1879.

274 - This statement was made by John Bright, a British politician and orator, in a speech he delivered in Birmingham in 1865.

275 - This statement was made by Clarence Darrow, an American lawyer and civil libertarian.

important social reformers. Did he think at the time of Glenrowan that there were existing wrongs that could be righted by wholesale murder and wanton destruction of property? As someone who had, at the very least, helped collect the material used in the Kelly armour, could he have been guided at the time by some higher motivation than just helping his friend Joe Byrne? Some historians (Arthur Hall and Len Pryor) believe so; however, the lack of evidence means we can only speculate.

By 1897 James and Barbara had been married for 23 very eventful years, but the marriage was under strain. On top of Prince's death, the *Kerang Times* was experiencing financial problems. It was about this time that James, then aged 43 years, commenced an affair with a woman named Bertha Litchfield (née Bonn) who was 16 years his junior.

Bertha was the 27-year-old wife of a Narraport farmer named David Litchfield,[276] and the daughter of a German couple who it appears emigrated to Australia after 1891.[277] Her parents were quite well off, with her father Jacob having come from a privileged and intellectual background. His occupation was listed as an electrician, and he and his family had previously spent several years living a comfortable middle-class lifestyle in London. How they came to be living in a Victorian wheat-belt town like Birchip is unknown.

The Litchfield family were Birchip pioneers, and the area they farmed near Narraport is to this day known as Litchfield. Nothing is known about the circumstances of Bertha's marriage to David Litchfield, who she married soon after the death of his first wife, but it is hard to

---

276 - Bertha was Litchfield's second wife, his first having died whilst giving birth to their second child. They were married in Birchip, Victoria, on 20 June 1893.

277 - Bertha Bonn was the daughter of Johan Victor Hubert Anton Jacob (Jacob) Bonn (1840–1925) and Johanna Sarah Margarethe Elise Elizabeth (Bertha) Wetters (1843–1932). Johan and Bertha were both from the Rhine Province of Prussia (Germany), and were married aged 24 and 21 years on 25 October 1864 in Middlesex England. They had four children (all girls), all born in London: Ludovica Anna Elise (Elise) Bonn (1866–1956); Anna Elizabeth Bonn (1867–1954); Bertha Bonn (1869–1911); and Amy Bonn (1872–1954). Ludovica and Anna were married in London in 1890 and 1891 respectively, and it is likely that Jacob and Bertha and their other two children (Bertha and Amy) came to Australia after those marriages. On the marriage certificate of John Litchfield and Bertha Bonn, both have recorded Birchip as being their current and usual place of residence. The marriage certificate records John as being a 34-year-old widower, and Bertha as being a 24-year-old spinster.

imagine that someone like her would have found fulfilment with a life on the land.

With Narraport being located about 10 miles from the town of Birchip and a long way (50 miles) from Kerang, it is not known how James and Bertha met, but Wallace family members believe it was a shared interest in spiritualism and an interest in the wider world that probably brought them together. Bertha was a spiritualist and was also known as a fortune teller, and it is possible James met her in that capacity.[278] Both shared an interest in all things intellectual. James, as befitting his former teaching role and his current role as a journalist, was well read and interested in the world at large, whilst Bertha was also highly educated.

Bertha with her husband David Litchfield.

---

278 - James had a life-long interest in mesmerism. When he was explaining his relationship with Aaron Sherritt to the Royal Commissioners, he said he had a power over Aaron due to his ability to subject him to mesmerism. Mesmerism is an element of spiritualism.

James's relationship with the woman he called Bonnie was the final insult for Barbara. She had suffered for years as a result of her husband having been a Kelly sympathiser. She had followed him to Yea and then to Queensland and then back to Beechworth and finally to Kerang, losing connections with family and friends as a result. She had had enough, and in early 1899, she and the seven young children still under her care took the train to Melbourne, leaving James behind in Kerang. The breakup caused a deep schism in the Wallace family. The couple's two eldest surviving sons – 24-year-old James who was now working as a journalist in Adelaide, and 21-year-old George – never forgave their father for his betrayal. George, who had been working at the Kerang State School as a pupil teacher also left Kerang at about this time, having accepted a position of junior master at Wesley College in Melbourne.[279]

With the departure of Barbara and the children, the *Kerang Times* and Bonnie were the only things keeping James in Kerang. The newspaper, however, was experiencing financial difficulties, and towards the end of 1900 James decided it was also time for him to leave Kerang.

A photograph of James Wallace taken at around the time of his departure from Kerang is the only known image of him that still exists. It shows Wallace and the proprietor of the competing newspaper posing with the Kerang Shire Councillors and some of the officers of the Council.[280] Wallace is standing in the back row to the right of the hatted man who is Mr WJ Davey of the Kerang Observer. In 1900, James was only 46 years old, but he looks a decade older. He seems less vital than most of the other men in the photograph. His hair has thinned and his beard is grey. His dress jacket is buttoned, with stretchmarks across the front exacerbating a portly frame – always

---

279 - George Wallace's acceptance of the teaching position at Wesley College was reported in the 17 February 1899 edition of the *Kerang Times*.

280 - Around the turn of the 20th century, the Kerang City councillors and officers would pose annually for group photographs with other important people from the Kerang community. One such photograph taken around 1900 shows the councillors and council officers posing with the managers of the two Kerang newspapers. A copy of the photograph held by the Kerang Library identifies those in the photograph – the two newspaper men are in the back row and are Mr WJ Davey of the *Kerang Observer* and Mr W Wallace of The *Kerang Times*. The reference to W Wallace is obviously an error – the fact that he is also identified as the editor of the *Kerang Times* leaves no doubt the man is James Wallace.

a man who liked to 'partake', perhaps he had become too used to the good life in Kerang. The emotional upheaval he had been through with the breakdown of his family, combined with the financial difficulties his newspaper was experiencing, had seemingly taken a toll.

Councillors, officers and pressmen, about 1900.
From the left – back row: WJ Davey (*The Kerang Observer*),
W Wallace (*Kerang Times* editor), DG Rattray (Shire Secretary),
Dr Simons (Health Officer), James Connelly (Thistle Inspector).
Middle Row: Crs Hamilton, D McDonald, FG Garden, T Curlett, Messrs.
JJ O'Connor (Shire Valuer), DJ McClelland (Shire Engineer),
Cr Williamson, CW Simms, Rattray junior.
Front row: Crs Richardson, Westblade, Cullen, Mr H Coleman (draughtsman),
Crs PJ O'Donnell, TF Hogan, Moore and W Dunstan.

30
Valedictory

About 50 gentlemen from the town and district assembled at Kerang's Commercial Hotel on the evening of 1 November 1900 to bid James Wallace, retiring editor and manager of the *Kerang Times*, farewell on the eve of his departure from the district. The *Kerang Times* reported on the event the following day.[281]

Mr GH Morton, a grazier from Benjeroop, chaired the event and gave apologies for those who could not be present, including the Hon. JH McColl, Minister for Lands, and Cr Curlett, president of the Kerang Shire. An apology letter from the Hon. JH McColl was read in which he praised the great ability with which Wallace had conducted his newspaper and thanked him for 'the courage he had displayed in battling always for what he considered honest and straightforward in public and private matters,' and noting that 'at times many may not have agreed with all he has written.'

Toasts were made to the Queen and the defence and volunteer forces, and the National Anthem was sung. Kind words about the guest of honour were then delivered by a number of dignitaries., including from a member of the Volunteer Reserve, a storekeeper, several justices of the peace, and a bank manager.

Mr John Kerr JP said he was a great admirer of Mr Wallace, despite quarrelling with him on occasions. 'The only fault he could find with him was that he was a bit too good as a fighter'. 'What he believed to be right he went for.'

Mr JW Neilson, manager of the London Bank, said, 'Mr Wallace had been a power for good and a most fearless writer – not always pleasing everyone but always writing what he thought best for the good of the district.'

---

281 - *Kerang Times*, Friday 2 November 1900. Page 2 report, 'Valedictory'.

Mr Geo. Adams JP endorsed the remarks of previous speakers. He had known Wallace since he had been in the town and 'always found that everything he did was straight and fair and above board.' Wallace, he said, 'was very expert with his pen and his efforts had been widely appreciated.' As editor, 'he had had a free hand and had sometimes gone further than he (Mr Adams) liked. He was sometimes a bit rough and trod heavily on people's toes, but everybody must give him credit for fighting in a straight-forward manner.'

The songs 'Boys of the Old Brigade', 'Pall Away', and 'Nancy Lee' had punctuated the various speakers. The chairman then presented Wallace with a set of gold and amethyst sleeve links as a memento.

Wallace replied that if an editor could blush, he would have blushed that night to hear so many kind things said. He then described his thoughts on his role as an editor, which the next day's edition of The Kerang Times summarised as follows:

> *An editor's position was a most responsible one. There was no power on earth at the present time so effective for good or evil as the power of the press. When a man spoke, he spoke to a limited number at the time within range of his voice. What he wrote travelled through the press to the farthest corners of the earth and had effect on the minds of readers not only in the present only, but in the future. What was written remained. Had he realised earlier his responsibilities and the power for good he might have exercised, he would in some instances have written differently. Still, he felt at all times he had tried to do justice to the shareholders, to the public and to himself. His position had not altogether been a bed of roses – he had had at times a pretty tough row to hoe – but he had received much pleasure from the kindly sympathy of his readers and contributors and the assistance of a loyal staff of officers.*

The breakup of his family may also have had something to do with Wallace's reasons for leaving. The Kerang Times reported that, 'For the past two years he had been living in exile from home and family and he thought his term should be about up.'

Further songs were then sung, a further toast was given by the chairman, after which the singing of Auld Lang Syne brought the function to a close.

31
A new life with Bonnie

Immediately after the valedictory function, James and Bertha left Kerang. The *Kerang Times* went bankrupt soon after.[282]

Although James had told those at his valedictory that there was a possibility he would continue to speak with his pen through the columns of another journal, his movements after leaving Kerang show that he and Bertha had other plans. Their first stop was Marrickville in Sydney to visit Bertha's parents and sister. From there, they took a steamer to Auckland. Despite the breakdown of both their marriages, money did not seem to be an issue.

In Auckland, Bertha established herself as a clairvoyant under the name Madame Spontini. The Spontini name was also taken on by James. From this point on, James faded into the background and let Bertha take the limelight. He was always there in the background, though, supporting his 'Bonnie' in all of her endeavours.

The couple spent two years in New Zealand as Madame Spontini honed her craft. With his background in newspapers, James advertised her services in the New Zealand papers.[283] Clairvoyants and spiritualists were common in these times and she was competing for business against many like her. With James assisting her and arranging publicity and placing advertisements in the right newspapers, she was able to hold her own against her competitors.

An early advertisement in Auckland's *Evening Post* described Madame Spontini as a 'Metaphysician, Masseuse and Medical Medium trained

---

282 - The *Kerang Times* went bankrupt in early 1901. After a restructure, the newspaper reappeared. The new manager was a man named H R Freeman.

283 - Advertisements for Madame Spontini appeared in the Evening Post, New Zealand Times, Thames Star, Gisborne Times, Poverty Bay Herald, and the Auckland Star.

in London and Paris, who was available for consultation by lady clients from 10 am to 10 pm daily'.[284]

Within weeks she had moved to new consulting rooms.[285] She offered lessons to ladies on 'Scientific Palmistry' and other branches of mental science, as well as 'Trance Psychometry', in addition to her usual range of services.[286]

At the same time, a new service was now available – Mr Spontini, described in the advertisements as a certified hypnotist and masseur, was available to treat male subjects!

Bertha was also busy giving her illustrated lecture on 'The Language of the Hand'. Notice of this lecture by the 'Scientific Palmist Madame Spontini' was advertised over multiple days in the *Evening Post* and *New Zealand Times*. Admission was 1 shilling, but 3 shillings entitled holders to a free public or private lesson or reading.

After several months in Auckland, the couple spent a few weeks plying the goldfields at Thames.[287] They took the coastal steamer from Auckland to Tauranga, and from there travelled by road, stopping en route for several weeks in the gold mining town of Waihi. At Waihi, Madame Spontini again delivered her 'Language of the Hand' lecture, reported by the *Thames Star* as featuring limelight illustrations of the palms of Madame Sarah Bernhard; Madame Melba; the late Lord Russell OG OM, Chief Justice of England; Mr Joseph Chamberlain; and Mr WT Stead.[288]

Having secured accommodation in Thames,[289] advertisements for Madame Spontini – 'Masseuse, Psychometrist and Character Reader, Lecturer on the Language of the Hand' – appeared in the *Thames Star* from the end of February to mid-April 1902. Madame was available for consultation every day except Sunday. Charts could be written and advice given on all subjects.

---

284 - *Evening Post* (Auckland), 31 October 1901.

285 - 12 Caroline Street, Auckland.

286 - *Evening Post*, 4 December 1901.

287 - *Thames Star*, 14 January 1902.

288 - *Thames Star*, 24 January 1902.

289 - The couple based themselves at 'The Bungalow' in Mackay Street, Thames.

One could be excused for thinking it was just money that was driving James and Bertha. However, a bereavement notice placed in the *New Zealand Herald* by the parents of a young man named Samuel Langford included a special acknowledgement of Madame Spontini and her husband for having so lovingly assisted Samuel's wife in nursing him, and for doing all in their power to alleviate his sufferings, regardless of expense or trouble and without any charge whatever.[290] Was the notice legitimate or just clever advertising? Interestingly, one of Bertha's sisters who had stayed behind in London had married into a family named Langford.

In late April 1902, the couple left for Rotorua. The *Thames Star* noted that during her short stay in Thames, Madame had given readings to over 1000 of Thames's citizens and had done a great deal to educate public opinion in regard to human science and human destiny.[291] But maybe the couple left Thames for other reasons – Brisbane's *Truth* newspaper would later publish an article titled 'Fortune-Telling Frauds',[292] which gave 'Madame from Maoriland' considerable attention. She was described as being comparatively young and as having a pleasant voice and talking manners, whilst her husband Mr Spontini was described as 'a smooth-faced, bald-headed man of unctuous and urbane manners' who acted as her assistant. The article noted Madame Spontini had found a certain degree of fame in Auckland, but that she occasionally needed to journey further afield in search of 'fresh dupes'.

The *Truth* described how Madame Spontini had generated quite a sensation in Thames by the knowledge she displayed of the adventures, experiences, occupations and tastes of her clients. It turns out, though, that she was using an old resident as her 'confederate' to surreptitiously signal her with the correct answers. It all went well until the day a stranger arrived and called her out. This caused an uproar followed by court proceedings, which caused the Spontini family to depart hastily.

---

290 - The bereavement notice appeared in the *New Zealand Herald* on 2 May 1902. It appears to be legitimate, but it is worth noting that Bertha's sister Anna, who had married and stayed behind in London when her parents and two younger sisters had left for Australia, had married into a family named Langford.

291 - *Thames Star*, 21 April 1902.

292 - *Truth* newspaper, Sunday 21 February 1904, article 'Fortune Telling Frauds'.

The reference in the Truth article to court proceedings is hard to verify, as there does not appear to be any reports of it in the New Zealand newspapers.

James and Bertha had worked hard in the six months they spent in New Zealand. They took some time off to relax in the spa town of Rotorua before returning to Auckland to work for a short time,[293] and then travelling back to Australia in June 1902 for a stint in Bathurst.[294] An advertisement headed 'What the World's a-seeking – Health & Happiness' in the *Bathurst Free Press and Mining Journal* on 26 June 1902 advised that 'Madame Spontini (From London, Paris & New Zealand), Scientific Palmist, Clairvoyante & Psychometrist' was available for a few days only for 'Short Readings at 1s and Long Readings 2s 6d'.

Madame Spontini's visit to Bathurst was later reported upon in the type of flowery language that had all the hallmarks of having been written by James Wallace:

PALMISTRY EXTRAORDINARY.

To the majority of people the very name of palmistry has been synonymous with humbug and suggestive rather of the confidence tricks on a racecourse or showground; but it would seem that the counterfeit only presupposes and postulates the genuine article which is counterfeited. Facts are stubborn things. Madame Spontini's short visit to Bathurst has shattered the scepticism of scores of the most intelligent and level headed of the citizens. The accuracy with which this modern mystic reads the record of the life, health, character, and environment of a client, as alleged to be written in the lines and markings of the human hand, is simply astonishing. The testimonies as to the genuineness of Madame Spontini's wonderful gifts are unimpeachable. It is

---

293 - *Auckland Star*, 12, 13 and 14 May, 1902.

294 - In Bathurst, Madame Spontini set herself up for consultations at 'The Elms' in Russell Street, Bathurst.

> *enough to make the uninitiated feel 'creepy' to hear the inmost secrets of the soul laid bare, or to listen to the tests given in medical and mining Psychometry. Madame Spontini brings her work back in Bathurst to a close tomorrow (Wednesday) evening.* [295]

After Bathurst, the couple headed back to New Zealand, where Bertha worked until mid-September from premises in Peel Street, Gisborne.[296] She also presented her 'Language of the Hand' lecture during this time in Gisborne.[297] A newspaper quoted her as describing the chief failings of the people of Gisborne as 'procrastination, lack of energy and too much 'tick' (idleness), which she attributed to climatic influences and the example set by the native race'.[298] Procrastination, lack of energy and too much tick were not accusations you could direct towards Bertha or James!

Later in September, James and Bertha returned to Auckland on the Waikare.[299] For the remainder of the year, advertisements for Madame Spontini ran in the *Auckland Star* and the *New Zealand Herald*. She was a masseuse and mental scientist, a chart writer, a character reader and a psychometrist. She had now also become an agent for Neil's Botanic Remedies.[300]

After a year in Auckland, it was time to return again to Australia – they departed on the Waikare on 21 September 1903. By late November, Bertha was working at No. 1 Arcade, Edward Street, Brisbane, with

---

295 - Bathurst Free Press and Mining Journal, dated 8 July 1902.

296 - Advertisements in the *Gisborne Times* advised that Madame Spontini was available to be consulted at her rooms in Peel Street.

297 - *The Poverty Bay Herald* advertised the lecture over the first half of September 1902.

298 - *The Gisborne Times*, 15 September 1902.

299 - *The Gisborne Times* dated 19 September 1902 reported that Madame Spontini would be departing for Auckland the following day on the Waikare. The shipping records show two bookings for Spontini arriving at Auckland on 21 September.

300 - James F Neil published a book titled *The New Zealand family herb doctor* (*also titled Family herb doctor & medical recipe book*), on the botanic eclectic system of medicine, containing the latest discoveries in medicine and surgery for the cure of disease. Also, a description of the herbs, roots, barks, seeds, extracts, essential oils, etc. The book contained 100 (six-coloured) plates of the most important medicinal plants growing in New Zealand, Australia, and elsewhere, together with numerous carefully selected valuable remedies, recipes, etc.

regular advertisements being placed in Brisbane's *Telegraph*.³⁰¹ She was one of numerous clairvoyants advertising such services – Madames Wallson, Rievaulex and Madelle were all competing for the same customers.

Back in Brisbane, Madame Spontini was advertised widely in the *Queensland Figaro* and *The Telegraph*. She worked by day in the city (2 Arcade, Edward Street) and in the evening at her home 'Edna Villa' in Musgrave Street, Red Hill. She even catered for those who lived at a distance – all they had to do was send a lock of hair or sample of handwriting. She didn't always have to advertise – sometimes her work was newsworthy. The *Queensland Figaro* edition of 11 February 1904 had this to say:

> *Madame Spontini, the wonderful clairvoyant and psychometrist, still continues to astonish and delight the Brisbane public with her knowledge of events, past and to come. She is well worth a visit, and No. 2 Arcade, Edward Street, is crowded daily with those whose friends have recommended them, on the strength of personal conviction, to hear what Madame Spontini has to tell them.*³⁰²

Other reports were not so glowing. The previously noted *Brisbane Truth* article titled 'Fortune-Telling Frauds' contained the sub-headings 'Madame from Maoriland', 'Herb Healing Horrors' and 'Palmistry Pests Promote Population Paucity'.³⁰³ Madame Spontini, assisted by Mr Spontini, was described as the leading soothsayer in Brisbane, who numbered among her clientele some of the elite of Brisbane. The article also had quite a bit to say about Mr Spontini's contributions, describing him as posing as a magnetic healer and massage practitioner. It noted that after Madame had diagnosed her clients' ailments (usually serious ailments like tuberculosis, kidney, heart or uterus diseases), she would advise the taking of certain drugs and persuasively suggest that Mr

---

301 - *The Telegraph*, 28 November 1903.

302 - The *Queensland Figaro and Punch* was a weekly newspaper published from 1885 to 1936 in Brisbane, Queensland, Australia.

303 - *Truth* newspaper, Sunday 21 February 1904, article 'Fortune Telling Frauds'.

Spontini should then take the case in hand. His role was to sell the medicine and, if the patient's means allowed, to apply the medicine at a charge of 10 shillings an hour. It was also noted that Madame Spontini would refer women who were producing too many children to her husband for advice, as he was able to supply much valuable information on that subject:

> *Madame Spontini never fails to express her horror when she finds that her lady applicants are doing their duty to the nation by producing little strangers at regular intervals and strongly advises that her husband should be consulted, as he is able to supply much valuable information on the subject.*

James, the smooth-faced, bald-headed man of unctuous and urbane manners, the magnetic healer and massage practitioner and supplier of medicines, was now also the giver of valuable information on the subject of birth control! As someone who had fathered 12 children, it was rather ironic.

The *Truth* also discredited another practitioner called Gypsy Lee. She was described as being clever with herbs for the cure of most things, but pregnancy in particular. Maybe some of Neil's botanic remedies sold by Madame Spontini shared similar pregnancy-curing properties? Perhaps that is the information Mr Spontini was providing to the women she was referring to him.

Articles like this in Brisbane's *Truth* and later in Perth's *Sunday Times* insinuated that practitioners like Madame Spontini and Gypsy Lee were associated with abortion or abortionists. The reference to Madame Spontini expressing horror at her lady applicants' lack of birth control and her strong advice that they should consult her husband on the subject is telling. One of the evils that many in these times associated with fortune tellers like Madame Spontini was that they were people to whom young women would go to see as a precursor to having an abortion. Herbs might be prescribed to deal with an early pregnancy, but a referral to someone else was on the cards if the pregnancy was more advanced.

Despite her notoriety, Madame Spontini continued to advertise in Brisbane newspapers.[304] By July 1904, she had relocated to new premises at 42 Tank Street, North Quay, and was working from 10 am until 9 pm daily, except for Wednesdays and Sundays, and Saturday nights. She charged 5 shillings for a consultation, and was still offering to analyse locks of hair and samples of handwriting sent to her from clients who lived too far to visit.

By the end of 1904, in addition to her massage, herbalist and clairvoyant services, her advertisements also extended to a range of Madame Spontini branded products, including:

- *Madame Spontini's Specialities – herbal mixtures for indigestion, nervous dyspepsia, rheumatism, paralysis, and all chronic complaints. 2s 6p per packet.*

- *Madame Spontini's Ruby Oil, the mother's friend, a sovereign remedy for outward application in all nervous affections, coughs, colds, etc, and a certain specific for chronic constipation. 2s 6p per bottle.*

- *Madame Spontini's healing ointment for all sores, cuts, wounds, bruises. 2s 6p.*

- *Madame Spontini's special eye Ointment. 2s 6 p.*

- *Madame Spontini's special Gargle for teachers and speakers relaxed throat; strengthens the vocal cords and restores the voice. 2s*

- *Madame Spontini's Pink Ointment for rheumatism, sciatica, and all muscular pains. 2s 6p.*

- *Madame Spontini's marvellous Paw-paw Ointment, for ulcerations, abscesses, sore throat, carache, chest weaknesses, etc. 2s. 6p.*

- *Madame Spontini's Urania Ointment, for inward complaints, dropsy, gravel, etc. 2s. 6p.*

- *Madame Spontini's Nasal Powder cures polypus, nasal catarrh, etc. 2s.*

- *Madame Spontini's Toilet Specialities, Urania face lotion, 2s 6p; Urania hair wash, 2s 6p.*

---

304 - Advertisements in *The Telegraph* and occasionally the *Queensland Figaro* continued through the remainder of 1904 and into 1905.

On 9 March 1905, readers of the *Queensland Figaro* 'Gossip from Woman's Clubland' column discovered that the famous palmist Madame Spontini had left by the Gabo for a trip to the south (Sydney). From there she headed for Perth. Advertisements in the Brisbane *Courier* advised her customers of how they could obtain her products during her absence.

From mid-April 1905 and for most of 1906, Madame Spontini worked from a small cottage called 'Tara' at 178 Aberdeen Street, Perth. Newspaper advertisements placed by James described her as a 'Clairvoyante, Herbalist and Consulting Masseuse, late of Auckland and Brisbane, who could be interviewed daily (except for Sundays) between the hours of 10 to 9'. She was described as an agent for Botanic Remedies prepared by Meyers of Melbourne and Neil of New Zealand. Health readings were also one of her specialities.

During this time in Perth, the *Sunday Times* ran an article headlined 'Prophets without Honor' similar to the one that appeared in the *Brisbane Truth* the previous year. The article excoriated 'The loafing crowd of soothsayers' who plied their trade in the neighbourhood of Perth.[305] A correspondent calling herself Miss Stinging Nettles recounted her experiences as she consulted the various palmists, clairvoyants and spiritualists, including Madame Spontini from whom she sought answers to questions regarding the whereabouts of a missing brother and her prospects of success in a pending fictitious court case:

> *As far as finance is concerned the most successful of the tribe of prophets appears to be the Aberdeen Street clairvoyante, who trades under the name of Madame Spontini. She is decorated with trinkets and jewels like a prize poodle, and sports a fashionable villa laden with Maori relics. After an hour's incessant chat concerning the riches, travels, and successes that lay before me, Madame, in reply to my first question found me my long lost brother on a stationary vessel in the NorWest quill driving, but thinking of coming home. 'But about, my court case?' I queried, whereupon she replied: 'Go straight ahead. You*

---

305 - The *Sunday Times*, Perth, WA, Sunday 10 December 1905, page 5.

> *have nothing to fear. You cannot meet with failure in anything you do for an Eastern sage, rich in the power of determination and force, is your daily spiritual guide.' I found scores of other guides as I went along, but Madame had reached me down one of those topmost creatures we poor folk cannot embrace every day.*

Just as the *Brisbane Truth* had done, after criticising Madame Spontini, the *Sunday Times* turned on a number of other clairvoyants who were practicing in the Perth area. Another one to get a serve was a Mrs Parker of Brisbane Street, the newly ordained head of the Spiritualistic Church. The reference to her in an article dismissive of Perth's fortune-telling frauds was interesting given that Madame Spontini was by this time also heavily involved in the Spiritualist Church, where she lectured on a wide range of subjects such as power of the mind. She was part of a movement the newspapers called 'The Truth', which was also known as the 'New Thought Movement'.

At this time, Perth was one of the earliest and most active centres for the New Thought movement in Australia. Madame Spontini conducted some of the early meetings. The same *Sunday Times* that had excoriated Madame Spontini in 1905 would later (in 1913) publish a piece about the story of the 'Higher Thought' movement. It noted that although the teaching at Madame Spontini's meetings was not given with absolute purity as regarded the New Truth foundation principles (savouring somewhat of the psychic plane instead), it was nevertheless a beginning. It also noted that the Perth Metaphysical Association also succeeded in holding together while Madame Spontini conducted it, with her dominant personality being a magnetic centre around which many gathered.[306]

Madame Spontini became well known in Perth for her activities with the New Thought Movement and her lectures at the Perth Metaphysical Association, with the newspapers regularly publishing details of her lectures. The *West Australian* newspaper of Sunday 15 September 1907 described how a very attentive and deeply interested

---

306 - *Sunday Times* (Perth, WA), Sunday 18 May 1913, page 14. Article titled 'The New Thought', an abbreviated history of the 'Higher Thought' movement in Perth, taken from an article in the *Truth Seeker*.

audience attended her lecture titled 'Varying planes and their relation to mental science' held in the Metaphysical Association's rooms.[307] In another lecture at the Perth Metaphysical Society on Sunday 26 October 1907, she spoke on the power inherent in members of the human race to uplift themselves and their fellow creatures to higher planes of thought and deed.[308] Heady stuff indeed! The positive reporting on Madame Spontini's lectures were not enough, however, to overcome the controversy that had been generated two years earlier by the *Sunday Times*.

On the last day of 1907, James and Bertha departed by sea for Sydney.[309] Bertha immediately set herself up for practice in Bull's Chambers at 14 Moore Street. Her advertisements now highlighted vibratory massage as one of her areas of expertise. An advertisement that appeared in the classified section of the Freeman's Journal on 25 February 1909 is typical of her publicity during this period:

VIBRATORY MASSAGE

> *Madame Spontini's bright rooms in Bull's Chambers, 14 Moore Street, are always thronged with people anxious to obtain a course of treatment according to her method. Madame Spontini claims to be a herbalist, dietician, and masseuse (a member of the Australian Union of Herbalists, Regd.). She depends for her cures on natural methods of treating her patients. Dieting is one of her specialities, and she has drawn up no less than twenty-seven different diet scales, with very definite instructions for the patient's daily diet. Splendid results have been obtained by this treatment, combined with Pulsator, Vibratory, and General Massage. Trained hospital nurses and experienced operators are constantly in attendance. Health conditions are read and advice given as to Naturopathic Treatment, Herbal Remedies, Diet,*

---

307 - As reported in the *West Australian*, 17 September 1907.

308 - As reported in *Daily News* (Perth WA), 2 November 1907.

309 - In the 31 December 1907 edition of the *Daily News*, the social page ('Mainly about People') announced that Madame Spontini was leaving Western Australia, sailing that night on the Monaro.

> *Massage, Physical Culture, Deep Breathing Exercise, etc. A few leading specialities are: – Madame Spontini's Mixed Herbs, special ointments, and some toilet creams and lotions and the celebrated Ruby oil, 'Marzol' for the relief and cure of pain by external application in rheumatism, sciatica, etc.*

Madame Spontini continued presenting lectures on a wide range of esoteric topics. Her 'Power of Color' lecture presented on 25 February 1909 to an audience at the Progressive Thought Hall is an example, in which she explained that there was a force and spiritual interpretation to colour because of the particles and electricity attracted to it.[310]

After two years in Sydney, it was time to return again to Perth. Madame Spontini's clients were notified that her rooms at Bull's Chambers would close on 11 December 1909 for the Christmas Holidays and during the proprietor's absence in Perth. Due notice of her return would be advertised.[311]

Back in Perth, Madame Spontini's business was booming, clearing an annual profit of £700 to £800. By comparison, the average annual wages at that time for employees in manufacturing industries was £107 for males and £51 13s for females. Western Australia paid the highest wages for both males (£150 15s per annum) and females (£58 68s per annum).[312]

Madame Spontini had also regained her status as a leading light in the Perth Metaphysical Society, in addition to the Women's Service Guild of Western Australia. She continued to be a much sought-after lecturer on a range of subjects. She and James were also active members of the Spiritualist Church at Subiaco. It was very much an intellectual and spiritual life.

---

310 - As reported in the Australian Star (Sydney, NSW), on 26 February 1909.

311 - *The Catholic Press*, page 11, 23 December 1909. Madame Spontini never did return to Sydney.

312 - Details of the Commonwealth Statistician's report were published in the *Sydney Morning Herald* dated 8 June 1914 in an article titled 'Average Wages – Factory Hands – Interesting Statistics'. The average annual wages for employees in manufacturing industries cited above were extrapolated from the average weekly wages listed in that report.

The couple's decision to return to Perth may also have had something to do with the fact that the New Thought Movement had just opened up its first Truth Centre and Healing Rooms.[313] The new healing rooms were there for the benefit of those who sought to be healed by the power of controlled thought and prayer. Despite only being in his mid-50s, James was by then suffering badly with diabetes and other ailments.

---

313 - The Truth Centre and Bethany Healing Rooms, opened in December 1909, at 181 St Georges Terrace, Perth. More information about the New Thought Movement in Perth and about this centre can be found in the article titled 'The New Thought, an abbreviated history of the "Higher Thought" movement in Perth', at page 14 of the 18 May 1913 edition of the *Sunday Times* (Perth, WA).

32

Death of James and Bonnie

In August 1910 Bertha purchased a little jarrah cottage in Thomas Street, Subiaco, directly opposite Kings Park and close to the Rokeby Street tram terminus.[314] However, the couple's happiness in their new home was short-lived. Only three months after moving in, James fell ill and died on 20 November 1910 at the age of only 56 years. His death certificate gave the cause of death as diabetes and exhaustion.[315] He was buried in the Spiritualist section of the Karrakatta Cemetery.

Bertha never recovered from the shock of James's death. Tragically, she followed him to the grave only three months later, at the age of only 40 years. Her death certificate gave the cause of death as brain fever and exhaustion.[316] However, a poignant obituary in the *Sunday Times* tells us it was her inability to cope with the loss of her soul mate James that was the real cause of death:

> *By the death of Madame Spontini, quite a remarkable personality has gone from among us. For some years a clairvoyant of remarkable powers, Madame Spontini later took up electric and vibratory treatment for many complaints, and is said to have effected cures. A strong advocate of psychic and spiritualistic force, the deceased lady was a prominent member of several societies dealing with these subjects. Madame Spontini's husband*

---

314 - The house was located at 143 Thomas Street, close to the intersection with Rokeby Road. The street numbering in Thomas Street was changed during the 20th century and bears no resemblance to the street numbering that existed in 1910.

315 - Death by exhaustion is an old medical expression that was often used to describe a death caused by a stress-related heart attack or stroke.

316 - Brain fever is an old medical expression for an inflammation of the brain, used to describe one of several different brain infections including encephalitis, meningitis and cerebritis.

predeceased her by about three months, and from the shock of his death she never rallied.[317]

Bertha was interred in the same grave as James. The grave was then marked with a large headstone faced with white marble and topped with a heavy marble cross bearing the name Bonnie. There is nothing to identify that a man named James Wallace also lies therein.

Madame Spontini's death was noted and deeply regretted at the 1911 AGM of the Women's Service Guild.[318] The Women's Christian Temperance Union (WCTU) also noted her passing at its 20th annual convention on 29 August 1911.[319]

James and Bertha may have passed themselves off as husband and wife, but the reality was that James was still officially married to Barbara. A death notice for James placed in Melbourne's *The Argus* newspaper described him as '...the beloved husband of Barbara Wallace, and father of Charles, George, William, Bert, Percy, Lily, Minnie, Ruby and Harold' (Martha, Ebenezer Arthur, and Barbara Eva Beatrice had all predeceased him).

Grave of James Wallace and Bertha Bonn, Karrakatta Cemetery, Perth, WA.

---

317 - *Sunday Times*, Perth, Sunday 26 February 1911, page 26.

318 - Details of the Women's Service Guild AGM were noted in the *Western Mail*, Saturday 15 April 1911 (page 41).

319 - Details of the WCTU's 20th convention were noted in the *West Australian*, Wednesday 30 August 1911 (page 8). The WCTU's business was described in the convention coverage as including visitations to the state's hospitals and infirmaries and delivery of flowers, fruit and literature to patients in those institutions, and visiting of prison inmates and the provision of assistance to inmates upon their discharge.

Most of James's surviving children had little to do with their father after he took up with Bertha. As he never left a will, it is not known if he made any financial provision for Barbara after their separation. It seems likely that he didn't, given there is resentment even to this day amongst some branches of the family about the financial and emotional burden that had been placed upon them due to their father's behaviour.

In the decade they were together, Bertha managed to build up considerable wealth as Madame Spontini, with James helping her behind the scenes. The wealth they accumulated was treated as Bertha's, perhaps as a way to ensure Barbara had no claim. Bertha's last will and testament shows that the couple did, however, maintain a relationship with at least two of James's children – Minnie (then aged 30) and Hubert (then aged 25).[320]

In Bertha's will, she bequeathed her assets as follows:

- Her Starr-Bowkett shares to a Miss Annie Udy of Rangiriri, NZ.[321]

- Her curios, Aboriginal weapons coWllection and books to James's younger brother Gilbert Murray Wallace.

- Her 'real and personal Estate' to her father Jacob Bonn (then living in Cambridge, Marrickville, Sydney).

- Her herbalist business was left in trust to Hubert John Wallace (James's eighth child) and William Paterson for them to sell and dispose as they thought fit – with the

---

320 - Marion Katherine Cleopatra Wallace (known as Minnie) was born in Yea on 4 December 1881 in the midst of the measles outbreak that caused James to close his school. Minnie never married. At the time of Bertha's death, Minnie and her mother Barbara were living with her brother George's family at the home they called 'Stranraer' at 6 Linacre Road, Hampton (the house being named after the town in Scotland that grandparents Charles and Marion Wallace left behind when they emigrated to Australia). Minnie died in 1935 at the Mont Park Asylum, a psychiatric hospital located in the Melbourne outer eastern suburb of Macleod. Hubert John Wallace was born in 1886 while the Wallace family were living in Brisbane.

321 - The author has not been able to definitively identify Miss Annie Udy. There is an Udy branch to Harriet (Hettie) Grigg's family tree (Harriet being the wife of James's brother John Wallace, who followed him to Kerang) and it is therefore possible that there was an Annie Udy who was related to Hettie. James and Bertha also spent several years living in New Zealand where a school teacher named Annie Udy appears in records.

proceeds to be distributed to Gilbert Murray Wallace (10 pounds) and the balance to be divided equally between Jacob Bonn (her father), Minnie Wallace (of 'Stranraer', Linacre Road, Sandringham) and Hubert John Wallace.[322]

Bertha's ownership of Starr-Bowkett shares is interesting. Starr Bowkett was a non-profit financial cooperative where members would pay subscriptions for an agreed period, after which, once the society had built up a certain amount of capital, subscribers would be eligible to participate in a ballot for an interest-free housing loan. The cooperative catered for people who would not otherwise have qualified for a loan from the mainstream financial sector (banks) due to low incomes, lack of collateral, and other reasons.[323] Without knowing the value or number of Star Bowkett shares she owned, it is impossible to say what they were worth. Likewise, without further details of her collection of curios, Aboriginal weapons and books, it is impossible to say what they might have been worth.

A number of notices appeared in *The Western Australian* newspaper relating to the sale of Bertha's 'real and personal Estate' and her herbalist business.

Bertha's home at 143 Thomas Street, Subiaco, together with the adjoining allotment was auctioned on 20 May 1911.[324] It is not known how much the house and adjoining lot returned at auction. As per Bertha's will, the proceeds would have been paid to her father Jacob Bonn.

---

322 - It is not known who William Patterson was. However, the transfer details on the Certificate of Title for Bertha Spontini's property at Thomas Street, Subiaco, states that probate of her will was granted by the Supreme Court to Herbert John Wallace alone, after the other executor had renounced his right to probate.

323 - The Starr Bowkett was a non-profit financial co-op based on the principle of self-help, and was an inspiration for modern micro credit movements. https://en.wikipedia.org/wiki/Starr-Bowkett_Society
The following article in the *West Australian* (Perth) newspaper dated Monday 19 September describes the operation of Starr-Bowkett societies and refers to the establishment of Starr-Bowkett Building Societies in Perth. https://trove.nla.gov.au/newspaper/article/3040167

324 - The house property (Lot 13 Section G) was described as having a 50 ft frontage to Thomas Street and a depth of 120 ft, upon which was erected a comfortable jarrah cottage of four rooms, with a verandah and electric light, and a stable, shed and outhouse. The adjoining allotment (Lot 14) had the same dimensions as the house lot and was enclosed with a picket fence. The property was described as being one minute from the Rokeby Road Tram Terminus and facing King's Park.

On the same day that Bertha's house and vacant lot were auctioned (20 May 1911), Madame Spontini's 'Furniture, Plant and business Stock in Trade' was also auctioned at her business premises in the Bookman's Buildings in Barrack Street, Perth. The business, which the auction notice stated was giving a clear profit of £700 to £800 per annum, was to be first offered as a going concern. If the business did not fetch the reserve price, everything (furniture, stock, plant, etc) would be sold in lots without reserve.

The auction notice also listed a stock, amongst other things, of 1000 bottles of 'Marsol', worth £88 at selling price, and the equivalent of £80 worth (selling price) of balm of figs, and a massage plant (table), which cost over £40.

It is not known if Madame Spontini's herbalist business was sold as a going concern, or if the furniture, plant and stock in trade was sold off as separate lots. As per her will, £10 of the proceeds would have been paid to James's brother Gilbert Wallace, with the balance paid equally between Jacob Bonn (her father) and to James's daughter Minnie Wallace and son Hubert Wallace.

On 24 May 1911, a further newspaper notice appeared inviting offers for the 'Goodwill, the two Trade Marks (Marsol and Urasis) and the recipes of Madame Spontini's business'. No information is to hand as to whether offers were received, or the outcome.

From the time they left Kerang, money never seemed to be an issue for James and Bertha. And yet, before moving to Kerang in 1892, James was virtually broke, with he and his family being forced out of necessity to live with his parents at their property in Chiltern. It is hard to believe that eight years of work at *The Kerang Times*, even if six of those years were as the manager, would have provided James with much in the way of a financial buffer given the size of his family. It is also unlikely that Bertha would have taken much away from her marriage to David Litchfield. Ultimately, though, Bertha's 'clairvoyancy' and obvious talents in business, combined with James's promotional abilities, saw the couple do very well for themselves.

Two years after Bertha's death, Madame Spontini's name was once again brought up by Perth's *Sunday Times* newspaper in an article headed 'The Fortune-Telling Fakir, an auxiliary of the abortionist'.[325] The article was written in response to the conclusion of what was known as the Bennett case, in which a man named Robert Bennett was found guilty of having conspired to procure an abortion in Subiaco in February 1913.[326]

The Bennett case attracted a lot of publicity in Western Australia. The girl had come to Perth to seek an abortion and to this end had proceeded to Bennett's Royal Herbal and Electric Institute in the Brookman's Building. Madame Spontini's business had been conducted from the same building, which the *Sunday Times* described as a place that many women resorted to in need. The girl had declared in court that she only happened to meet Bennett because she had gone to find Madame Spontini to consult her about a lost purse. Madame Spontini was dead by this time, but the *Sunday Times* seized upon the reference to her as something that emphatically endorsed its view of the fortune telling evil, which it had been bringing to the public's attention periodically over several years. The article expressed the view that if some of those so-called fortune tellers were not allowed so much licence, there would be fewer 'professional abortionists' of the moral calibre of 'Doctor' Bennett in their midst.

Clearly there was an inference that 'fortune-tellers' like Madame Spontini had strong links to the abortionist trade. That is probably the case.

* * *

This book was written to document the life of James Wallace, a man who would have been forgotten to history had it not been for the significant role he played in the story of the Kelly Gang. Covering James's life in the post-Kelly years gives us a more complete appreciation and understanding of the man.

---

325 - 'The Fortune-Telling Fakir, an auxiliary of the abortionist', *Sunday Times* (Perth), 13 April 1913 edition.

326 - Refer to *Western Mail*, Friday 18 April 1913 'The Bennett case'. Robert Bennett was sentenced to imprisonment with hard labour for seven years, while the young girl named Helena Lily Griffiths on whom the abortion was performed was also found guilty of having conspired with Bennett, and sentenced to three months with hard labour.

The last 10 years of James's extraordinary life were spent travelling with the clairvoyant and spiritualist Madame Spontini. During this time, James faded into the background while she stole the limelight. He was always there in the background, though, supporting his 'Bonnie' in all her business and spiritual endeavours. Whilst a reader of the final chapters of this book could be excused for thinking the book was more about Bertha than James, this is only because there is a lot of information available about Madame Spontini during this period and a paucity of information about James. They were very much a couple, though, with James living a life far removed from those early years he spent growing up in the rough-and-tumble Woolshed Valley and then as the head teacher at that little state school at Bobinawarrah, smack-bang in the thick of the troubles during the tumultuous years when the Kelly Gang had their short reign.

33
Wallace family cover-up

Victor Wallace wrote *The Wallace Story* in 1973, commencing with his family's Scottish origins.[327] As the son of John (Jack) Wallace, one of the two brothers who accompanied James to Kerang, Victor's family history places a greater emphasis on his own father's line than on James Wallace and his line. His reference to James and Barbara is for the most part confined to the information that could be obtained from their birth, marriage and death certificates.[328] He does acknowledge, though, that James was the first of the family to take up teaching – and that his 'Licence to Teach' parchment-like scroll was then in the possession of Gretta Wallace, the widow of another of James's brothers. There is also mention that James took up Life Insurance work in Queensland, before returning to Melbourne, and that he also became a journalist in Kerang.

The Wallace Story contains no information at all about James's activities in North-Eastern Victoria during the Kelly years, or about him being a Kelly sympathiser. Nor is there any mention of him having left his wife and children to take up with his mistress Bertha Bonn. The omission of information about the Wallace family connections to the Kelly story was apparently deliberate.[329] Victor was a prominent gynaecologist and was concerned the story would show the family in a negative light. He was also concerned to cover-up the role played by his own father John (Jack) Wallace.

John Wallace died in 1937 (aged 74 years) at his home in Bendigo Street, Elwood. The family say he had connections with the State

---

327 - Victor Wallace was the third child of John (Jack) Wallace and his wife Harriet (Grigg).

328 - *The Wallace Story* by Victor H Wallace, pages 9 and 10 deal with James Wallace and his wife Barbara.

329 - This is the view of Arthur Hall, author of *The Headmaster of Hurdle Creek*.

Library of Victoria (SLV), which was at one time the custodian of the Kelly records now in the Public Records Office of Victoria.[330] Family history has it that John 'borrowed' many records that implicated the Wallace family with the Kellys, and that his house in Elwood was jokingly known to some in the family as the 'Elwood Annexe' of the SLV. The documents borrowed by John ('the Kelly file') were apparently still there at the time of his death in 1937, but have not been seen since.

Gilbert, the youngest of the Wallace brothers, wrote to John's widow Hetty after John's death asking her not to destroy Jack's manuscripts. Victor Wallace simply noted in his family history that 'Unfortunately, the manuscripts mentioned by Uncle Gilbert had not been preserved'.[331] He did not allude, however, as to what the missing manuscripts entailed, although the Wallace family believe that some of the missing documents comprised letters that had been written by Joe Byrne to Jack Sherritt and which had been held in the Kelly file that John Wallace removed to his home in Elwood. After Jack's death, the story goes that the documents were destroyed because the family did not know how to return the material while at the same time keeping 'Dad's good name'.

The Wallace family maintain that James Wallace was a sympathiser due to his friendship with Joe Byrne, although there were also other reasons at play. It is not known what James thought of Ned Kelly, but the Wallace family say that Ned was appreciative of all James had done to keep them safe during the time they were on the run. The family say that Ned expressed his appreciation by gifting James a stock whip, a neck piece on a leather chain, another neck piece (made of bronze), and a policeman's shriller whistle. The items had no monetary value, but were considered important enough to have been kept by

---

330 - According to some Wallace family members, John (Jack) Wallace worked for a time at the SLV. The author has not been able to verify this.

331 - The author wrote to the current owner of the Bendigo Street property with the suggestion that they might like to search the property (e.g. below the floor or in the roof) to see what might be found on the off-chance that the documents may have been hidden away out of sight. However, the owner was not interested.

James's youngest son (Harold Wallace).³³² Harold kept the items in an old leather case, which was stored wrapped in a parchment-like material that had masonic temple-like patterns on it.³³³ That branch of the Wallace family placed considerable value on the items as they had no doubt about how they had come into the family's possession.

---

332 - The items were said to have been passed from James (or perhaps his wife Barbara) to his youngest son Harold Wallace. Harold's wife Gretta (née Martin) passed them on to her brother Lionel Martin, who in turn passed them to his daughter Lily (later to become Lily Wheeler). Lily was always aware of the item's provenance, and at the age of 86 tried to sell the items to the National Museum of Australia. The museum was interested but ultimately declined the opportunity to purchase the items due to a mistake Lily made in her description of the chain of ownership. After Lily Wheeler's death, it seems that the significance of the items was not appreciated by her children and grandchildren and the items have been lost or disposed of. Photographs of the items were taken by the Curator of the Collections Department at the National Museum, and are the only evidence that the items existed.

333 - It is not known whether the items were handed to James in the leather case, or whether the case was simply used by James or subsequent custodians to keep the items in.

34

Conclusion

At the time of writing this book, James Wallace has been dead for 114 years and it has been 143 years since the destruction of the Kelly Gang at Glenrowan. The Kelly story lives on in popular culture of course, whereas James Wallace's part in that story has been largely ignored or forgotten, which is curious given the attention he was given by the Royal Commissioners.

James grew up in interesting times. The Woolshed Valley in the 1860s was a wild and wondrous place for young boys like him and his mates to grow up in. Future Kelly Gang member Joe Byrne was one of those mates, as was Aaron Sherritt who would one day be murdered by Byrne after the gang had come to the realisation that he was betraying them. James was an accessory to that murder.

James was a complex man. He was highly intelligent, charismatic, forceful and energetic. He liked to be noticed, was opinionated and filled with a sense of his own self-importance. From a young age, he had no hesitation in using politicians and power-brokers to his advantage. He succeeded in getting himself appointed as the head teacher of a new State School at Hurdle Creek at the age of only 19, and by the age of 24 he was running that school and another as part-time schools, and was also running the local post office. Married with a young family, he had also selected 152 acres at the edge of the Hurdle Creek settled area.

After the Kelly Gang murdered three policemen at Stringybark Creek, James became one of the gang's most trusted allies. He was a sympathiser, as were hundreds of others in North-Eastern Victoria at the time. There were a lot of social and economic dynamics at play that resulted in men like him siding with the Kellys; however, the main reason James was a sympathiser was his friendship with Joe Byrne. 'I am firmly convinced he would never sell his old pal, Joe Byrne,' wrote Captain Standish, the much-maligned Chief Commissioner of Police, after Wallace's removal from Kelly country but prior to the Kelly Gang's final showdown at Glenrowan.

James Wallace was an inveterate letter writer. In the early days the Kelly Gang was at large, he is believed to have been the writer of a number of letters and articles that sought to present the gang in a more positive light. The most famous of these letters would become known as the Cameron and Jerilderie letters, but were suppressed at the time by the authorities. A book titled *The Outlaws of the Wombat Ranges,* which was published by the proprietor of the *Mansfield Guardian,* included information about 'the other side of the story' that this author believes is likely to have been written by Wallace.

After Assistant Commissioner Nicolson recruited James as a police agent, he embarked on a 'perfect deluge of writing', sending Nicolson some 21 letters over the period of August 1879 to March 1880. James revelled in this extracurricular activity. It was like a game for him, where he would continuously tantalise Nicolson with new information that seemed promising but that was actually of no use at all. James knew Nicolson was also receiving reports from others like Detective Ward who knew that his sympathies actually lay with the gang, and enjoyed the battle of wits that was required to keep one step ahead.

After giving evidence before the Royal Commission on the Police Force of Victoria, James was dismissed from the public service on the recommendation of the Commissioners. Forced to flee Victoria under the threat of prosecution, six years would pass before James decided it was safe to return. After an unsuccessful campaign to clear his name and regain employment as a teacher, he eventually acquired a job as a journalist at the *Kerang Times* where he would soon become the manager and editor. The Kerang years were a relatively settled and secure time for the family. However, the death of a son in 1897, followed by James's relationship with a woman named Bertha (Bonnie) Litchfield saw the end of his marriage, with his wife Barbara and the children leaving him in 1899.

James and Bertha left Kerang themselves and embarked on a new life together shortly before the bankruptcy of the *Kerang Times* in 1901.

Bertha established herself as a clairvoyant who called herself Madame Spontini, while James faded into the background and provided support. The couple moved around extensively, to New Zealand first, and then between Sydney, Brisbane and Perth. Madame Spontini became highly successful in her professional life, despite newspaper articles that claimed she was a charlatan and suggestions that she and others like her had links to abortionists. Madame Spontini also became prominent in the New Thought Movement, the Metaphysical Association and the Spiritualist Church. James was also known to have an interest in these matters, which dated back to his schooldays in Woolshed where he said he practiced mesmerism on Aaron Sherritt.

It is ironic, given a significant part of Madame Spontini's business entailed the promotion of healthy living practices, that both she and James died young. James had been suffering for some time from diabetes and other ailments when he died in 1910 at the age of only 56 years. Compared to most people of the times, he had lived a full and adventurous life, though not necessarily an easy life. The decision he made in his twenties to support the Kelly Gang sympathiser caused him and his family more than 10 years of emotional and financial hardship that only ended when he managed to secure employment as a journalist in Kerang. But even then, after all he had put his family through, he was still restless. It seems he was always in need of some kind of intellectual and perhaps even spiritual stimulation, which he eventually found with the woman he called Bonnie.

At the end of his publication *The Headmaster of Hurdle Creek*, the author Arthur Hall, to whom this book is dedicated, wrote that his research into James Wallace was just a beginning, and that much research remained for those who were interested. Hopefully this book fills in many gaps in the story.

APPENDIX 1
Wallace's land selection dealings

Application for License

James Wallace forwarded an application form on 27 October 1875 for a License to Occupy. It was accompanied by a letter dated 25 October 1875:

> Sir,
>
> *I desire to make application for a license to occupy under the Land Act 1869, the block of land situated on the east side of catherine McGreggor's selection on Hurdle Creek in the Parish of Moyhu as 'Allotments 5A and 5B section 1 containing 152 acres 3 roods 26 perches and I therefore request that you will forward me the necessary forms on which to apply and also kindly inform me how much money it will be necessary for me to send in as rent, & costs of survey along with the application.*
>
> *I have to request that you will inform me whether the application can be sent by post or whether it is necessary for me to take it in person to your office at Benalla.*

James Wallace made an application for License under Part II of the Land Act 1869 by declaring on the ninth day of November 1875 that at 9.30 o'clock that day he had dug a trench not less than two feet long, six inches wide, and four inches deep in the direction of the continuing sides, and placed conspicuous posts or cairns of stones with notices thereon at the corners of the allotment for which he was making application to lease (being Allotment 5A & 5B, Section 1, County of Delatite, Parish of Moyhu). The Allotment concerned had an area of 152 acres 3 roods and 26 perches.

The application includes statements in response to various questions, from which we learn that:

- James's occupation was school teacher at Bobinawarrah.
- His family resided at Bobinawarrah.
- He did not own any land in fee simple.
- He did not hold any land under license or lease from the Crown.
- He had not selected any other land under the Land Act 1869.

On 6 December 1875, James Wallace wrote to the Lands & Survey Department Melbourne as follows:

Sir,

I have the honor to respectfully request that you will kindly inform me whether there is any objection by your department to my commencing improvements before I have received 'License to occupy' my selection (allotments 5A & 5B Section 1 Parish of Moyhu). My application was recommended at the Local Land Board at Wangaratta on the 3rd instant and there was no objection that I know of.

I wish if possible to get my residence erected and fencing laid down before the wet weather.

I have the honor to be Sir,

Your obedient servant

James Wallace

(address Bobinawarrah)

Department of Lands and Survey (Occupation Branch) internal memo acknowledges receipt of James's letter. The memo states: 'Inform that application cannot be dealt with until report is delivered from Mining Department. Ask him how he proposes to comply with the conditions especially that of residence.'

On 24 December 1975, James Wallace wrote to Secretary for Lands Melbourne as follows:

Sir,

Referring to your letter of the 16th instant in which you request me to inform you how I propose complying with the conditions of my license (if granted) especially that of residence, I beg to state that I intend to build a house on the land and reside there in my own proper person, walking to and from my school daily – a distance of about a mile – to fence it with a substantial two-rail split post & rail fence, to cultivate about 20 acres and clear the rest for pasture. I have the greater part of the fencing split already and only wait your permission to erect it in the ground.

I shall be much obliged if you will kindly inform me whether there will be any other objection that what may arise from the Mining Department (for I am certain there will be none from that quarter) so that I may be enabled to get my fencing carted on the line before the ground is too soft.

I have the honor to be Sir,

Your obedient servant

James Wallace

Requests form to apply for lease

On 23 January 1879, James wrote to the Secretary, Crown Law Office Melbourne as follows:

Sir,

As my License (3908) under the Land Act 1869 for Allotment 5 section 1 Parish of Moyhu, County of Delatite will terminate in a week from this date I have the honor to request that you will supply me with a form on which to make application for a Lease of the same.

I have also to apply for Certificate of Improvements.

Crown Lands Bailiff C King Witt visited the selection some time ago. On that time I had improvements on it to the amount of 1 pound per acre but had not then cultivated any of it. I have since complied with the cultivation clause, and request that you will direct your officer to call and report on same so that no delay may take place in the issue of Lease.

I have the honor to be Sir,

Your obedient servant

James Wallace

Application for Lease

This Indenture (entered in the register Book, Vol. 301 Fol. 60171) made between Her Most Gracious Majesty Queen Victoria and James Wallace of Bobinawarrah Teacher for (the land) was for the term of seven years. Equal half yearly payments in advance on the first day of February and the first day of August, with the next payment thereof to be made on the first day of August next ...

On 4 February 1879, James applied for Crown Grant (or Lease) under Section 20 of the Land Act 1869. The application contained the following 'further particulars':

- The land was enclosed by 141 chains of post and 2-rail fencing costing 123 pounds, 7 shillings and 6 pence, and 20 chains of brush costing 3 pounds. He indicated that the 141 chains of post and 2-rail fencing included fencing along the boundary of Catherine McGreggor's adjoining property for which they shared the cost.

- As far as cultivation, he had planted 12 acres with maize at a cost of 18 pounds. This had only been planted in August 1878 and had not yet been harvested.

- As far as buildings, he had erected a Dwelling House measuring 20 ft x 12 ft with a verandah 20 ft x 4 ft. The materials of construction were slab and bark. The cost was 15 pounds.

- Water storage – comprised a well with fixtures, measuring 12 ft (deep) x 4 ft x 4ft. Cost was 2 pounds and 10 shillings.

- Other improvements – clearing line for fencing @ about 5 pounds; ringing timber and cutting and burning scrub on 120 acres at 5 shillings per acre for a cost of 30 pounds; and a stockyard @ 1 pound 10 shillings.

- The dwelling contained two rooms and was permanently attached to the soil of the allotment.

- In response to a question about whether he had resided here continuously, James answered that he worked on the grounds almost daily from February 1876 and occupied it in the fullest sense of the term with the exception that he did not sleep there continuously.

- That he had another place of abode, being at the State School Hurdle Creek, one and a half miles from the selection, this being where his family resided.

- In answer to a question about why the conditions of cultivation had not been complied with, James answered: The land (is) utterly unfit for cultivation with the exception of the 12 acres under tillage. As evidence of the quality of the land I respectfully beg to direct attention to the fact that the cultivation condition has been dispensed with on this account by the Department in the three adjoining selections – i.e. C W Lloyd and Miss McGreggor.

On 4 July 1879, James writes to the District Surveyor, Benalla:

Sir,

I have the honor to transmit herewith my application for a Lease of 153 acres of land (allot 1 sec 5) in the Parish of Moyhu and I request that you will forward it on as soon as possible to headquarters.

I am Sir,

Your obedient servant

James Wallace

Wallace's land selection dealings

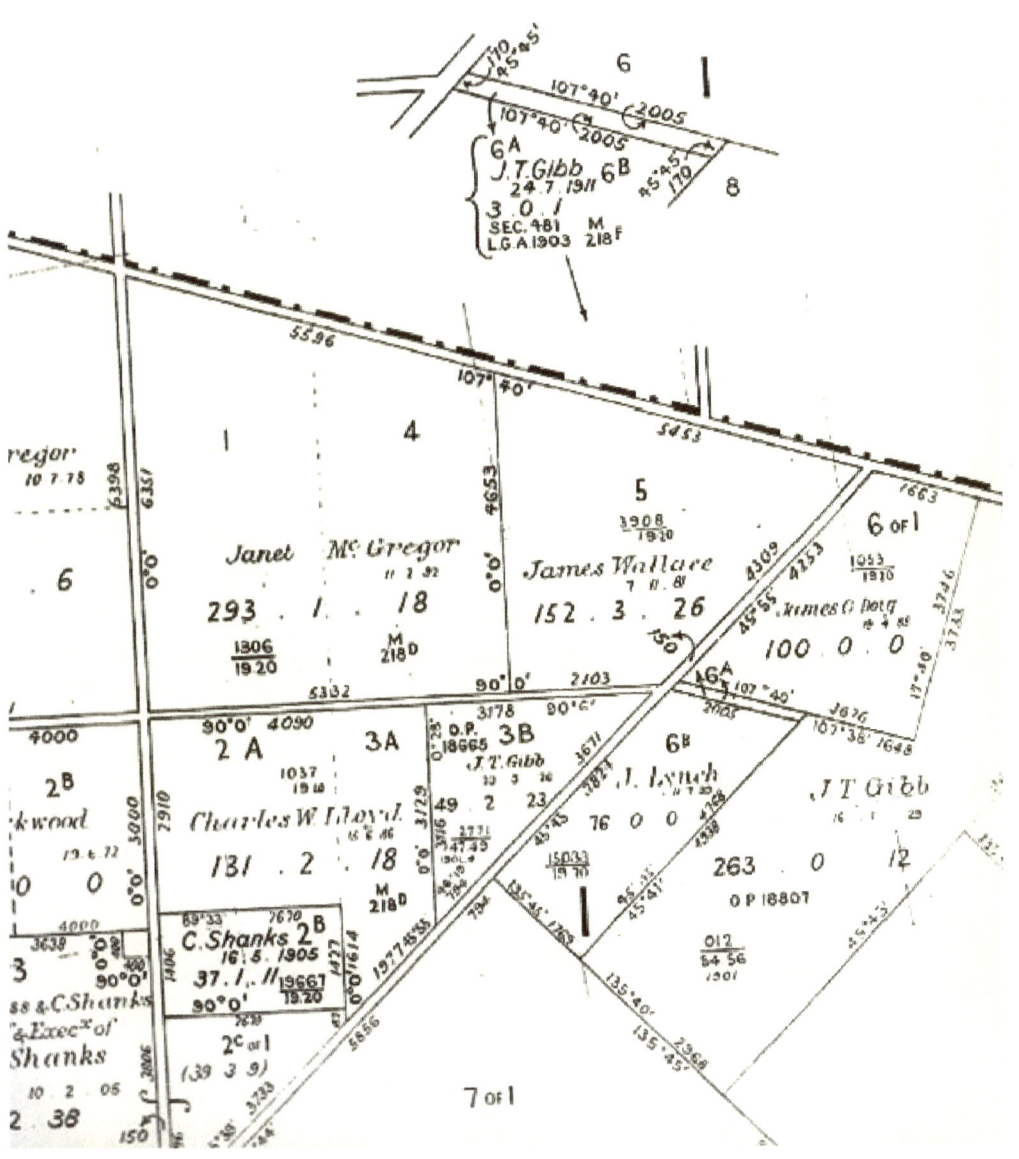

APPENDIX 2
Transcript of the Cameron Letter

Mr. Donald Cameron, M.L.C.,

Dear Sir,

Take no offense if I take the opportunity of writing a few lines to you, wherein I wish to state a few remarks concerning the case of Trooper Fitzpatrick against Mrs. Kelly, W. Skillon and W. Williamson, and to state the facts of the case to you. It seems to me impossible to get any justice without I make a statement to someone that will take notice of it, as it is no use in me complaining about anything that the police may choose to say or swear against me, and the public, in their ignorance and blindness, will undoubtedly back them up to their utmost. No doubt I am now placed in very peculiar circumstances, and you might blame for it, but if you knew how I have been wronged and persecuted, you would say I cannot be blamed.

In April last, an information was (which must have come under your notice) sworn against me for shooting Trooper Fitzpatrick, which was false, and my mother, with an infant baby, and brother-in-law and another neighbour, were taken for aiding and abetting and attempting to murder him, a charge for which they are as purely innocent as the child unborn.

During my stay on the King River I run in a wild bull, which I gave to Lydicher, who afterwards sold him to Carr, and he killed him for beef. Some time afterwards I was told I was blamed for stealing this bull from Whitty. I asked Whitty on Moyhu Racecourse why he blamed me for stealing his bull, and he said that he had found the bull and he never blamed me for stealing him. He said it was Farrell who told him I stole the bull. Some time afterward I heard again I was blamed for stealing a mob of calves from Whitty and Farrell, which I had never had anything to do with, and along with this and the other talk, I began to think they wanted something to talk about.

Whitty and Burns, not being satisfied with all the picked land on King River and Boggy Creek, and the run of their stock on the certificate ground free, and no one interfering with them, paid heavy rent for all the open ground, so as a poor man could not keep his stock, and impounded every beast they could catch, even off Government roads. If a poor man happened to leave his horse or a bit of poddy calf outside his paddock, it would be impounded. I have known over sixty head of horses to be in one day impounded by Whitty and Burns, all belonging to poor men of the district. They would have to leave their harvest or ploughing and go to Oxley, and then perhaps not have money enough to release them, and have to give a bill of sale or borrow the money, which is no easy matter.

Along with all this sort of work, Farrell, the policeman, stole a horse from George King (my stepfather) and had him in Whitty and Jeffrey's paddock until he left the force, and this was the cause of me and my stepfather, George King, stealing Whitty's horses and selling them to Baumgarten and those other men. The pick of them was sold at Howlong, and the rest was sold to Baumgarten, who was a perfect stranger to me, and, I believe, an honest man. No man had anything to do with the horses but me and George King. William Cooke, who was convicted for Whitty's horses, had nothing to do with them, nor was he ever in my company at Peterson's, the German's, at Howlong.

The brand was altered by me and George King, and the horses were sold as straight. Any man requiring horses would have bought them the same as those men, and would have been potted the same. I consider Whitty ought to do something towards the release of those innocent men, otherwise there will be a collision between me and him, as I can to his satisfaction prove I took J. Welshe's black mare and the rest of the horses, which I will prove to him in next issue, and after those had been found and the row being over them, I wrote a letter to Mr. Swanhill of Lake Rowan, to advertise my horses for sale, as I was intent to sell out. I sold them afterwards at Benalla, and the rest in New South Wales, and left Victoria as I wished to see certain parts of the country. Very shortly afterwards there was a Warrant for me, and as I since hear, the Police Sergeant Steele, Straughan and Fitzpatrick and others searched the eleven mile and every other place in the district for me and a man named Newman, who had escaped from the Wangaratta.

Police for months before the 15th of April. Therefore it was impossible for me to be in Victoria, as every schoolboy knows me, and on the 15th of April, Fitzpatrick came to the Eleven Mile and had some conversation with Williamson who was splitting on the hill. Seeing my brother and another man, he rode down and had some conversation with this man whom he swore was William Skillion. This man was not called in Beechworth as he could have proved Fitzpatrick's falsehood, as Skillion and another man was away after horses at this time, which can be proved by eight or nine witnesses.

The man who the troopers swore was Skillion can prove Williamson's innocence, besides other important evidence which can be brought on the prisoner's behalf. The trooper, after speaking to this man, rode to the house and Dan came out. He asked Dan to go to Greta with him. Dan asked him what for and he said he had a warrant for him for stealing Whitty's horses. They both went inside, and Dan was having something to eat.

The trooper was impatient and Mrs. Kelly asked him what he wanted Dan for. He said he had a warrant for him. Dan said 'Produce your Warrant', and he said he had none, it was only a telegram from Chiltern. Mrs. Kelly said he need not go unless he liked without a warrant. She told the trooper he had no business on her premises without some Authority besides his word. He pulled out his revolver, and said he would blow her brains out if she interfered in the arrest. Mrs. Kelly said that if Ned was here he would ram the revolver down his throat. To frighten the trooper Dan said, 'Ned is coming now.' The trooper looked around to see if it was true. Dan dropped the knife and fork, which showed he had no murderous intention, clapped Heenan's Hug on him, took his revolver and threw him and part of the door outside and kept him there until Skillion and Ryan came with horses which Dan sold that night.

The trooper left and invented some scheme to say he got shot, when any man can see it was impossible for him to have been shot. He told Dan to clear out; that Sergeant Steele or Detective Brown would be there before morning. Straughan was over the Murray trying to get up a case against Dan and the Lloyds, as the Germans over the Murray would swear to anyone, and they will lag you, guilty or not. Next day Skillion, Williamson and Mrs. Kelly, with an infant were taken and thrown into prison and were six months awaiting trial and no bail allowed, and was convicted on the evidence of the meanest man that ever the sun shone on. I have been told by police that he is hardly ever sober. Also, between him and his father they sold his sister to a Chinaman.

He seems a strapping and genteel looking young man, and more fit to be a starcher to laundress than a trooper, but to a keen observer he has the wrong appearance to have anything like a clear conscience or a manly heart. The deceit is to plainly be seen in the white cabbage-hearted looking face. I heard nothing of this transaction until very close on the trial, I then being over 400 miles from Greta. I heard that I was outlawed and £100 reward for me in Victoria, and also hundreds of charges of horse stealing was against me, beside shooting a trooper. I came into Victoria and enquired after my brother and found him working with another man in Bullock Creek.

Heard how the police use to be blowing that they would shoot me first and then cry surrender; how they used to come to the house when there was no one there but women, and Superintendent Smith used to say 'See all the men I have today – I will have as many more tomorrow and blow him into pieces as small as the paper that is in our guns.' They used to repeatedly rush into the house revolver in hand and upset milk dishes, empty the flour out onto the ground, break tins of eggs, throw the mat out of the cask onto the floor, and dirty and destroy all the provisions, which can be proved; and shove the girls in front of them into the rooms like dogs and abuse and insult them. Detective Ward and Constable Hayes took out their revolvers and threatened to shoot the girls and children whiles Mrs. Skillion was absent, the oldest being with her. The greatest murderers and ruffians would not be guilty of such an action. This sort of cruelty and disgraceful conduct to my brothers and sisters who had no protection, coupled with the conviction of my Mother and those innocent men certainly made my blood boil as I don't think there is a man born could have the patience to suffer what I did.

They were not satisfied with frightening and insulting my sisters night and day, and destroying their provisions and lagging my Mother with an infant baby and those innocent men, but should follow me and my brother, who was innocent of having anything to do with those stolen horses, into the wilds where he had been quietly digging and doing well, neither molesting or interfering with anyone. I was not there long when on October 25 I came on the track of police horses between Table Top and the Bogs, and crossed them and went to Emu Swamp, and returning home I came on more police tracks making for our camp. I told my mates, and me and my brother went out next morning and found police camped at the Shingle Hut with long fire-arms. We came to the conclusion that our doom was sealed unless we could take their fire-arms. As we had nothing but a gun and a rifle, if they came on us at our work or camp, we had no chance, only to die like dogs.

We thought our country was woven with police, and we might have a chance of fighting them if we had fire-arms, as it generally takes forty to one. We approached the spring as close as we could get to the camp, the intervening space being clear. We saw two men at the log. They got up, and one took a double-barrel fowling piece and one drove the horses down and hobbled them against the tent. We thought there was more men in the tent, those being on sentry. We could have shot these two men without speaking, but not wishing to take life, we waited.

McIntyre laid the gun against the stump, and Lonigan sat on the log. I advanced, my brother Dan keeping McIntyre covered. I called on them to throw up their hands. McIntrye obeyed and never attempted to reach for his gun and revolver. Lonigan ran to a battery of logs and put his head up to take aim at me when I shot him, or he would have shot me, as I knew well. I asked who was in the tent. McIntyre replied 'No one.' I approached the camp and took possession of their revolvers and fowling piece, which I loaded with bullets instead of shot. I told McIntyre I did not want to shoot him or any man that would surrender. I explained Fitzpatrick's falsehood, which no policeman can be ignorant of. He said he knew Fitzpatrick had wronged us, but he could not help it. He said he intended to leave the Force on account of his bad health; his life was insured.

The other two men, who had no fire-arms, came up when they heard the shot fired and went back to our camp for fear the police might call there in our absence and surprise us on our arrival. My brother went back to the spring and I stopped at the log with McIntyre. Kennedy and Scanlon came up. McIntyre said he would get them to surrender if I spared their lives as well as his. I said I did not know either him, Scanlon or Kennedy, and had nothing up against them, and would not shoot any of them if they gave up their fire-arms and promised to leave the Force, as it was the meanest billet in the world. They are worse than cold-blooded murderers and hangmen.

He said he was sure they would never follow me anymore. I gave him my word I would give them a chance. McIntyre went up to Kennedy, Scanlon being behind with a rifle and revolver. I called on them to throw up their hands. Scanlon slewed his horse round to gallop away, but turned again, and as quick as thought, fired at me with the rifle, and was in the act of firing again when I shot him. Kennedy alighted on the off side of his horse and got behind a tree and opened hot fire. McIntyre got on Kennedy's horse and galloped away. I could have shot him if I chose, as he was right against me, but rather than break my word I let him go.

My brother advanced from the spring. Kennedy fired at him and ran, and he found neither of us were dead. I followed him. He got behind another tree and fired at me again. I short him in the armpit as he was behind the tree. He dropped his revolver and ran again, and slewed round; I fired with the gun again and shot him through the right chest, as I did not know that he had dropped his revolver and was turning to surrender. He could not live, or I would have let him go. Had they been my own brothers I could not help shooting them, or else lie down and let them shoot me, which they would have done had their bullets been ear off, or brutally treating any of them, it is a cruel falsehood. If Kennedy's ear was cut off, it had been done since. I put his cloak over him and left him as honourable as I could, and if they were my own brothers I could not be more sorry for them.

With the exception of Lonigan. I did not begrudge him what bit of lead he got, as he was the flashest, meanest man that I ever had any account against, for him Fitzpatrick, Sergeant Whelan, Constable Day, and King the bootmaker once tried to handcuff me at Benalla, and when they could not, Fitzpatrick tried to choke me. Lonigan caught me by the privates and would have killed me, but was not able. Mr. McInnes came up and I allowed him to put the handcuffs on me when the police were bested. This cannot be called wilful murder, for I was compelled to shoot them in my own defence, or lie down like a cur and die. Certainly their wives and children are to be pitied, but those men came into the bush with the intention of shooting me down like a dog, yet they know and acknowledge I have been wronged.

And is my mother and her infant baby and my poor little brothers and sisters not to be pitied? More so, who has got no alternative, only to put up with brutal and unmanly conduct of the police, who have never had any relations or a mother, or must have forgot them. I was never convicted of horse stealing. I was once arrested by Constable Hall and 14 more men in Greta, and there was a subscription raised for Hall by persons who had too much money about Greta, in honour of Hall arresting Wild Wright and Gunn. Wright and Gunn were potted, and Hall could not pot me for horse stealing, but with the subscription money he gave £20 to James Murdock, who has been recently hung in Wagga Wagga. On Murdock's evidence I was found guilty of receiving knowing it to be stolen, which J. Wright, W. Ambrose, J. Ambrose, T.H. Hatcher and W. Williamson and others can prove.

I was innocent of knowing the mare to be stolen, and I was once accused of taking a hawker by the name of McCormack's horse to pull another hawker named Ben Gould out of a bog. Mr. Gould got up in the morning to feed his horses, seen Mr. McCormack's horse, knew he had strayed and sent his man with him about two miles to where McCormack was camped in Greta. Mr. and Mrs. McCormack came out and seen the wagon bogged and accused him of using the horse. I told Gould that was for his good nature. Mrs. McCormack turned on me and accused me of catching the horse for Gould, as Gould knew that he was wicked and could not catch him himself.

Me and my uncle was cutting and branding calves, and Ben Gould wrapped up a pair of testicles, wrote a note and gave it to me to give to Mrs. McCormack. McCormack said he would fight me. I was then fourteen years of age. I was getting off my horse and Mrs. McCormack hit the horse, he jumped forward and my fist came in collision with Mr. McCormack's nose, who swore he was standing twenty yards away from another man and the one hit knocked the two men down. However ridiculous the evidence may seem, I received three months or £10, for hitting him and 3 months for delivering the parcel and bound to the peace for 12 months.

At the time I was taken by Hall and his 14 assistants, therefore I dare not strike any of them, as Hall was a great cur, and as for Dan, he never was tried for assaulting a woman. Mr. Butler, P.M., sentenced him to 3 months without the option of a fine and one month or 2 pounds fine for wilfully destroying property, a sentence which there is no law to uphold, and yet they had to do their sentence and their prosecutor, Mr. D. Goodman since got 4 years for perjury concerning the same property.

The minister of justice should enquire into this respecting their sentence, and he will find a wrong jurisdiction given by Butler, P.M. on October 19, 1877 at Benalla, and these are the only charges was ever proved against either of us, therefore we are falsely represented. The reports of bullets being fired into the bodies of the Troopers after death is false, and the coroner should be consulted. I have no intention of asking mercy for myself or any mortal man, or apologising, but wish to give timely warning that if my people do not get justice, and those innocents released from prison, and the police wear their uniform, I shall be forced to seek revenge of everything of the human race for the future. I will not take innocent life if justice is given, but as the police are afraid or ashamed to wear their uniform, therefore every man's life is in danger, as I was outlawed without cause, and cannot be no worse, and have but once to die. If the public do not see justice done I will seek revenge for the name and character which has been given to me and my relations, while God gives me strength to pull a trigger.

The witness which can prove Fitzpatrick's falsehood can be found by advertising, and if this is not done immediately, horrible disasters shall follow. Fitzpatrick shall be the cause of greater slaughter to the rising generation than St. Patrick was to the snakes and toads of Ireland. Had I robbed, plundered, ravished and murdered everything I met my character could not be painted blacker than it as present, thank God my conscience is as clear as the snow in Peru.

As I hear, a picked jury, amongst which was a retired Sergeant of Police was empanelled on the trial of my mother, and David Lindsay who gave evidence for the crown, is a shanty keeper having no licence, and is liable to a heavy fine, and keeps a book of information for the police, and his character needs no comment. He is capable of rendering Fitzpatrick any assistance he required for a conviction, as he could be broke any time Fitzpatrick chose to inform on him.

I am really astonished to see Members of the Legislative Assembly led astray by such articles as the police,

for a while an outlaw reigns their pocket swells

'Tis double pay and country girls.

by concluding, as I have no more paper unless I rob for it, if I get justice I Will cry a go.

For I need no lead or powder

to avenge my cause,

and if words be louder

I will appose your laws.

With no offence (remember your railroads), and a sweet good bye from

Edward Kelly
enforced outlaw

APPENDIX 3
Transcript of the Jerilderie Letter

Page 1

Dear Sir

I wish to acquaint you with some of the occurrences of the present, past and future. In or about the Spring of 1870 the ground was very soft. A Hawker named Mr Gould got his waggon bogged between Greta and my mother's place house on the eleven mile creek. The ground was that rotten it would bog a duck in places so Mr Gould had to abandon his waggon for fear of losing his horses in the spewy ground. He was stopping at my mother's awaiting finer or dryer weather. Mr McCormack and his wife (Hawkers' also) were camped in Greta and the mosquitoes were very bad which they generally are in a wet spring, and to help them Mr Johns had a horse called Ruita Cruta. Although a gelding was as clever as old Wombat or any other Stallion

Page 2

at running horses away and taking them on his beat, which was from Greta swamp to the seven mile creek, consequently he enticed McCormack's horse away from Greta. Mr Gould was up early finding his horses, heard a bell and seen McCormack's horse for he knew the horse well. He sent his boy to take him back to Greta, when McCormack's got the horse, they came straight out to Gould and accused him of working the horse.

This was false and Gould was amazed at the idea. I could not help laughing to hear Mrs McCormack accusing him of using the horse after him being so kind as to send his boy to take him from the Ruita Cruta and take him back to him. I pleaded Gould's innocence and Mrs McCormack turned on me and accused me of

Page 3

bringing the horse from Greta to Gould's waggon to pull him out of the bog. I did not say much to the woman as my mother was present, but that same day me and my uncle was cutting calves. Gould wrapped up a note and a pair of the calves testicles and gave them to me to give them to Mrs McCormack. I did not see her and I gave the parcel to a boy to give to her when she would come. Instead of giving it to her he gave it to her husband. Consequently McCormack said he would summons me. I told him neither me or Gould used their horse. He said I was a liar and he could welt me or any of my breed. I was about 14 years of age but accepted the challenge and dismounting when Mrs McCormack

Page 4

struck my horse in the flank with a bullocks shin it jumped forward and my fist came in collision with McCormack's nose and caused him to lose his equilibrium and fall prostrate. I tied up my horse to finish the battle but McCormack got up and ran to the police .camp Constable Hall asked me what the row was about. I told him they accused me and Gould of using their horse and I hit him and I would do the same to him if he challenged me. McCormack pulled me and swore their lives against me. I was sentenced to three months for hitting him and three months for the parcel and bound to keep the peace for 12 months. Mrs McCormack gave good substantial evidence as she is well acquainted

Page 5

with that place called Tasmania better known as the Dervon or Van Dieman's land. And McCormack being a policeman over the convicts and w omen being scarce released her from that land of bondage and tyranny. And they came to Victoria and are at present, residents of Greta and on the 29th of March I was released from prison and came home. Wild Wright came to the eleven mile to see Mr Gunn, stopped all night and lost his mare. Both him and me looked all day for her and could not get her. Wright who was a stranger to me was in a hurry to get back to Mansfield and I gave him another mare and he told me if I found his mare to keep her until he brought mine back. I was going to Wangaratta

Page 6

and seen the mare I caught her and took her with me. All the police and Detective Berrill seen her as Martain's girls used to ride her about the town during several days that I stopped at Peter Martain's Star Hotel in Wangaratta. She was a chestnut mare, white face, docked tail, very remarkable. Branded as plain as the hands on a town clock. The property of a Telegraph master in Mansfield, he lost her on the 6th, gazetted her on the 12th of March and I was a prisoner in Beechworth Goal until the 29th March. Therefore I could not have stole the mare. I was riding the mare through Greta. Constable Hall came to me and said he wanted me to sign some papers that I did not sign at Beechworth concerning my

Page 7

bail bonds. I thought it was the truth. He said the papers was at the Barracks and I had no idea he wanted to arrest me or I would have quietly rode away instead of going to the Barracks. I was getting off when Hall caught hold of me and thought to throw me but made a mistake and came on the broad of his back, himself in the dust. The mare galloped away and instead of me putting my foot on Hall's neck and taking his revolver and putting him in the lockup, I tried to catch the mare. Hall got up and snapped three or four caps at me and would have shot me but the Colts patent refused. This is well known in Greta. Hall never told me he wanted to

Page 8

arrest me until after he tried to shoot me. When I heard the caps snapping, I stood until Hall came close. He had me covered and was shaking with fear and I knew he would pull the trigger before he would be game to put his hand on me so I duped and jumped at him, caught the revolver with one hand and Hall by the collar with the other. I dare not strike him or my sureties would loose the bond money. I used to trip and let him take a mouthful of dust now and again as he was as helpless as a big guano after leaving a dead horse or bullock. I kept throwing him in the dust until I got him across the street, the very spot where Mrs O'Brien's hotel stands now. The cellar was just

Page 9

dug then. There was some brush fencing where the post and rail was taking down and on this I threw big cowardly Hall on his belly. I straddled him and rolled both spurs into his thighs. He roared like a big calf attacked by dogs and shifted several yards of the fence. I got his hands at the back of his neck and tried to make him let the revolver go but he stuck to it like grim death to a dead volunteer. He called for assistance to a man named Cohan and Barnett Lewis, Thompson Jewell, two blacksmiths who was looking on. I dare not strike any of them as I was bound to keep the peace or I could have spread those curs like dung in a paddock. They got ropes, tied my hands and feet and Hall beat me over the head

Page 10

with his six chambered colts revolver. nine stitches were put in some of the cuts by Dr Hastings And when Wild Wright and my Mother came they could trace us across the street by the blood in the dust and which spoiled the lustre of the paint on the gate post of the Barracks. Hall sent for more police and Dr Hastings next morning. I was handcuffed, a rope tied from them to my legs and to the seat of the cart and taken to Wangaratta Hall. He was frightened I would throw him out of the cart so he tied me whilst Constable Arthur laughed at his cowardice for it was he who escorted me and Hall to Wangaratta. I was tried and committed as Hall swore I claimed the mare the

Page 11

Doctor died or he would have proved Hall a perjurer. Hall has been tried several times for perjury but got clear. As this is no crime in the police force it is a credit to a policeman to convict an innocent man but any muff can pot a guilty one. Hall's character is well known about El Dorado and Snowy Creek and Hall was considerably in debt to Mr L O'Brien and as he was going to leave Greta, Mr O'Brien seen no other chance of getting his money so there was a subscription collected for Hall and with the aid of this money he got James Murdock who was recently hung in Wagga Wagga to give false evidence against me. But I was acquitted on the charge of horse stealing and on Hall and Murdock's evidence,

Page 12

I was found guilty of receiving and got 3 years experience in Beechworth Pentridges dungeons. This is the only charge ever proved against me. Therefore I can say I never was convicted of horse or cattle stealing. My Brother Dan was never charged with assaulting a woman but he was sentenced to three months without the option of a fine and one month and two pounds fine for damaging property by Mr Butler PM, a sentence that there is no law to uphold. Therefore the Minister of Justice neglected his duty in that case but there never was such a thing as justice in the English laws. But any amount of injustice to be had. Out of over thirty head of the very best horses the land

Page 13

could produce, I could only find one when I got my liberty. Constable Flood stole and sold the most of them to the navvies on the railway line. One bay cob he stole and sold four different times, the line was completed and the men all gone when I came out and Flood was shifted to Oxley. He carried on the same game, there all the stray horses that was any time without an owner and not in the police Gazette Flood used to claim. He was doing a good trade at Oxley until Mr Brown of the Laceby Station got him shifted as he was always running his horses about. Flood is different to Sergeant Steel. Strachan Hall and the most of police as they have to hire cads and if they fail they,

Page 14

the police are quite helpless but Flood can make a cheque single handed he is the greatest horse stealer with the exception of myself and George King I know of. I never worked on a farm. A horse and saddle was never traced to me after leaving employment since February 1873. I worked as a faller at Mr J Saunders and K. Rules Sawmills then for Heach and Dochendorf. I never worked for less than two pounds ten a week since I left Pentridge and in 1875 or 1876 I was overseer for Saunders and Rules. Bourke's water holes sawmills in Victoria since then I was on the King River during my stay there I ran in a wild bull which I gave to Lydicher, a farmer.

Page 15

He sold him to Carr, a publican and butcher who killed him for beef some time afterwards. I was blamed for stealing this bull from James Whitty Boggy Creek. I asked Whitty Oxley racecourse why he blamed me for stealing his bull. He said he had found his bull and never blamed me but his son-in-law Farrell told him he heard I sold the bull to Carr. Not long afterwards I heard again I was blamed for stealing a mob of calves from Whitty and Farrell which I knew nothing about. I began to think they wanted me to give them something to talk about. Therefore I started wholesale and retail horse and cattle dealing. Whitty and Burns not being satisfied with all the picked land on the

Page 16

Boggy Creek and King river and the run of their stock on the certificate ground free and no one interfering with them paid heavy rent to the Banks for all the open ground so as a poor man could keep no stock. And impounded every beast they could get even off Government roads. If a poor man happened to leave his horse or a bit of poddy calf outside his paddock they would be impounded. I have known over 60 head of horses impounded in one day by Whitty and Burns all belonging to poor farmers. They would have to leave their ploughing or harvest or other employment to go to Oxley. When they would get there perhaps not have money enough to release them

Page 17

and have to give a bill of sale or borrow the money which is no easy matter. And along with all this sort of work, Farrell the policeman stole a horse from George King and had him in Whitty and Farrell's paddock until he left the force and all this was the cause of me and my stepfather George King taking their horses and selling them to Baumgarten and Kennedy. The pick of them was taken to a good market and the culls were kept in Peterson's paddock and their brands altered by me two was sold to Kennedy and the rest to Baumgarten who were strangers to me and I believe honest men.

Page 18

They paid me full value for the horses and could not have known they were stolen. No person had anything to do with the stealing and selling of the horses but me and George King William Cooke who was convicted for Whitty's horses was innocent. He was not in my company at Peterson's. But it is not the place of the police to convict guilty men, as it is by them they get their living. Had the right parties been convicted it would have been a bad job for the police as Berry would have sacked a great many of them, only I came to their aid and kept them in their billets and good employment and got them double pay. And yet the ungrateful articles my mother and an infant, my brother-in-law and another

Page 19

man who was innocent, and still annoy my brothers and sisters and the ignorant unicorns, even threaten to shoot myself. But as soon as I am dead they will be heels up in the muroo, there will be no more police required. They will be sacked and supplanted by soldiers on low pay in the towns and special constables made of some of the farmers to make up for this double pay and expense. It will pay Government to give those people who are suffering innocence justice and liberty. If not I will be compelled to show some colonial stratagem which will open the eyes of not only the Victorian police and inhabitants but also the whole British army, and no doubt

Page 20

they will acknowledge their hounds were barking at the wrong stump, and that Fitzpatrick will be the cause of greater slaughter to the Union Jack than Saint Patrick was to the snakes and toads in Ireland. The Queen of England was as guilty as Baumgarten and Kennedy, Williamson and Skillion of what they were convicted for. When the horses were found on the Murray River I wrote a letter to Mr Swanhill of Lake Rowan to acquaint the auctioneer and to advertize my horses for sale, brought some of them to that place but did not sell. I sold some of them in Benalla, Melbourne and other places and left the colony and became a rambling gambler soon after

Page 21

I left – there was a warrant for me and the police searched the place and watched night and day for two or three weeks and they could not snare me. They got a warrant against my brother Dan and on the 15 April, Fitzpatrick came to the Eleven Mile Creek to arrest him. He had some conversation with a horse dealer whom he swore was William Skillion, this man was not called in Beechworth. Besides several other witnesses who alone could have proved Fitzpatrick's falsehood after leaving this man he went to the house asked was Dan in. Dan came out. I hear previous to this Fitzpatrick had some conversation with Williamsons on the hill he asked Dan to come to Greta with him as he had a warrant for him for stealing Whitty's horses. Dan said all right, they both went inside. Dan was having something to eat. His mother asked Fitzpatrick what he wanted Dan for. The Trooper said he had a warrant for him. Dan then asked him to produce it. He said it was only a telegram sent from Chiltern but Sergeant Whelan ordered him to relieve Steel at Greta and call and arrest Dan and take him into Wangaratta next morning and get him remanded. Dan's mother said Dan need not go without a warrant unless he liked and that the trooper had no business on her premises without some authority besides his own word. The trooper pulled out his revolver and said he would blow her brains out if she interfered in the arrest. She told him it was a good job for him Ned was not there or he would ram the revolver down his throat. Dan looked out and said Ned is

Page 22

coming now. The trooper being off his guard looked out and when Dan got his attention drawn, he dropped the knife and fork which showed he had he had no murderous intent and slapped Leenan's hug on him, took his revolver and kept him there until Skillion and Ryan came with horses which Dan sold that night. The trooper left and invented some scheme to say that he got shot which any man can see is false. He told Dan to clear out that Sergeant Steel and Detective Brown and Strachan would be there before morning. Strachan had been over the Murray trying to get up a case against him and they would convict him if they caught him as the stock society offered an enticement for witnesses to swear anything and the Germans over the Murray would swear to the wrong man as well as the right. Next day Williamson and my mother were arrested and Skillion the day after who was not there at all at the time of the row which can be proved by 8 or 9 witnesses. And the police got credit and praise in the papers for arresting the mother of 12 children, one an infant on her breast and those two quiet hardworking innocent men who would not know the difference in a revolver and a saucepan handle, and kept them six months awaiting trial and then convicted them on the evidence of the meanest article that ever the sun shone on. It seems that the jury were well chosen by the police as there was a discharged sergeant amongst them which is contrary to law. They thought it impossible for a policeman to swear a lie but I can assure them it is by that means and hiring cads they get promotion. I have heard from a trooper that he never

Page 23

knew Fitzpatrick to be one night sober and that he sold his sister to a China man. But he looks a young strapping (fellow), rather genteel, more fit to be a starcher to a laundress than policeman for to a keen observer he has the wrong appearance or a manly heart. The deceit and cowardice is too plain to be seen in the puny cabbage hearted looking face. I heard nothing of this transaction until very close on the trial. I being then over 400 miles from Greta when I heard I was outlawed and a hundred pounds reward for me for shooting at a trooper in Victoria and a hundred pound reward for any man that could prove a conviction of horse stealing against me. So I came back to Victoria, knew I would get no justice if I gave myself up. I enquired after my brother Dan and found him digging on Bullock Creek, heard how the police used to be blowing that they would not ask me to stand, they would shoot me first and then cry surrender and how they used to rush into the house upset all the milk dishes break tins of eggs, empty the flour out of the bags on to the ground and even the meat out of the cask and destroy all the provisions, and shove the girls in front of them into the rooms like dogs so as if any one was there they would shoot the girls first. But they knew well I was not there or I would have scattered their blood and brains like rain. I would manure the Eleven Mile with their bloated carcasses and yet remember there is not one drop of murderous blood in my veins. Superintendent Smith used to say to my sisters, see all the

Page 24

men I have out today, I will have as many more tomorrow and we will blow him into pieces as small as paper that is in our guns. Detective Ward and Constable Hays took out their revolvers and threatened to shoot the girls and Children in Mrs Skillion's absence the greatest ruffians and murderers no matter how depraved would not be guilty of such a cowardly action, and this sort of cruelty and disgraceful and cowardly conduct to my brothers and sisters who had no protection coupled with the conviction of my mother. And those men certainly made my blood boil as I don't think there is a man born could have the patience to suffer it as long as I did or ever allow his blood to get cold cold while such insults as these were unavenged. And yet in every paper that is printed I am called the blackest and coldest blooded murderer ever on record. But if I hear any more of it I will not exactly show them what cold blooded murder is but wholesale and retail slaughter something different to shooting three troopers in self defence and robbing a bank. I would have been rather hot blooded to throw down my rifle and let them shoot me and my innocent brother. They were not satisfied with frightening my sisters night and day and destroying their provisions and lagging my mother and infant and those innocent men but should follow me and my brother into the wilds where he had been quietly digging neither molesting or interfering with any one he was making good wages as the creek is very rich within half a mile from where I shot Kennedy. I was not there long and on the 25 October, I came on police tracks between Tabletop and the bogs. I crossed

Page 25

them and returning in the evening I came on a different lot of tracks making for the shingle hut. I went to our camp and told my brother and his two mates and my brother went and found their camp at the shingle hut, about a mile from my brother's house, saw they carried long firearms and we knew our doom was sealed if we could not beat those before the others would come as I knew the other party of police would soon join them. And if they came on us at our camp they would shoot us down like dogs at our work as we had only two guns. We thought if best to try and bail those up, take their firearms and ammunition and horses and we could stand a chance with the rest. We approached the spring as close as we could get to the camp, as the intervening space being clear ground and no battery we saw two men at the logs. They got up and one took a double barrelled fowling piece and fetched a horse down and hobbled him at the tent, and we thought there were more men in the tent asleep, those being on sentry. We could have shot those two men without speaking but not wishing to take their lives we waited. McIntyre laid the gun against a stump and Lonigan sat on the log. I advanced, my brother Dan keeping McIntyre covered which he took to be Constable Flood. And had he not obeyed my orders or attempted to reach for the gun or draw his revolver, he would have been shot dead. But when I called on them to throw up their hands, McIntyre obeyed and Lonigan ran some six or seven yards to a battery of logs instead of dropping behind the one

Page 26

he was sitting on. He had just got to the logs and put his head up to take aim when I shot him that instant, or he would have shot me as I took him to be Strachan, the man who said he would not ask me to stand, he would shoot me first like a dog. But it happened to be Lonigan the man who in company with Sergeant Whelan Fitzpatrick and King, the boot maker and Constable O'Day that tried to put a pair of handcuffs on me in Benalla, but could not and had to allow McInnes the Miller to put them on. Previous to Fitzpatrick swearing, he was shot. I was fined two pounds for not allowing five curs like Sergeant Whelan, O'Day, Fitzpatrick, King and Lonigan, and would have sent me to kingdom come. Only I was not ready and he is the man that blowed before he left Violet Town. If Ned Kelly was to be shot, he was the man that would shoot him and no doubt he would shoot me even if I threw up my arms and laid down as he knew four of them could not arrest me single handed, not to talk of the rest of my mates. Also either him or me would have to die, this he knew well therefore he had a right to keep out of my road. Fitzpatrick is the only one I hit out of the five in Benalla. This shows my feelings towards him as he said we were good friends and even swore it. But he was the biggest enemy I had in the country with the exception of Lonigan, and he can be thankful I was not there when he took a revolver and threatened to shoot my mother in her own house. It is not fire three shots and miss him at a yard and a half. I don't think I would use a revolver to shoot a man like him when I was within a yard and a half of him or attempt to

Page 27

fire into a house where my mother, brothers and sisters was. And according to Fitzpatrick's statement, all around him a man that is such a bad shot as to miss a man three times at a yard and a half would never attempt to fire into a house where my mother brothers among a houseful of women and children while I had a pair of arms and a bunch of fives on the end of them that never failed to peg at anything they came in contact with. And Fitzpatrick knew the weight of one of them only too well as it run against him once in Benalla and cost me two pound odd as he is very subject to fainting. As soon as I shot Lonigan he jumped up and staggered some distance from the logs with his hands raised and then fell. He surrendered but too late I asked McIntyre who was in the tent. He replied no one. I advanced and took possession of their two revolvers and fowling piece which I loaded with bullets instead of shot. I asked McIntyre where his mates was. He said they had gone down the creek and he did not expect them that night. He asked me was I going to shoot him and his mates. I told him no I would shoot no man if he gave up his arms and leave the force. He said the police all knew Fitzpatrick had wronged us and he intended to leave the force as he had bad health and his life was insured. He told me he intended going home and that Kennedy and Scanlon were out looking for our camp and also about the other police he told me the New South Wales police had shot a man for shooting Sergeant Walling. I told him if they did, they had shot the wrong man and I expect your gang came

Page 28

to do the same with me. He said no they did not come to shoot me, they came to apprehend me. I asked him what they carried, spencer rifles and breech loading, fowling places, and so much ammunition for, as the police was only supposed to carry one revolver and six cartridges in the revolver but they had eighteen rounds of revolver cartridges, each three dozen for the fowling piece and twenty one spencer rifle cartridges. And God knows how many they had away with the rifle this looked as if they meant not only to shoot me, only to riddle me. but I don't know either Kennedy, Scanlan or him and had nothing against them. He said he would get them to give up their arms if I would not shoot them as I could not blame them, they had to do their duty. I said I did not blame them for doing honest duty but I could not suffer them blowing me to pieces in my own native land and they knew Fitzpatrick wronged us and why not make it public and convict him. But no, they would rather riddle poor unfortunate creoles. But they will rue the day ever Fitzpatrick got among them. Our two mates came over when they heard the shots fired but went back again for fear the police might come to our camp while we were all away, and manure bullock flat with us. On our arrival, I stopped at the logs and Dan went back to the spring, for the troopers would come in that way. But I soon heard them coming up the creek. I told McIntyre to tell them to give up their arms. He spoke to Kennedy who was some distance in front of Scanlan he reached for his revolver and jumped off on the off side of his horse and got behind a tree when I

Page 29

called on them to surrender, throw up their arms, and Scanlon who carried the rifle slewed his horse around to gallop away. But the horse would not go and as quick as thought fired at me with the rifle without unslinging it, and was in the act of firing again when I had to shoot him and he fell from his horse. I could have shot them without speaking but their lives was no good to me. McIntyre jumped on Kennedy's horse and I allowed him to go as I did not like to shoot him after he surrendered or I would have shot him as he was between me and Kennedy. Therefore I could not shoot Kennedy without shooting him first. Kennedy kept firing from behind a tree. My brother Dan advanced and Kennedy ran I followed him, he stopped behind another tree and fired again. I shot him in the armpit and he dropped his revolver and ran. I fired again with the gun as he slewed around to surrender. I did not know he had dropped his revolver the bullet passed through the right side of his chest and he could not live or I would have let him go. Had they been my own brothers, I could not help shooting them or else let them shoot me which they would have done had their bullets been directed as they intended them. But as for handcuffing Kennedy to a tree or cutting his ear off or brutally treating any of them is a falsehood. If Kennedy's ear was cut off, it was not done by me, and none of my mates was near him after he was shot. I put his cloak over him and left him as well as I could. And were they my own brothers, I could not have been more sorry for them. This cannot be called wilful murder for I was compelled to shoot them or lie down and let them shoot me, it would not be wilful murder if they packed our remains in shattered into a mass of animated gore to Mansfield. They would have got great praise and credit as well as promotion but I

Page 30

am recorded a horrid brute because I had not been cowardly enough to lie down for them under such trying circumstances, and insults to my people. Certainly their wives and children are to be pitied but they must remember those men came into

the bush with the intention of scattering pieces of me and my
brother all over the bush and yet they know and acknowledge
I have been wronged. And my mother and four or five men
lagged innocent, and is my brothers and sisters and my mother
not to be pitied also who was has no alternative only to put up
with the brutal and cowardly conduct of a parcel of big ugly,
fat necked, wombat headed, big bellied, magpie legged, narrow
hipped splaw-footed sons of Irish bailiffs or English landlords
which is better known as officers of justice or Victorian police
who some calls honest gentlemen. But I would like to know
what business an honest man would have in the police as it is
an old saying, 'it takes a rogue to catch a rogue' and a man that
knows nothing about roguery would never enter the force and
take an oath to arrest brother, sister, father or mother if required.
And to have a case and conviction if possible, any man knows it
is possible to swear a lie. And if a policeman looses a conviction
for the sake of swearing a lie he has broke his oath, therefore he
is a perjurer. Either ways a policeman is a disgrace to his country
and ancestors and religion, as they were all Catholics before
the Saxons and Cranmore yoke held sway since then they were
persecuted massacred, thrown into martyrdom and tortured
beyond the ideas of the present generation. What would people
say if they saw a strapping big lump of an Irishman shepparding
sheep for fifteen bob a week or tailing turkeys in Tallarook
ranges for a smile from Julia or even begging his tucker.

Page 31

They would say he ought to be ashamed of himself and tar and
feather him. But he would be a king to a policeman who for
a lazy loafing cowardly billet left the ash corner, deserted the
Shamrock, the emblem of true wit and beauty to serve under a
flag and nation that has destroyed, massacred and murdered their
forefathers by the greatest of torture as rolling them down hill

in spiked barrels, pulling their toes and finger nails, and on the wheel and every torture imaginable. More was transported to Van Dieman's Land to pine their young lives away in starvation and misery among tyrants worse than the promised hell itself. All of true blood, bone and beauty that was not murdered on their own soil or had fled to America or other countries to bloom again another day, were doomed to Port McQuarie, Toweringabbie and Norfolk Island and Emu Plain. And in those places of tyranny and condemnation, many a blooming Irishman rather than subdue to the Saxon yoke were flogged to death and bravely died in servile chains, but true to the Shamrock and a credit to Paddy's land. What would people say if I became a policeman and took an oath to arrest my brothers, sisters and relations, and convict them by fair or foul means after the conviction of my mother, and the persecutions and insults offered to myself. And people would they say I was a decent gentleman

Page 32

and yet a policeman is still in worse and guilty of meaner actions than that the Queen must surely be proud of such heroic men as the police and Irish soldiers. As it takes eight or eleven of the biggest mud crushers in Melbourne to take one poor little half starved larrikin to a watch house. I have seen as many as eleven big and ugly enough to lift Mount Macedon out of a crab hole, move like the species of a baboon or guerrilla than a man actually come into a court house and swear they could not arrest one eight stone larrikin. And them, armed with battens and neddies without some civilian's assistance and some of them going to the hospital from the effects of hits from the fists of the larrikin. And the magistrate could send the poor little larrikin into a dungeon for being a better man than such a parcel of armed curs. What would England do if America declared war and hoisted a green flag as it is all Irishmen that has got command army forts of her batterys, even her very life guards and beef tasters are Irish. Would they not slew round and fight her with their own arms for the sake of the color they dare not wear for years and to reinstate it and rise old Erin's isle once more from the pressure and tyrannism of the English yoke, and which has kept in poverty and starvation and caused them to wear the enemy's coat. What else can England expect, is there not big fat necked unicorns enough paid to torment and drive me to do things which I don't wish to do without the public assisting them.

Page 33

I have never interfered with any person unless they deserved it and yet there are civilians who take firearms against me for what reason I do not know. Unless they want me to turn on them and exterminate them. Without medicine I shall be compelled to make an example of some of them if they cannot find no other employment. If I had robbed and plundered, ravished and murdered everything I met, young and old, rich and poor, the public could not do anymore than take firearms and assisting the police as they have done. But by the light that shines pegged on an ant bed with their bellies opened, their fat taken out, rendered and poured down their throat boiling hot, will be fool to what pleasure I will give some of them. And any person aiding or harbouring or assisting the police in any way whatever or employing any person whom they know to be a detective, or cad or those who would be so depraved as to take blood money, will be outlawed and declared unfit to be allowed human burial. Their property either consumed or confiscated and them and theirs and all belonging to them exterminated of the face of the earth, the enemy I cannot catch myself. I shall give a payable reward for I would like to know who put that article that reminds me of a poodle dog half clipped in the lion fashion called Brooker Smith superintendent of police he knows as much about commanding police

Page 34

as Captain Standing does about mustering mosquitoes and boiling them down for their fat on the back blocks of the Lachlan, for he has a head like a turnip, a stiff neck as big as his shoulders, narrow hipped and pointed towards the feet like a vine stake. And if there is any one to be called a murderer regarding Kennedy, Scanlan and Lonigan it is that misplaced poodle he gets as much pay as a doz good troopers, if there is any good in them. And what does he do for it he cannot look behind him without turning his whole frame. It take three or four police to keep sentry while he sleep in Wangaratta for fear of body snatchers. Do they think he is a superior animal to the men that has to guard them him. If so why not send the men that gets big pay and rec k oned superior to the common police after me and you shall soon save the country of high salaries to men that is fit for nothing else but getting better men than himself shot, and sending orphan children to the industrial school to make prostitutes for the detectives, and other evil disposed persons send the high paid men that receive big salaries for years in a gang by themselves after me, as it will make no difference to them but it will give the public a chance of showing whether they are worth more pay than a common trooper or not. And I think the public will soon find out they are only in the road of good men. That is if there

Page 35

is any good men among them and obtaining money under false pretences.

Page 36

PLEASE NOTE: Page 36 of the original document is a blank page.

Page 37

I do not call McIntyre a coward as he is as good a man, as wears the jacket he had the presence of mind to know his position directly he was spoken to, it is only foolishness to disobey an outlaw, it was cowardice and foolhardiness , made Lonigan fight, it was is foolhardiness to disobey an outlaw as it means a speedy dispatch to kingdom come. I would advise all those who joined the Stock Protection to withdraw their money and give it to the poor of Greta where I have spent and will again spend many happy days fearless free and bold.

Page 38

As it only aids the police to procure false witnesses to lag innocent men. I would advise them to subscribe a sum and give it to the poor of their district, as no man could steal their horse or cattle without the knowledge of the poor, and they would rise as one man and find it if it was on the face of the earth. The police can't protect you,

Page 39

all those that have reason to fear me had better sell out and give £10 out of every hundred to the widow and orphan fund. And do not attempt to reside in Victoria but as short a time as possible after reading this notice, neglect this and abide by the consequence which shall be worse than rust in wheat in Victoria or the drought of a dry season to the grasshoppers in New South

Wales. I do not wish to give the order full force without giving timely warning but I am a Widow's Son, outlawed and my orders must be obeyed.

Page 40

[blank on the original document].

APPENDIX 4
The Traveller

The Kelly Gang or The Outlaws of the Wombat Ranges was published by George Wilson Hall in February 1879. The work was published shortly after the Jerilderie bank robbery of February 1879 (the preface is dated 22 February 1879).

George W Hall was the publisher of the work, but its authors are not named. The preface is signed 'The Authors' as plural, so it is most likely a collaboration between Hall and the unnamed 'traveller' (see the text, page 123; Mr Blank, page 131).

Peter Newman, author of *James Wallace: The Kelly Gang Sympathiser*, believes it is highly likely that James Wallace was the writer of the material in Chapters XXIV and XXV that relate the story of the unnamed traveller (or else that he was a significant contributor to the material). Peter's reasons are set out in Chapter 11 of this book.

Stuart Dawson has made a transcription of the publication, which he has made freely available at https://gutenberg.net.au/ebooks19/1900581p.pdf The following reproduces in full Chapters XXIV and XXV that relate to the unnamed traveller.

[123]
CHAPTER XXIV

"Mystery, half veiled and half revealed". – SCOTT
"For hosts may in these wilds abound,
 Such as are better missed than found". – *Ibid.*

It was about noontide on one of those warm, exhausting, sweltry days which, in Victoria, marked the close of the January succeeding the date of the murders, when not a breeze stirred the leaves of the forest, and all nature seemed hushed in breathless repose; when the azure vault of heaven could not boast one little cloud to shelter, even for a moment, in its passage, the parched and weary wayfarer from the fierce and nearly perpendicular rays of an almost tropical sun, that a traveller might have been seen slowly climbing, with weary steps, one of the steepest and most tedious spurs of the south-western slope of the Wombat Ranges. And as, at short and frequent intervals, his feet would slip backwards on the treacherously shifting shingle with clothed the ascent, the objurgatory observations, "not loud but deep", which he occasionally vented relative to the soil he was then treading would have led any unprejudiced listener to the conclusion that the pedestrian, in the course of a nomadic – and probably checkered – existence, had made a choice and varied collection of the rarest oaths and most objective curses that could be found under the flags of Great Britain and the United States of America, or, by any possibility, conceived in that juratory magazine and matrix of anathemas – the Anglo-Saxon brain.

There was nothing strikingly peculiar in the general appearance of the stranger – nothing to make him an object of special notice, had he been met on any ordinary highway or in a settled quarter. Yet his dress and belongings had been
[124] carefully considered, and judiciously selected with a special object – namely, the non-attraction of observation in his journey through the bush, by the presentation of hues corresponding as much as possible with the tints displayed by the surface and vegetation of that part of the country through which he desired to pass. For although he was in search of a party of men to whom, notwithstanding the dangerous character they

bore, he brought credentials that he felt confident would ensure him not only safety, but welcome, yet there were larger parties, in the service of law and order, to be met with, occasionally traversing the neighbourhood, who were occupied in a similar pursuit – at least it was so said – but with different motives, and whose credentials consisted of central-fire ball cartridges. These he did not wish to come in contact with; not that he had any grounds for fearing them on the score of personal safety, but lest the purpose for which he was making the long and hazardous journey might be frustrated, or, at least, ruinously delayed, by their legalized mode of satisfying their curiosity.

There was nothing marked about the physiognomy or figure of the stranger; of medium height and build, somewhat past middle age, with dark brown hair and beard, hazel eyes, and a fair skin, save for the effects of the weather, he offered no point either of attraction or repulsion likely to induce a passer-by to take a second look at him under every-day circumstances.

In his equipment, however, might have been found sundry articles to excite surprise and speculation in the eyes of many. His dress, to commence at the top, consisted of a broad-leafed, tall, soft felt *sombrero*, of an obfusc greyish-brown;[26] an ordinary flannel singlet, covered by an olive-green Crimean shirt;

[125] trousers of a kind known in the slop-shops as "coloured moles", kept in position by leathern waist-belt, and of a neutral shade, which might be described as dirty chocolate; grey military socks, and a pair of strong lace-up boots – all baggage with which he was encumbered had nothing externally to mark it as unusually strange, but its interior would have discovered some articles not strictly in keeping with the ostensible character of the bearer – namely, a man seeking work; and some would have seemed utterly useless. He carried on his shoulder a single coarse brown blanket, rolled up swag fashion, within the folds of which snugly reposed some tobacco, a maiden bottle of "Three star" brandy, and a bottle, which, though three parts filled with "Long John" whiskey, showed evident signs of having been tampered with and tapped since its purchase. The bottles were carefully wrapped in a few of the most recent copies of the *Argus* and *Age* newspapers.

From the two ends of this, fastened together with a saddle strap, depended what is known as a "Sydney pot", containing water, and consisting of a quart billy, the close-fitting lid of which formed a pannican. On the opposite side, slung to a strap passing over the other shoulder, hung a well-worn tourist's bag, made of leather, in one compartment of which were a few well-baked, solid scones, and a lump of hard corned beef; while the other contained two small calico bags, with tea and sugar, also a diminutive binocular field-glass, a good-sized note-book, the four of diamonds from a new pack, an ordinary large empty cardboard pill box, a few long hairs from the tail of a horse, and a bright white-metal table spoon. A coloured cotton pocket-handkerchief in his hat, and a strong clasp knife, some twine, a box of matches, a short black clay pipe, and a

[126] small compass in his trousers pockets, bring the inventory to a conclusion.

---

[26] Obfusc - late 19th century; probably shortened from obfuscous or obfuscate; here, a muddled colour.

The traveller continued to pursue his journey up the steep, winding, and – save for woody vegetation – barren spur until, after many involuntary deviations, which caused him to retrace his steps for considerable distances, and drew forth appropriate remarks, he reached the highest summit of the principal elevation in those ranges, known as "Wombat Hill".

Here, after looking round for a while, as if in search for some landmark, he unhitched his swag, and throwing himself wearily at the foot and under the shade of a giant gum tree, he proceeded to indulge in a meditative smoke, after first refreshing exhausted nature with a modest quencher of qualified "Long John".

Reclining thus, drowsily comfortable, under the combined and soothing influences of tobacco and whiskey, his thoughts began to shape themselves into muttered soliloquy, the burden of which seemed to be, "I wonder if it's a sell"; after repeating which two or three times, at intervals, he sprung up sharply, exclaiming, while he re-adjusted his traps, "Well, here goes! I'll see it out anyway, hit or miss". His next act would have appeared highly mysterious, if not idiotic, to a looker-on, for he proceeded to cut sundry small boughs or springs from the green suckers that were growing around, and these he hastily twisted into a sort of wreath or crown, with which he invested his hat; then, taking out the polished spoon, which reflected the rays of the sun from the back of its bowl, like a convex mirror, he fixed it firmly and diagonally across the front of his novel head-dress, thus leaving himself open – should he meet any of the uninitiated – to the suspicion of having recently escaped from the precincts of the Yarra Bend or some

[127] other lunatic asylum. He then took out of his pocket compass, placing it on the ground beside the tree under which he had camped, and stood over it, watching the oscillations of the needle, until that unerring guide subsided into a state of absolute repose.

As soon as this point had been reached, he took up the instrument, and, retaining it in his hand, walked away at a comparatively smart rate, towards the east, evidently counting his paces as he went. When he had achieved the limit he desired, some two hundred yards or more, he stopped, and carefully examined his surroundings for a few minutes; then, having apparently satisfied himself, and made up his mind as to the direction he required to take, he plunged down a rocky declivity which led to the ranges on the north-eastern side of the eminence he had occupied.

CHAPTER XXV

"For his particular I'll receive him,
But not one stranger". - Shakespeare.

We may here permit ourselves to imagine the wanderer, for some three hours or so, struggling with the average difficulties which beset a man in such a region while endeavouring to discover a point hitherto unvisited by him, while guided only by verbal instructions referring to natural features of the country – features not only difficult of

recognition by a stranger, but also not easily discoverable by anyone, owing to the thickly-timbered, and frequently scrubby, character of the locality. Availing ourselves, then, of the "presto" privilege accorded

[128] to anecdotical writers, we next present the mysterious stranger to our readers, standing, with a doubtful and puzzled expression of countenance, in the dry bed of a small and shallow water-course which originated at the convergence of two deep, dark, and thickly timbered gullies, the interstices between the trees being filled with close-growing wattle scrub, interlaced in places, with tough and tangled creepers, which formed an almost impenetrable mass.

After moving several times to the right and left of the stream bed, anxiously and earnestly scrutinizing the details surrounding his position, not only with the naked eye, but also through his field-glass, his face suddenly lighted up with an expression of genuine satisfaction and triumph, on catching a glimpse of the summit of an immense moss-covered and dome-shaped rock that lay embowered, and almost concealed, amid the redundant foliage of the trees on the closely-timbered spur which divided, and at the same time, helped to form the two gloomy gullies recently described.

Opening his travelling bag, he quickly extracted from it the four of diamonds card, and taking off his hat and detaching the spoon from it, he replaced the latter with the playing card, which he fixed firmly, the unsullied face of the pasteboard being turned to the front, and he then put on his hat.

This done, he returned the spoon to his haversack, and sitting down on a log, facing the rock, he pulled out the pillbox and horsehair, which he placed on the log. His next step was to select a long and strong horsehair from his bundle, and after fastening a short piece of rush, from one growing beside him, to one end of it by a loop and knot, pass the hair through a pin-hole in the bottom of the pill box, the piece of [129] rush being inside it, and the hair projecting through the hole in its bottom.

This might, at first sight, have appeared to be a preparation for constructing a simple bush telephone, like that used by the Cingalese, and, in good truth, it was intended to answer a somewhat simular purpose, as will be surmised presently; for, taking the box in his left hand, and drawing the hair steadily between the forefinger and thumb of the right, moistened with saliva, the operator succeeded in producing, at intervals of about a minute, exact imitation of the "Caw-aw-a-w-w" of a crow, which was distinguishable at a long distance in the silence of the forest, and which would have been good enough to defy competition on the part of the most accomplished mockingbird to be found amid the leafy solitudes of the Australian Alps.

He had not been more than a quarter of an hour indulging in this apparently harmless bird-like harmony (?) (which added to the appearance of insanity suggested by his head-gear),[27] when two young men, attired in ordinary stockman's style, but displaying two revolvers each at their belts, stepped lightly forward, simultaneously, from the leafy screen at the mouth of the right hand gully, distant about three chains off, and with guns pointed at the corvine minstrel, cried out – "Put up your hands and stand up!" an order promptly and cheerfully obeyed, as though in gratitude for being allowed

---

[27] Both sets of bracketed comments, the (?) and the next, are as per the original text.

---

the privilege of looking straight into the barrels of two loaded smooth-bores at full-cock, with the animating reflection that there was no sufficiently established guarantee against either or both going off while the inspection proceeded.

The younger of these two new arrivals on the scene, who looked quite a youth, with a feminine, beardless face and a mild [130] expression, lowering his muzzle, then walked up to the traveller, and after convincing himself, by a rapid and skilful search, that he was unarmed (unless he chanced to have utilized his swag as a magazine) told him to drop his hands, and then put his question to him, "How is the pound getting on?" to which the reply was, "There hasn't been any more 'gully-raking' lately, and six head have been released". With an abrupt but civil, "All right, come on", the youth led the way to where his mate (who, seeing all was correct, had thrown his gun across his right shoulder) was standing, and introduced the visitor with the brief remark, "This is the cove".

The three men then, forming Indian file, the traveller in the middle, disappeared amid the intricacies of the gully as suddenly and completely as though the mountain gorge had fairly swallowed them up – or down.

The subsequent movements of that trio on that evening, through the bush, being totally inexplicable without the adjunct of an accurate topographical map of the features of the locality, and such not being in existence, we must leave their peregrinations to the fancies of our readers.

Suffice it to say that in about an hour after they vanished they reached their camping place, which was on an eminence, from whence ran four deep, winding gullies, distant about two miles from their starting point, where the tourist, thoroughly exhausted, was made acquainted by his guide with two other men, who, though not quite so young, were decorated, in the prevailing fashion affected by the clique, with that useful, if not chastely ornamental, style of jewellery manufactured largely by Dean and Adams, Webly, Tranter and Colt.

It was remarkable that the eldest of the party, who seemed [131] about twenty-four years of age, and evidently "bossed" the whole concern, was obviously of the same inquiring turn of mind as his younger comrade; for, of the arrival of him whom, at this stage, we may distinguish as the guest, the following dialogue took place:–

Host – "Have you many hawks down your way?" *Guest* – "Yes, about the stations". *Host* – "Did you meet any in these ranges?" *Guest* – "No". *Host* – "How's that, do you think?" *Guest* (after a minute or two's anxious thought, the host whiling away the time by playing with a six-shooter) – "I suppose they'd rather tackle a crippled sheep than a lively wombat". *Host* – "Right you are, my sonny; chuck down your dunnage. Joe's just going to sling the billy in the cave; we never light a fire here".

Acting instantaneously on the welcome permission, or rather invitation, Mr. Blank went to work to unroll his blanket, and bring to view the unexpected liquid treasures that were so cosily ensconced within its voluminous folds.

These were received with low but earnest acclamation, and the purveyor was favoured with a request from head quarters, which amounted to a command, to set the company an example by indulging in a reasonable "snorter" (and no heeltaps)[28] from each bottle, as a preliminary to the flasks making the round of the mob. This he did, nothing loathe; and while the cordial balm was being distributed among the captain, the guest, and the crew, including the lookout man, the scene became gradually enveloped in the dusky robe of night, scarcely relieved by the cheese-paring of a moon then in existence.

For imperative reasons, which could in no way interest the reader, we are bound to draw the curtain of judicious [132] silence over the minutes of the further proceedings; but we are at liberty to state that the guest was treated with the utmost consideration, and the next morning, after a sound and refreshing night's sleep, having been furnished with all the comforts obtainable from a larder so limited in variety, though plenteous in contents, had a final interview with the host, to whose earnest and impressive remarks he might have been seen attentively listening, notebook in hand, while ever and anon he made a hurried but careful entry therein, in each case repeating them aloud for confirmation or correction.

The last fact we have to record relating to this rather mysterious affair, the unravelment of which we leave to the perspicuity of our readers, is that the adventurous being whose hazardous enterprise we have endeavoured partially to chronicle reached his home safe and well, though rather foot-sore, some two days after the date of the last scene depicted, well satisfied both with the reception he met with, and the results of his trip through the wilds of the Wombat Ranges, with the outskirts of which only he was previously acquainted; and he declares that, while he lives, he will bear a lively recollection of the best of the weather, as well as a grateful remembrance of the warm reception he met among the hills; the latter, he is wont to say, he made sure he would meet with, *either of one kind or the other.*

APPENDIX 5
Wallace letters to Nicolson

Wallace letter, Monday 18 August 1879

I agree with you as to them not being 'identical' for the following reasons:

1. I have ascertained that the horseman has passed here on the morning of the 11th was the senior brother beyond a doubt. Therefore he would not have time to reconnoitre, plan, and carry out the Lancefield affair.
2. The descriptions do not correspond at all.
3. The modus operandi was altogether different to that of our boys.

I have not been idle since seeing you. The boys are or were for the past few weeks in the vicinity. During that time they have visited a house within three miles of Beechworth on several occasions.

The poet seems to have been ill. The exposure and occasional prolonged frosts not agreeing with his naturally delicate constitution.

The others are in good fettle and they are all in good spirits. I had hoped to have come across them last night but my horse is 'played out' and I have not yet come across another one to suit.

I will try to run down to Benalla to see you on Thursday evening next.

I think it more desirable to communicate details to you personally as there is a 'screw loose' in your department somewhere.

Even the list of places that I gave you at our first interview is now in the hands of our friends' friends and they 'would like to know who the b____ he _ gave him that rigmarole.'

There is a delightful game of cross purposes being played on both sides that is worth the trouble of watching if there were no other motive.

I think I can persuade someone to return the chronometer to the widow per post but he is avaricious and would rather melt it down.

You have frightened his brother a bit. He is shy and will have to be played with 'finesse'.

Wallace letter, Wednesday 27 August 1879

Sorry to say I've not managed to ascertain anything worthwhile since seeing you. Interviewed Mr Hare's protégé on Saturday in fact spent the night with him. He has National Bank notes – at least he had two on Saturday evening but whether they come from Euroa or not is not easy to determine. He said they were 'square' and that he had obtained them in payment for services rendered to the police. I changed one of them for him and cashed it purposely in Ward's presence at Wertheims Beechworth. I jocularly drew that gentleman's attention to it as being a 'National' and asked him what he would give to be told where that came from. As to the watch in the early part of the evening he of his own accord proposed that I should go home with him that night and he would show it to me to get my opinion as to the feasibility of getting it altered so as to defy identification. He said it was at his mother's that he had taken it in and given it to her for safe keeping in case the police played him double and let him in for stealing Mrs Byrne's horse. He said that there was a dark stain on the case and a sovereign pendant on the chain. He had an interview with Ward after this and I fancy he was put on his guard by that gentleman. At any rate we stayed in Beechworth all night.

In the night or rather towards morning – for we slept together – he asked me if I could imitate Byrne's handwriting. I replied in the affirmative. He said he wanted a threatening letter written to Mr A Crawford of Beechworth purporting to come from Byrne and warning him to prepare for his latter end as they were informed that he had informed on G Baumgarten for supplying them with sugar etc. In this letter to Crawford he wanted one – 'a terror' as he called it, enclosed for himself (Sherritt). At his request I wrote a draft of the proposed letters and showed them to him. Went down to the old peoples next morning (Sunday) and stayed to dinner. The old lady was not at all communicative but appeared nervous and frightened. Had a walk out with Jack for his father's horse (K K's lost chestnut). He was rather reticent and distrustful at first. I asked him how the outlaws were as foolish as to go into the house while the children were there. He said they could not well help it. They wanted tucker. He had heard Byrne's whistle during the day and knew they were about but was afraid the man who was with him might suspect something if he (Jack) went out to them and in the evening he and his brother were from home. He said he would take care they were not so foolish again. His account of their visit tallies with his mothers. He said the police were on a new 'lay' hoping to get Mrs B to persuade Joe to turn informer. He said they might save themselves the trouble as the old woman declared 'she would rather see him shot or hanged any day rather turn traitor'. He (Jack) says the outlaws are well aware of the 'move', but are not at all afraid of Byrne selling them. Jack evidently distrusts Aaron, he shepherded him closely while in my company. He says though he has not tried sell them yet, he would not trust him. He said Aaron had told (word obscured by paper fold) their visit, but says he did it to get some cash as he knew it was too late for the information to injure the boys.

Was out in the ranges all last night. I will reconnoitre Black Range Creek tomorrow night and interview Mr B on Saturday morning.

Wallace letter, Monday 1 September 1879

I have not yet had the pleasure of wiring you a telegram though I had strong hopes of being able to do something in that time soon.

There is no doubt as to their being about; and from unguarded expressions let drop by the Sherritts A & J, I think they have been bivouacking in some of the terribly ranges between Sebastopol and El Dorado without horses. I think they very seldom remain long in one place, moving about at night and sleeping in scrub or caves during the day is just in their line. On Tuesday last from 11 pm till 3 the next morning I ran through the likely places in the Hurdle Creek Range and reconnoitered Black Range Ck. On Thursday night I went to Mackay's Springs and up the ranges as far as Bullock Camp. Starting from here at about 11pm on Friday evening I rode along their stolen horses track under the railway arch above Everton and along the ridges at the back of the Golden Ball. Had a peep at Sherritt's various establishments between 2 and 4am and then rode down on to Byrne's look out. Rested and fed my horse and watched Chappells & Mrs Brynes till sunrise. From there, crossed the creek (word unclear) below Bachelor's and went by way of Salisbury's & Smith's gullies down into the Pilot Flat and along Deep Creek and got to the Upper Black Dog Creek about noon my horse thoroughly knocked up. Camped until dark at a Chinamans hut whom I recognised as from Sebastopol a great friend of the Byrnes. He was loud in his expression of sympathy and ridiculed the search party style of hunting outlaws. He said the outlaws were in these ranges some time ago. (By the way, speaking of Chinamen, Aaron told me that he had heard from some Chinaman that Ned had purchased some stores lately at a Chinese shop at Bright. It is not unlikely, and doubtless there are many celestials about there who would supply the outlaws with food and hold their tongues about it. How would it do to let Fook Shing do a weeks duty on the business?).

On Saturday night went in and saw Lord Byron. Got him under the influence of wine. He evidently knows a thing or two about them and would have let out more than he did if he had not been checked by his wife.

Towards morning something startled my horse. He broke his hobbles and made tracks for home leaving me in the lurch. He was too long gone when I noticed he was missing in the morning (Sunday) so I made up my mind to foot it back here and improve the opportunity by visiting some of their old horse stealing dens and camps during the night. Left the Black Dog about 11 on Sunday night walked up to Mitchells at the Gap. Thence through Wall's Gully about midnight, and visited some camping places about the Woolshed. Salisburys Camp, Kennedys Camp etc. Thence cross and over the range to Sherritts (junior) then to the old man's about from 2 till 3, thence to some of the huts about but all was quiet. Cruised round the ridges a bit and then went down Stony Ck & Yellow Creek for a bit till daylight but saw nothing. Got home about 9.30 this morning thoroughly knocked up.

I will recruit tonight and visit Whorouley tomorrow night, and put in a couple of days in Rat's Castle Saty & Sunday where Byrne has offered to show me through the caves (Kelly's and other bushranger plants) if I will swear 'to keep it dark'. You'll have to do something with Aaron soon. He is 'sweating' horses right and left. If he don't get into some steady billet where he can make an honest living he'll develop into another outlaw before long. There is not the least doubt about his playing you double.

Mrs B has been pestered so much about Joe's pardon (?) lately that I think it will be better to wait for a week or fortnight before I interview her in regard to it. I have strong hopes of being able to put Jumbo and Barney on the trail soon.

Wallace letter, Tuesday 9 September 1879

Poet Sneak & Co were up in the Sebastopol ranges again on Saturday evening and had a jolly carouse with two of the young S's. They got a pack of provender (word unclear) out of Beechworth that day. The pack horse carrying it was met when coming out by Brooke Smith & another const. who were going in; but it would seem no suspicions were aroused.

It was Byrne who wrote the letter read by Ward last week. Byrne will never turn traitor. He swears 'to fight like a demon and die like a man with the assistance of God almighty'.

I can't understand how I have missed them hitherto. They must be on foot and very wary. On Saty night I was down on the Black Dog, and on Sunday and Sunday night round the

Barambogie. On Monday searched the Pilot, Barries Gully, Scarred Rock etc. Found traces on the Pilot of a recent camp fire. On Monday night I went to (word unclear) where I read the information from J. Will give you particulars when I see you. I will be down on Friday evening and will call on you at your rooms at 7pm.

Young Jack S is very desirous to see you. He says his business is of great importance to you. I have promised to introduce him to you or the Captain at the Wangaratta Show if either of you are there. I think it will be better to take him down to Benalla to see you. We can go down from the Show by the train which leaves Wratta at 4.46pm and returns by the 8pm train from Benalla. There is not the slightest danger of his selling the boys. I cannot guess what business he can have with you.

Mrs E Byron was paid for her good offices at the late trial in National Bank notes. The boys have been at her place but not recently. With reference to that I will speak when I see you. I think their present position is in the neighbourhood of Surface gully, below Sebastopol. There is ground cover there.

If you please do not let Ward know that you received news that they were there until I see you on Friday. There are strong reasons why he should be kept in the dark as regards my position in the matter which I will explain when I see you. I will very likely find them tomorrow night. If I do you will get a telegram at once from El Dorado or Beechworth. I will want a few more rounds of ammunition and perhaps a few pounds in cash. We are bound to have them soon now. I fancy I have got their routes and tactics correct.

Wallace letter, Friday night, 19 September 1879

Just rec'd your note undated which was posted at Benalla on the 15th. It must have been mislaid at some of the intermediate post offices. Since coming home I have met a large number of people who were at the ploughing match on the 16th. If there had been such a rumour current as you told me I would be sure to have heard it by this time. Rumours of that kind soon travel. I do not believe that Ward heard anything of the kind. If he did he alone is responsible for it.

It has turned out as I feared. I knew well that if he found out what relations existed between you and me he would do his best to spoil any chance of being useful to you. I have it on the very best authority from two different sources that he stated at the Ploughing match that I 'was a detective', that he 'was certain of it', that he 'had seen my name on the list'. He also told a Mr James Doig a farmer of this place that 'I was trying to get on as a detective' that he 'had seen my name on a departmental list'.

How is it possible that my name could be seen on a list by him? He must just have conjectured it or else Captain Standish may have let him know. In any case he was not justified in any way in publishing the fact abroad in this manner.

As far as anything I have said is concerned no one – not even my wife – could suspect that there is any communication between myself and the Department on the subject. If he has told the Sherritts or other Kelly Sympathisers the same story, he will have greatly lessened my chances of being of service to you, just when I thought I was about certain of success.

If you have anyone else who bears the same relation to you that I do take care that Ward does not find out. If he does, he would do all in his power to spoil success. If he has told Aaron, the outlaws will be possessed of the rumour by this time and I may expect a reminder from Byrne per post.

In regard to what I spoke to you of last night, I have a lot of information on Jack Barry's authority as to the outlaws being on visiting terms with Ned Burke of Black Range Creek. Independent of Barry's yarns I have also a little collateral evidence in support of my belief that he (Burke) is their commissary in that quarter.

Barry (my informant) was also a great friend of Joe Byrnes. He used to work at Byrnes uncle's farm on Whorouley. He has just now returned from Byrne's cousin's place at Wagga. Barry is also a confidential friend of Burkes & (word unclear – looks like Dunns) and can do a little on the 'crooked' himself.

I think I will do well to devote a little more attention to the Black Ranges than I have done hitherto. There is ground cover there and it has not been half searched.

I could do nothing last night it rained incessantly and was as dark as pitch – not a star visible.

Try to make Ward hold his libellous tongue if you can.

Since writing the rest, I have met Doig. He says that Ward publicly stated that I was a detective in Gardiners Hotel Milawa in the presence of Colin Gardner J.P., James Kelly teacher, John Barrie farmer, A McCormick farmer.

Wallace letter, Sunday evening, 21 September 1879

Friday night & Saturday morning I went through the Hurdle Creek & Meadow ranges. Found nothing but the tracks of a heavy shod horse on the ranges near the One Tree Hill crossing over from the Hurdle Creek above McCallums in the direction of the Lower Meadow Creek. The track was a few days old. I also found traces of a camp fire at the head of Saw Pit Gully but a week or fortnight old if not older.

Last night (Saturday) I was detained at home till 10pm by a meeting being held here. Left then for Sebastopol ranges. It was a beautifully clear starlit night – much preferable for my purpose to a moonlit one. Rode and walked quietly through the hills behind Hargreaves & Hodges and above Sebastopol – but neither saw or heard anything of note. Visited the huts of the Sherritt Bros on Crawford selection, but all was quiet. A fire was still blazing brightly at one of the huts at the time of my visit (3 am) as other lads had been up later. Went down Sebastopol Gully along the bed of the streamlet – a rough spot to ride through in the dark, and got to Mrs Byrne's just at day break. At the mouth of the gully at the back of Mrs Byrne's I came on the very fresh tracks of two shod horses and two men with heavy boots.

They were either the tracks of two horsemen leading their horses or else two mounted men accompanied by two pedestrians. I am inclined to believe the latter for several reasons. I ran the tracks round and round. The kept the path along the foot of the hill going east for about ½ a mile, then struck north to the track passing close to Mrs Byrnes house which they followed in a westerly direction. These were evidently police watching Mrs Byrnes. If they were they showed great indiscretion in keeping on the footpath where their heavy tracks could not fail to be seen. They should be instructed when doing duty of this kind to avoid the footpaths where their tracks are too quickly noticed and to keep on the grass. If they are afraid of losing their way they can keep in sight of the path without going on it. Another thing – they should not take their horses to the house but should tie them to a tree in the scrub at a convenient distance and then reconnoitre the house on foot with greater ease and with less danger of being observed.

At this time just after day break all was quiet at Mrs Byrnes. Leaving there and going westward I struck on the fresh trail of a solitary individual in on foot and ran his footprints for about two miles & a half down the creek along the foot of the range where they appeared to go into a Chinamans hut at the foot of Surface Gully. The man's tracks were fresh and he had walked with more discretion than the others. After leaving Byrnes he kept on the grass for some distance before he took the path. He walked lightly and wore neat strong boots (about number 7 in size). He had as was evident from tracks come up the same road the night before and had returned down the road positively between dawn and sunrise and therefore could have only preceded me by a few minutes as the sun was just rising when I abandoned the trail at the Chinaman's hut. I should have gone into the hut but all these confounded Chinamen know me and since Ward has libelled me so it might do your cause more harm than good for to discover myself.

I then went up the ranges. There were several tracks discernible both horse & foot of a pretty recent date all on the footpaths & other ground but none in the scrub & cover. I put in about an hour & a half through these hills and then made for the El Dorado road below the Kangaroo Bridge. Here I again came on similar horse tracks to those I observed near Byrnes and ran them into the El Dorado Police Camp.

Let me know per post whether I should beat up that Chinkie's hut at Surface Gully or not – you will know by the reports whether the tracks were made by one of your men or not.

Jack & Bill Sherritt both rode into El Dorado one day last week – Thursday, I think. In cantering out again Jack's horse fell & threw him. In the shock of the fall a revolver he had concealed on him dropped on the road and was seen by a bystander. It is just possible that Bill was also armed. If so the fact is significant.

I have heard nothing yet of the rumour reported to you by Ward. I believe he told you a falsehood.

The school inspector is to examine my pupils on Thursday – it will take all my time to prepare for it. As it is I think I shall lose from £5 to £10 in results through being so much engrossed in your affair.

After Thursday I will again be at work.

Wallace brief letter, Thursday 25 September 1879

Const. Alexander called here on the 25th. He stated that he was sent to make enquiries in regard to a rumour which had been communicated to Constable Arthur at Milawa, to the effect that the outlaws were seen here – some more of Ward's pleasantries I reckon.

Wallace letter, Monday 29 September 1879

Rec'd your reply this evening. I am glad you warned W. He may find it advisable to hold his tongue for the future. The fact that the tracks I reported were not made by police puts a different complexion on the matter entirely. I was so confident from the appearance of them and the way they moved about that I did not pay as much attention to them as I otherwise would have done. The chances are that they were your missing friends. Who else would it have been manoeuvring round there at that suspicious hour? There could not possibly be any mistake as to the age of the tracks. They had positively been made between midnight and daylight. I arrive at this conclusion in this way! – Up till 12 o'clock on the Saturday evening the sky was cloudy. On a cloudy night no dew falls. There was a heavy dew on the grass on Sunday morning which had fallen since midnight. These tracks were very plainly to be seen on the dewy grass, therefore they must have left the trail after the dew had fallen. Nothing could be plainer.

Another reason why I judged the trail to be that of police was that they were accompanied by a large dog (a hound I think by the trail). I thought it most unlikely that the outlaws would have a dog with them. And picking up the trail of one of the horses on the El Dorado road and running it to the Post Office (next door to the Police Camp) where I abandoned it, I thought was circumstantial evidence sufficient to prove they were police.

With regard to the tracks of the pedestrian which I followed nearly into the Chinese hut, it is just possible as you suggest that it might have been a Chinaman. I will visit the hut and ascertain.

Ah Shin a Chinese tobacco grower residing at Hedi today informed me that on the Saturday after the Wangaratta Show (13th Sept) as he was walking through the Boggy Creek ranges (Moyhu) he was met about 2 miles from Tyrells and accosted by a man whose description very nearly tallies with that of the senior outlaw – about six foot high – pretty well made, reddish beard & whiskers, black eyes, tweed trousers, top boots, dark coat, brownish felt hat worn down over his eyes with black band on chin, armed with no less than four revolvers hung around his belt – one of the revolvers of very unusual length – rode a red (bay or chestnut) horse. This man came down from a hill to the road leading his horse and cross-questioned the Chinaman pretty severely – made him tell his name, occupation, etc, where he came from, where he was going etc. The Chinaman replied that he was looking for a job and the stranger said that he too was looking for work. The Chinaman mustered up courage to ask the stranger where he lived. The man answered 'anywhere'.

Being too frightened to ask any further questions Ah Shin cut the interview as short as he could with civility and went on his way – he mentioned nothing to anyone about his interview with the stranger, thinking it possible that he might be one of the bushrangers. He feared that if such was the case that if he spoke of it he might be murdered by the Kellys or some of their numerous friends.

Of course there may be nothing in it. The man may have been a policeman in disguise. Ah Shin estimated his age at about 40.

I cannot understand how the man came to have a revolver of such a length – 2 ft or 2 ½ ft as described by Ah Shin. Perhaps fear exaggerated it.

I am afraid there is leaking somewhere in your dept. Young Handcock (Jack) *(indescipherable)* told Jack Barry that 'the Police had got scent of the boys about Greta a couple of months ago'.

I have discovered nothing new since last writing. I have to be very careful since Ward floated the report, and have to work almost wholly at night. I am confident of finding them soon.

You spoke of being able to bring pressure to bear on the Minister for Education through the political head of your Dept. I have applied for the head teachership of the Three Mile School near Beechworth and am pretty secure of getting it. I will then be in a better position to work this business for you. I will have more leisure and be more centrally situated. I want to get my brother William Wallace of the El Dorado school appointed as my successor here. He is well qualified and eligible for the position. Perhaps you could assist me to work the thing so. If it can be done I will guarantee, with his assistance, to pin down the outlaws within a month, or die in the attempt. Apart from this particular business I could assist you in many ways in stamping out the horse stealing game for instance which has been as long carried on, and will consider myself bound to do so if you assist me in the above matter.

Wallace letter, Monday 6 October 1879

I have been out almost incessantly since I last wrote, and have worked this side of Hedi, Meadow Ck, Hurdle Ck Ranges, Sebastopol Ranges & between Sebastopol and El Dorado. The only discovery of interest was on Thursday morning. I left home on horseback on Wednesday night reached Everton in time for to catch the train for Beechworth. Left my horse at Everton and went into Beechworth by rail. I then went on foot and carefully reconnoitred the vicinity of Sherritts on Sheep Station Ck and the adjoining #### camps. At about 2.30 am I visited Aron's hut on his selection – the place where the boys used to camp before the Jerilderie raid. I cautiously approached the place and finding that there was no one within it, I opened the door and went in, found traces of someone having been here within the last 3 days previous. The last time I went into the hut about 3 weeks ago, the floor was dirty and litter was scattered around. On Thursday morning I found that the floor was quite clean having been carefully swept up in a heap. I raked them aside and found there had been a recent fire on, the traces of which had been carefully covered up. Embedded in the cinders I found a few green strips of wild broom which had been used to sweep out the house, these were quite fresh and green not more than a couple of days pulled, proving by their scorched ends that the fire had been recent. I visited the place – rode past it – on Saty night but all was quiet. I visited the hut (Chinese) before referred to but there was no one in, and I did not feel justified in ransacking the place in the absence of the owner.

Wallace letter, Monday 27 October 1879

Nothing new to report of any importance. Been knocking around as usual but have not dropped across your calls. Stayed a night with Walsh of Hedi who was reported to have seen the Brothers. Slept with him and had a long conversation. He is an ardent admirer. He did see the Brothers, but it is some time ago, shortly before the Jerilderie exploit. He met them on a Sunday afternoon between Moyhu & Hedi on the main road about 3 o'clock, one riding a few hundred yards in front of the other. He says he has not seen them since but I doubt him much. He has lately acquired a very neat silver mounted Breech-loading pistol, rifled, or American manufacture – has a range of 150 yards. He says it was given to him by a friend. Perhaps you may have some record of such a toy from Euroa or Jerilderie. Things are quiet on Black Range Creek – I don't think they have been there within a fortnight.

I think there is something suspected at Sherritts. The last time I called there I only saw the old man. He told me the boys were not at home, which was not strictly true, for I saw Master William make tracks for the bedroom and hide there as I rode up to the house. The old man was very constrained in his manner towards me, notwithstanding that I called at his urgent solicitation to give him the pedigree of a particular horse he wanted. I saw Jack and Aaron at a distance the same Sunday on the Woolshed killing a bullock.

Met young Pat Byrne on Sebastopol, had a yarn and a drink with him. He asked me where I thought the boys were. I replied 'Beating about between here (Sebastopol) and Greta looking for the police'. He laughed and said he 'supposed they were'. I told him he should caution them about being as careless as they had been during the past few days, for if they didn't be more careful they would soon be reined in. He said he would caution them. He admitted that they would have to make another rise soon as their funds were low.

I noticed that he had a black greyhound bitch with him. This animal will account for the hound's tracks reported by me as showing with the horsemen on the Sunday morning before referred to. Doubtless young Pat was with them, or perhaps the dog might have followed Joe.

I beat round that quarter all night the night before last, but all was quiet.

I saw Pat and his do about midnight on the Woolshed. He was accompanied by another whom I took to be Jack Sherritt. They were coming from the Chinese Camp and went in the direction of his brother's cottage on Sebastopol.

Oh, by the way, in speaking to Pat on Sebastopol in reference to the police search parties, he remarked that on the previous evening (Saturday 18th) that three or four strangers came in to Beechworth by the late train. He said they looked like 'traps' in disguise and were enquiring the way to the Hibernian Hotel.

I fancy they are still on your side of the King R. I will do Stricklands tonight, and Burkes and Whalleys tomorrow night, and will either go to Glenmore or to Beechworth on Saturday & Sunday.

Wallace letter, Friday 31 October 1879

On Thursday morning (Oct 30) about 2.30 am <u>five</u> horsemen riding pretty fast crossed the Hurdle Creek Bridge opposite the Bobinawarrah State School. They came from the direction of Hedi and were making towards Milawa (they were going too fast to [word unclear] identify [word unclear]).

On Tuesday (28) Jack Johnson of Black Range Creek Hedi was seen about 4pm near the Pioneer Bridge making in the Beechworth direction.

Last Sunday (26th) Francis Harty of Greta (or a man like him passed through El Dorado) and went up the Sebastopol road.

Wallace letter, Wednesday 12 November 1879

(This letter is partially written over pages from a school enrolment form.)

Since writing to you last I have been working hard and incessantly in your interests. I am afraid your precautions at Beechworth have been too conspicuous as the Gang appear to have relinquished that idea for the present at least.

I have beaten up their haunts in the Sebastopol Ranges on three different nights since seeing you but have found no traces of recent date and their friends around there appeared to be paying attention to their sleeping. On each occasion I passed through the arch above Everton where they used to cross and was careful to look for tracks but none were observable. I also visited Hart & Co's hut at the 'Disputed Camp' on the Hurdle Creek run between here and Whorouley and paid attention to Burkes, Johnsons, Walshe's and Stricklands.

On last Sunday week I met Aaron Sherritt on the Woolshed and had a long conversation with him. He said the Police were going to have more than one mustering match and run in all the sympathisers again. He taxed me with having let out something about Kennedy's watch and said that you had been persecuting him about it. He remarked that Ward and he were on bad terms and that you negotiated with him personally now. He lamented the loss of his revolver and handcuffs and detailed with much relish his playful eccentricities with the same. He boasted that he knew all about the outlaws and kindly promised to drop me a few hundred some of these fine days.

Since seeing you I have twice seen Jack Sherritt but on each occasion he carefully avoided me. From this I infer that he suspects me of having played him false. Either your precautions at Beechworth were too evident, or else you have tried to 'get at' him yourself. Or perhaps you have told Ward – if so, I firmly believe that that individual would do all in his power to prevent the outlaws coming within shot of him. If the outlaws suspect me of working for you either directly or indirectly they will take care to be careful of Sebastopol. I heard from two different sources on the Woolshed of 'special constable Sherritt's' vagaries with the revolver and the handcuffs among the Chinamen. I ascertained from whom he obtained them.

There was a Ball here on Monday night. Mr William Burke of Black Range Creek Hedi honoured us with his company. He paid for his ticket with a Bank of New South Wales £1 note dated Sydney October 1878.

He said he had come down purposely to see me. He wanted me to do him a favour. I replied that I should be most happy if it lay in my power. Some time back his brother Tom pegged out a selection of 50 acres. His application was dealt with at the Land Board at Tarrawingee on the 2nd October. When his case was called on the Officer in Charge informed him that he had received a telegram from Melbourne on the previous evening directing him to refuse the application. It was refused accordingly and recommended to again be thrown out for selection. No reason was given at the time for this refusal but they ascertained afterwards through a friend in Melbourne that he was suspected by the police of being a Kelly Sympathiser and that his name along with the names of about 100 other residents of this district were registered in a Blacklist at the Land Office. William says that he is positive that his brother Tom (the applicant) was not connected in any way with the outlaws. He could take his oath that Tom had not spoken to them since the murders and that if he had seen them it was purely by accident and not through any wish or fault of his own. He admitted that a number of those in the vicinity whose names were marked richly deserved it as they were guilty of aiding and abetting the outlaws. He therefore wished his brother Tom's case dealt with apart from the others – apart even from his own or his other brother Ned's, as Tom was totally innocent, and being so it was not right that the innocent should suffer for the guilty. I thoroughly believe him. Tom is a decent, honest, hardworking lad always employed about home doing the farm work and looking after the horses, and very seldom going out anywhere.

Knowing I was acquainted with some of the Members of Parliament he wished me to write to them on his brother's account. He wished me to write to Graves, Gaunson, Cooper M L and to Reid, Wallace and Wilson MLC and also to draw out a petition to Parliament respectfully worded for the respectful presidents of the district to sign saying that Thomas Burke's case be enquired into. I agreed to do what he desired, but suggested that he should first write a letter to the Chief Commissioner of Police stating the facts of the case and requesting him to enquire into it, for as he was positively certain that his brother was innocent the Comm on enquiry would soon find out where the mistake had been made and as both Captain Standish and Commissioner Nicolson were reputed to be honourable and humane gentlemen I was sure they would withdraw their objection. He coincided (?) with me and said he would take my advice as it would be a much easier and simpler course than petitioning Parliament and enlisting the advocacy of MPs and thus bringing their name into public. I therefore wrote a letter for him to the Comm which young Tom was to forward on by first post. That letter will probably have reached you before this. We arranged it will give me a sort of claim on their friendship and gratitude, which I can then abuse in your interest. I could almost take my oath that young Tom is innocent while I could almost as surely swear that Ned knows all and William a great deal about them.

Please contrive that your reply, if reply you do, leaves Benalla by the first mail on Friday. He will then be sure to get it and I will be able to work him on the strength of it.

I have gleaned some more very interesting information in reference to a proposed bank raid on the Lancefield style of business but I think it best to withhold it for a day or two. I fancy if I had withheld the information I gave you about the proposed Beechworth raid for a week or so I might have been more fortunate.

You will remember that when you requested me to act in your interests you promised to make good any extra expense I might be put to in consequence. The amount of expense I have incurred since last pay is £7-10. I have to request that you will remit me that amount by return post if you can. If you will send me £10 (ten pounds) I will promise not to ask for any more until the business is finished which will be very shortly and you can deduct that amount and what I have before received from my share of the plunder – (paper tear). Please send it in a regular letter (paper tear) a ten pound note would be most convenient (paper tear) send a cheque.

I interviewed Jack Barry of Hedi last night. Had a conversation in re the outlaws. He was rather more reticent than he usually is, and would let out nothing tangible. I am sure he knows something about them But I think it is indirectly through Ned Burke.

Barry said that if was Byrne he would ride into Beechworth and shoot Ward at the first opportunity. I asked him why? What reason had Byrne to dislike Ward more than another? He replied that Ward had seduced Byrne's sister Kate. I asked him how he (Barry) knew? He said he knew all about it – that the information had come through Byrne himself and that he got to know it indirectly.

I have strong suspicions that young Jack Lewis of Glenmore could tell a thing or two if he liked. I had a few words with him and his brother Wm. Lewis just on Monday. They warmly pressed me to go up to Glenmore station occasionally and have a hunt with them. Of course I'll go. I think the Black Range, Upper King, and Moyhu districts will be the best fields for my labours for the next week or so.

I trust you will see your way clear to secure a favourable reply to young Burke's letter, and that you will withdraw to his application for land. If you can do so it will (assist?) me wonderfully as that if a favourable reply was not received by

Friday's post, I was to write for him the above-mentioned gentleman and draw up the petition for him.

I had then a long conversation with William about the outlaws. He was very wary and reticent at first but soon changed out when I began to find excuses for them and to run down the police. And when I told him how they had persecuted me – how Arthur had prowled about here at night and how Alexander had annoyed me by day and how Ward had invented imperious slanders against me, the bod of union was complete and he talked freely. Without exactly speaking out ('splitting') he gave me to understand in a rather roundabout way that the boys were still about – that they had now a much stronger party and were in a better position to deal with their pursuers, that they would have to make another break soon as their cash was running low. He said there was splendid grass now and they could feed their horses like fighting cocks. From what he said or rather hinted, I fancy the gang are reinforced by two others – Tommy Lloyd jnr., and an elderly man (possibly Evans the Avoca desperate who has been in the district before). If such is the case they will form a strong party as Evans is reported to be a determined ruffian – 'as game as a piss-ant' as they say – and young Lloyd in addition to being the best rider in Victoria without exception knows the ranges better than any.

Of course I expressed great admiration to Burke for the outlaws and boasted of my acquaintance with Byrne. Burke says that his mother (Old Mrs Burke) was very intimately acquainted with Joe's father and mother in the old country. He warmly pressed me to come up to their place and see them soon. I promised to go up on Saturday and go out on the Black Range on Sunday with Ned and himself to run wild horses. There is to be a Dance too up the river on Friday night – I need an invitation and intend going up to it. I may chance to learn something as there will be a number of Kelites there.

APPENDIX 6
Letter to the *Herald*

The following is a reproduction of the front-page article 'The Kelly Gang' published in the *Ovens and Murray Advertiser* (Beechworth) on Saturday 12 July 1879. The article was an abridged version of a letter sent by a 'Kelly Gang sympathiser' to the *Melbourne Herald*. The only change made to the article is the inclusion of paragraph breaks to improve readability.

THE KELLY GANG
[HERALD]

We have received from an anonymous correspondent who is evidently a sympathiser with, and a near associate of the Kelly's and their companions, a long but rambling statement of the case as it is put by the outlaws. The document, which contains sixteen pages, came by post simply addressed to 'The editor of the Herald newspaper, Melbourne.' It is evidently written by an illiterate person, the orthography being defective, the calligraphy in some portions almost undecipherable, and the composition rambling and sometimes unintelligible. Sufficient can be gathered, however, to show that there is a very bitter feeling of animosity among the sympathisers of the outlaws against the police, and reasons are stated why they should exist. An inquiry is anxiously demanded, and as the statements made are of a serious character, and the demand for an inquiry apparently a justifiable one, we give some particulars from the citation of our anonymous correspondent, who, for aught we know, may be one of the gang.

He commences by drawing attention to the Monk inquiry, and as might be expected, fully endorses the decision of Mr Panton, asserting positively that Monk's statements that he was shot at were false. In this matter the anonymous writer thinks the authorities acted with wisdom, as the statements were such as to demand inquiry. He then proceeds to argue that a similar inquiry into the whole circumstances that led up to the police murders is necessary, and that it would save the Government money if they appointed Mr Panton to make, not only that inquiry but to also investigate the conduct of the police in the North-Eastern district, not only before, but since the outrage, in support of this, it is alleged, as has before been stated, that the whole cause of the tragedy and the subsequent events was the conviction of Mrs Kelly, Skillian and Williamson, on the unsupported testimony of Constable Fitzpatrick, which it is affirmed, was false. Justice is claimed for these three persons, and it is boldly stated that had it been accorded in the first instance, there would have been no necessity for persons like Monk to go in search of the bodies of police who were sent out to shoot men who, on false evidence, were banished to the wilds, and their mother, brother-in-law, and friends, on the word of one man alone, convicted of a serious crime.'

The writer goes on to say that on the jury that tried Mrs Kelly, Skillian and Williamson, was a discharged sergeant of police, 'which is contrary to law.' To quote again from our correspondent, 'The Kelly's were then outlawed, and a price of £200 offered for their apprehension, for firing three shots at Fitzpatrick, as he said, at a yard and a half distance; and yet he was hit only once, the bullet entering the middle of the back of his wrist, but not even injuring a sinew of touching the bone, but passing simply along the skin. Kelly's arm and a revolver would go a long way towards a yard and a half, and Fitzpatrick must have had good eyesight to see bullets and revolvers all round him. In fact his statement was simply ridiculous.

From the 13th April, 1878, to the 23rd October in the same year, the Kelly's were not seen or heard of. During that time they were not interfering with or harming anyone, but were digging on Bullock Flat, quietly trying to make a living, when the police came to shoot them down like dogs, as they stated they would do before they would ask them to stand. Three different parties of police, numbering in all some 12 or 15, supplied with the best firearms, were sent out to take the Kellys in dead or alive. Kennedy's party camped within a mile of the Kelly's, and the latter had nothing for it but to coolly wait and be shot like dogs, or bail the police up and take their firearms from them. And when they called on the police to surrender, one obeyed, and was not injured, but the rest fought and were shot.

If the Queen of England was in in the place of the Kellys, she could have done no less than they did. Let anyone consider the circumstances of the persecution of the Kelly's. Their mother and friends convicted, and themselves banished and pursued by blacktrackers, police, and even English bloodhound's, on the evidence of Fitzpatrick; and for what cause? In the first place, if the Kellys intended to murder Fitzpatrick, they could easily have done so, as, according to his statement, there were enough of them to eat him without salt; and yet there was no mark on him but a small cut on the back of his wrist, which any man could see was never done by a bullet fired from a revolver. Fitzpatrick would not stand long before Mr Panton.'

Our anonymous correspondent then goes on to give his version of the characters of the Kelly's. He says : – 'The Kellys are termed thieves and cold-blooded murderers, but those that term them this would be guilty of far worse crimes than they are. No case of horse stealing was ever proved against any of the Kelly's. Ned got six months for striking a man named McCormack, and three years for receiving a stolen horse. This was on the evidence of Constables – ------and---------- . The swearing abilities of the first are well known, as he has been twice tried for perjury, and the latter has himself since been sentenced to three years for horse stealing.

Dan Kelly was sentenced to three months for smashing a door with his fist. These are the only convictions on the roll against the Kelly's. I guess there was not much cold-bloodness about the shooting of the police. It was the police who went out to murder for the reward. If other men were treated as the Kelly's have been, they would not spare nothing in human shape, as both the public and the Government have done their best against them, and laws have been made to suit the police.'

Having thus lauded the outlaws, the writer comes to his great grievance – the conduct of the police in the North-Eastern District. He writes : – 'The policeman business has been a good one during the last fourteen months that Kelly's has been outlawed. Any scapgrace can get a pound a-day now. I know a great many of the special constables, not one of whom could earn their tucker before, but now can sport silk coats, and calls themselves mounted -constables. Two, in particular, I could mention. One is well-known in the Beechworth and Greta districts, and his character needs no comment. But he is a good man for Ned Kelly, as he can draw the police where-ever he chooses, and clears the road for a man that knows

how to work him better than all the police-detectives put together. When a drove of police are getting tired of watching about the Beechworth hills this man will steal a horse from some of the neighbors, ride him down to Greta or Sandy Creek, or some other place; there style himself Byrne, the bushranger; ride through a railway gate and threaten to shoot the gate keeper, so that the police will make a rush in that direction after the

Kelly's. When they start on his tracks, he cuts the horse's throat and doubles back, while the police keep in hot pursuit, especially when they find the dead horse, and hear the testimony of the people the supposed Byrne threatened to shoot. The special constable on his way back steals a couple of horses, takes them with him to near Byrne's house, and when the police return, tells them that Byrne has been visiting his home and has left strange horses. In fact, this man tries the mettle of the blacktrackers, and even the blood hounds, and gets great credit from the inspectors for his supposed cleverness in getting information of the Kelly's. Some of the police officers are as bad as this man himself, as they are aware that it was he who fired at several persons in the Beechworth district, and also that he rode a grey horse belonging to a Chinaman at the Woolshed.

If an inquiry should he held there are plenty of members of the police force who could give important evidence, and could show the public the true character of the special constables and others supposed to be hunting for the Kelly's. In fact, if things are not altered there will be plenty bushrangers besides the Kelly's. As it is, the whole force ought to be outlawed instead of the Kelly's. If the police are allowed to threaten to shoot respectable men, women, and even children, break down fences, turn stolen horses into peoples' paddocks, and a lot of drunken police, dressed like bushrangers, to surround quiet homes, threatening to shoot the inmates and ransacking the house; yelling, roaring and galloping through the crops, shouting at the trees, who can tell if they are the police or the Kelly's? It is the place of the public to insist that the police should wear their uniforms, or at least something to distinguish them from bushrangers or civilians. As it is, no man dare fire at anyone surrounding his house, for fear of shooting a policeman, as the police are in the habit of bailing people up and be having in a most ruffianly manner. A certain inspector of police a fortnight before Fitzpatrick alleged he was shot at, told an editor that he knew the Kelly's were armed, and that there would be shooting between the police and the Kelly's before a fortnight. If he thought that it is very strange to me that he should send a drunken trooper to arrest them without a warrant.

I believe I write the opinion of thousands, when I say an inquiry should be held, and all the particulars brought to light. Unless this is done the Kelly's will certainly revenge the insult offered to themselves and their mother. At present they are painted as black as print can paint them, but they harmed no man, woman, or child. Their actions are more like those of four sisters of charity, than four outlaws. If they had robbed, and plundered, and ravished and murdered the public and every man and woman they met, it would have been a very different thing, but in the way they have acted, after being treated as they have been, they deserve to be called men instead of outlaws. Their robberies are confined to banks, the police, and the Government. If this sort of thing goes on, the Chief Secretary will soon have to go home for a new loan.' Of course the above extracts are not given' verbatim et literatim,' but they have only been altered sufficiently to render them intelligible. With the writer's opinions as to the angelic nature of the Kelly's we have nothing to do, but the public is concerned to know whether his allegations against the police are true or false. Sooner or later a most searching inquiry will have to be made, and it is to be hoped that when the proper time comes, those who can give evidence will come boldly forward.

APPENDIX 7
M Connor letter to Mr Graves MLA

Melbourne, 19th. April, 1880.

J.H.Graves, Esquire.

Dear Sir,

In laying before you the following statement relative to the police force and the Kelly Gang, I trust you will excuse the liberty I have taken, but I hope to justify my action by the following facts. As you are aware, the outlaws have now been at large over eighteen months, and the question arises in one's mind -- are they ever to be captured? Well, I will endeavour to the best of my ability to explain: the cause of their being still at large, from the time of the police murders at Mansfield up to the present, has been but a complete failure of the Police Department. I will begin my narrative at the Euroa bank robbery. How the outlaws eluded the police there can only be accounted for in one way, and that was negligence of duty by Mr. Nicolson, who was then in charge of the search party there. There should be an enquiry instituted about this particular case. Why the members of the force were delayed at Euroa for hours after the outlaws were gone, is a serious matter, and ought in justice to every member of the force to be cleared up. That a serious blunder was committed there can be no doubt, and it is the only reason the Chief Commissioner had for ordering him to Melbourne on a pretext of having bad eyes.

Another case similar happened shortly afterwards at Beechworth, when valuable information reached the constable in charge that the outlaws were in the vicinity. The constables, five or six in number, decided to proceed at once, and when everything was complete and ready to start, an officer dropped in, and ordered them to remain in barracks, and went for orders, which they were obliged to obey. The consequence of this delay was, that when all the usual red tape routine was gone through, they surrounded the hut, in three days after the information reached Beechworth. The Kelly Gang had decamped the day previous. There is something very singular in this case. When this particular hut was surrounded there was almost as many officers present as constables. The question arises – were these constables delayed for the purpose of collecting all the officers in the district to be present at the great charge of Sebastopol, as it is now termed? Had these six constables been allowed to proceed at once with the informer, the Kelly Gang would now be a thing of the past, as it has been proved beyond a doubt since that the outlaws were there twenty-four hours after the information reached Beechworth. This is two instances in which if proper and prompt steps had been taken, the gallows would have had its victims.

Mr. Nicolson has resumed his old position in charge, and what he has done towards capturing the outlaws, I am not in a position to say. There has been a secret party of police in charge of Detective Ward at Beechworth for the last four months, watching Mrs. Byrne's house. This party of police were going to succeed at once. The gang, who were always supposed to be visiting Mrs. Byrne, were to be sold by Aaron Sherritt, who is engaged at a very high salary by the Police Department. And it is well known that Sherritt did assist these outlaws when they first turned out, and will assist them again, and I would not be the least surprised but what he carries all the information about the police movements to the Kellys: yet this is the man that AC. Police places his confidence in. The party is now withdrawn, on account of the outlaws' friends knowing what the police were up to. And it seems to me that the party was nothing more nor less than a complete farce, as the Byrne and Sherritt families are great friends, and both know as much as the police about the secret party. In fact Detective Ward has expressed himself on several occasions to some of his friends in Beechworth, previous to the party going out, that he knew there was nothing in it, but he must do something to curry favour with Nicolson. And at the proper time evidence will be brought forward to prove my statement true. At the present time there are men in the district who had been picked out for their smartness and activity, and they are not allowed outside barracks, for fear of them hearing anything about the murderers.

There are also stationed in the district six black trackers from Queensland. The Government finds them in good clothing, and also a constable and sub-inspector to look after them. To me it seems monstrous that a sub-inspector is required to look after six black trackers at £50 per month, also horses to sport his figure on. At the lowest estimate, the trackers cost the country about £130 a month without horses, and in their first attempt at tracking, two men escaped from Lancefield to Sandhurst on foot. That does not speak much for their abilities as black trackers, and I may state that those members of the force who have had an opportunity of judging of their capabilities are of opinion that they will be the cause of the outlaws escaping on the next attempt at sticking-up a bank, as no one was allowed to go in pursuit of the robbers at Lancefield for fear of obliterating the track. The same thing will occur again. The members of the Victorian police force, who are all desirous of meeting their comrades' murderers, are to wait behind, these trackers crawling along at the rate of three or four miles an hour after men who are travelling at the rate of fifteen or twenty miles an hour until they are safe in their old haunts again with their plunder: there to remain and laugh at the futile efforts of the police to capture them.

Unless some changes are made very shortly, I am afraid that very little security to life or property we need expect from the police. If the police require strengthening in the North-Eastern District, it is not for the purpose of confining the members from where the crime is committed: and in place of the Kelly Gang being allowed to rest and mature their plans for the future, the police should be allowed to exert themselves to their utmost to capture them, and not wait for the Kellys to walk into some police station and give themselves up as prisoners. I will now finish my remarks with a few suggestions, and I beg that you will be good enough to use your influence on behalf of the many who are of the same opinion as myself on this subject, and I trust you will bring under the notice of the Chief Secretary the present helplessness of the police force to capture the Kellys. In my opinion, those men that are hired at a high salary should be dispensed with. If Aaron Sherritt, or any of his class ever intended to sell the Kellys, they would have done so long ago for the £8,000, and the department would not be the laughing-stock of the outlaws and their Sympathisers. Fancy a man in his proper senses engaging Aaron Sherritt to sell the outlaws. Why, he would rather cut his arm off.

The fact is Ned Kelly's best friends are engaged by the department, but why they are engaged is the question. If there are not men in the force capable of doing any duty required of them, the whole force should be disbanded. Are the trackers required? If they are not, they ought to be sent to Coranderrk, and it would save the country £130 a month at the very least, and the sub-inspector could return to Queensland, as he is never troubled with the trackers. Is Detective Ward and the Assistant-Commissioner capable of outwitting the outlaws? My answer is they are not. What they have done up to the present time is nothing, and I believe they will continue doing nothing, and the Kellys will reign until they die a natural death. I will now conclude, hoping that you will bring this subject before

Parliament, or under the notice of the Chief Secretary, and save the country from further needless expense, as I am certain that, with a change of officers, and a very little skill, the Kellys will soon be brought to justice.

I am, in the meantime, yours obediently -

M. Connor.

APPENDIX 8
Detectives Reports on Wallace investigations

Detective Department

Beechworth 22nd December 1881

Re Special enquiry re James Wallace

We beg to report for your information that on the 8th of Dec. inst. we proceeded to Beechworth with reference to enquiries as above. We first saw a Mr Kelly a schoolmaster near Beechworth who we knew had an intimate knowledge of Wallace's friends both in the neighbourhood of Beechworth, Hurdle Creek and the King. After seeing him we proceeded on the following day to Oxley and Milawa. At this stage we only made cautious inquiries the result of which we heard that he Wallace had purchased at the stores a greater quantity of tinned fish etc than he or his family which at that time consisted only of three (3) persons, himself included, could consume. We also heard that on a certain night during the time the Kellys were at large, that he (Wallace) asked a man named James O'Neil if he would go to Mrs Connors (* This Mrs Connor referred to was an aunt by marriage to the late outlaw Joe Byrne) at Whorouly as the Kellys were to be at her place on that night and he (Wallace) wanted to warn them that the tropers would be there as Captain Standish (late Chief Commissioner) had informed him that such was to be the case. O'Neil refused and he (Wallace) asked him if he could get a man from Mrs McGreggors where he was working. O'Neil said he did not know whether a man named John Dwyer would go or not. Wallace then accompanied him O'Neil to Mrs

McGreggors the latter called out Dwyer and he Wallace asked him if he would go to Whorouly for the purpose of warning the outlaws of the projected police raid on Mrs Connor's house but Dwyer refused to go.

We did not at this stage deem it advisable to question either O'Neil or Dwyer but the information coming from a reliable source we had no doubt of its truth. We were also informed that on a date during the time the outlaws were at large viz. the latter end of 1879, that a youth named McGreggor aged about 17 years then at the Grammar School Ballarat received a letter from James Wallace (to whom he was personally known) enclosed in which was a letter addressed to Miss Kate Byrne Post Office Beechworth with instructions to post it which young McGreggor did. McGreggor on his return home from school spoke to Wallace about the danger he incurred in sending such a letter. Wallace passed it off as a joke. McGreggor on receiving this letter from Wallace showed it to a school mate named Munro now assistant Clark of Petty Sessions at Wangaratta.

Having heard of the discovery of a hut in the bush near Hurdle Creek we proceeded there and found that a bushfire had destroyed the hut 15 x 11 feet situate at the foot of One Tree Hill, opposite a gap leading into Saw Mill gully through which there is a direct track leading to Wallace's late school Bobinawarrah at a distance of about four (4) miles, through an unsettled district. The hut we were informed was built some six or seven ago by some splitters and fencers who occupied it at that time, but since then we failed to find out any person who occupied or heard of its being inhabited. We searched round the neighbourhood of the hut but failed to find any traces of a horse camp or of splitters or bee hunters having been working in that vicinity, in fact the neighbourhood appears a most isolated one the nearest house being about three (3) miles where the herdsman David McCallum resides, he it was in company with a neighbour named Doig discovered the recent occupation of the hut. They state it contains three (3) bunks, two (2) large and the (1) double over which attached to the roof were grab rope loops as if used for hanging up guns, there was a quantity of empty bottles both inside and outside the hut, none of which had any labels. (We ourselves saw a number outside the hut). There were also a few tins but not many. There is a spring of fresh water close to the hut, the only one within miles. Both McCallum and Doig have no hesitation in saying that the hut had the appearance of having been occupied within the last two (2) years, though by whom they cannot say, but on being questioned as to their opinion on the subject they said there could be but little doubt but that it was occupied by the outlaws as had anyone been working such as splitters etc in that neighbourhood they could not help knowing it.

We then worked our way back to Beechworth but failed to find anything important relative to this matter, further than that it was the opinion of several respectable residents that Wallace was an active sympathiser of the outlaws.

We next saw Mrs John Sherritt. She states Wallace called at her place about August and borrowed one of the saddles but did not return it and subsequently paid her the sum of £3.0.0 for it. She can identify the saddle, she further states that at the time Wallace borrowed the old saddle he had a good saddle of his own. She further states that on a date subsequent to this, but not long after Wallace again called at her place he came in a buggy, he asked her in her daughter Mary Jane's presence whether she had any mouldboards for sale, giving as an excuse that his father was a dealer in old metals and he was purchasing for him. At the same time he showed her one he had in a bag with him. Mrs Sherritt also remembers Wallace calling at her place on or about the 23rd August 1879, he came in a buggy in which she saw a quantity of stores consisting of bread etc and a case of brandy, he had dinner at her house and left in company with Aaron Sherritt now deceased.

Mary Jane Sherritt can corroborate her mother's statement with regard to Wallace borrowing the saddle and wanting to purchase mouldboards etc and adds that she frequently saw Wallace at Mrs Byrne's (mother of Joe Byrnes outlaw) house, where he (Wallace) had various meals and usually slept on the sofa, this was during the time the outlaws were at large, viz. 1879.

Owing to Detective Ward having to attend the Criminal Sessions in Melbourne the inquiry was discontinued till Saturday the 17th inst. on which day we proceeded to Moyhu but failed to gain anything of importance there. We on the following day proceeded to John Dwyer's selection on the King River. We saw Dwyer and questioned him relative to what we had heard had passed between him and Wallace at Mrs McGreggor's and he at first refused to give us any information on the subject stating as an excuse that he did not wish to injure any one, but on our pointing out to him that the circumstance of Wallace being at Mrs McGreggor's on the night referred to was known to several persons he admitted that James O'Neil did call him out of Mrs McGreggor's house where he was playing cards, and that he then saw Wallace who asked him to do a certain thing, he would not tell us what passed between him and Wallace adding I did not go where I was asked, I did not do anything wrong, and I will not injure anyone. Though this man Dwyer was extremely (indecipherable) we would here beg to point that the information we had previously received proved to be correct by Dwyer's own admissions, but his refusal to tell us what actually passed between him and Wallace is a still stronger proof.

On leaving Dwyer's we at once proceeded to Hedi for the purpose of seeing Edward Burke referred to in Wallace's evidence before Commission page 350 question 14547 etc.[334] We failed to see Burke owing to his absence from home, then fearing that John Dwyer would endeavour to communicate with James O'Neil, we having been compelled to use the latter's name in our interview with Dwyer, we at once proceeded that evening to Hurdle Creek where we saw James O'Neil who is now in the employ of Andrew Reid farmer Hurdle Creek. After a good deal of pressure and a little strategy on our part, he stated as follows: 'I remember calling at Wallace's house at Bobinawarrah I do not recollect the date but it was some time in 1879. I saw Wallace there after some conversation he said to me Jim will you do me a favour. I replied I would if it was in my power. He said would you like to see the Kellys (indecipherable) I replied it is nothing to do with me. He said I hear the Kellys are at Mrs Connors at Whorouly will you go and warn them that a body of police are to be sent there. I declined to go giving as an excuse that I could not ride out there didn't know the road to Whorouly. He then turned to his wife who was present and said I will go myself. She commenced to cry and implored him not to go, saying that if he persisted in going he would not find her then on his return. He then asked me if I could get someone to go to Whorouly. I said I could not. He then said who is working with you at Mrs McGreggors (at this time I was employed there). I replied John Dwyer. Wallace said do you think he will go. I replied I do not know. He then said I will go with you to Mrs McGreggors at once and we left for there. On arriving there he asked me to go to the house and call Dwyer out as he did not wish any of the McGreggors to see him. I consented and called Dwyer out where he and Wallace had a conversation which I did not hear, however I know that Dwyer did not go as I saw him (Dwyer)

---

334 - The reference here to the Royal Commission Minutes of Evidence is incorrect. Wallace's evidence about Edward Burke was given in response to question 14550 and is at page 529 of the Minutes of Evidence.

re-enter the house. I did not see any more of Wallace after his conversation with Dwyer on that night.'

Mrs McGreggor of Hurdle Creek (a most respectable person) remembers James O'Neil calling John Dwyer out of her house one night during the time the Kellys were at large, and Dwyer returning shortly afterwards and being extremely reticent in his manners. This circumstance is more distinctly impressed on her memory from the fact that on the following morning mysterious hints as to the speedy capture of the Kelly Gang were thrown out by James O'Neil at the breakfast table.

Alexander McGreggor, son of Mrs and Mr McGreggor, Hurdle Creek stated in reply to questions put by us as follows: 'I remember whilst at school at Ballarat in 1879 (indecipherable) receiving a letter from James Wallace then a schoolteacher at Bobinawarrah and to whom I was personally known asking me to post a letter which he enclosed. The letter was addressed to Miss Kate Byrne Post Office Beechworth, which I showed the letter to a school mate of mine named Munro, now assistant Clerk of Petty Sessions at Wangaratta. On my return home from school and whilst working at a bushfire I met Wallace. This was the first time I had seen him since I received his letter. He asked me if I got his letter all right, and did I do what he asked me viz. to post enclosed letter. I replied that I posted the letter but that I thought he was very foolish on his part as I might have taken the letter to the police. He said I knew you would not do that and then laughed the matter off. I have since mislaid the letter but possibly I can find it.

I am acquainted with Wallace's handwriting and the letter I refer to was written by him and has his signature.

After making these enquiries at Hurdle Creek we on the following day returned to Hedi and on the day after saw Edward Burke referred to in Wallace's evidence given before the Royal Commission. He (Burke) of course denies in toto Wallace's allegation that he was in communication with the late outlaws and states that he had no conversation with Wallace relative to them at all. He admits to going on a trip with Wallace about Xmas 1879 but says they only went to the Wonnangatta River, Gippsland calling at the township of Hawkesdale. They took a pack horse with them.

At the outset we had little or no hope of obtaining any information from the man Burke as from our knowledge of his character, he being a reported cattle duffer and an associate of the criminal class in this district, but his name having been mentioned by Wallace in his evidence before the Commission we deemed it advisable to see him.

With reference to the purchase of stores at Oxley and Milawa we find that between the 24th of June and 11th of September 1879, he Wallace purchased tea and sugar at Dunlop's store, Oxley largely in excess of what he would require for his own private use and that subsequently he made various cash purchases one of which Mr Dunlop remembers particularly being about £2 worth of tinned fish. Owing to the destruction of the hut at the foot of the One Tree Hill by fire and consequently the destruction of the tins etc we did not deem it advisable to push this portion of the inquiry as had we done so someone in the neighbourhood would have been cognisant of the nature of our inquiries and Wallace having friends there would be at once put on his guard and up to the present time our inquiries have been made in such a manner that no one has suspected what was really our object. Owing to our knowledge of Mr Dunlop we were able to put questions to him which we could not put to the store keepers at Milawa.

We would here point the fact that Wallace in his statement in his reply says 'That I can solemnly swear and am prepared to swear that it is over fifteen (15) years as far as I can recollect since I spoke to Mrs Byrne on any subject whatsoever'.

This is distinctly contradicted by Miss Sherritt's statement which was given to us prior to the receipt of Wallace's printed reply.

We propose having the saddles taken possession of by the police at Glenrowan after the capture of the Kelly Gang sent from Benalla to Beechworth in order that they may be shown to Mrs Sherritt and her daughter to ascertain that they can identify any of them as the saddle Wallace purchased from her.

Senior Constable Mullane will endeavour to ascertain from Mrs Byrne Wallace's connection with the family. He has already visited at the house but owing to some neighbours being present he was unable to make the enquiry without exciting suspicion, but as Mrs Byrne will be at Beechworth on Monday next, he will then be able to make the enquiry without exciting suspicion and the (indecipherable) told in due course. Senior Constable Mullane has been selected to make his position of the enquiry owing to his being very friendly with Mrs Byrne.

Detective Ward proceeds to Yea tomorrow in order to complete the inquiry there.

In conclusion we would beg to state that if the object of this inquiry is to prosecute Wallace, we do not think that sufficient evidence can be obtained to sustain a conviction for the following reasons. 1st owing to the length of time that has elapsed and the inability of people to fix or remember dates. 2nd

the unwillingness of persons to come forward and give evidence in a public court.

That in the present state of feeling on the matter in this District such a prosecution would be anything but advisable. If on the other hand the result of this inquiry is to justify the findings of the Commission and action taken by the Government in Wallace's case, sufficient evidence can be obtained to prove beyond a doubt that Wallace was an active sympathiser of the late Kelly Gang.

Considine

Ward

* * *

Detective Department

Beechworth December 29/81 (29th December 1881)

Re Special enquiry re James Wallace

I beg to report that on Friday the 23rd inst. I proceeded to (Yea) for the purpose of making inquiries in the above case. I there saw Constable Fitzgerald. I made careful enquiries but could obtain no information. James Wallace and his three (3) brothers were in Yea and carefully watched my movement. I left Yea on Saturday and gave instructions to Constable Fitzgerald to try to elicit something from the publican there. There is a publican named Purdy who Wallace told that he (Wallace) often carried tinned fish and preserved meat to the outlaws. Constable Fitzgerald is of the opinion that in case of a prosecution if Purdy was subpoenaed he would when in the box speak the truth and give good evidence for the prosecution although at the present time he will say nothing.

Proceeded to Beechworth and interviewed Senior Constable Mullane who willingly gave me (indecipherable) and he (Mullane) rode down to Sheep Station Creek and made arrangements with the members of the Sherritt family who could identify the saddle bought from them by James Wallace and afterwards found in possession of the Kelly Gang of outlaws at Glenrowan on the 28th and 29th June 1880.

On the 28th inst. John Sherritt called at Senior Constable Mullane's private residence Beechworth. Was there shown three (3) saddles he carefully examined them, and after some time he picked out one of the saddles and said that is my saddle but it has been greatly knocked about. On the same day but later on Anne Jane Sherritt (daughter of John Sherritt) called at the Senior Constable's private residence and was shown the three (3) saddles. She carefully examined them and after some little time she picked out the same saddle and said that was her father's saddle, and the saddle Wallace took away from her father's place in July or August 1879. She knew it because she often rode on it. She also said that she remembered Wallace taking the saddle away while the Kellys were at large.

Mrs Sherritt has a sick child at the present time is unable to attend in Beechworth but as soon as she does Senior Constable Mullane will report progress. I made inquiries in and about Beechworth, Black Springs, Woolshed and Sebastopol but was unable to obtain any information. Senior Constable Mullane has promised me to leave nothing undone in this matter, as he is very friendly with Mrs Byrnes, Dick Murphy, James Chappel and Cornelius O'Donaghue, who may be likely to give some information of Wallace's movements during the time the Kellys were at large unless they have been got at by Wallace or his brothers. Previously there are several reports to check out with reference to Wallace assisting the Kelly Gang but on enquiry they come to be mere heresay and I fail to trace them to any (indecipherable).

M E Ward

Det. 2838

* * *

Police Department

Shepparton 21st January 1882

Confidential

Re James Wallace, suspected of aiding and abetting the late Kelly Gang

I beg to report for your information that I have obtained some particulars relative to James Wallace late schoolteacher at Bobinawarrah from Mrs Cox of Katamatite and forward her statement herewith, with the request that you will be good enough to forward it to the A.C.C. of Police for transmission to Mr Harriman.

M. Considine

Det. No. ???

Mrs Cox's statement read as follows:

I am a married woman and reside with my husband who is a Police Constable at Katamatite. In September 1879 when my maiden name was Rogers my father kept an Hotel at Beechworth and I managed a shop there for him. I know James Wallace late schoolteacher at Bobinawarrah he used frequently stay at my father's hotel whilst in Beechworth and he has purchased tinned fish from me on several occasions I cannot recollect how much. He generally used to leave the hotel at Beechworth very late at night or early in the morning how I know this is he used to ask me to leave the back door open saying he would be off early. In September previously mentioned, I was staying at a Mr Allan's at Oxley (Wallace's father in law). Whilst there I went on one Saturday to have tea at James Wallace's house at Bobinawarrah. Wallace was there. Whilst at tea Wallace's little boy a child about six years old was sitting next me at the table, he was playing with my watch chain, he whispered to me Ned Kelly has not got a watch and chain like you. I asked 'do you know Ned Kelly' I said to the child. 'No I don't know him' he said, 'he was here the other day and gave me a shilling'. I think Wallace must have overheard what the child said as he Wallace said to me 'what has the child been saying to you Miss Rogers'. I said 'he has been telling me that the Kellys have paid you a visit'. Wallace then said don't take any notice of what the child has been saying. He appeared very much annoyed and told Mrs Wallace to put the child to bed, and I heard the child being slapped afterwards.

* * *

Police Department

Benalla January 1882

Re Special enquiry re James Wallace

We beg to report for your information, that on Saturday the 7th inst. we proceeded to El Dorado with a view of making enquiries relative to James Wallace's father ever having been a dealer in old metal. In our previous report of 22nd December 1881, we found that Wallace Senr. was at present absent at Yea but Constable (Beard informed us that Wallace only dealt in butter, eggs and such (and) that he never heard of him dealing in old metals.

We instructed Constable Beard who knows nothing of the nature of the enquiry, to see Wallace Snr of his return and put the following questions to him, viz. whether he Wallace within the last three (3) years has ever dealt in old metals etc. We gave as a pretext to Constable Beard that we were making enquiries relative to copper plates stolen some time ago, and he was to make enquiries on the ground of the old Metal Dealers Act.

On Sunday we proceeded to Hurdle Flat and Stanley to interview a State School master named Mr McAlice whose friends do reside in Oxley near Hurdle Creek. He informed us that James Wallace late schoolmaster had purchased several pairs of mole skin trousers of a larger size than he Wallace could wear himself from a storekeeper in Wangaratta. Being questioned on his authority he could give no answer as it was only commonly reported since James Wallace's suspension.

On Monday we continued our enquiries at Black Springs and there interviewed Mr Vale school master Hillsborough who we had heard could give us assistance in our enquiries. He informed us that Mr Hugh Ferguson of Hurdle Creek told him on a day during the time the Kelly Gang were at large, he in company with others, were at the Bobinawarrah Post Office at that time it was reported that Joe Byrne the bushranger was sick. They were speaking about Byrne. Wallace came out of the Post Office and said it could not be true and I saw Joe Byrne last night and he was all right then.

On Tuesday we continued our enquiries at the Woolshed of Mrs Sherritt Junior but failed to find out anything of significance. With the exception of that she informed us that that (sic) James Wallace was very thick with a blacksmith named Straughair on the Woolshed who was suspected by the people there of making Joe Byrne's armour. Straughair was particularly intimate with Mrs Byrnes. We endeavoured to obtain some further information on this subject but failed to do so.

On Wednesday we continued our enquiries and proceeded to Wooragee where John Sherritt Senior is employed working in the bush for the purpose of obtaining his statement to enable us to make out our report but were unable to see him.

On the following day Thursday we saw him and obtained a statement from him (indecipherable) brief.

Friday we had an interview with a confidential person at the Woolshed re the connection between Wallace and Straughair black smith, Woolshed relative to the making of Byrne's armour. We ascertained that Wallace was on very intimate terms with Straughair and used to leave his horse there when visiting Mrs Sherritts or Byrnes and also that Straughair used to work late at night. We have very little doubt that Straughair made Joe Byrne's armour but from the length of time that has elapsed there is no feasible chance of obtaining any proof about him.

On Saturday we left for Wangaratta. On arriving there we tried to obtain any corroboration of the statement that we had heard at Beechworth relative to the purchase of trousers (moleskins) which Wallace was alleged to have purchased in Wangaratta. Though we made every possible inquiry we failed in this effort. We next proceeded to Milawa and met all the store keepers there, viz Mr Colin Gardiner and Mr Warren, could give relative to this matter was that Wallace was a customer of his, and supplies for the family were entered in fact he was a credit customer and had a running account; but he does not appear to have had any suspicious items booked to him; but that Mr Gardiner and his daughter Isabelle told us that Wallace had made frequent purchases of tinned fish, such as sardines, salmon, etc, also bread and sometimes a bottle of brandy for all of which he paid cash and he always used to make these purchases at night after the store was closed. This occurred during the time the Kelly Gang were at large but they cannot give dates.

We next saw Mr Warren who kindly allowed us to see his books, but they disclosed nothing suspicious with reference to Wallace's purchases with the exception that on the 11th, 16th and 18th of August 1879, he purchased bread to the amount of 29 loaves which seems largely in excess of what he required for his (personal) use. We questioned Mr Warren as to whether Wallace had made any cash purchases to which he replied in the negative.

The following day we proceeded to Oxley but failed to elicit anything much there. From there we proceeded to Moyhu and saw the store keepers there. Wallace does not appear to have dealt with either of them, although he frequently visited the Hotel and store.

On talking over the Kelly business with Mr Lewis he informed us that the only suspicious transaction he had about that time was when a young man named McAuliffe (well-known sympathiser of the Kelly Gang) made some (indecipherable) purchases at his store and in payment thereof tendered a New South Wales five (5) £ note which was doubtless one of the Jerilderie bank notes.

We next saw Mr Ferguson of Hurdle Creek referred to in a previous part of this report. He admitted to having had a conversation to the with Mr McAliece schoolmaster relative to Wallace having said something about the outlaw Joe Byrne, but denied that he himself had heard Wallace say anything and had only repeated what he had heard, but could not give us his authority or the names of any one who heard or took part in the alleged conversation and this must be put down to one of the idle rumours which are flying about with reference to this matter on which no reliance can be placed.

On Monday we returned to Wangaratta enroute to Benalla. Whilst there we saw Mr Munro who denies that Mr McGreggor ever showed him the letter referred to in our previous report, but states that he had a conversation with Mr McGreggor at Hurdle Creek on the subject but this was after they both left school. Mr McGreggor must have been mistaken in his statement to us and any conversation he had with Mr Munro re this subject. Wallace (indecipherable) not being admissible as evidence.

On reaching Benalla we set to work to trace the saddle which has been identified by Mrs Sherritt and experienced great difficulty and it is very doubtful if the saddle can be traced to the possession of the Kelly Gang.

We proceeded to Glenrowan today and obtained the names of all the Constables who were stationed there at and immediately after the capture of the Kelly Gang with a view of ascertaining who eventually took possession of the saddles and other property at Glenrowan supposed to have belonged to the Kelly Gang and when and where they found them, thus (indecipherable) to the settlement that existed at the time appears to us to be very difficult as none of the saddles were marked and as some eight (8) saddles were taken possession of by the police at Glenrowan various Constables two (2) of which have been given up to Mrs Skillion (sister To Ned Kelly) the remainder being in the possession of the Benalla Police.

The Constables through whose hands the saddles are supposed to have passed are scattered over this and other districts, but they will be all seen in detail and every effort made to endeavour to trace the saddles, one identifiable in particular, with the view of tracing it as near possible to the possession of the late Kelly Gang.

The only hope we have of effecting this is which two (2) of the murdered police saddles were recovered at Glenrowan, and if we can ascertain that the saddle which has been identified by Mrs Sherritt, was found at the same time and place as the two (2) police saddles previously mentioned, it will to our idea prove conclusively that they were one and all bought there by the Kelly Gang. As soon as this can be ascertained a further report will be at once furnished. We proceed to Shepparton tomorrow, to make enquiries there from which Police Detective Ward having, to proceed to Wallan Wallan, will return to Melbourne with a file of the Wangaratta Despatch 1880 containing copies of Christmas in Kelly Land of which Wallace is the author. The file was lent for a few days and will have to be returned within the week.

Considine

Ward

* * *

Benalla Police Station

January 27th 1882

Re Special enquiry pertaining James Wallace

We have the honour to report for your information that on Tuesday 17th inst. we proceeded to Glenrowan to interview Mounted Constable Alexander with reference the property found at Glenrowan on the 28th and 29th June 1880 the day the Kelly Gang were captured.

Robert Alexander stated that on the morning of the 28th he in company with Constable Millard, Meehan, Dowling and I were directed to remain at the Glenrowan station with Constable Bracken. On the following morning the 29th Constable Meehan, Millard, Major and Dowling bought forward (2) horses and stables to the police station and handed them over to me (Constable Bracken was absent at Benalla at the time). They said they found them at McDonalds Railway Inn Glenrowan and that they were the property of the late Kelly Gang; the horses were placed in the police yard and the saddles remained on the station until Constable Bracken returned from Benalla about 1 o'clock midday.

When Constable Bracken returned, he despatched Constable Meehan and myself with the four 4 horses and four (4) saddles to Benalla Police station. On the way to Benalla one of the horses broke away from us and was not recovered for some days. After Meehan and I delivered the four (4) saddles and three (3) horses over the Sergeant Whelan on the evening of the 29th I have not seen them since then. I do not think I could be able to identify either the saddles or the horses as I did not mark them. But I can positively prove the saddles I gave up to Sgt. Whelan are the same saddles that was handed to me by Constables Dowling, Meehan, Major & Millard as having been found at McDonalds Railway Inn Glenrowan on the same morning the 29th June 1880.

On Wednesday we proceeded to Wallan Wallan to interview Constable Bracken. Bracken states that on the morning of the 29th of June 1880 the day after the Kelly Gang were captured he left Glenrowan for to attend an inquest on the body of [there is an unfilled space in the letter] at Benalla, and the inquest being adjourned he returned to Glenrowan about 1 o'clock same day. On his return to the station he was informed by the

Constables stationed there that they found four (4) horses and four (4) saddles at McDonalds Inn Glenrowan left there by the Kelly Gang. He at once despatched Constables Alexander and Meehan to Benalla police station for them to hand them over to Sgt. Whelan; Bracken states he took no particular notice of the saddles found and would not be able to identify them again.

On the same day we returned to Shepparton to interview Constable Millard, who is stationed there and who states as follows hereunder the 28th of June the day the Kelly Gang were captured at Glenrowan, I remember a brown mare being shot said to be Dan Kelly's mare she had on her a police saddle. I also remember a chestnut mare with a good bullock hide saddle (indecipherable) Wangaratta. She was taken charge of Sgt. Sadleir. I also remember a horse and pack saddle being found that were all forwarded to Benalla. I remember the following morning the 29th in company with Constables Meehan, Dowling and Major going to McDonalds Glenrowan Inn from information received, and there found four (4) horses and four (4) saddles. We were advised that they were left there by the Kelly Gang. We took the horses and saddle to the Glenrowan police station. On examination of the saddles, I discovered a police saddle, and I said to the Constables present that this is one of the saddles taken from the murdered police at Stringybark Creek. There was two old saddles amongst and one good saddle then other saddles I think I would know again.

Constables Alexander and Meehan were despatched with the horses and saddles to Benalla. I also went to Benalla that morning the 29th. I rode the horse found with the pack saddle and handed it over to Sgt. Whelan at Benalla. I believe Alexander and Meehan lost one of the four (4) horses on the road to Benalla, at least they told me so before I met them in Benalla the same night. On the 30th of the same month I found another horse and saddle and took it to Benalla and handed it over to Sgt. Whelan. I did not mark any of the saddles at the time and I cannot say until I see them whether I would be able to identify any of the saddles or horses. The only horse and saddle I think I would be able to identify as I placed the saddle on the horse and he (indecipherable) it off.

On Friday I proceeded to Colac there saw Constable (Major) who states as follows. I remember the morning of the 29th of June 1880 the day the Kellys were captured. I remember (indeciperhable) to Melbourne at Glenrowan at 8.30. Once there saw Detective Ward (indecipherable) who informed me that there were four (4) horses and four (4) saddles the property of ther Kelly Gang at McDonalds public house. In company with Constables Meehan, Dowling and Millard we proceeeded to McDonalds stables there found four (4) horses and four (4) saddles. The police saddle one fairly good saddle and two (2) old saddles we took possession of all and conveyed them to the Glenrowan police station later on the same day. Constables Meehan and Alexander removed the horses and saddles to Benalla, and did not pay any special attention to ther saddles. I did not mark them and I did not think I would be able to identify any of them again as the saddles were found at McDonalds stables.

On Monday I proceeded to Glenrowan Railway Station for the purpose of interviewing Mr and Mrs Stanistreet, the latter I heard could give me some good information. On examination Mrs Ann Stanistreet states that she is the wife of Mr J Stanistreet and remembers the morning of the 27th of June the day the Kelly gang of outlaws stuck up the Glenrowan Railway Station. She remembered Ned Kelly, Jas Byrne, Dan Kelly and Steve Hart coming to her place between 2 or 3 am on the morning of the 27th June 1880. She also remembers Ned

Kelly telling Jas. Byrne and Steve Hart to put the horses into McDonald's Stables. She saw Jas. Byrne and Steve Hart go into the bush at the rear of McDonald's and bring four (4) horses and saddles and place them in McDonald's Stables. She did not see the horses again until she saw the police take possession of them on the morning of the 29th and lead them to the Glenrowan Police Station. She identified the horses as the same horses Jas. Byrne and Hart placed in the stables as one of these was a small grey pony. The saddles she would not be able to identify.

Patrick Dowling

On Tuesday of the 24th I interviewed Patrick Dowling now stationed at Sandridge, who I also remember the morning of the 29th of June 1880, the day after the Kellys were captured at Glenrowan. I remember being in company with Constables Meehan, Major and Millard. We went to McDonald's Public House and in his stables we found four (4) horses and four (4) stables which we took possession of. I heard some of the Constables say that one of the Stringybark Creek murdered police saddles were amongst them. I did not examine the saddles. I would not know again. I believe the horses and saddles were forwarded to Benalla but I would not swear.

J. J. Sherritt

On the same day 24th I interviewed J. J. Sherritt who states, I known James Wallace for many years. We were school mates. I remember 1878 when the police were murdered at Stringy Bark Creek by the Kelly Gang. I knew the Kelly Gang as Byrne was a school mate of Wallace's and mine. I remember all the time the Kellys were at large, and I know James Wallace was an active sympathiser of the gang. I had a very good opportunity of judging it as Wallace frequently came to me and my brothers William and Aaron and wanting us to go out into the bush with him on horse back to make tracks to deceive the police and to try what the black trackers were made of but on all occasions I declined to have anything to do with him. I remember Wallace borrowing a saddle from my mother in the month of August 1879 he promised to return it but he failed to do so. About a fortnight after this he paid my mother £3 for the saddle and said he could not return it. I also saw Wallace at our place on a Sunday in August 1879. He came from the direction of Beechworth he had a horse and buggy with him. In the buggy he had a bag of bread, a case of brandy and a quantity of preserved meats and tinned fish. He had dinner at our place on that day and left going in the direction of Hurdle Creek. Wallace was constantly annoying me with questions, viz. if I could tell him the movements of the police, to try to ascertain for him how many were stationed in Beechworth and what was their opinion as to whether the Kellys had left the country or not. Wallace told me that Joe Byrne was in the habit of calling at his place that he was a good fellow and would do him no harm. On the occasion when annoyed by Wallace as to the movements of the police, I told him that I saw four (4) mounted men going down the old El Dorado Road, he (Wallace) immediately went to Mrs Byrnes and informed her of what I had told him. This I am certain of for Patsy Byrne told me immediately. Wallace was on the most intimate terms with Mrs Byrne and all her family and was a frequent visitor during the time the Kelly Gang were at large.

The Wednesday after returned to Benalla to complete the enquiry and make out the brief. I expect to have all complete and be able to hand the brief to you on Monday the 30th instant.

M. E. Ward

Det. No. 2358

P.S. Detective Considine is about, he may have some news from Katamatite, when he returns tomorrow.

***

Police Department: Benalla

Detective Office: 30/1/82

Mr Harriman Esq

Crown Law Department,

Melbourne

Re Special enquiry pertaining James Wallace

We have the honour to report for your information that we have completed as far as is in our power a brief of all the evidence obtainable for the prosecution of the person whose name appears in the margin. Since our last reports we have not been able to obtain any fresh information with the exception of Mrs Cox's statement which may be of some value.

As regards the voluminous nature of the police evidence we had to insist it in order to trace the saddles etc which were found at Glenrowan and taken possession of the by the police and passed through many hands, the evidence connecting the saddle purchased by James Wallace from Sherritt to the possession of the Kellys is weak as none of the property was actually found in their (Kelly's) possession and the only hope we have in tracing the saddle was to connect it to the saddle which belonged to Kit No. 730 which was in possession of Constable Lonigan at the time of his murder at Stringybark Creek and was stolen by the Kellys there. This saddle was found in McDonald's Stable (presumably) as we can account for the other police saddle viz. Constable Scanlan's forming portion of Kit No. 960.

M Considine Det. No. 2413

M Ward Det. No. 2358